VHDL

Douglas L. Perry

Second Edition

McGraw-Hill, Inc.
New York   San Francisco   Washington, D.C.   Auckland   Bogotá
Caracas   Lisbon   London   Madrid   Mexico City   Milan
Montreal   New Delhi   San Juan   Singapore
Sydney   Tokyo   Toronto

Library of Congress Cataloging-in-Publication Data

Perry, Douglas L.
    VHDL / Douglas L. Perry. — 2nd ed.
      p.   cm. — (Computer engineering series)
    Includes index.
    ISBN 0-07-049434-7 :
      1. VHDL (Computer hardware description language).   I. Title.
    II. Series.
    TK7885.7.P47   1993
    621.39′2—dc20   93-23153
                                                   CIP

      6 7 8 9 0   DOC/DOC   9 9 8 7 6 5

ISBN 0-07-049434-7

The sponsoring editor for this book was Jeanne Glasser and the production supervisor was Donald F. Schmidt. This book was set in Century Schoolbook by North Market Street Graphics.

Printed and bound by R. R. Donnelley & Sons Company.

LIMITS OF LIABILITY AND DISCLAIMER OF WARRANTY

The author and publisher have exercised care in preparing this book and the programs contained in it. They make no representation, however, that the programs are error-free or suitable for every application to which the reader may attempt to apply them. The author and publisher make no warranty of any kind, expressed or implied, including the warranties of merchantability or fitness for a particular purpose, with regard to these programs or the documentation or theory contained in this book, all of which are provided "as is." The author and publisher shall not be liable for damages in amount greater than the purchase price of this book, or in any event for incidental or consequential damages in connection with, or arising out of the furnishing, performance, or use of these programs or the associated descriptions or discussions.

    Readers should test any program on their own systems and compare results with those presented in this book. They should then construct their own test programs to verify that they fully understand the requisite calling conventions and data formats for each of the programs. Then they should test the specific application thoroughly.

To my wife, Debbie, and my son, Brennan—
thanks for all your patience and support.

Contents

Preface

This second version of the book has some significant differences from
the first. All of the examples in the book now use the IEEE standard
1164 value system. This provides greater compatibility with other
models. Also, the book now includes a discussion of VHDL synthesis.
Chapters 9 and 10 discuss the basics of the synthesis process, and give
a number of synthesis examples. The vending machine controller
design example from the first version was modified so that it could be
synthesized. There were a number of syntax errors due to the text processor used for the last version of the book. These have been eliminated
and the graphics have been greatly improved.

This book was written to help hardware design engineers learn how
to better model their designs. It will provide guidance in writing VHDL
descriptions for every level of a hardware design, from the initial specification to the gate-level implementation.

It will also attempt to bring the designer with little or no knowledge
of VHDL to the level of writing complex VHDL descriptions. It is not
intended to show every possible construct of VHDL in every possible
use, but rather to show the designer how to write concise, efficient, and
correct VHDL descriptions of hardware designs.

This book is organized into three logical sections. The first section of
the book will introduce the features of VHDL; the second section discusses the VHDL synthesis process; and the third walks through a
design example of a vending machine controller from initial specification to final synthesizable implementation. At the back of the book are
included a number of appendices that contain useful information about
the language and examples used throughout the book.

In the first section, VHDL features are introduced one or more at a
time. As each feature is introduced, one or more real examples are
given to show how the feature would be used. The first section com-
prises Chapters 1 through 8, and each chapter introduces a basic

description capability of VHDL. Chapter 1 discusses how VHDL design relates to typical computer-aided engineering (CAE) methodologies, and introduces the basic terms of the language. Chapter 2 describes some of the basic concepts of VHDL, including the different delay mechanisms available, how to use instance-specific data, and talks about VHDL drivers. In Chapter 2 concurrent statements are discussed, while in Chapter 3 the reader is introduced to VHDL sequential statements. Chapter 4 talks about the wide range of types available for use in VHDL. Examples are given for each of the types showing how they would be used in a real example. In Chapter 5 the concepts of subprograms and packages are introduced. The different uses for functions are given, as well as the features available in VHDL packages.

Chapter 6 introduces the five kinds of predefined attribute categories available for use in VHDL. Each of the categories has examples describing how to use the specific attribute to the designer's best advantage. Examples are given which describe the purpose of each of the attributes. Chapter 7 discusses how configurations are used to specify how a design is constructed. Each of the types of configurations are discussed, along with some examples to illustrate the point. Chapter 8 walks the reader through some of the more advanced topics of VHDL. This chapter discusses overloading, user-defined attributes, generate statements, and TextIO. All of these topics are advanced features of the language that will be used when the designer becomes more familiar with VHDL.

The second section of the book consists of Chapters 9 and 10. These two chapters describe the basics of the synthesis process. Discussed are such topics as how to write synthesizable VHDL, what a technology library is, what the synthesis process looks like, what constraints and attributes are, and what the optimization process looks like.

The third section of the book walks through a description of a vending machine controller from the behavioral level to a synthesized gate-level output. Chapter 11 describes the vending machine from a behavioral level. Chapter 12 decomposes the vending machine into three synthesizable components and discusses the synthesis output.

Finally, there are four appendices at the end of the book to provide reference information. Appendix A is a listing of the IEEE 1164 STD_LOGIC package used throughout the book. Appendix B provides the gate-level netlists from the vending machine synthesis process in Chapter 12. Appendix C is a set of useful tables that condense some of the information in the rest of the book into quick reference tables. Finally, Appendix D discusses how to read BNF. I can only hope that the reader will have as much fun reading this book and working with VHDL as I did in writing it.

Acknowledgments

This book would not have been possible without the help of a number of people, and I would like to express my gratitude to all of them. Rod Farrow, Cary Ussery, Alec Stanculescu, and Ken Scott answered a multitude of questions about some of the vagaries of VHDL. Ken Scott and Kjell Nielsen reviewed the first manuscript, and Dierdre Hanford reviewed the synthesis portions for the second manuscript. Their comments were both helpful and insightful. Rick Herrick supplied the idea of using a vending machine controller as an instructive example. It is an easy-to-understand example, yet still complex enough to show off some interesting features of the language. Paul Krol developed the chart that describes generics in Chapter 7. Keith Irwin helped define the style of some of the chapters. Brent Gregory and Russ Segal contributed a lot to my understanding of how to synthesize VHDL. I would like to thank all of the members of the team at Vantage Analysis Systems, Synopsys, and Redwood Design Automation for providing the tools that made verification of the concepts in the book possible. I would also like to thank the management of Redwood Design Automation for supporting this effort even though the company was very young.

Douglas L. Perry

Introduction to VHDL

The VHSIC Hardware Description Language is an industry standard language used to describe hardware from the abstract to the concrete level. VHDL is rapidly being embraced as the universal communication medium of design. Computer-aided engineering workstation vendors throughout the industry are standardizing on VHDL as input and output from their tools. These tools include simulation tools, synthesis tools, layout tools, etc.

In this chapter we will examine the basics of VHDL. The history of VHDL will be presented, and then some basic terms will be defined. Finally, VHDL design will be contrasted with traditional design methods.

VHSIC Program

VHDL is an offshoot of the very high speed integrated circuit (VHSIC) program that was funded by the Department of Defense in the late 1970s and early 1980s. The goal of the VHSIC program was to produce the next generation of integrated circuits. Program participants were urged to push technology limits in every phase of the design and manufacture of integrated circuits.

The goals were accomplished admirably but, in the process of developing these extremely complex integrated circuits, the designers found out that the tools used to create these large designs were inadequate for the task. The tools that were available to the designers were mostly based at the gate level. Creating designs of hundreds of thousands of gates using gate level tools was an extremely challenging task and, therefore, a new method of description was in order.

VHDL as a Standard

A new hardware description language was proposed in 1981 called the VHSIC Hardware Description Language, or as we know it now, VHDL. The goals of this new language were twofold. First, the designers wanted a language that could describe the complex circuits that they were trying to describe. Second, they wanted a language that was a standard, so that all of the players in the VHSIC program could distribute designs to other players in a standard format. Also, any subcontractors would be able to talk to their main contractors with a single standard format.

In 1986 VHDL was proposed as an IEEE standard. It went through a number of revisions and changes until it was adopted as the IEEE 1076 standard in December 1987. The IEEE 1076-1987 standard VHDL is the VHDL that will be used in this book. All of the examples have been described in IEEE 1076 VHDL and compiled and simulated with the VHDL simulation environment from Vantage Analysis Systems. The synthesis examples were synthesized with the Synopsys synthesis tools.

Learning VHDL

VHDL can be a very difficult language to learn by reading the *VHDL Language Reference Manual* (also called the LRM) from cover to cover. The LRM describes VHDL for the VHDL implementor, and was never intended to be a VHDL user's guide. VHDL itself is a large language, however, and learning all of it can be a very large task. The entire language does not need to be learned initially to write useful models. A subset of the language can be learned initially and, as more complex models are required, the more complex features can be learned and used.

VHDL contains levels of representations that can be used to represent all levels of description from the bidirectional switch level to the system level, and any level in between. The best way to approach VHDL is to learn enough of the language to try some small designs. When you become familiar enough with this subset of VHDL that you feel very comfortable writing it, move on to some of the other features of the language and try new things.

VHDL Terms

Before we go any further, let's define some of the terms that we will be using throughout the book. These are the basic VHDL building blocks that are used in almost every description, along with some terms that are redefined in VHDL to mean something different to the average designer.

Entity.   All designs are expressed in terms of entities. An entity is the most basic building block in a design. The uppermost level of the design is the top-level entity. If the design is hierarchical, then the top-level description will have lower-level descriptions contained in it. These lower-level descriptions will be lower-level entities contained in the top-level entity description.

Architecture.   All entities that can be simulated have an architecture description. The architecture describes the behavior of the entity. A single entity can have multiple architectures. One architecture might be behavioral, while another might be a structural description of the design.

Configuration.   A configuration statement is used to bind a component instance to an entity-architecture pair. A configuration can be considered as a parts list for a design. It describes which behavior to use for each entity, much like a parts list describes which part to use for each part in the design.

Package.   A package is a collection of commonly used data types and subprograms used in a design. Think of a package as a toolbox that contains tools used to build designs.

Bus.   The term bus usually brings to mind a group of signals or a particular method of communication used in the design of hardware. In VHDL a bus is a special kind of signal that may have its drivers turned off.

Driver.   This is a source on a signal. If a signal is driven by two tri-state inverters, when both inverters are active the signal will have two drivers.

Attribute.   An attribute is data that is attached to VHDL objects or predefined data about VHDL objects. Examples are the current drive capability of a buffer or the maximum operating temperature of the device.

Generic.   A generic is VHDL's term for a parameter that passes information to an entity. For instance, if an entity is a gate level model with a rise and a fall delay, values for the rise and fall delays could be passed into the entity with generics.

Process.   A process is the basic unit of execution in VHDL. All operations that are performed in a simulation of a VHDL description are broken into single or multiple processes.

Traditional Design Methods

When a design engineer develops a new piece of hardware today, it is probably designed on a computer-aided engineering (CAE) workstation. To create a design on a typical CAE workstation, the designer will create a schematic for the design. (HDL-based design methods will be described later.)

A typical schematic consists of symbols representing the basic units of the design connected together with signals. The symbols come from a library of parts that the designer uses to build the schematic. The type of symbols available depends on the type of design that the designer is creating. If the designer is creating the schematic for a board design that uses standard logic parts, then the symbols used in the schematic represent the standard parts that the designer has available. If the designer is creating a schematic for an application-specific integrated circuit (ASIC), then the symbols available are the library macros available for use on this specific type of ASIC.

The symbols are wired together using signals (or *nets*—short for networks). The interconnection of the symbols by signals creates the connections needed to specify the design such that a netlist can be derived from the connections. A netlist can be used to create a simulation model of the design to verify the design before it is built. Once the design has been verified, the netlist can be used to provide the information needed by a routing software package to complete the actual design. The routing software will create the physical connection data to either create the trace information needed for a PC board or the layer information needed for an ASIC.

Figure 1.1 illustrates an example of a symbol used in a schematic. It is the symbol for a reset-set flip-flop (RSFF). The symbol describes the following pieces of information to the designer:

The number of input pins for the device. In this example, the number is 2, set and reset.

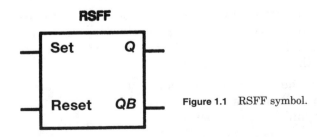

Figure 1.1   RSFF symbol.

The number of output pins for the device.   In this example, the number of output pins is 2, Q, and QB.

The function of the device.   In this example, the function of the device is described by the name of the symbol. In the case of simple gates, the function of the symbol is described by the shape of the symbol.

Symbols specify the interface and the function to the designer. When the symbols are placed on a schematic sheet and wired together with signals, a schematic for the design is formed. An example of a simple schematic for an RSFF is shown in Fig. 1.2.

Traditional Schematics

The schematic contains two NAND gate symbol instances and four port instances. Four nets connect the symbols and ports together to form the RS flip-flop. Each port has a unique name which also specifies the name of the signal (net) connected to it. Each symbol instance has a unique instance identifier (U1, U2). The instance identifier is used to uniquely identify an instance for reference.

When this schematic is compiled into a typical gate-level simulator, it will function as an RSFF. A '0' level on the reset port will cause the reset signal to have the value '0'. This will cause NAND gate U2 to output a '1' value on signal QB independent of the value on the other input of the NAND gate. The '1' value on QB feeds back to one input of the NAND gate U1. If the set input is at an inactive value ('1'), then NAND gate U1 will have two '1' values as input, causing it to output a value of '0' on the output Q. The RSFF will have been reset.

How would this same design look in VHDL? First of all, how do you represent a symbol in VHDL? What does a schematic look like in VHDL?

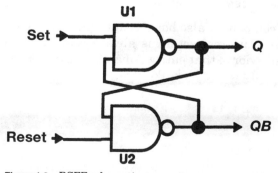

Figure 1.2   RSFF schematic.

Symbols versus Entities

All designs are created from entities. An entity in VHDL corresponds directly to a symbol in the traditional CAE workstation design methodology. Let's look at the top-level entity for the *rsff* symbol described earlier. An entity for the *rsff* would look like this:

```
ENTITY rsff IS
  PORT ( set, reset : IN BIT;
         q, qb : BUFFER BIT);
END rsff;
```

The keyword ENTITY signifies that this is the start of an entity statement. In the descriptions shown throughout the book, keywords of the language and types provided with the STANDARD package will be shown in all CAPITAL letters. For instance, in the preceding example, the keywords are ENTITY, IS, PORT, IN, BUFFER, etc. The standard type provided is BIT. Names of user-created objects, such as *rsff* in the preceding example, will be shown in lowercase italics.

The name of the entity is *rsff,* as was the name of the symbol described earlier. The entity has four ports in the PORT clause. Two ports are of mode IN and two ports are of mode BUFFER. The reason for port mode BUFFER instead of just OUT will be described later. The two input ports correspond directly to the two input pins on the symbol from the CAE workstation. The two buffer ports correspond directly to the two output ports for the symbol. All of the ports have a type of BIT.

The entity describes the interface to the outside world. It specifies the number of ports, the direction of the ports, and the type of the ports. A lot more information can be put into the entity than is shown here, but this will give us a foundation upon which we can later build.

Schematics versus Architectures

The schematic for the *rsff* component also has a counterpart in VHDL. It is called an *architecture.* An architecture is always related to an entity and describes the behavior of that entity. An architecture for the *rsff* device described previously would look like this:

```
ARCHITECTURE netlist OF rsff IS
  COMPONENT nand2
    PORT ( a, b : IN BIT;
           c : OUT BIT);
  END COMPONENT;
BEGIN
```

```
U1: nand2
   PORT MAP (set, qb, q);

U2: nand2
   PORT MAP (reset, q, qb);
END netlist;
```

The keyword ARCHITECTURE signifies that this statement will describe an architecture for an entity. The architecture name will be *netlist*. The entity that the architecture is describing is called *rsff*.

The reason for the connection between the architecture and the entity is that an entity can have multiple architectures describing the behavior of the entity. For instance, one architecture could be a behavioral description, and another, like the one preceding, could be a structural description.

The textual area between the keyword ARCHITECTURE and the keyword BEGIN is where local signals and components are declared for later use. In this example, there are two instances of a *nand2* gate placed in the architecture. The compiler needs to know what the interface to the components placed in the architecture are. The component declaration statement will describe that information to the compiler.

The statement area of the architecture starts with the keyword BEGIN. All statements between the BEGIN and the END *netlist* statement are called *concurrent statements,* because all of the statements execute concurrently. This concept will be discussed in great detail later.

Component Instantiation

In the statement area are two component instantiation statements. Each statement creates an instance of a component in the model. In this example, each statement creates an instance of a nand2 gate. The first instance U1 corresponds directly with the nand2 gate U1 in the schematic in Fig. 1.2. The way to read the component instantiation statement is as follows. The first statement creates an instance called U1 of a nand2 component, with the first port connected to signal *set,* the second port connected to signal *qb,* and the last port connected to signal *q.*

If we look again at the nand2 component declaration we will see that the first port is an IN port called *a,* the second port is an IN port called *b,* and the last port is an OUT port called *c.* Therefore, the component instantiation would connect the *a* port of the nand2 component to signal *set,* the *b* port to signal *qb,* and the *c* port to signal *q.* We have thus matched the actual parameters *set, qb,* and *q* of the instantiation with the corresponding formal parameters *a, b,* and *c* of the declaration.

There is another way to map the ports if the ports are not in a particular order. Component instantiation statements as demonstrated here can be used:

```
U1: nand2 port map (a => set, b => qb, c => q);
```

This form is called *named association,* and maps the ports directly, without concern for the order. In fact, the following statement would work perfectly well, also.

```
U1: nand2 port map ( b => qb, c => q, a => set);
```

The second component instantiation statement of architecture *netlist* creates another instance of the nand2 component with an instance identifier, U2. These instances correspond directly with the instance identifiers of the schematic in Fig. 1.2. This model matches the schematic in Fig. 1.2. This type of VHDL representation is called a *structural model,* or *structural representation.* What makes this description a structural one is the fact that it has components instantiated in it. In the next few chapters we will be discussing structural, behavioral, and mixed structural-behavioral descriptions.

The structural architecture *netlist* is very similar to a netlist in a typical CAE workstation simulator. Some of the examples in this book will use structural parts to describe the functionality, but behavioral modeling and synthesizable RTL descriptions will be the main focus.

Behavioral Descriptions

Another way to describe this same circuit is by using a behavioral architecture. An example of a behavioral architecture is shown in the architecture example following. This architecture uses concurrent signal assignment statements. As the name implies, the statements contained in the model assign values to signals. What makes these statements different from assignment statements in typical programming languages is the fact that these statements execute in parallel (concurrently), not serially.

```
ARCHITECTURE behave OF rsff IS
BEGIN
  q <= NOT( qb AND set ) AFTER 2 ns;
  qb <= NOT( q AND reset ) AFTER 2 ns;
END behave;
```

Concurrent signal assignment

In a typical programming language such as C or Pascal, each assignment statement executes one after the other in a specified order. The order of execution is determined by the order of the statements in the source file. Inside a VHDL architecture, there is no specified ordering of the assignment statements. (We will look later at process statements in which signal assignment statements are ordered.) The order of execution is solely specified by events occurring on signals to which the assignment statements are sensitive.

Examine the first assignment statement from architecture *behave,* as shown here:

```
q <= NOT( qb AND set ) AFTER 2 ns;
```

A signal assignment is identified by the symbol <=. The logical AND of *qb* and *set* is complemented and assigned to signal *q*. This statement will be executed whenever either *qb* or set has an event occur on it. An event on a signal is a change in the value of that signal. A signal assignment statement is said to be sensitive to changes on any signals that are to the right of the <= symbol. This signal assignment statement is sensitive to *qb* and *set*. The other signal assignment statement in architecture *behave* is sensitive to signals *q* and *reset*.

The AFTER clause in the signal assignment is used to emulate propagation delay in the circuit. Any event (change in value) on *qb* or *set* may cause a change on signal *q* 2 ns later.

Let's take a look at how these statements actually work. Suppose that we have a steady-state condition where both *set* and *reset* are at a '1' value, and signal *q* is currently at a '0' value. Signal *qb* will be at a '1' value because it will be opposite of q except when both *set* and *reset* are at a '0' value. Now, assume that we place an event on the *set* signal that causes its value to change to a '0'. When this happens, the first signal assignment statement will wake up and execute. This happens because *set* is on the right side of the <= and is therefore in the *implied sensitivity list* for the first signal assignment statement.

When the first statement executes it will compute the new value to be assigned to *q* from the current value of the signal expression on the right side of the <= symbol. The expression value calculation will use the current values for all signals contained in it.

What will the signal expression calculate? Signal *set* is now equal to '0' since its value just changed. Signal *qb* is equal to '1' because it did not change. The new value for signal *q* will be the complement of the two values, ANDed together. This will result in a '1' value to be assigned to signal *q*.

Event scheduling

The assignment to signal *q* does not happen instantly, however. The AFTER clause we discussed earlier will delay the assignment of the new value to *q* by 2 ns. The mechanism for delaying the new value is called *scheduling an event.* By assigning *q* a new value, an event was scheduled 2 ns in the future that contains the new value for signal *q*. When the event matures (2 ns in the future), signal *q* will receive the new value.

Statement concurrency

The first assignment is the only statement to execute at the current time when the event on *set* happens. The second signal assignment statement will not execute until the event on signal *q* happens, or an event happens on signal *reset.* If no event happens on signal *reset,* then the second assignment statement will not execute for 2 ns. This will be when the event on signal *q* that was scheduled by the first signal assignment occurs.

When the event on signal *q* occurs, the second signal assignment statement will execute. It will calculate a new value from *q* and *reset.* Assuming *reset* stays at a '1', then the new value for *qb* will be a '0'. This value will be scheduled to occur on signal *qb* 2 ns in the future.

When the event occurs on signal *qb,* the first signal assignment will wake up, execute again, and calculate the new value for *q* based on the values of *qb* and *set.* If *set* is still a '0', then the '0' value of *qb* will not change the value of *q*. Signal *q* will already be at a '1' value from the *set* signal at a '0'. No new event will be scheduled on the *q* output signal, because signal *q* does not change its value.

The two signal assignment statements in the architecture *behave* form a behavioral model, or architecture, for the *rsff* entity. The *behave* architecture contains no structure. There are no components instantiated in the architecture. There is no further hierarchy and this architecture can be considered a leaf node in the hierarchy of the design.

Sequential Behavior

There is yet another way to describe the functionality of an *rsff* device in VHDL. The fact that VHDL has so many possible representations for similar functionality is what makes learning the entire language a big task. The third way to describe the functionality of the *rsff* will be to use a process statement to describe the functionality in an algorithmic representation. This is shown in architecture *sequential* as follows:

```
ARCHITECTURE sequential OF rsff IS
BEGIN
  PROCESS (set, reset )
BEGIN
    IF set = '1' AND reset = '0' THEN
    q <= '0' AFTER 2 ns;
```

```
        qb <= '1' AFTER 4 ns;
    ELSIF set = '0' AND reset = '1' THEN
      q <= '1' AFTER 4 ns;
      qb <='0' AFTER 2 ns;
    ELSIF set = '0' AND reset = '0' THEN
      q <= '1' AFTER 2 ns;
      qb <= '1' AFTER 2 ns;
    END IF;
  END PROCESS;
END sequential;
```

The architecture contains only one statement, called a *process state-ment*. It starts at the line beginning with the keyword PROCESS and ends with the line that contains END PROCESS. All of the statements between these two lines are considered part of the process statement.

Process statements

The process statement consists of a number of parts. The first part is called the *sensitivity list*. The second part is called the *process declarative part;* and the third is the *statement part*. In the example shown above, the list of signals in parentheses after the keyword PROCESS is called the sensitivity list. This list enumerates exactly which signals will cause the process statement to be executed. In this example the list consists of *set* and *reset*. Only events on these signals will cause the process statement to be executed.

Process declarative region.   The process declarative part consists of the area between the end of the sensitivity list and the keyword BEGIN. In this example, the declarative part is empty. This area is used to declare local variables or constants that can be used only inside of the process.

Process statement part.   The statement part of the process starts at the keyword BEGIN and ends at the END PROCESS line. All of the statements enclosed by the process are sequential statements. This means that any statements enclosed by the process are executed one after the other in a sequential order, just like a typical programming language. Remember that the order of the statements in the architecture did not make any difference; however, inside of the process this is not true. *The order of execution is the order of the statements in the process statement.*

Process execution.   Let's see how this works by walking through the execution of the example in architecture *sequential,* line by line. To be consistent, let's assume that *set* changes to a '0' and *reset* remains at a '1'. Because set is in the sensitivity list for the process statement, the process will be invoked. Each statement in the process will then be executed sequentially. In this example, however, there is only one IF statement. Each check that the IF statement performs is done sequentially, starting with the first in the model.

The first check is to see if *set* is equal to a '1' and *reset* is equal to a '0'. This statement will fail because *set* is equal to a '0' and *reset* is equal to a '1'. The two signal assignment statements that follow the first check will not be executed. Instead, the next check will be performed. This check will succeed and the signal assignment statements following the check for *set* = '0' and *reset* = '1' will be executed. These statements are:

```
q <= '1' AFTER 2 ns;
qb <= '0' AFTER 2 ns;
```

Sequential statements

These two statements will execute sequentially. They may look exactly the same as previous signal assignment statements that we have examined but, because of the context (they are inside the process statement), they are different. These two assignment statements are called *sequential signal assignment statements,* and they execute one after the other inside the process statement. The first statement may schedule an event on signal *q,* and then the second statement may schedule an event on signal *qb.* However, if signal *q* is already at a '1' value, no change in value will occur and, therefore, no event will be scheduled.

After these two statements are executed, the next check of the IF statement is not performed. Whenever a check succeeds, no other checks are done. Since the IF statement was the only statement inside the process, the process terminates.

Architecture Selection

So far three architectures have been described for one entity. Which architecture should be used to model the *rsff* device? It depends on the accuracy wanted, and whether structural information is required. If the model is going to be used to drive a printed circuit board layout tool, then probably the structural architecture *netlist* is most appropriate. If a structural model is not wanted for some other reason, then a more efficient model can be used. Either of the other two methods (architectures *behave* and *sequential*) are probably more efficient in terms of memory space required and speed of execution. How to choose between these two methods may come down to a question of programming style. Would the modeler rather write concurrent or sequential

VHDL code? If the modeler wants to write concurrent VHDL code, then the style of architecture *behave* is the way to go; otherwise, architecture *sequential* should be chosen. Typically, modelers are more familiar with sequential coding styles, but concurrent statements are very powerful tools to write small, efficient models, as we shall illustrate later.

We will also look at yet another architecture that can be written for an entity. This is the architecture that can be used to drive a synthesis tool. Synthesis tools convert a Register Transfer Level (RTL) VHDL description into an optimized gate level description. Synthesis tools can offer greatly enhanced productivity compared to manual methods. The synthesis process will be discussed in Chaps. 9 and 10.

Configuration statements

An entity can have more than one architecture, but how does the modeler choose which architecture to use in a given simulation? The configuration statement maps component instantiations to entities. With this powerful statement, the modeler can pick and choose which architectures are used to model an entity at every level in the design.

Let's look at a configuration statement using the *netlist* architecture of the *rsff* entity. An example configuration is as follows:

```
CONFIGURATION rsffcon1 OF rsff IS
   FOR netlist
      FOR U1,U2 : nand2 USE ENTITY WORK.mynand(version1);
      END FOR;
   END FOR;
END rsffcon1;
```

The function of the configuration statement is to spell out exactly which architecture to use for every component instance in the model. This occurs in a hierarchical fashion. The highest-level entity in the design needs to have the architecture specified, as well as any components instantiated in the design.

The preceding configuration statement reads as follows. This is a configuration named *rsffcon1* for entity *rsff*. Use architecture *netlist* as the architecture for the topmost entity, which is *rsff*. For the two component instances U1 and U2 of type nand2 instantiated in the *netlist* architecture, use entity *mynand,* architecture *version1* from the library called WORK. All of the entities now have architectures specified for them. Entity *rsff* has architecture *netlist,* and component *nand2* has entity *mynand* and architecture *version1*.

Power of configurations. By compiling the entities, architectures, and the configuration specified previously, you can create a simulatable model. But what if you did not want to simulate at the gate level? What if you really wanted to use architecture BEHAVE instead? The power of the configuration is that you do not need to recompile your complete design; you need only to recompile the new configuration. An example configuration is as follows:

```
CONFIGURATION rsffcon2 OF rsff IS
    FOR behave
    END FOR;
END rsffcon2;
```

This is a configuration named *rsffcon2* for entity *rsff*. Use architecture *behave* for the topmost entity, which is *rsff*. By compiling this configuration, the architecture *behave* will be selected for entity *rsff* in this simulation.

This configuration is not necessary, in standard VHDL, but gives the designer the freedom to specify exactly which architecture will be used for the entity. The default architecture used for the entity is the last one compiled into the working library.

In this chapter we have had a basic introduction to VHDL and how it can be used to model the behavior of devices and designs. The first example showed how a larger design can be made of smaller designs; in this case, an RSFF was modeled using NAND gates. The first example provided a structural view of VHDL.

The second example showed a more abstract view that did not include the gate level view of the RSFF, but had more of a data-flow flavor to it. In the third example, an algorithmic, or behavioral, view of the RSFF was presented. All of these views of the RSFF successfully model the functionality of an RSFF and all can be simulated with a VHDL simulator. Ultimately, however, a designer will want to use the model to facilitate building a piece of hardware. The most common use of VHDL in actually building hardware today is through synthesis tools. Therefore, the focus of the rest of the book will be not only the simulation of VHDL, but also the synthesis of VHDL.

In this chapter we have had a basic introduction to VHDL and to some of the description styles available in the language. In the next chapter we will examine behavioral modeling in greater detail.

Behavioral Modeling

In Chap. 1 we discussed structural modeling with traditional CAE systems and touched briefly on behavioral modeling. In this chapter we will discuss behavioral modeling more thoroughly, as well as some of the issues relating to the simulation and synthesis of VHDL models.

Introduction to Behavioral Modeling

The signal assignment statement is the most basic form of behavioral modeling in VHDL. An example follows.

```
a <= b;
```

This statement is read as follows: *a* gets the value of *b*. The effect of this statement is that the current value of signal *b* will be assigned to signal *a*. This statement will be executed whenever signal *b* changes value. Signal *b* is in the *sensitivity list* of this statement. Whenever a signal in the sensitivity list of a signal assignment statement changes value, the signal assignment statement is executed. If the result of the execution is a new value that is different than the current value of the signal, then an event is scheduled for the target signal. If the result of the execution is the same value, then no event will be scheduled but a transaction will still be generated (transactions are discussed in Chap. 3). A transaction is always generated when a model is evaluated, but only signal changes cause events to be scheduled.

The next example shows how to introduce a nonzero delay value for the assignment.

```
a <= b after 10 ns;
```

This statement is read as follows: a gets the value of b when 10 ns of time have elapsed.

Both of the preceding statements are concurrent signal assignment statements. Both statements are sensitive to changes in the value of signal b. Whenever b changes value, these statements will execute and new values will be assigned to signal a.

Using a concurrent signal assignment statement, a simple AND gate can be modeled as follows:

```
ENTITY and2 IS
  PORT (a, b : IN BIT;
        c : OUT BIT );
END and2;

ARCHITECTURE and2_behav OF and2 IS
BEGIN
  c <= a AND b AFTER 5 ns;
END and2_behav;
```

The AND gate has two inputs a, b and one output c, as shown in Fig. 2.1. The value of signal c may be assigned a new value whenever either a or b changes value. With an AND gate, if a is a 0 and b changes from a 1 to a 0, output c will not change. If the output does change value, then a transaction occurs which causes an event to be scheduled on signal c; otherwise, a transaction occurs on signal c.

The entity design unit describes the ports of the *and2* gate. There are two inputs a and b, as well as one output c. The architecture *and2_behav* for entity *and2* contains one concurrent signal assignment statement. This statement is sensitive to both signal a and signal b by the fact that the expression to calculate the value of c includes both a and b signal values.

The value of the expression a and b will be calculated first, and the resulting value from the calculation will be scheduled on output c, 5 ns from the time the calculation is completed.

The next example shows more complicated signal assignment statements and demonstrates the concept of concurrency in greater detail. In Fig. 2.2, the symbol for a four-input multiplexer is shown.

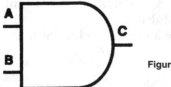

Figure 2.1   AND gate symbol.

This is the behavioral model for the mux.

```
USE WORK.std_logic_1164.ALL;

ENTITY mux4 IS
  PORT (i0, i1, i2, i3, a, b : IN std_logic;
          q : OUT std_logic);

END mux4;

ARCHITECTURE mux4 OF mux4 IS
  SIGNAL sel: INTEGER;
BEGIN
  WITH sel SELECT
    q <= i0 AFTER 10 ns WHEN 0,
      i1 AFTER 10 ns WHEN 1,
      i2 AFTER 10 ns WHEN 2,
      i3 AFTER 10 ns WHEN 3,
      'X' AFTER 10 ns WHEN OTHERS;

  sel <= 0 WHEN a = '0' AND b = '0' ELSE
      1 WHEN a = '1' AND b = '0' ELSE
      2 WHEN a = '0' AND b = '1' ELSE
      3 WHEN a = '1' AND b = '1' ELSE
      4;
END mux4;
```

The entity for this model has six input ports and one output port. Four of the input ports (*i0, i1, i2, i3*) represent signals that will be assigned to the output signal *q*. Only one of the signals will be assigned to the output signal *q* based on the value of the other two input signals *a* and *b*. The truth table for the multiplexer is shown in Fig. 2.3. To implement the preceding functionality, we will use a conditional signal assignment statement and a selected signal assignment.

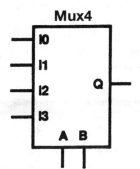

Figure 2.2   Mux4 symbol.

A	B	Q
0	0	I0
1	0	I1
0	1	I2
1	1	I3

Figure 2.3   Mux functional table.

The second statement type in this example is called a *conditional signal assignment statement.* This statement will assign a value to the target signal based on conditions that are evaluated for each statement. The statement WHEN conditions are executed one at a time in sequential order until the conditions of a statement are met. The first statement that matches the conditions required will assign the value to the target signal. The target signal for this example is the local signal *sel.* Depending on the values of signals *a* and *b,* the values 0 through 4 will be assigned to *sel.*

If more than one statement's conditions match, the first statement that matches will do the assign, and the other matching statements values will be ignored.

The first statement is called a *selected signal assignment* and will select among a number of options to assign the correct value to the target signal. The target signal in this example is the signal *q.*

The expression (the value of signal *sel* in this example) will be evaluated, and the statement that matches the value of the expression will assign the value to the target signal. All of the possible values of the expression must have a matching choice in the selected signal assignment (or an OTHERS clause must exist).

Each of the input signals can be assigned to output *q,* depending on the values of the two select inputs, *a* and *b.* If the values of *a* or *b* are unknown values, then the last value, 'X' (unknown), is assigned to output *q.* In this example, when one of the select inputs is at an unknown value, the output is set to unknown.

Looking at the model for the multiplexer, it looks as though the model will not work as written. It looks as though the value of signal *sel* is used before it is computed. This impression is received from the fact that the second statement in the architecture is the statement that actually computes the value for *sel.* The model will work as written, however, because of the concept of concurrency.

The second statement is sensitive to signals *a* and *b.* Whenever either *a* or *b* changes value, the second statement is executed, and signal *sel* will be updated. The first statement is sensitive to signal *sel*. Whenever signal *sel* changes value, the first signal assignment will be executed.

If this example is processed by a synthesis tool, the resulting gate structure created will resemble a 4 to 1 multiplexer. If the synthesis library contains a 4 to 1 multiplexer primitive, that primitive may be generated based on the sophistication of the synthesis tool and the constraints put on the design.

Transport versus Inertial Delay

In VHDL there are two types of delays that can be used for modeling behaviors. Inertial delay is the most commonly used, while transport delay is used where a wire delay model is required.

Inertial delay

Inertial delay is the default in VHDL. If no delay type is specified, then inertial delay is used. Inertial delay is the default because in most cases it behaves similarly to the actual device.

In an inertial delay model, the output signal of the device has inertia which must be overcome in order for the signal to change value. The inertia value is equal to the delay through the device. If there are any spikes, pulses, etc., that have periods where a signal value is maintained for less than the delay through the device, the output signal value will not change. If a signal value is maintained at a particular value for longer than the delay through the device, the inertia is overcome and the device will change to the new state.

Figure 2.4 is an example of a very simple buffer symbol. The buffer has a single input A and a single output B. The waveforms are shown for input A and the output B. Signal A changes from a '0' to a '1' at time 10 ns and from a '1' to a '0' at 20 ns. This creates a pulse or *spike* that is 10 ns in duration. The buffer has a 20 ns delay through the device.

The '0' to '1' transition on signal A causes the buffer model to be executed, and will schedule an event with the value '1' to occur on output B at time 30 ns. At time 20 ns, the next event on signal A occurs. This will execute the buffer model again. The buffer model will predict a new event on output B of a 0 value at time 40 ns. The event scheduled on output B for time 30 ns still has not occurred. The new event predicted by the buffer model clashes with the currently scheduled event, and the simulator will preempt the event at 30 ns.

The effect of the preemption is that the spike is swallowed. The reason for the cancellation is that, according to the inertial delay model,

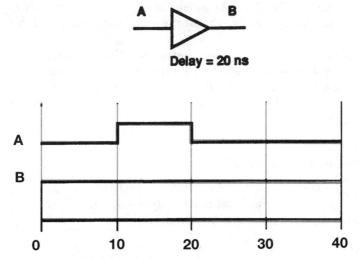

Figure 2.4   Inertial delay buffer waveforms.

the first event at 30 ns did not have enough time to overcome the inertia of the output signal.

The inertial delay model is by far the most commonly used in all currently available simulators. Part of the reason for this is that, in most cases, the inertial delay model is accurate enough for the designer's needs. One more reason for the widespread use of inertial delay is that it prevents prolific propagation of spikes throughout the circuit. In most cases, this is the behavior wanted by the designer.

Transport delay

Transport delay is not the default in VHDL and must be specified. It represents a wire delay in which any pulse, no matter how small, is propagated to the output signal delayed by the delay value specified. Transport delay is especially useful for modeling delay line devices, wire delays on a PC board, and path delays on an ASIC.

If we look at the same buffer circuit that was shown in Fig. 2.4, but replace the inertial delay waveforms with the transport delay waveforms, we get the result shown in Fig. 2.5. The same waveform is input to signal A, but the output from signal B is quite different. With transport delay, the spikes are not swallowed, but the events are ordered before propagation.

At time 10 ns, the buffer model will be executed and will schedule an event for the output to go to a 1 value at 30 ns. At time 20 ns, the buffer model will be reinvoked and predict a new value for the output at time

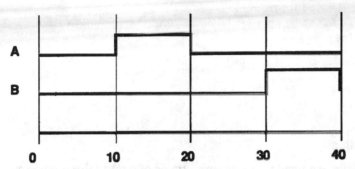

Figure 2.5 Transport delay buffer waveforms.

40 ns. With the transport delay algorithm, the events are put in order. The event for time 40 ns will be put in the list of events after the event for time 30 ns. The spike is not swallowed, but propagated intact after the delay time of the device.

Inertial delay model

The following model shows how to write an inertial delay model. It is the same as any other model that we have been looking at. The default delay type is inertial; therefore, it is not necessary to specify the delay type to be inertial.

```
USE WORK.std_logic_1164.ALL;
ENTITY buf IS
  PORT ( a : IN std_logic;
         b : OUT std_logic);
END buf;

ARCHITECTURE buf OF buf IS
BEGIN
    b <= a AFTER 20 ns;
END buf;
```

Transport delay model

The following is an example of a transport delay model. It is similar in every respect to the inertial delay model except for the keyword

TRANSPORT in the signal assignment statement to signal *b*. When this keyword exists, the delay type used in the statement is the transport delay mechanism.

```
USE WORK.std_logic_1164.ALL;
ENTITY delay_line IS
  PORT ( a : IN std_logic;
         b : OUT std_logic);
END delay_line;

ARCHITECTURE delay_line OF delay_line IS
BEGIN
  b <= TRANSPORT a AFTER 20 ns;
END delay_line;
```

Simulation Deltas

Simulation deltas are used to order some types of events during a simulation. Specifically, zero-delay events must be ordered to produce consistent results. If zero delay events are not properly ordered, results can be disparate between different simulation runs. An example of this will be shown using the circuit shown in Fig. 2.6. This circuit could be

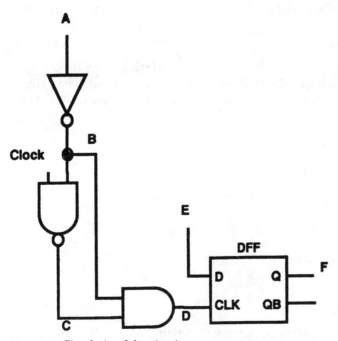

Figure 2.6 Simulation delta circuit.

part of a clocking scheme in a complex device being modeled. It probably would not be the entire circuit, but only a part of the circuit used to generate the clock to the D flip-flop.

The circuit consists of an inverter, a NAND gate, and an AND gate driving the clock input of a flip-flop component. The NAND gate and AND gate are used to gate the clock input to the flip-flop.

Let's examine the circuit operation, using a delta delay mechanism and using another mechanism. By examining the two delay mechanisms, we will better understand how a delta delay orders events.

To use delta delay, all of the circuit components must have zero delay specified. The delay for all three gates is specified as zero. (Real circuits do not exhibit such characteristics, but sometimes modeling is easier if all of the delay is concentrated at the outputs.) Let's examine the nondelta delay mechanism first.

When a falling edge occurs on signal A, the output of the inverter will change in 0 time. Let's assume that such an event occurred at time 10 ns. The output of the inverter, signal B, will change to reflect the new input value. When signal B changes, both the "and" gate and the nand gate will be reevaluated. For this example, the clock input is assumed to be a constant value '1'. If the nand gate is evaluated first, its new value will be '0'.

When the AND gate evaluates, signal B will be a '0', and signal C will be a '1'; therefore, the AND gate will predict a new value of '0'. But what happens if the AND gate evaluates first. The AND gate will see a '1' value on signal B, and a '1' value on signal C before the NAND gate has a chance to reevaluate. The AND gate will predict a new value of '1'.

The NAND gate reevaluates and calculates its new value as '0'. The change on the output of the NAND gate causes the AND gate to reevaluate again. The AND gate will now see the value of B, a '1' value, and the new value of signal C, a '0' value. The AND gate will now predict a '0' on its output. This process is summarized in Table 2.1.

TABLE 2.1 Comparison of Two Evaluation Mechanisms

AND first	NAND first
evaluate inverter	evaluate inverter
B <= 1	B <= 1
evaluate AND (C = 1)	evaluate NAND
D <= 1	C <= 0
evaluate NAND	evaluate AND
C <= 0	D <= 0
evaluate AND	
D <= 0	

Both circuits arrive at the same value for signal D. However, when the AND gate is evaluated first, a rising edge, one delta delay wide, occurs on signal D. This rising edge can clock the flip-flop, depending on how the flip-flop is modeled.

The point of this discussion is that without a delta synchronization mechanism, the results of the simulation can depend on how the simulator data structures are built. For instance, compiling the circuit the first time might make the AND gate evaluate first, while compiling again may make the NAND gate evaluate first—clearly not desirable results—and simulation deltas prevent this behavior from occurring.

The same circuit evaluated using the VHDL delta delay mechanism would evaluate as shown in Table 2.2.

The evaluation of the circuit does not depend on the order of evaluation of the NAND gate or AND gate. The sequence in Fig. 2.8 will occur irrespective of the evaluation order of the AND or NAND gate.

During the first delta time point of time 10 ns, signal A will receive the value '0'. This will cause the inverter to reevaluate with the new value. The inverter will calculate the new value for signal B, which will be the value '1'. This value will not be propagated immediately, but will be scheduled for the next delta time point (delta 2).

The simulator will then begin execution of delta time point 2. Signal B will be updated to a '1' value, and the AND gate and NAND gate will be reevaluated. Both the AND gate and NAND gate will now schedule their new values for the next delta time point (delta 3).

When delta 3 occurs, signal D receives a '1' value, and signal C receives a '0' value. Since signal C also drives the "and" gate, the "and" gate will be reevaluated and will schedule its new output for delta time point 4.

TABLE 2.2   Delta Delay Evaluation Mechanism

Time	Delta	Activity
10 ns	(1)	A <= 0
		evaluate inverter
	(2)	B <= 1
		evaluate AND
		evaluate NAND
	(3)	D <= 1
		C <= 0
		evaluate AND
	(4)	D <= 0
11 ns		

To summarize, simulation deltas are an infinitestimal amount of time used as a synchronization mechanism when zero-delay events are present. Delta delay is used whenever zero delay is specified, as follows:

```
a <= b AFTER 0 ns;
```

Another case for using delta delay is when no delay is specified:

```
a <= b;
```

In both cases, whenever signal *b* changes value from an event, signal *a* will have a delta-delayed signal assignment to it.

An equivalent VHDL model of the circuit shown in Fig. 2.6, except for the flip-flop, is as follows:

```
ENTITY reg IS
  PORT( a, clock : in bit;
        d : out bit);
END reg;
ARCHITECTURE test OF reg IS
  SIGNAL b, c : bit;
BEGIN
  b <= NOT(a); -- notice no delay
  c <= NOT( clock AND b);
  d <= c AND b;
END test;
```

Drivers

VHDL has a unique way of handling multiply-driven signals. Multiply-driven signals are very useful for modeling a data bus, a bidirectional bus, etc. To correctly model these kinds of circuits in VHDL requires the concept of signal drivers. A VHDL driver is one contributor to the overall value of a signal.

A multiply-driven signal has many drivers. The values of all of the drivers are resolved together to create a single value for the signal. The method of resolving all of the contributors into a single value is through a resolution function (resolution functions are discussed in Chap. 5). A resolution function is a designer-written function that will be called whenever a driver of a signal changes value.

Driver creation

Drivers are created by signal assignment statements. A concurrent signal assignment inside of an architecture produces one driver for each signal assignment. Multiple signal assignments therefore produce multiple drivers for a signal. Consider the following architecture:

```
ARCHITECTURE test OF test IS
BEGIN
  a <= b AFTER 10 ns;
  a <= c AFTER 10 ns;
END test;
```

Signal a is being driven from two sources, b and c. Each concurrent signal assignment statement will create a driver for signal a. The first statement will create a driver that contains the value of signal b delayed by 10 ns. The second statement will create a driver that contains the value of signal c delayed by 10 ns. How these two drivers are resolved is left to the designer. The designers of VHDL did not want to arbitrarily add language constraints to signal behavior. Synthesizing the preceding example would short c and b together.

Bad multiple driver model

Let's look at a model that seems correct enough at first glance, but will not function as the user intended. The model is for the four-to-one multiplexer discussed earlier.

```
USE WORK.std_logic_1164.ALL;
ENTITY mux IS
  PORT (i0, i1, i2, i3, a, b: IN std_logic;
        q : OUT std_logic);
END mux;

ARCHITECTURE bad OF mux IS
BEGIN
  q <= i0 WHEN a = '0' AND b = '0' ELSE '0';
  q <= i1 WHEN a = '1' AND b = '0' ELSE '0';
  q <= i2 WHEN a = '0' AND b = '1' ELSE '0';
  q <= i3 WHEN a = '1' AND b = '1' ELSE '0';
END BAD;
```

This model assigns $i0$ to q when a is equal to a 0 and b is equal to a 0, $i1$ when a is equal to a 1 and b is equal to a 0, etc. From a first glance, the model looks as if it will work. However, each assignment to signal q creates a new driver for signal q. Four drivers to signal q will be created by this model.

Each driver will be driving either the value of one of the $i0$, $i1$, $i2$, $i3$ inputs, or '0'. The value driven will be dependent on inputs a and b. If a is equal to '0', and b is equal to '0', the first assignment statement will put the value of *i0* into one of the drivers of *q*. The other three assignment statements will not have their conditions met and, therefore, will be driving the value '0'. Three drivers will be driving the value 0, and one driver will be driving the value of *i0*. Typical resolution functions would have a difficult time predicting the desired output on *q*, which is the value of *i0*.

A better way to write this model is to create only one driver for signal *q*, as shown here:

```
ARCHITECTURE better OF mux IS
BEGIN
  q <= i0 WHEN a = '0' AND b = '0' ELSE
       i1 WHEN a = '1' AND b = '0' ELSE
       i2 WHEN a = '0' AND b = '1' ELSE
       i3 WHEN a = '1' AND b = '1' ELSE
       'X';   --- unknown
END better;
```

Generics

Generics are a general mechanism used to pass information to an instance of an entity. The information passed to the entity can be of most types allowed in VHDL. (Types are covered in detail in Chap. 4.)

Why would a designer want to pass information to an entity? The most obvious, and probably most used, information passed to an entity are delay times for rising and falling delays of the device being modeled. Generics can also be used to pass any user-defined data types, including information such as load capacitance, resistance, etc. For synthesis parameters such as data-path widths, signal widths, etc., can be passed in as generics.

All of the data passed to an entity is instance-specific information. The data values pertain to the instance being passed the data. In this way, the designer can pass different values to different instances in the design.

The data passed to an instance is static data. Once the model has been elaborated (linked into the simulator), the data will not change during simulation. Generics cannot be assigned information as part of a simulation run. The information contained in generics passed into a component instance or a block can be used to alter the simulation results, but results cannot modify the generics.

Following is an example of an entity for an AND gate that has three generics associated with it.

```
ENTITY and2 IS
  GENERIC(rise, fall : TIME; load : INTEGER);
```

```
  PORT( a, b : IN BIT;
        c : OUT BIT);
END AND2;
```

This entity would allow the designer to pass in a value for the rise and fall delays, as well a the loading that the device has on its output. With this information, the model can correctly model the AND gate in the design. The architecture for the AND gate is as follows:

```
ARCHITECTURE load_dependent OF and2 IS
  SIGNAL internal : BIT;
BEGIN
  internal <= a AND b;
  c <= internal AFTER (rise + (load * 2 ns)) WHEN internal =
'1'
    ELSE internal AFTER (fall + (load * 3 ns));

END load_dependent;
```

The architecture declares a local signal called *internal* to store the value of the expression *a* and *b*. Precomputing values used in multiple instances is a very efficient method for modeling.

The generics *rise, fall,* and *load* contain the values that were passed in by the component instantiation statement. Let's look at a piece of a model that will instantiate the components of type AND2 in another model.

```
USE WORK.std_logic_1164.ALL;
ENTITY test IS
  GENERIC(rise, fall : TIME; load : INTEGER);
  PORT ( ina, inb, inc, ind : IN std_logic;
         out1, out2 : OUT std_logic);
END test;

ARCHITECTURE test_arch OF test IS
  COMPONENT AND2
    GENERIC(rise, fall : TIME; load : INTEGER);
    PORT ( a, b : IN std_logic;
           c : OUT std_logic);
  END COMPONENT;
BEGIN
  U1: AND2 GENERIC MAP(10 ns, 12 ns, 3)
    PORT MAP (ina, inb, out1 );

  U2: AND2 GENERIC MAP(9 ns, 11 ns, 5)
    PORT MAP (inc, ind, out2);
END test_arch;
```

The architecture statement first declares any components that will be used in the model. In this example, component AND2 is declared.

Next, the body of the architecture statement contains a couple of component instantiation statements for components U1 and U2. Port *a* of component U1 is mapped to signal *ina,* port *b* is mapped to signal *inb,* and port *c* is mapped to *out1.* In the same way, component U2 is mapped to signals *inc, ind,* and *out2.*

Generic *rise* of instance U1 is mapped to 10 ns, generic *fall* is mapped to 12 ns, and generic *load* is mapped to 3. The generics for component U2 are mapped to values 9 and 11 ns and value 5.

Generics can also have default values that are overridden if actual values are mapped to the generics. In the example following are two instances of component type AND2.

In instance U1, actual values are mapped to the generics, and these values will be used in the simulation. In instance U2, no values are mapped to the instance and, therefore, the default values will be used to control the behavior of the simulation, if specified; otherwise, an error will occur.

```
USE WORK.std_logic_1164.ALL;
ENTITY test IS
  GENERIC(rise, fall : TIME;
          load : INTEGER);
  PORT ( ina, inb, inc, ind : IN std_logic;
         out1, out2 : OUT std_logic);
END test;

ARCHITECTURE test_arch OF test IS
  COMPONENT and2
    GENERIC(rise, fall : TIME := 10 NS;
            load : INTEGER := 0);
    PORT ( a, b : IN std_logic;
           c : OUT std_logic);
  END COMPONENT;
BEGIN

  U1: and2 GENERIC MAP(10 ns, 12 ns, 3 )
    PORT MAP (ina, inb, out1 );

  U2: and2 PORT MAP (inc, ind, out2 );

END test_arch;
```

As we have seen, generics have many uses. The uses of generics are limited only by the creativity of the model writer.

Block Statements

Blocks are a partitioning mechanism within VHDL that allows the designer to logically group areas of the model. The analogy with a typical CAE system is a schematic sheet. In a typical CAE system, a level or a portion of the design can be represented by a number of schematic sheets. The reason for partitioning the design may relate to design standards about how many components are allowed on a sheet, or it may be a logical grouping that the designer finds more understandable.

The same analogy holds true for block statements. The statement area in an architecture can be broken into a number of separate logical areas. For instance, if you were designing a CPU, one block might be an ALU; another, a register bank; and another, a shifter.

Each block represents a self-contained area of the model. Each block can declare local signals, types, constants, etc. Any object that can be declared in the architecture declaration section can be declared in the block declaration section. An example follows.

```
USE WORK.std_logic_1164.ALL;
PACKAGE bit32 IS
  TYPE tw32 IS ARRAY(31 DOWNTO 0) OF std_logic;
END bit32;

USE WORK.std_logic_1164.ALL;
USE WORK.bit32.ALL;
ENTITY cpu IS
  PORT( clk, interrupt : IN std_logic;
        addr : OUT tw32; data : INOUT tw32 );
END cpu;

ARCHITECTURE cpu_blk OF cpu IS
  SIGNAL ibus, dbus : tw32;
BEGIN
  ALU : BLOCK
    SIGNAL qbus : tw32;
  BEGIN
    -- alu behavior statements
  END BLOCK ALU;

  REG8 : BLOCK
    SIGNAL zbus : tw32;
  BEGIN
    REG1: BLOCK
      SIGNAL qbus : tw32;
    BEGIN
      -- reg1 behavioral statements
    END BLOCK REG1;

      -- more REG8 statements

  END BLOCK REG8;
END cpu_blk;
```

Entity *cpu* is the outermost entity declaration of this model. (This is not a complete model, only a subset.) Entity *cpu* declares four ports that are used as the model interface. Ports *clk* and *interrupt* are input ports, *addr* is an output port, and *data* is an inout port. All of these ports are visible to any block declared in an architecture for this entity. The input ports can be read from, and the output ports can be assigned values.

Signals *ibus* and *dbus* are local signals declared in architecture *cpu_blk*. These signals are local to architecture *cpu_blk* and cannot be referenced outside of the architecture. However, any block inside of the architecture can reference these signals. Any lower-level block can reference signals from a level above, but upper-level blocks cannot reference lower-level local signals.

Signal *qbus* is declared in the block declaration section of block ALU. This signal is local to block ALU and cannot be referenced outside of the block. All of the statements inside of block ALU can reference *qbus*, but statements outside of block ALU cannot use *qbus*.

In exactly the same fashion, signal *zbus* is local to block REG8. Block REG1 inside of block REG8 has access to signal *zbus*, and all of the other statements in block REG8 also have access to signal *zbus*.

In the declaration section for block REG1, another signal called *qbus* is declared. This signal has the same name as the signal *qbus* declared in block ALU. Won't this cause a problem? To the compiler, these two signals are separate, and this is a legal, although confusing, use of the language. The two signals are declared in two separate declarative regions and are valid only in those regions; therefore, they are considered to be two separate signals with the same name. Each *qbus* can be referenced only in the block that has the declaration of the signal, except as a fully qualified name, discussed later in this section.

Another interesting case is shown as follows:

```
BLK1 : BLOCK
  SIGNAL qbus : tw32;
BEGIN

  BLK2 : BLOCK
    SIGNAL qbus : tw32;
  BEGIN
    -- blk2 statements
  END BLOCK BLK2;

    -- blk1 statements

END BLOCK BLK1;
```

In this example, signal *qbus* is declared in two blocks. The interesting feature of this model is that one of the blocks is contained in the other. It would seem that BLK2 has access to two signals called *qbus:* the first from the local declaration of *qbus* in the declaration section of BLK2 and the second from the declaration section of BLK1.BLK1 is also the parent block of BLK2. However, BLK2 will see only the *qbus* signal from the declaration in BLK2. The *qbus* signal from BLK1 has been overridden by a declaration of the same name in BLK2.

The *qbus* signal from BLK1 can be seen inside of BLK2 if the name of signal *qbus* is qualified with the block name. For instance, in this example, to reference signal *qbus* from BLK1, use *BLK1.qbus.*

In general, this can be a very confusing method of modeling. The problem stems from the fact that you are never quite sure which *qbus* is being referenced at a given time without fully analyzing all of the declarations carefully.

As mentioned earlier, blocks are self-contained regions of the model. But blocks are unique because a block can contain ports and generics. This allows the designer to remap signals and generics external to the block to signals and generics inside the block. But why, as a designer, would I want to do that?

The capability of ports and generics on blocks allows the designer to reuse blocks written for another purpose in a new design. For instance, let's assume that you are upgrading a CPU design and need extra functionality in the ALU section. Let's also assume that another designer has a new ALU model that performs the functionality needed. The only trouble with the new ALU model is that the interface port names and generic names are different than the names that exist in the design being upgraded. With the port and generic mapping ability within blocks, this is no problem. Map the signal names and the generic parameters in the design being upgraded to ports and generics created for the new ALU block. An example illustrating this follows

```
USE WORK.std_logic_1164.ALL
PACKAGE math IS
  TYPE tw32 IS ARRAY(31 DOWNTO 0) OF std_logic;
  FUNCTION tw_add(a, b : tw32) RETURN tw32;
  FUNCTION tw_sub(a, b : tw32) RETURN tw32;
END math;

USE WORK.math.ALL;
USE WORK.std_logic_1164.ALL;
ENTITY cpu IS
  PORT( clk, interrupt : IN std_logic;
        addr : OUT tw32; cont : IN INTEGER;
        data : INOUT tw32 );
END cpu;
ARCHITECTURE cpu_blk OF cpu IS
```

```
        SIGNAL ibus, dbus : tw32;
     BEGIN
       ALU : BLOCK
         PORT( abus, bbus : IN tw32;
               d_out : OUT tw32;
               ctbus : IN INTEGER);
         PORT MAP ( abus => ibus, bbus => dbus, d_out => data,
                    ctbus => cont);
         SIGNAL qbus : tw32;
       BEGIN
         d_out <= tw_add(abus, bbus)   WHEN ctbus = 0 ELSE
                  tw_sub(abus, bbus)  WHEN ctbus = 1 ELSE
                  abus;
       END BLOCK ALU;
     END cpu_blk;
```

Basically, this is the same model as that shown earlier, except for the port and port map statements in the ALU block declaration section. The port statement declares the number of ports used for the block, the direction of the ports, and the type of the ports. The port map statement maps the new ports with signals or ports that exist outside of the block. Port abus is mapped to architecture CPU_BLK local signal *ibus,* port *bbus* is mapped to *dbus.* Ports *d_out* and *ctbus* are mapped to external ports of the entity.

Mapping implies a connection between the port and the external signal such that whenever there is a change in value on the signal connected to a port, the port value changes to the new value. If a change occurs in the signal *ibus,* the new value of *ibus* will be passed into the ALU block and port *abus* will obtain the new value. The same is true for all ports.

Guarded blocks

Block statements have another interesting behavior known as *guarded blocks.* A guarded block contains a guard expression which can enable and disable drivers inside the block. The guard expression is a boolean expression: when true, drivers contained in the block are enabled and, when false, the drivers are disabled. Let's look at an example to show some more of the details.

```
USE WORK.std_logic_1164.ALL;
ENTITY latch IS
  PORT( d, clk : IN std_logic;
        q, qb : OUT std_logic);
END latch;
```

```
ARCHITECTURE latch_guard OF latch IS
BEGIN
  G1 : BLOCK( clk = '1')
  BEGIN
    q <= GUARDED d AFTER 5 ns;
    qb <= GUARDED NOT(d) AFTER 7 ns;
  END BLOCK G1;
END latch_guard;
```

This model illustrates how a latch model could be written using a guarded block. This is a very simpleminded model; however, more complex and more accurate models will be shown later. The entity declares the four ports needed for the latch, and the architecture has only one statement in it. The statement is a guarded block statement. A guarded block statement looks like a typical block statement except for the guard expression after the keyword BLOCK. The guard expression in this example is (clk = '1'). This is a boolean expression that will return TRUE when clk is equal to a '1' value, and will return FALSE when clk is equal to any other value.

When the guard expression is true, all of the drivers of guarded signal assignment statements will be enabled, or turned on. When the guard expression is false, all of the drivers of guarded signal assignment statements are disabled, or turned off. There are two guarded signal assignment statements in this model. One is the statement that assigns a value to q, and the other is the statement that assigns a value to qb. A guarded signal assignment statement is recognized by the keyword GUARDED between the <= and the expression part of the statement.

When port clk of the entity has the value '1', the guard expression will be true, and the value of input d will be scheduled on the q output after 5 ns, and the NOT value of d will be scheduled on the qb output after 7 ns. When port clk has the value '0', or any other legal value of the type, outputs q and qb will turn off and the output value of the signal will be determined by the default value assigned by the resolution function. When clk is not equal to '1' the drivers created by the signal assignments for q and qb in this architecture are effectively turned off. The drivers do not contribute to the overall value of the signal.

Signal assignments can be guarded by using the keyword GUARDED. A new signal is implicitly declared in the block whenever a block has a guard expression. This signal is called GUARD. Its value is the value of the guard expression. This signal can be used to trigger other processes to occur.

Blocks are useful for partitioning the design into smaller, more manageable units. They allow the designer the flexibility to create large designs from smaller building blocks and provide a convenient method of controlling the drivers on a signal. At the time of this writing, guarded blocks are currently not supported by synthesis tools.

In the first chapter, concepts of structurally building models were discussed. This chapter is the first of many that discuss behavioral modeling. In this chapter we discussed the following:

- Signal assignments are the most basic form of behavioral modeling.

- Signal assignment statements can be selected or conditional.

- Signal assignment statements can contain delays.

- VHDL contains inertial delay and transport delay.

- Simulation delta time points are used to order events in time.

- Drivers on a signal are created by signal assignment statements.

- Generics are used to pass data to entities.

- Block statements allow grouping within an entity.

- Guarded block statements allow the capability of turning off drivers within a block.

3

Sequential Processing

In Chap. 2 we examined behavioral modeling using concurrent statements. We discussed concurrent signal assignment statements, as well as block statements and component instantiation. In this chapter we will focus on sequential statements. Sequential statements are statements that execute serially, one after the other. Most programming languages such as C and Pascal support this type of behavior. In fact, VHDL has borrowed the syntax for its sequential statements from ADA.

Process Statement

In an architecture for an entity, all statements are concurrent. So, where do sequential statements exist in VHDL? There is a statement called the *process statement* that contains only sequential statements. The process statement is itself a concurrent statement. A process statement can exist in an architecture and define regions in the architecture where all statements are sequential.

A process statement has a declaration section and a statement part. In the declaration section, types, variables, constants, subprograms, etc., can be declared (for a full list, see appendix A in the LRM). The statement part contains only sequential statements. Sequential statements consist of CASE statements, IF THEN ELSE statements, LOOP statements, etc. We will examine these statements later in this chapter. First, let's look at how a process statement is structured.

Sensitivity list

The process statement can have an explicit sensitivity list. This list defines the signals that will cause the statements inside the process statement to execute whenever one or more elements of the list change value. The sensitivity list is a list of the signals that the process is sensitive to. Changes in the values of these signals will cause the process to be invoked. The process has to have an explicit sensitivity list or, as we will discuss later, a WAIT statement.

As of this writing, synthesis tools have a difficult time with sensitivity lists that are not fully specified. Synthesis tools think of process statements as either describing sequential logic or combinational logic. If a process contains a partial sensitivity list, one that does not contain every input signal used in the process, there is no way to map that functionality to either sequential or combinational logic.

Process example

Let's look at an example of a process statement in an architecture to see how the process statement fits into the big picture, and discuss some more details of how it works. Shown here is a model of a two-input nand gate:

```
USE WORK.std_logic_1164.ALL;
ENTITY nand2 IS
  PORT( a, b : IN std_logic;
        c : OUT std_logic);
END nand2;

ARCHITECTURE nand2 OF nand2 IS
BEGIN
  PROCESS( a, b )
    VARIABLE temp : std_logic;
  BEGIN
    temp := NOT (a and b);

    IF (temp = '1') THEN
      c <= temp AFTER 6 ns;
    ELSIF (temp = '0') THEN
      c <= temp AFTER 5 ns;
    ELSE
      c <= temp AFTER 6 ns;
    END IF;

  END PROCESS;
END nand2;
```

This example shows how to write a model for a simple two-input NAND gate using a process statement. The USE statement declares a VHDL package that provides the necessary information to allow modeling this NAND gate with 9-state logic. (This package is described in

App. A.) We will discuss packages in Chap. 5. The USE statement was included so that the model could be simulated with a VHDL simulator without any modifications.

The entity declares three ports for the *nand2* gate. Ports *a* and *b* are the inputs to the *nand2* gate and port *c* is the output. The name of the architecture is the same name as the entity name. This is legal and can save some of the headaches of trying to generate unique names.

The architecture contains only one statement, a concurrent process statement. The process declarative part starts at the keyword PRO-CESS and ends at the keyword BEGIN. The process *statement* part starts at the keyword BEGIN and ends at the keywords END PRO-CESS. The process *declaration* section declares a local variable called *temp*. The process *statement* part has two sequential statements in it; a variable assignment statement

```
temp := NOT (a AND b);
```

and an IF THEN ELSE statement.

```
IF (temp = '1') THEN
   c <= temp AFTER 6 ns;
ELSIF (temp = '0') THEN
   c <= temp AFTER 5 ns;
ELSE
   c <= temp AFTER 6 ns;
END IF;
```

The process contains an explicit sensitivity list with two signals contained in it.

```
PROCESS( a, b)
```

The process is sensitive to signals *a* and *b*. In this example, *a* and *b* are input ports to the model. Input ports create signals that can be used as inputs; output ports create signals that can be used as outputs; and inout ports create signals that can be used as both. Whenever port *a* or *b* has a change in value, the statements inside of the process will be executed. Each statement will be executed in serial order, starting with the statement at the top of the process statement and working down to the bottom. After all of the statements have been executed once, the process will wait for another change in a signal or port in its sensitivity list.

The process declarative part declares one variable called *temp*. Its type is *std_logic*. This type will be explained in App. A, as it is used throughout the book. For now, assume that the type defines a signal that is a single bit and can assume the values 0, 1, and X. Variable *temp* is used as temporary storage in this model to save the precomputed value of the expression (*a* and *b*). The value of this expression is precomputed for efficiency.

Signal Assignment versus Variable Assignment

The first statement inside of the process statement is a variable assignment that assigns a value to variable *temp*. In the previous chapter we discussed how signals received values that were scheduled either after an amount of time or after a delta delay. A variable assignment happens immediately when the statement is executed. For instance, in this model the first statement has to assign a value to variable *temp* for the second statement to use. Variable assignment has no delay; it happens immediately.

Let's look at two examples that illustrate this point more clearly. Both examples are models of a four-to-one multiplexer device. The symbol and truth table for this device are shown in Fig. 3.1. One of the four input signals is propagated to the output, depending on the values on inputs *a* and *b*.

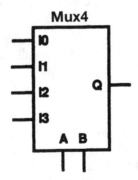

A	B	Q
0	0	I0
1	0	I1
0	1	I2
1	1	I3

Figure 3.1   Four-input mux symbol and function.

The first model for the multiplexer is an incorrect model and the second is a corrected version of the model.

Incorrect mux example

The incorrect model of the multiplexer has a flaw in it that will cause the model to produce incorrect results. This is shown by the following model:

```
USE WORK.std_logic_1164ALL;
ENTITY mux IS
   PORT (i0, i1, i2, i3, a, b : IN std_logic;
         q : OUT std_logic);
END mux;

ARCHITECTURE wrong of mux IS
   SIGNAL muxval : INTEGER;
BEGIN
PROCESS (i0, i1, i2, i3, a, b )
BEGIN
   muxval <= 0;
   IF (a = '1') THEN
     muxval <= muxval + 1;
   END IF;

   IF (b = '1') THEN
     muxval <= muxval + 2;
   END IF;

   CASE muxval IS
     WHEN 0 =>
       q <= I0 AFTER 10 ns;
     WHEN 1 =>
       q <= I1 AFTER 10 ns;
     WHEN 2 =>
       q <= I2 AFTER 10 ns;
     WHEN 3 =>
       q <= I3 AFTER 10 ns;
     WHEN OTHERS =>
       NULL;
   END CASE;
END PROCESS;
END wrong;
```

Whenever one of the input signals in the process sensitivity list changes value, the sequential statements in the process are executed. The process statement in the first example contains four sequential statements. The first statement initializes the local signal *muxval* to a known value (0). The subsequent statements add values to the local signal, depending on the value of the a and b input signals. Finally, the case statement will choose an input to propagate to the output based on the value of signal *muxval*. This model has a significant flaw, however. The first statement,

```
muxval <= 0;
```

causes the value 0 to be scheduled as an event for signal *muxval*. In fact, the value 0 is scheduled in an event for the next simulation delta because no delay was specified. When the second statement,

```
IF (a = '1') THEN
  muxval <= muxval + 1;
END IF;
```

is executed, the value of signal *muxval* will be whatever was last propagated to it. The new value scheduled from the first statement will not have propagated yet. In fact, when multiple assignments to a signal occur within the same process statement, the last assigned value will be the value propagated.

The signal *muxval* will have a *garbage* value when entering the process. Its value will not be changed until the process has completed execution of all of the sequential statements contained in the process. In fact, if signal b is a '1' value, then whatever garbage value the signal had when entering the process will have the value 2 added to it.

A better way to implement this example is shown in the next example. The only difference between this next model and the previous one is the declaration of *muxval* and the assignments to *muxval*. In the previous model, *muxval* was a signal, and signal assignment statements were used to assign values to it. In the next example, *muxval* is a variable and variable assignments are used to assign to it.

Correct mux example

In this example, the incorrect model will be rewritten to reflect a solution to the problems with the last model.

```
USE WORK.std_logic_1164.ALL;
ENTITY mux IS
  PORT (i0, i1, i2, i3, a, b : IN std_logic;
        q : OUT std_logic);
END mux;

ARCHITECTURE better OF mux IS
BEGIN
  PROCESS ( i0, i1, i2, i3, a, b )
```

```
      VARIABLE muxval : INTEGER;
  BEGIN
    muxval := 0;
    IF (a = '1') THEN
      muxval := muxval + 1;
    END IF;

    IF (b = '1') THEN
      muxval := muxval + 2;
    END IF;

    CASE muxval IS
      WHEN 0 =>
        q <= I0 AFTER 10 ns;
      WHEN 1 =>
        q <= I1 AFTER 10 ns;
      WHEN 2 =>
        q <= I2 AFTER 10 ns;
      WHFN 3 =>
        q <= I3 AFTER 10 ns;
      WHEN OTHERS =>
        NULL;
    END CASE;
  END PROCESS;
END better;
```

This simple coding difference makes a tremendous operational difference. When the first statement,

```
muxval := 0;
```

is executed, the value 0 is placed in variable *muxval* immediately. The value is not scheduled because *muxval* in this example is a variable, not a signal. Variables represent local storage, as opposed to signals, which represent circuit interconnect. The local storage is updated immediately, and the new value can be used later in the model for further computations.

Since *muxval* is initialized to 0 immediately, the next two statements in the process will use 0 as the initial value and add appropriate numbers, depending on the values of signals *a* and *b*. These assignments are also immediate and, therefore, when the CASE statement executes, variable *muxval* contains the correct value. From this value, the correct input signal can be propagated to the output.

Sequential Statements

Sequential statements exist inside the boundaries of a process statement, as well as in subprograms. In this chapter, we are most concerned with sequential statements inside of process statements. In Chap. 5, we will discuss subprograms and the statements contained within them.

The sequential statements that we will discuss are:

IF

CASE

LOOP

ASSERT

WAIT

IF statements

In App. A of the LRM, all VHDL constructs are described using a variant of the Bachus-Naur format (BNF) that is used to describe typical programming languages. If you are not familiar with BNF, App. D in this book gives a cursory description. Becoming familiar with the BNF will help you to better understand how to construct complex VHDL statements.

The BNF description of the IF statement is listed in App. A of the LRM and looks like this:

```
if_statement ::=
  IF condition THEN
    sequence_of_statements
  {ELSIF condition THEN
    sequence_of_statements}
  [ELSE
    sequence_of_statements]
END IF;
```

From the BNF description, we can conclude that the IF statement starts with the keyword IF and ends with the keywords END IF, spelled out as two separate words. There are also two optional clauses; they are the ELSIF clause and the ELSE clause. The ELSIF clause is repeatable such that more than one ELSIF clause is allowed, but the ELSE clause is optional, and only one is allowed. The condition construct in all cases is a boolean expression. This is an expression that evaluates to either true or false. Whenever a condition evaluates to a true value, the sequence of statements following is executed. If no condition is true, then the sequence of statements for the ELSE clause is executed, if one exists. Let's analyze a few examples to get a better understanding of how the BNF relates to the VHDL code.

The first example shows how to write a simple IF statement.

```
IF (x < 10) THEN
  a := b;
END IF;
```

The IF statement starts with the keyword IF. Next is the condition (x < 10), followed by the keyword THEN. The condition will be true when the value of x is less than 10; otherwise, it will be false. When the condition is true, the statements between the THEN and END IF will be executed. In this example, the assignment statement ($a := b$) will be executed whenever x is less than 10. What happens if x is greater than or equal to 10? In this example, there is no ELSE clause, so no statements will be executed in the IF statement. Instead, control will be transferred to the statement after the END IF.

Let's look at another example where the ELSE clause is useful.

```
IF (day = sunday) THEN
  weekend := TRUE;
ELSIF (day = saturday) THEN
  weekend := TRUE;
ELSE
  weekday := TRUE;
END IF;
```

In this example, there are two variables, *weekend* and *weekday,* that get set depending on the value of a signal called *day.* Variable *weekend* gets set to TRUE whenever *day* is equal to *saturday* or *sunday.* Otherwise, variable *weekday* gets set to TRUE. The execution of the IF statement starts by checking to see if variable *day* is equal to *sunday.* If this is true, then the next statement is executed and control is transferred to the statement following END IF. Otherwise, control is transferred to the ELSIF statement part and *day* is checked for *saturday.* If variable *day* is equal to *saturday,* then the next statement is executed and control is again transferred to the statement following the END IF statement. Finally, if *day* is not equal to *sunday* or *saturday,* then the ELSE statement part is executed.

The IF statement can have multiple ELSIF statement parts, but only one ELSE statement part. Between each statement part can exist more than one sequential statement.

CASE statements

The CASE statement is used whenever a single expression value can be used to select between a number of actions. The BNF for the CASE statement is as follows:

```
case_statement ::=
  CASE expression IS
    case_statement_alternative
    {case_statement_alternative}
END CASE;

case_statement_alternative ::=
  WHEN choices =>
    sequence_of_statements
sequence_of_statements ::=
  {sequential_statement}

choices ::=
  choice{| choice}

choice ::=
  SIMPLE_expression|
  discrete_range|
  ELEMENT_simple_name|
  OTHERS
```

A CASE statement consists of the keyword CASE followed by an expression and the keyword IS. The expression will either return a value that matches one of the CHOICES in a WHEN statement part, or match an OTHERS clause. If the expression matches the CHOICE part of a WHEN *choices => clause,* the *sequence_of_statements* following will be executed. After these statements are executed, control is transferred to the statement following the END CASE clause.

Either the CHOICES clause must enumerate every possible value of the type returned by the expression, or the last choice must contain an OTHERS clause.

Let's look at some examples to reinforce what the BNF states.

```
CASE instruction IS
  WHEN load_accum =>
    accum <= data;
  WHEN store_accum =>
    data_out <= accum;
  WHEN load|store =>
    process_IO(addr);
  WHEN OTHERS =>
    process_error(instruction);
END CASE;
```

The CASE statement will execute the proper statement depending on the value of input *instruction.* If the value of *instruction* is one of the choices listed in the WHEN clauses, then statement following the WHEN clause is executed. Otherwise, the statement following the

OTHERS clause is executed. In this example, when the value of *instruction* is *load_accum,* the first assignment statement is executed. If the value of *instruction* is *load* or *store,* the *process_IO* procedure is called.

If the value of *instruction* is outside the range of the choices given, then the OTHERS clause will match the expression, and the statement following the OTHERS clause will be executed. It is an error if an OTHERS clause does not exist and the choices given do not cover every possible value of the expression type.

In the next example, a more complex type (types are discussed in Chap. 4) is returned by the expression. The CASE statement uses this type to select among the choices of the statement.

```
TYPE vectype IS ARRAY(0 TO 1) OF BIT;
VARIABLE bit_vec : vectype;
    .
    .
    .
CASE bit_vec IS
  WHEN "00" =>
    RETURN 0;
  WHEN "01" =>
    RETURN 1;
  WHEN "10" =>
    RETURN 2;
  WHEN "11" =>
    RETURN 3;
END CASE;
```

This example shows one way to convert an array of bits into an integer. When both bits of variable *bit_vec* contain '0' values, the first choice "00" will match and the value 0 will be returned. When both bits are '1' values, the value 3, or "11", will be returned. This CASE statement does not need an OTHERS clause because all possible values of variable *bit_vec* are enumerated by the choices.

LOOP statements

The LOOP statement is used whenever an operation needs to be repeated. LOOP statements are used when powerful iteration capability is needed to implement a model. The BNF for the LOOP statement is as follows:

```
loop_statement ::=
  [LOOP_label : ] [iteration_scheme] LOOP
    sequence_of_statements
  END LOOP[LOOP_label];
```

```
iteration_scheme ::=
  WHILE condition | FOR LOOP_parameter_specification

LOOP_parameter_specification ::=
  identifier IN discrete_range
```

The LOOP statement has an optional label which can be used to identify the LOOP statement. The LOOP statement has an optional *iteration_scheme* that determines which kind of LOOP statement is being used. The *iteration_scheme* includes two types of LOOP statements, a "WHILE condition" LOOP statement and a "FOR identifier IN *discrete_range*" statement. The FOR loop will loop as many times as specified in the *discrete_range,* unless the loop is exited from (discussed later). The WHILE condition LOOP statement will loop as long as the condition expression is TRUE.

Let's look at a couple of examples to see how these statements work.

```
WHILE (day = weekday) LOOP
  day := get_next_day(day);
END LOOP;
```

This example uses the "WHILE condition" form of the LOOP statement. The condition is checked each time before the loop is executed. If the condition is TRUE, the LOOP statements are executed. Control will then be transferred back to the beginning of the loop. The condition will be checked again. If TRUE, the loop will be executed again; if not, statement execution will continue on the statement following the END LOOP clause.

The other version of the LOOP statement is the FOR loop.

```
FOR i IN 1 to 10 LOOP
  i_squared(i) := i * i;
END LOOP;
```

This loop will execute 10 times whenever execution begins. Its function is to calculate the squares from 1 to 10 and insert them into the *i_squared* signal array. The index variable, *i,* will start at the leftmost value of the range and will be incremented until the rightmost value of the range.

In some languages, the loop index (in this example, *i*) can be assigned a value inside the loop to change its value. VHDL does not allow any assignment to the loop index. This also precludes the loop index existing as the return value of a function, or as an out or inout parameter of a procedure.

Another interesting point about FOR LOOP statements is the fact that the index value *i* is locally declared by the FOR statement. The variable *i* does not need to be declared explicitly in the process, function, or procedure. By virtue of the FOR LOOP statement, the loop index is declared locally. If another variable of the same name exists in the process, function, or procedure, then these two variables are treated as separate variables and are accessed by context. Let's look at an example to illustrate this point.

```
PROCESS(i)
BEGIN

  x <= i + 1; -- x is a signal

  FOR i IN 1 to a/2 LOOP
    q(i) := a; -- q is a variable
  END LOOP;

END PROCESS;
```

Whenever the value of the signal *i* in the process sensitivity list changes value, the process will be invoked. The first statement will schedule the value *i* + 1 on the signal *x*. Next, the FOR loop will be executed. The index value *i* is not the same object as the signal *i* that was used to calculate the new value for signal *x*. These are separate objects that are each accessed by context. Inside the FOR loop, when a reference is made to *i*, the local index is retrieved. But outside the FOR loop, when a reference is made to *i*, the value of the signal *i* in the sensitivity list of the process is retrieved.

The values used to specify the range in the FOR loop need not be specific integer values, as has been shown in the examples. The range can obtain any discrete range. A *discrete_range* can be expressed as a *subtype_indication* or a range statement. Let's look at a few more examples of how FOR loops can be constructed with ranges.

```
PROCESS(clk)
  TYPE day_of_week IS (sun, mon, tue, wed, thur, fri, sat);
BEGIN
  FOR i IN day_of_week LOOP
    IF i = sat THEN
      son <= mow_lawn;
    ELSIF i = sun THEN
      church <= family;
    ELSE
      dad <= go_to_work;
```

```
    END IF;
  END LOOP;
END PROCESS;
```

In this example, the range is specified by the type. By specifying the type as the range, the compiler will determine that the leftmost value is *sun* and the rightmost value is *sat*. The range will then be determined as from *sun* to *sat*.

If an ascending range is desired, use the *to* clause. The *downto* clause can be used to create a descending range. An example would be:

```
PROCESS(x, y)
BEGIN
  FOR i IN x downto y LOOP
    q(i) := w(i);
  END LOOP;
END PROCESS;
```

When different values for *x* and *y* are passed in, different ranges of the array *w* are copied to the same place in array *q*.

NEXT statement

There are cases when it is necessary to stop executing the statements in the loop for this iteration and go to the next iteration. VHDL includes a construct that will accomplish this. The NEXT statement allows the designer to stop processing this iteration and skip to the successor. When the NEXT statement is executed, processing of the model stops at the current point and is transferred to the beginning of the LOOP statement. Execution will begin with the first statement in the loop but the loop variable will be incremented to the next iteration value. If the iteration limit has been reached, processing will stop. If not, execution will continue.

The following is an example showing this behavior:

```
PROCESS(A, B)
  CONSTANT max_limit : INTEGER := 255;
TYPE d_type is ARRAY (0 TO max_limit OF BOOLEAN;
VARIABLE done : d_type;
BEGIN
  FOR i IN 0 TO max_limit LOOP
    IF (done(i) = TRUE) THEN
      NEXT;
    ELSE
      done(i) := TRUE;
    END IF;

    q(i) <= a(i) AND b(i);

  END LOOP;
END PROCESS;
```

The process statement contains one LOOP statement. This LOOP statement will logically "and" the bits of arrays *a* and *b* and put the results in array *q*. This behavior will continue whenever the flag in array *done* is not true. If the *done* flag is already set for this value of index *i*, then the NEXT statement is executed. Execution will continue with the first statement of the loop, and index *i* will have the value *i* + 1. If the value of the *done* array is not true, then the NEXT statement is not executed, and execution will continue with the statement contained in the ELSE clause for the IF statement.

The NEXT statement allows the designer the capability to stop execution of this iteration and go on to the next iteration. There are other cases when the need exists to stop execution of a loop completely. This capability is provided with the EXIT statement.

EXIT statement

During the execution of a LOOP statement, it may be necessary to jump out of the loop. This can occur because a significant error has occurred during the execution of the model or all of the processing has finished early. The VHDL EXIT statement allows the designer to exit or jump out of a LOOP statement currently in execution. The EXIT statement causes execution to halt at the location of the EXIT statement. Execution will continue at the statement following the LOOP statement.

Here is an example illustrating this point:

```
PROCESS(a)
  variable int_a : integer;
BEGIN
  int_a := a;

  FOR i IN 0 TO max_limit LOOP
    IF (int_a <= 0) THEN -- less than or
      EXIT;            -- equal to
    ELSE
      int_a := int_a -1;
      q(i) <= 3.1416 / REAL(int_a * i); -- signal
    END IF;                    -- assign
  END LOOP;

  y <= q;

END PROCESS;
```

Inside this process statement, the value of *int_a* is always assumed to be a positive value greater than 0. If the value of *int_a* is negative or zero, then an error condition results and the calculation should not be completed. If the value of *int_a* is less than or equal to 0, then the IF statement will be true and the EXIT statement will be executed. The loop will be immediately terminated and the next statement executed will be the assignment statement to *y* after the LOOP statement.

If this were a complete example, the designer would also want to alert the user of the model that a significant error had occurred. A method to accomplish this function would be with an ASSERT statement, which is discussed later in this chapter.

The EXIT statement has three basic types of operations. The first involves an EXIT statement without a loop label, or a WHEN condition. If these conditions are true, then the EXIT statement will behave as follows: The EXIT statement will exit only from the most current LOOP statement encountered. If an EXIT statement is inside a LOOP statement that is nested inside another LOOP statement, the EXIT statement will exit only the inner LOOP statement. Execution will still remain in the outer LOOP statement. The exit statement will exit only from the most recent LOOP statement. This case was shown by the preceding example.

If the EXIT statement has an optional loop label, then the EXIT statement, when encountered, will complete the execution of the loop specified by the loop label. Therefore, the next statement executed will be the one following the END LOOP of the labeled loop. The following is an example:

```
PROCESS(a)
BEGIN
  first_loop: FOR i IN 0 TO 100 LOOP
    second_loop:FOR j IN 1 TO 10 LOOP
      ......
      EXIT second_loop; -- exits the second loop only
      ......
      EXIT first_loop; -- exits the first loop and second loop
    END LOOP;
  END LOOP;
END PROCESS;
```

The first EXIT statement will exit only the innermost loop because it only completes execution of the loop labeled *second_loop*. The last EXIT statement completes execution of the loop labeled *first_loop*, which exits from the first loop and the second loop.

If the EXIT statement has an optional WHEN condition, then the EXIT statement will exit the loop only if the condition specified is true. The next statement executed depends on whether the EXIT statement has a loop label specified or not. If a loop label is specified, the next statement executed will be contained in the LOOP statement specified by the loop label. If no loop label is present, the next statement executed is in the next outer loop. An example of an EXIT statement with a WHEN condition is as follows:

```
EXIT first_loop WHEN (i < 10);
```

This statement will complete the execution of the loop labeled *first_loop* when the expression $i < 10$ is true.

The EXIT statement provides a quick and easy method of exiting a LOOP statement when all processing is finished or an error or warning condition occurs.

ASSERT statement

The ASSERT statement is a very useful statement for reporting textual strings to the designer. The ASSERT statement checks the value of a boolean expression for true or false. If the value is true, the statement does nothing. If the value is false, the ASSERT statement will output a user-specified text string to the standard output to the terminal.

The designer can also specify a severity level with which to output the text string. The four levels are, in increasing level of severity: *note, warning, error,* and *failure.* The severity level allows the designer the capability to classify messages into proper categories.

The *note* category is useful for relaying information to the user about what is currently happening in the model. For instance, if the model had a giant loop that took a long time to execute, an assertion of severity level *note* could be used to notify the designer when the loop was 10 percent complete, 20 percent complete, 30 percent complete, etc.

Assertions of category *warning* can be used to alert the designer of conditions that, while not catastrophic, can cause erroneous behavior later. For instance, if a model expected a signal to be at a known value while some process was executing, but the signal was at a different value, it may not be an error as in the exit statement example, but a warning to the user that results may not be as expected.

Assertions of severity level *error* are used to alert the designer of conditions that will cause the model to work incorrectly, or not work at all. If the result of a calculation was supposed to return a positive value, but instead returned a negative value, depending on the operation, this could be considered an error.

Assertions of severity level *failure* are used to alert the designer of conditions within the model that can have disastrous effects. An example of such a condition was discussed in the EXIT statement section. Division by 0 is an example of an operation that could cause a failure in the model. Another is addressing beyond the end of an array. In both cases, the severity level *failure* can let the designer know that the model is behaving incorrectly.

The severity level is a good method for classifying assertions into informational messages to the designer that can describe conditions during execution of the model.

The ASSERT statement is currently ignored by synthesis tools. Since the ASSERT statement is used mainly for exception handling while writing a model, no hardware is built.

Assertion BNF. The BNF description for the ASSERT statement is shown as follows:

```
assert_statement ::=
  ASSERT condition
  [REPORT expression]
  [SEVERITY expression];
```

The keyword ASSERT is followed by a boolean-valued expression called a *condition*. The condition determines whether the text expression specified by the REPORT clause is output or not. If false, the text expression is output; if true, the text expression is not output.

There are two optional clauses in the ASSERT statement. The first is the REPORT clause. The REPORT clause allows the designer the capability to specify the value of a text expression to output. The second is the SEVERITY clause. The SEVERITY clause allows the designer to specify the severity level of the ASSERT statement. If the report clause is not specified, the default value for the ASSERT statement is *assertion violation*. If the severity clause is not specified, the default value is *error*.

Let's look at an example of an ASSERT statement in a practical use to illustrate how it works. The example performs a data setup check between two signals that control a D flip-flop. Most flip-flops require the *din* (data) input to be at a stable value a certain amount of time before a clock edge appears. This time is called the *setup time* and will guarantee that the *din* value will be clocked into the flip-flop if the setup time is met. This is shown in the model following. The assertion example will issue an error message to the designer if the setup time is violated (*assertion is false*).

```
PROCESS(clk, din)
  VARIABLE last_d_change : TIME := 0 ns;
  VARIABLE last_d_value : std_logic := 'X';
  VARIABLE last_clk_value : std_logic := 'X';
BEGIN
  IF (last_d_value /= din) THEN -- /= is not equal
```

```
     last_d_change := NOW;
     last_d_value := din;
  END IF;

  IF (last_clk_value /= clk) THEN
     last_clk_value := clk;

    IF (clk = '1') THEN
      ASSERT (NOW - last_d_change >= 20 ns)
        REPORT "setup violation"
        SEVERITY WARNING;
    END IF;
  END IF;
END PROCESS;
```

The process makes use of three local variables to record the time and last value of signal *din* as well as the value of the *clk* signal. By storing the last value of *clk* and *din*, we can determine if the signal has changed value or not. By recording the last time that *din* changed, we can measure from the current time to the last *din* transition to see if the setup time has been violated or not. (An easier method using attributes will be shown in Chap. 5.)

Whenever either *din* or *clk* changes, the process is invoked. The first step in the process is to see if the *din* signal has changed. If it has, the time of the transition is recorded using the predefined function NOW. This function returns the current simulation time. Also, the latest value of *din* is stored for future checking.

The next step is to see if signal *clk* has made a transition. If the *last_clk_value* variable is not equal to the current value of *clk*, then we know that a transition has occurred. If signal *clk* is a '1' value, then we know that a rising edge has occurred. Whenever a rising edge occurs on signal *clk*, we need to check the setup time for a violation. If the last transition on signal *d* was less than 20 ns ago, then the expression

```
(NOW - last_D_change)
```

will return a value that is less than 20 ns. The ASSERT statement will trigger and report the assertion message *setup violation* as a warning to the designer. If the last transition on signal *d* occurred more than 20 ns in the past, then the expression will return a value larger than 20 ns and the ASSERT statement will not write out the message. Remember, the ASSERT statement writes out the message when the assert condition is false.

The message reported to the user will have, at a minimum, the user string and the error classification. Some simulators will also include the time of the assertion report as well as the line number in the file of the assertion.

The ASSERT statement used in this example was a sequential ASSERT statement, because it was included inside of a PROCESS statement. A concurrent version of the ASSERT statement also exists. It has exactly the same format as the sequential ASSERT statement and exists only outside of a PROCESS statement or subprogram.

The concurrent ASSERT statement will execute whenever any signals that exist inside of the condition expression have an event upon them. This is as opposed to the sequential ASSERT statement in which execution occurs when the sequential ASSERT statement is reached inside the PROCESS statement or subprogram.

WAIT statements

The WAIT statement allows the designer the capability of suspending the sequential execution of a process or subprogram. The conditions for resuming execution of the suspended process or subprogram can be specified by three different means. These are:

WAIT ON signal changes

WAIT UNTIL an expression is true

WAIT FOR a specific amount of time

WAIT statements can be used for a number of different purposes. The most common use today is for specifying clock inputs to synthesis tools. The WAIT statement specifies the clock for a process statement that is read by synthesis tools to create sequential logic such as registers and flip-flops. Other uses are to delay process execution for an amount of time or to modify the sensitivity list of the process dynamically.

Let's take a look at a process statement with an embedded WAIT statement that is used to generate sequential logic. An example is as follows:

```
PROCESS
BEGIN
  WAIT UNTIL clock = '1' AND clock'EVENT;
  q <= d;
END PROCESS;
```

This process is used to generate a flip-flop that will clock the value of d into q when the clock input has a rising edge. The attribute 'EVENT attached to input clock will be true whenever the clock input has had an event during the current delta time point. ('EVENT will be discussed in great detail in Chap. 5.) The combination of looking for a '1' value and a change on clock will create the necessary functionality to look for a rising edge on input clock. The effect is that the process is held at the WAIT statement until the clock has a rising edge. Then the current value of d is assigned to q.

Reading this description into a synthesis tool will create a D flip-flop without a set or reset input. A synchronous reset can be created by the following:

```
PROCESS
BEGIN
  WAIT UNTIL clock = '1' AND clock'EVENT;
  IF (reset = '1') THEN
    q <= '0';
  ELSE
    q <= d;
  END IF;
END PROCESS;
```

When the clock occurs, the reset signal is tested first. If it is active, then the reset value ('0') is assigned to q; otherwise, the d input is assigned.

Finally an asynchronous reset can be added as follows:

```
PROCESS
BEGIN
  IF (reset = '1') THEN
    q <= '0';
  ELSIF clock'EVENT AND clock = '1' THEN
    q <= d;
  END IF;

  WAIT ON reset, clock;
END PROCESS;
```

This process statement contains a WAIT ON statement that will cause the process to halt execution until an event occurs on either reset or clock. The IF statement is then executed and, if reset is active, the flip-flop is asynchronously reset; otherwise, the clock is checked for a rising edge with which to transfer the d input to the q output of the flip-flop.

A WAIT statement can also be used to control the signals a process or subprogram is sensitive to at any point in the execution. An example is as follows:

```
PROCESS
BEGIN
```

```
WAIT ON a; -- 1.
  .
  .
  .
WAIT ON b; -- 2.
  .
  .
END PROCESS;
```

Execution of the statements in the PROCESS statement proceeds until point 1 in the VHDL fragment shown here. The WAIT statement will cause the process to halt execution at that point. The process will not continue execution until an event occurs on signal a. The process is therefore sensitive to changes in signal a at this point in the execution. When an event occurs on signal a, execution will start again at the statement directly after the WAIT statement at point 1. Execution will proceed until the WAIT statement at point 2 is encountered. Once again, execution is halted, and the process is now sensitive to events on signal b. Therefore, by adding in two WAIT statements, we can alter the process sensitivity list dynamically.

Next, let's discuss the three different options available to the WAIT statement. Again, they are:

```
WAIT ON signal [,signal]
WAIT UNTIL boolean_expression
WAIT FOR time_expression
```

WAIT ON signal. We have already seen an example of the first type in the preceding process example. The WAIT ON signal clause specifies a list of one or more signals upon which the WAIT statement will wait for events. If any signal in the signal list has an event occur on it, execution will continue with the statement following the WAIT statement. An example is as follows:

```
WAIT ON a, b;
```

When an event occurs on either a or b, the process will resume with the statement following the WAIT statement.

WAIT UNTIL expression. The WAIT UNTIL *boolean_expression* clause will suspend execution of the process until the expression returns a value of true. This statement will effectively create an implicit sensitivity list of the signals used in the expression. When any of the signals in the expression have events occur upon them, the expression will be evaluated. The expression must return a boolean type or the compiler will complain. When the expression returns a true value, execution will continue with the statement following the WAIT statement. Otherwise, the process will continue to be suspended. An example is as follows:

```
WAIT UNTIL ((x * 10 ) < 100 );
```

In this example, as long as the value of signal *x* is greater than or equal to 10, the WAIT statement will suspend the process or subprogram. When the value of *x* is less than 10, execution will continue with the statement following the WAIT statement.

WAIT FOR time_expression. The WAIT FOR *time_expression* clause will suspend execution of the process for the time specified by the time expression. After the time specified in the time expression has elapsed, execution will continue on the statement following the WAIT statement. A couple of examples are as follows:

```
WAIT FOR 10 ns;
WAIT FOR ( a * (b + c));
```

In the first example, the time expression is a simple constant value. The WAIT statement will suspend execution for 10 ns. After 10 ns has elapsed, execution will continue with the statement following the WAIT statement.

In the second example, the time expression is an expression that first must be evaluated to return a time value. Once this value is calculated, the WAIT statement will use this value as the time value to wait for.

Multiple WAIT conditions. The WAIT statement examples that we have examined so far have shown the different options of the WAIT statement used separately. The different options can be used together. A single statement can include an ON signal, UNTIL expression, and FOR *time_expression* clauses. An example is as follows:

```
WAIT ON nmi,interrupt UNTIL ((nmi = TRUE) or
                    (interrupt = TRUE)) FOR 5 usec;
```

This statement will wait for an event on signals *nmi* and *interrupt* and will continue only if *interrupt* or *nmi* is true at the time of the event, or until 5 μs of time has elapsed. Only when one or more of these conditions are true will execution continue.

When using a statement such as:

```
WAIT UNTIL (interrupt = TRUE) OR ( old_clk = '1');
```

be sure to have at least one of the values in the expression contain a signal. This is necessary to ensure that the WAIT statement does not wait forever. If both *interrupt* and *old_clk* are variables, the WAIT statement will not reevaluate when these two variables change value. (In fact, the variables cannot change value, because they are declared in the suspended process.) Only signals have events on them, and only signals can cause a WAIT statement or concurrent signal assignment to reevaluate.

WAIT timeout.   There are instances while designing a model when you are not sure that a condition will be met. To prevent the WAIT statement from waiting forever, add a timeout clause. The timeout clause will allow execution to proceed whether or not the condition has been met. Be careful, though, because this method can cause erroneous behavior unless properly handled. The following example shows this problem.

```
ARCHITECTURE wait_example of wait_example IS
  SIGNAL sendB, sendA : std_logic;
BEGIN
  sendA <= '0';
  A : PROCESS
  BEGIN
    WAIT UNTIL sendB = '1';
    sendA <= '1' AFTER 10 ns;

    WAIT UNTIL sendB = '0';
    sendA <= '0' AFTER 10 ns;

  END PROCESS A;

  B : PROCESS
  BEGIN
    WAIT UNTIL sendA = '0';
    sendB <= '0' AFTER 10 ns;

    WAIT UNTIL sendA = '1';
    sendB <= '1' AFTER 10 ns;

  END PROCESS B;
END wait_example;
```

This architecture has two processes that communicate through two signals *sendA* and *sendB*. This example does not do anything real but is a simple illustration of how WAIT statements can wait forever, a condition commonly referred to as *deadlock*.

During simulator initialization, all processes are executed exactly once. This allows the processes to always start at a known execution point at the start of simulation. In this example, the process labeled *A* will execute at start-up and stop at the following line:

```
WAIT UNTIL sendB = '1';
```

The process labeled *B* will also execute at start-up. Execution starts at the first line of the process and continues until the following line:

```
WAIT UNTIL sendA = '1';
```

Execution will stop at the first WAIT statement of the process even though the expression sendA = '0' is satisfied by the first signal assignment of signal *sendA*. This is because the WAIT statement needs an event to occur on signal *sendA* to cause the expression to be evaluated. Both processes are now waiting for each other. Neither process can continue, because they are both waiting for a signal set by the other process. If a timeout interval is inserted on each WAIT statement, execution can be allowed to continue. There is one catch to this last statement. Execution will continue when the condition is not met. An ASSERT statement can be added to check for continuation of the process without the condition being met. The following example shows the previous architecture *wait_example* rewritten to include timeout clauses.

```
ARCHITECTURE wait_timeout OF wait_example IS
  SIGNAL sendA, sendB : std_logic;
BEGIN
  A : PROCESS
  BEGIN
    WAIT UNTIL (sendB = '1') FOR 1 us;

    ASSERT (sendB = '1')
      REPORT "sendB timed out at '1' "
      SEVERITY ERROR;

    sendA <= '1' AFTER 10 ns;

    WAIT UNTIL (sendB = '0') FOR 1 us;

    ASSERT (sendB = '0')
      REPORT "sendB timed out at '0' "
      SEVERITY ERROR;

    sendA <= '0' AFTER 10 ns;
  END PROCESS A;
```

```
B : PROCESS
BEGIN
  WAIT UNTIL (sendA = '0') FOR 1 us;

  ASSERT (sendA = '0')
    REPORT "sendA timed out at '0' "
    SEVERITY ERROR;

  sendB <= '0' AFTER 10 ns;
  WAIT UNTIL (sendA = '1') FOR 1 us;

  ASSERT (sendA = '1')
    REPORT "sendA timed out at '1' "
    SEVERITY ERROR;

  sendB <= '1' AFTER 10 ns;

  end PROCESS B;
END wait_timeout;
```

Each of the WAIT statements now has a timeout expression specified as 1 μsec. However, if the timeout does happen, the ASSERT statement will report an error that the WAIT statement in question has timed out.

Sensitivity list versus WAIT statement.   A process with a sensitivity list is an implicit WAIT ON the signals in the sensitivity list. This can be shown as follows:

```
PROCESS (clk)
  VARIABLE last_clk : std_logic := 'X';
BEGIN
  IF (clk /= last_clk ) AND (clk = '1') THEN
    q <= din AFTER 25 ns;
  END IF;

  last_clk := clk;

END PROCESS;
```

This example can be rewritten using a WAIT statement:

```
PROCESS
  VARIABLE last_clk : std_logic := 'X';
BEGIN
  IF (clk /= last_clk ) AND (clk = '1') THEN
    q <= din AFTER 25 ns;
  END IF;

  last_clk := clk;

  WAIT ON clk;
END PROCESS;
```

The WAIT statement at the end of the process is equivalent to the sensitivity list at the beginning of the process. But why is the WAIT statement at the end of the process and not at the beginning? During initialization of the simulator, all processes are executed once. To mimic the behavior of the sensitivity list, the WAIT statement must be at the end of the process to allow the PROCESS statement to execute once.

Concurrent assignment problem

One of the problems that most designers using sequential signal assignment statements will encounter is that the value assigned in the last statement will not appear immediately. This can cause erroneous behavior in the model if the designer is depending on the new value. An example with this problem is as follows:

```
USE WORK.std_logic_1164.ALL;
ENTITY mux IS
  PORT (I0, I1, I2, I3, A, B : IN std_logic;
        Q : OUT std_logic);
END mux;

ARCHITECTURE mux_behave OF mux IS
  SIGNAL sel : INTEGER RANGE 0 to 3;
BEGIN
  B1 : PROCESS(A, B, I0, I1, I2, I3)
  BEGIN

    sel <= 0;
    IF (A = '1') THEN sel <= sel + 1; END IF;
    IF (B = '1') THEN sel <= sel + 2; END IF;

    CASE sel IS
      WHEN 0 =>
        Q <= I0;
      WHEN 1 =>
        Q <= I1;
      WHEN 2 =>
        Q <= I2;
      WHEN 3 =>
        Q <= I3;
    END CASE;
  END PROCESS;
END mux_behave;
```

This model is for four-to-one multiplexer. Depending on the values of *A* and *B*, one of the four inputs, I0 through I3, will be transferred to output *Q*.

The architecture starts processing by initializing internal signal *sel* to the value 0. Then, based on the values of *A* and *B*, the values 1 or 2 are added to *sel* to select the correct input. Finally, a CASE statement selected by the value of *sel* will transfer the value of the input to output *Q*.

This architecture will not work as presently implemented. The value of signal sel will never be initialized by the first line in the architecture:

```
sel <= 0;
```

This statement inside of a process statement will schedule an event for signal *sel* on the next delta time point, with the value 0. However, processing will continue in the process statement with the next sequential statement. The value of *sel* will remain at whatever value that it had at the entry to the process. Only when the process has completed will this current delta have finished and the next delta time point be started. Only then will the new value of *sel* be reflected. By this time, however, the rest of the process will already have been processed using the wrong value of *sel*.

There are two ways to fix this problem. The first is to insert WAIT statements after each sequential signal assignment statement as follows:

```
ARCHITECTURE mux_fix1 OF mux IS
  SIGNAL sel : INTEGER RANGE 0 TO 3;
BEGIN
  PROCESS
  BEGIN
    sel <= 0;
    WAIT FOR 0 ns; -- or wait on sel

    IF (a = '1') THEN sel <= sel + 1; END IF;
    WAIT for 0 ns;

    IF (b = '1') THEN sel <= sel + 2; END IF;
    WAIT FOR 0 ns;

    CASE sel IS
      WHEN 0 =>
        Q <= I0;
      WHEN 1 =>
        Q <= I1;
      WHEN 2 =>
        Q <= I2;
      WHEN 3 =>
        Q <= I3;
```

```
    END CASE;

    WAIT ON A, B, I0, I1, I2, I3;
  END PROCESS;
END mux_fix1;
```

The WAIT statements after each signal assignment cause the process to wait for one delta time point before continuing with the execution. By waiting for one delta time point, the new value has a chance to propagate. Therefore, when execution continues after the WAIT statement, signal sel has the new value.

One consequence of the WAIT statements, however, is that the process can no longer have a sensitivity list. A process with WAIT statements contained within it or within a subprogram called from within the process cannot have a sensitivity list. A sensitivity list implies that execution will start from the beginning of the procedure, while a WAIT statement allows suspending a process at a particular point. The two are mutually exclusive.

Since the process can no longer have sensitivity list, a WAIT statement has been added to the end of the process that will exactly imitate the behavior of the sensitivity list. This is the statement:

```
WAIT ON A, B, I0, I1, I2, I3;
```

The WAIT statement will proceed whenever any of the signals on the right side of the keyword ON have an event upon them.

This method of solving the sequential signal assignment problem will cause the process to work, but a better solution is to use an internal variable instead of the internal signal, as shown:

```
ARCHITECTURE mux_fix2 OF mux IS
BEGIN
  PROCESS(A, B, I0, I1, I2, I3)
    VARIABLE sel : INTEGER RANGE 0 TO 3;
  BEGIN
    sel := 0;
    IF (A = '1') THEN sel := sel + 1; END IF;
    IF (B = '1') THEN sel := sel + 2; END IF;

    CASE sel IS
      WHEN 0 =>
        Q <= I0;
      WHEN 1 =>
        Q <= I1;
      WHEN 2 =>
```

```
        Q <= I2;
      WHEN 3 =>
        Q <= I3;
    END CASE;
  END PROCESS;
END mux_fix2;
```

The signal *sel* from the preceding example has been converted from an internal signal to an internal variable. This was accomplished by moving the declaration from the architecture declaration section to the process declaration section. Variables can be declared only in the process or subprogram declaration section.

Also, the signal assignments to *sel* have been changed to variable assignment statements. Now when the first assignment to sel is executed, the value is updated immediately. Each successive assignment is also executed immediately, so that the correct value of *sel* is available in each statement of the process.

Passive Processes

Passive processes are processes that exist in the entity statement part of an entity. They are different from a normal process in that no signal assignment is allowed. These processes are used to do all sorts of checking functions. For instance, one good use of a passive process is to check the data setup time on a flip-flop.

The advantage of the passive process over the example discussed in the ASSERT statement section is that, since the passive process exists in the entity, it can be applied to any architecture of the entity. Take a look at the following example:

```
USE WORK.std_logic_1164.ALL;
ENTITY dff IS
  PORT( CLK, din : IN std_logic;
        Q, QB : OUT std_logic);
BEGIN
  PROCESS(CLK, din)
    VARIABLE last_d_change : TIME := 0 ns;
    VARIABLE last_clk, last_d_value : std_logic := 'X';
  BEGIN
    IF (din /= last_d_value) THEN
      last_d_change := now;
      last_d_value := din;
    END IF;

    IF (CLK /= last_clk) THEN
      IF (CLK = '1') THEN
```

```
      ASSERT(now - last_d_change >= 15 ns)
        REPORT "setup error"
        SEVERITY ERROR;
    END IF;

    last_clk := CLK;
  END IF;
 END PROCESS;
END dff;

ARCHITECTURE behave OF dff IS
BEGIN
  .
  .
  .
  .
END behave;

ARCHITECTURE struct OF dff IS
BEGIN
  .
  .
  .
  .
END struct;

ARCHITECTURE switch OF dff IS
BEGIN
  .
  .
  .
  .
END switch;
```

This example shows the entity for a D flip-flop with a passive process included in the entity that performs a data setup check with respect to the clock. This setup check function was described in detail in the ASSERT statement description. What this example shows is that when the setup check function is contained in the entity statement part, each of the architectures for the entity will have the data setup check performed automatically. Without this functionality, each of the architectures would have to have the setup check code included. This introduces more code to maintain, and can introduce inconsistencies between architectures.

The only restriction on these processes, as mentioned earlier, is that no signal assignment is allowed in a passive process. In the preceding example a process statement was used to illustrate a passive process. A passive process can also exist as a concurrent statement that does not do any signal assignment. Examples of such statements are concurrent assert statements and concurrent subprogram invocations. An example of two concurrent assert statements as passive processes follows.

```
ENTITY adder IS
  PORT( A, B : IN INTEGER;
        X : OUT INTEGER);
BEGIN
  ASSERT (A < 256)
    REPORT "A out of range"
    SEVERITY ERROR;

  ASSERT (B < 256)
    REPORT "B out of range"
    SEVERITY ERROR;

END adder;
```

The first ASSERT statement checks to make sure that input A is not out of range, and the second assertion checks that input B is not out of the range of the adder. Each of these statements acts as an individual process that is sensitive to the signal in its expression. For instance, the first assertion is sensitive to signal A since that signal is contained in its expression.

In this chapter we discussed the following:

- Process statements are concurrent statements that delineate areas of sequential statements.

- Process statements can be used to control when a process is activated.

- Signal assignments are scheduled and variable assignments happen immediately within a process statement.

- IF, CASE, and LOOP statements can be used to control the flow of execution within a model.

- ASSERTION statements can be used to check for error conditions, or to report information to the user.

- The three forms of the WAIT statement. WAIT UNTIL is used for specifying clocks for synthesis. WAIT ON can be used to modify the sensitivity list.

- Passive processes can be used to perform error checking and other tasks across a number of architectures by existing in an ENTITY statement.

The next chapter will focus on all of the different data types of VHDL that can be used in models.

Data Types

In this chapter we will examine the object types used in VHDL. The types allowed in VHDL consist of everything from scalar numeric types, to composite arrays and records, to file types. The first step in looking at the varied VHDL types, will be to review the VHDL objects that can attain the varied types. Then we will use examples to show how many types of descriptions can be made easier to read by using the power of enumerated and composite data types.

Object Types

A VHDL object consists of one of the following:

1. *Signal* represents interconnection wires that connect component instantiation ports together.
2. *Variable* is used for local storage of temporary data, visible only inside a process.
3. *Constant* names specific values.

Signal

Signal objects are used to connect entities together to form models. Signals are the means for communication of dynamic data between entities. A signal declaration looks like this:

```
SIGNAL signal_name : signal_type [:=initial_value];
```

The keyword SIGNAL is followed by one or more signal names. Each signal name will create a new signal. Separating the signal names from the signal type is a colon. The signal type specifies the data type of the information that the signal will contain. Finally, the signal can contain an initial value specifier so that the signal value may be initialized.

Signals can be declared in entity declaration sections, architecture declarations, and package declarations. Signals in package declarations are also referred to as *global signals* because they can be shared among entities.

An example of signal declarations is as follows:

```
USE WORK.std_logic_1164.ALL;
PACKAGE sigdecl IS
  TYPE bus_type IS ARRAY(0 to 7) OF std_logic;

  SIGNAL vcc  : std_logic := '1';
  SIGNAL ground : std_logic := '0';

  FUNCTION magic_function( a : IN bus_type) RETURN bus_type;

END sigdecl;

USE WORK.sigdecl.ALL;
USE WORK.std_logic_1164.ALL;
ENTITY board_design is
  PORT( data_in : IN bus_type;
        data_out : OUT bus_type);

  SIGNAL sys_clk : std_logic := '1';

END board_design;

ARCHITECTURE data_flow OF board_design IS
  SIGNAL int_bus : bus_type;
  CONSTANT disconnect_value : bus_type
      := ('X', 'X', 'X', 'X', 'X', 'X', 'X', 'X');
BEGIN
  int_bus <= data_in WHEN sys_clk = '1'
    ELSE int_bus;
  data_out <= magic_function(int_bus) WHEN sys_clk = '0'
    ELSE disconnect_value;

  sys_clk <= NOT(sys_clk) after 50 ns;
END data_flow;
```

Signals *vcc* and ground are declared in package *sigdecl*. Because these signals are declared in a package, they can be referenced by more than one entity and are therefore *global signals*. For an entity to reference these signals, the entity will need to use package *sigdecl*. To use the package requires a VHDL USE clause as follows:

```
USE work.sigdecl.vcc;
USE work.sigdecl.ground;
```

or

```
USE work.sigdecl.ALL;
```

In the first example, the objects are included in the entity by specific reference. In the second example, the entire package is included in the entity. In the second example, problems may arise because more than what is absolutely necessary is included. If more than one object of the same name results because of the USE clause, none of the objects is visible, and a compile operation that references the object will fail.

Signals global to entities. Inside the entity declaration section for entity *board_design* is a signal called *sys_clk*. This signal can be referenced in entity *board_design* and any architecture for entity *board_design*. In this example there is only one architecture, *data_flow,* for *board_design.* The signal *sys_clk* can therefore be assigned to and read from in entity *board_design* and architecture *data_flow.*

Architecture local signals. Inside of architecture *data_flow* is a signal declaration for signal *int_bus.* Signal *int_bus* is of type *bus_type,* a type defined in package *sigdecl.* The *sigdecl* package is used in entity board; therefore, the type *bus_type* is available in architecture *data_flow.* Since the signal is declared in the architecture declaration section, the signal can be referenced only in architecture *data_flow* or in any process statements in the architecture.

Variables

Variables are used for local storage in process statements and subprograms (subprograms are discussed in Chap. 6). As opposed to signals which have their values scheduled, all assignments to variables occur immediately. A variable declaration looks as follows:

```
VARIABLE variable_name {,variable_name} : variable_type[:= value];
```

The keyword VARIABLE is followed by one or more variable names. Each name creates a new variable. The construct *variable_type* defines the data type of the variable, and an optional initial value can be specified.

Variables can be declared in the process declaration section and sub-program declaration sections only. An example using two variables is as follows:

```
USE WORK.std_logic_1164.ALL;
ENTITY and5 IS
  PORT ( a, b, c, d, e : IN std_logic;
         q : OUT std_logic);
END and5;

ARCHITECTURE and5 OF and5 IS
BEGIN
  PROCESS(a, b, c, d, e)
    VARIABLE state : std_logic;
    VARIABLE delay : time;
  BEGIN

    state := a AND b AND c AND d AND e;

    IF state = '1' THEN
      delay := 4.5 ns;
    ELSIF state = '0' THEN
      delay := 3 ns;
    ELSE
      delay := 4 ns;
    END IF;

    q <= state AFTER delay;

  END PROCESS;
END and5;
```

This example is the architecture for a five-input AND gate. There are two variable declarations in the process declaration section: one for variable *state* and one for variable *delay*. Variable *state* is used as a temporary storage area to hold the value of the AND function of the inputs. Temporary-storage value *delay* is used to hold the delay value that will be used when scheduling the output value. Both of these values cannot be static data because their values depend on the values of inputs *a, b, c, d,* and *e.* Signals could have been used to store the data, but there are several reasons why a signal was not used.

- Variables are inherently more efficient because assignments happen immediately, while signals must be scheduled to occur.
- Variables take less memory, while signals need more information to allow for scheduling and signal attributes.
- Using a signal would have required a WAIT statement to synchronize the signal assignment to the same execution iteration as the usage.

When any of the input signals *a, b, c, d,* or *e* change, the process is invoked. Variable *state* is assigned the AND of all of the inputs. Next, based on the value of variable *state,* variable *delay* is assigned a delay value. Based on the delay value assigned to variable *delay,* output signal *q* will have the value of variable *state* assigned to it.

Constants

Constant objects are names assigned to specific values of a type. Constants allow the designer the capability to have a better-documented model, and a model that is easy to update. For instance, if a model requires a fixed value in a number of instances, a constant should be used. By using a constant, the designer can change the value of the constant and recompile, and all of the instances of the constant value will be updated to reflect the new value of the constant.

A constant also provides a better-documented model by providing more meaning to the value being described. For instance, instead of using the value 3.1414 directly in the model, the designer should create a constant as follows:

```
CONSTANT PI: REAL := 3.1414;
```

Even though the value is not going to change, the model becomes more readable.

A constant declaration looks like this:

```
CONSTANT constant_name {,constant_name} : type_name[:= value];
```

The value specification is optional, because VHDL also supports deferred constants. These are constants declared in a package declaration, whose value is specified in a package body.

A constant has the same scoping rules as signals. A constant declared in a package can be global if the package is used by a number of entities. A constant in an entity declaration section can be referenced by any architecture of that entity. A constant in an architecture can be used by any statement inside the architecture, including a process statement. A constant declared in a process declaration can be used only in a process.

Data Types

All of the objects that we have been discussing until now—the signal, the variable, and the constant—can be declared using a type specification to specify the characteristics of the object. VHDL contains a wide range of types that can be used to create simple or complex objects.

To define a new type, you must create a type declaration. A type declaration defines the name of the type and the range of the type. Type declarations are allowed in package declaration sections, entity declaration sections, architecture declaration sections, subprogram declaration sections, and process declaration sections.

A type declaration looks like this:

```
TYPE type_name IS type_mark;
```

A *type_mark* construct encompasses a wide range of methods for specifying a type. It can be anything from an enumeration of all of the values of a type to a complex record structure. In the next few sections, type marks will be examined. All of the scoping rules that were defined for signals and variables also apply to type declarations.

Figure 4.1 is a diagram showing the types available in VHDL. The four broad categories are scalar types, composite types, access types, and file types. Scalar types include all of the simple types, such as integer and real. Composite types include arrays and records. Access types are the equivalent of pointers in typical programming languages. Finally, file types give the designer the capability to declare file objects with designer-defined file types.

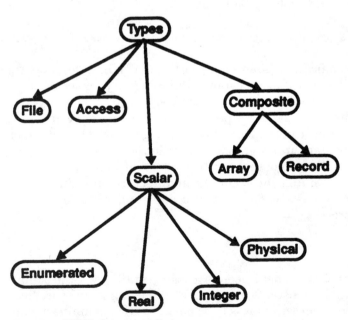

Figure 4.1   VHDL data types diagram.

Scalar Types

Scalar types describe objects that can hold, at most, one value at a time. The type itself can contain multiple values, but an object that is declared to be a scalar type will hold, at most, one of the scalar values at any point in time. Referencing the name of the object references the entire object. Scalar types encompass these four classes of types:

1. Integer types
2. Real types
3. Enumerated types
4. Physical types

Integer types

Integer types are exactly like mathematical integers. All of the normal predefined mathematical functions like add, subtract, multiply, and divide apply to integer types. The VHDL LRM does not specify a maximum range for integers, but does specify the minimum range: from $-2,147,483,647$ to $+2,147,483,647$. The minimum range is specified by the Standard package which is contained in the Standard Library.

The Standard package defines all of the predefined VHDL types provided with the language. The Standard library is used to hold any packages or entities provided as standard with the language. The Standard package appears in chapter 14 of the *VHDL 1076-1987 Language Reference Manual*.

It may seem strange to some designers who are familiar with two's complement representations that the integer range is specified from $-2,147,483,647$ to $+2,147,483,647$ when two's complement integer representations usually allow one smaller negative number, $-2,147,483,648$. The language defines the integer range to be symmetric around 0.

Some examples of integer values are shown here:

```
ARCHITECTURE test OF test IS
BEGIN
  PROCESS(X)
    VARIABLE a : INTEGER;
    VARIABLE b : int_type;
  BEGIN
    a := 1;   -- Ok 1
    a := -1;  -- Ok 2
    a := 1.0;  -- error 3
  END PROCESS;
END test;
```

The first two statements (1 and 2) show examples of a positive integer assignment and a negative integer assignment. Line 3 shows a noninteger assignment to an integer variable. This line will cause the compiler to issue an error message. Any numeric value with a decimal point is considered a real number value. Because VHDL is a strongly typed language, for the assignment to take place either the base types must match or a type-casting operation must be performed.

Real types

Real types are used to declare objects that emulate mathematical real numbers. They can be used to represent numbers out of the range of integer values as well as fractional values. The minimum range of real numbers is also specified by the Standard package in the Standard Library, and is from $-1.0E+38$ to $+1.0E+38$. These numbers are represented by the following notation:

```
+ or - number.number[E + or - number]
```

A few examples of some real numbers are shown here:

```
ARCHITECTURE test OF test IS
  SIGNAL a : REAL;
BEGIN
  a <= 1.0;      -- Ok 1
  a <= 1;        -- error 2
  a <= -1.0E10;  -- Ok 3
  a <= 1.5E-20;  -- Ok 4
  a <= 5.3 ns;   -- error 5
END test;
```

Line 1 shows how to assign a real number to a signal of type REAL. All real numbers have a decimal point to distinguish them from integer values. Line 2 is an example of an assignment that will not work. Signal a is of type REAL, and a real value must be assigned to signal a. The value 1 is of type INTEGER, so a type mismatch will be generated by this line.

Line 3 shows a very large negative number. The numeric characters to the left of the character E represent the mantissa of the real number, while the numeric value to the right represents the exponent.

Line 4 shows how to create a very small number. In this example, the exponent is negative, so the number is very small.

Line 5 shows how a type TIME cannot be assigned to a real signal. Even though the numeric part of the value looks like a real number, because of the units after the value, the value is considered to be of type TIME.

Enumerated types

An enumerated type is a very powerful tool for abstract modeling. A designer can use an enumerated type to represent exactly the values required for a specific operation. All of the values of an enumerated type are user-defined. These values can be identifiers or single-character literals. An identifier is like a name. Examples are *a, abc,* and *black*. Character literals are single characters enclosed in quotes, such as 'X', '1', and '0'.

A typical enumerated type for a four-state simulation value system is as follows:

```
TYPE fourval IS ( 'X', '0', '1', 'Z' );
```

This type contains four character-literal values that each represent a unique state in the four-state value system. The values represent the following conditions:

'X'   unknown value

'0'   logical 0 or false value

'1'   logical 1 or true value

'Z'   tristate or open-collector value

Character literals are needed for values '1' and '0' to separate these values from the integer values 1 and 0. It would be an error to use the values 1 and 0 in an enumerated type, because these are integer values. The characters X and Z do not need quotes around them because they do not represent any other type, but the quotes were used for uniformity.

Another example of an enumerated type is as follows:

```
TYPE color IS ( red, yellow, blue, green, orange );
```

In this example, the type values are very abstract, that is, not representing physical values that a signal might attain. The type values in type *color* are also all identifiers. Each identifier represents a unique value of the type; therefore, all identifiers of the type must be unique.

Each identifier in the type has a specific position in the type determined by the order in which the identifier appears in the type. The first identifier will have a position number of 0, the next a position number of 1, and so on. (In Chap. 5 are some examples using position numbers of a type.)

A typical use for an enumerated type would be representing all of the instructions for a microprocessor as an enumerated type. For instance, an enumerated type for a very simple microprocessor could look as follows:

```
TYPE instruction IS ( add, sub, lda, ldb, sta, stb, outa, xfr );
```

The model that uses this type might look like this:

```
PACKAGE instr IS
 TYPE instruction IS ( add, sub, lda, ldb, sta, stb, outa, xfr );
END instr;

USE WORK.instr.ALL;
ENTITY mp IS
  PORT (instr : IN instruction;
        addr : IN INTEGER;
        data : INOUT INTEGER);
END mp;

ARCHITECTURE mp OF mp IS
BEGIN
  PROCESS(instr)
    TYPE regtype IS ARRAY(0 TO 255) OF INTEGER;
    VARIABLE a, b : INTEGER;
    VARIABLE reg : regtype;
  BEGIN
              -- select instruction to
    CASE instr is  -- execute
      WHEN lda =>
        a := data; -- load a accumulator

      WHEN ldb =>
        b := data; -- load b accumulator

      WHEN add =>
        a := a + b; -- add accumulators

      WHEN sub =>
        a := a - b; -- subtract accumulators

      WHEN sta =>
        reg(addr) := a; -- put a accum in reg array

      WHEN stb =>
        reg(addr) := b; -- put b accum in reg array

      WHEN outa =>
        data <= a;    -- output a accum

      WHEN xfr =>        -- transfer b to a
        a := b;

    END CASE;
  END PROCESS;
END mp;
```

The model receives an instruction stream (*instr*), an address stream (*addr*), and a data stream (*data*). Based on the value of the enumerated value of *instr*, the appropriate instruction is executed. A CASE statement is used to select the instruction to execute. The statement is executed and the process will then wait for the next instruction.

Another common example using enumerated types is a state machine. State machines are commonly used in designing the control logic for ASICs. They represent a very easy and understandable method for specifying a sequence of actions over time, based on input signal values.

```
USE WORK.std_logic_1164.ALL;
ENTITY traffic_light IS
  PORT(sensor : IN std_logic;
       clock : IN std_logic;
       red_light : OUT std_logic;
       green_light : OUT std_logic;
       yellow_light : OUT std_logic);
END traffic_light;


ARCHITECTURE simple OF traffic_light IS
  TYPE t_state is (red, green, yellow);
  SIGNAL present_state, next_state : t_state;
BEGIN
  PROCESS(present_state, sensor)
  BEGIN
    CASE present_state IS
      WHEN green =>
        next_state <= yellow;
        red_light <= '0';
        green_light <= '1';
        yellow_light <= '0';
      WHEN red =>
        red_light <= '1';
        green_light <= '0';
        yellow_light <= '0';
        IF (sensor = '1') THEN
          next_state <= green;
        ELSE
          next_state <= red;
        END IF;
      WHEN yellow =>
        red_light <= '0';
        green_light <= '0';
        yellow_light <= '1';
        next_state <= red;
```

```
    END CASE;
  END PROCESS;

  PROCESS
  BEGIN
    WAIT UNTIL clock'EVENT and clock = '1';
    present_state <= next_state;
  END PROCESS;
END simple;
```

The state machine is described by two processes: the first calculates the next state logic and the second latches the next state into the current state. Notice how the enumerated type makes the model much more readable because the state names represent the color of the light that is currently being displayed.

Physical types

Physical types are used to represent physical quantities such as distance, current, time, etc. A physical type provides for a base unit, and successive units are then defined in terms of this unit. The smallest unit representable is one base unit; the largest is determined by the range specified in the physical type declaration. An example of a physical type for the physical quantity *current* is as follows:

```
TYPE current IS RANGE 0 to 1000000000

UNITS
  na;           -- nano amps
  ua = 1000 na; -- micro amps
  ma = 1000 ua; -- milli amps
  a  = 1000 ma; -- amps
END UNITS;
```

The type definition begins with a statement that declares the name of the type (*current*) and the range of the type (0 to 1,000,000,000). The first unit declared in the UNITS section is the base unit. In the preceding example, the base unit is *na*. After the base unit is defined, other units can be defined in terms of the base unit or other units already defined. In the preceding example, the unit *ua* is defined in terms of the base unit as 1000 base units. The next unit declaration is *ma*. This unit is declared as 1000 *ua*. The units declaration section is terminated by the END UNITS clause.

More than one unit can be declared in terms of the base unit. In the preceding example, the *ma* unit can be declared as 1000 *ma* or 1,000,000 *na*. The range constraint limits the minimum and maximum values that the physical type can represent in base units. The unit identifiers all must be unique within a single type. It is illegal to have two identifiers with the same name.

Predefined physical types. The only predefined physical type in VHDL is the physical type TIME. This type is as follows:

```
TYPE TIME IS RANGE <impelementation defined>
  UNITS
    fs;          -- femtosecond
    ps  = 1000 fs; -- picosecond
    ns  = 1000 ps; -- nanosecond
    us  = 1000 ns; -- microsecond
    ms  = 1000 us; -- millisecond
    sec = 1000 ms; -- second
    min = 60 sec; -- minute
    hr  = 60 min; -- hour
END UNITS;
```

The range of time is implementation-defined, but has to be at least the range of integer, in base units. This type is defined in the Standard package.

An example using a physical type:

```
PACKAGE example IS
  TYPE current IS RANGE 0 to 1000000000
    UNITS
      na;          -- nano amps
      ua = 1000 na; -- micro amps
      ma = 1000 ua; -- milli amps
      a = 1000 ma; -- amps
    END UNITS;

  TYPE load_factor IS (small, med, big );
END example;

USE WORK.example.ALL;
ENTITY delay_calc IS
  PORT ( out_current : OUT current;
         load : IN load_factor;
         delay : OUT time);
END delay_calc;

ARCHITECTURE delay_calc OF delay_calc IS
BEGIN
  delay <= 10 ns WHEN (load = small) ELSE
           20 ns WHEN (load = med) ELSE
           30 ns WHEN (load = big) ELSE
           10 ns;
```

```
   out_current <= 100 ua WHEN (load = small)ELSE
                  1 ma WHEN (load = med) ELSE
                  10 ma WHEN (load = big) ELSE
                  100 ua;
END delay_calc;
```

Here, two examples of physical types are represented. The first is of predefined physical type TIME and the second of user-specified physical type *current*. This example will return the *current* output and delay value for a device based on the output load factor.

Composite Types

Looking back at the VHDL types diagram in Fig. 4.1, we see that composite types consist of array and record types. Array types are groups of elements of the same type, while record types allow the grouping of elements of different types. Arrays are useful for modeling linear structures such as RAMs and ROMs, while records are useful for modeling data packets, instructions, etc.

Composite types are another tool in the VHDL toolbox that allows very abstract modeling of hardware. For instance, a single array type can represent the storage required for a ROM.

Array types

Array types group one or more elements of the same type together as a single object. Each element of the array can be accessed by one or more array indices. Elements can be of any VHDL type. For instance, an array can contain an array or a record as one of its elements.

In an array, all elements are of the same type. The following example shows a type declaration for a single dimensional array of bits.

```
TYPE data_bus IS ARRAY(0 TO 31) OF BIT;
```

This declaration declares a data type called *data_bus* that is an array of 32 bits. Each element of the array is the same as the next. Each element of the array can be accessed by an array index. An example of how to access elements of the array is as follows:

```
VARIABLE X: data_bus;
VARIABLE Y: BIT;

Y := X(0); -- line 1
Y := X(15); -- line 2
```

This example represents a small VHDL code fragment, not a complete model. In line 1, the first element of array X is being accessed and assigned to variable *Y*, which is of bit type. The type of *Y* must match the base type of array *X* in order for the assignment to take place. If the types do not match, the compiler will generate an error.

In line 2, the sixteenth element of array *X* is being assigned to variable *Y*. Line 2 is accessing the sixteenth element of array *X* because the array index starts with 0. Element 0 is the first element, element 1 is the second, and so on.

Another more comprehensive example of array accessing is as follows:

```
PACKAGE array_example IS
  TYPE data_bus IS ARRAY(0 TO 31) OF BIT;
  TYPE small_bus IS ARRAY(0 TO 7) OF BIT;
END array_example;

USE WORK.array_example.ALL;
ENTITY extract IS
  PORT (data : IN data_bus;
        start : IN INTEGER;
        data_out : OUT small_bus);
END extract;

ARCHITECTURE test OF extract IS
BEGIN
  PROCESS(data, start)
  BEGIN
    FOR i IN 0 TO 7 LOOP
      data_out(i) <= data(i + start);
    END LOOP;
  END PROCESS;
END test;
```

This entity will take in a 32-bit array element as a port and return 8 bits of the element. The 8 bits of the element returned depend on the value of index *start*. The 8 bits are returned through output *port data_out*. (There is a much easier method to accomplish this task—with functions—described in Chap. 5.)

A change in value of *start* or *data* will trigger the process to execute. The FOR loop will loop 8 times, each time copying a single bit from port *data* to port *data_out*. The starting point of the copy takes place at the integer value of port start. Each time through the loop the *i*th element of *data_out* is assigned the (i + start) element of *data*.

The examples shown so far have been simple arrays with scalar base types. In the next example, the base type of the array will be another array.

```
USE WORK.std_logic_1164.ALL;
PACKAGE memory IS
  CONSTANT width : INTEGER := 3;
```

```
  CONSTANT memsize : INTEGER := 7;

  TYPE data_out IS ARRAY(0 TO width) OF std_logic;
  TYPE mem_data IS ARRAY(0 TO memsize) OF data_out;
END memory;

USE WORK.std_logic_1164.ALL;
USE WORK.memory.ALL;
ENTITY rom IS
PORT( addr : IN INTEGER;
      data : OUT data_out;
      cs : IN std_logic);
END rom;

ARCHITECTURE basic OF rom IS
  CONSTANT z_state : data_out := ('Z', 'Z', 'Z', 'Z');
  CONSTANT x_state : data_out := ('X', 'X', 'X', 'X');
  CONSTANT rom_data : mem_data :=
     ( ( '0', '0', '0', '0'),
       ( '0', '0', '0', '1'),
       ( '0', '0', '1', '0'),
       ( '0', '0', '1', '1'),
       ( '0', '1', '0', '0'),
       ( '0', '1', '0', '1'),
       ( '0', '1', '1', '0'),
       ( '0', '1', '1', '1') );
BEGIN
  ASSERT addr <= memsize
    REPORT "addr out of range"
    SEVERITY ERROR;
data <= rom_data(addr) AFTER 10 ns WHEN cs = '1' ELSE
        z_state AFTER 20 ns WHEN cs = '0' ELSE
        x_state AFTER 10 ns;
END basic;
```

Package memory uses two constants to define two data types that form the data structures for entity *rom*. By changing the constant width and recompiling, we can change the output width of the memory. The initialization data for the ROM would also have to change to reflect the new width.

The data types from package memory are also used to define the data types of the ports of the entity. In particular, the *data* port is defined to be of type *data_out*.

The architecture defines three constants used to determine the output value. The first defines the output value when the *cs* input is a '0'. The value output is consistent with the *rom* being unselected. The second constant defines the output value when *rom* has an unknown value on the *cs* input. The value output by *rom* will be unknown as well. The last constant defines the data stored by *rom* (this is a very efficient method to model the ROM, but if the ROM data changes, the model will need to be recompiled). Depending on the address to *rom,* an appropriate entry from this third constant will be output. This will happen when the *cs* input is a '1' value.

The *rom* data type in this example is organized as 8 rows (0 to 7) and 4 columns (0 to 3). It is a two-dimensional structure, as shown in Fig. 4.2.

To initialize the constant for the *rom* data type an aggregate initialization is required. The table after the *rom_data* constant declaration is an aggregate used to initialize the constant. The aggregate value is constructed as a table for readability; it could have been all on one line. The structure of the aggregate must match the structure of the data type for the assignment to occur. A simple example of an aggregate assignment:

```
PROCESS(X)
   TYPE bitvec IS ARRAY(0 TO 3) OF BIT;
   VARIABLE Y : bitvec;
BEGIN
   Y := ('1', '0', '1', '0');
   .
   .
   .
END PROCESS;
```

Variable *Y* has an element of type BIT in the aggregate for each element of its type. In this example, the variable *Y* is 4 bits wide, and the aggregate is 4 bits wide as well.

Addr	Bit 3	Bit 2	Bit 1	Bit 0
0	0	0	0	0
1	0	0	0	1
2	0	0	1	0
3	0	0	1	1
4	0	1	0	0
5	0	1	0	1
6	0	1	1	0
7	0	1	1	1

Figure 4.2 ROM data representation.

The constant *rom_data* from the *rom* example is an array of arrays. Each element of type *mem_data* is an array of type *data_out*. The aggregate assignment for an array of arrays can be represented by the following form:

```
value := ((e1, e2,...,en),...,(e1, e2,...,en));
                E1          ...          En
```

However a much more readable form is shown as follows:

```
value := ((e1, e2,..., en),   -- E1
          (e1, e2,...,en),    -- E2
          .  .  ...  .
          .  .  ...  .
          (e1, e2,..., en) )  -- En
```

In the statement part of the *rom* example, there is one conditional signal assignment statement. The output port *data* is assigned a value based on the value of the *cs* input. The data type of the value assigned to port *data* must be of type *data_out* because port *data* has a type of *data_out*. By addressing the *rom_data* constant with an integer value, a data type of *data_out* will be returned.

A single value can be returned from the array of arrays by using the syntax shown here:

```
bit_value := rom_data(addr) (bit_index);
```

The first index (*addr*) will return a value with a data type of *data_out*. The second index (*bit_index*) will index the *data_out* type and return a single element of the array.

Multidimensional arrays. The constant *rom_data* in the *rom* example was represented using an array of arrays. Another method for representing the data is with a multidimensional array, as follows:

```
TYPE mem_data_md IS ARRAY(0 TO memsize, 0 TO width) OF
std_logic;
CONSTANT rom_data_md : mem_data_md :=
  ( ( '0', '0', '0', '0'),
    ( '0', '0', '0', '1'),
    ( '0', '0', '1', '0'),
    ( '0', '0', '1', '1'),
    ( '0', '1', '0', '0'),
    ( '0', '1', '0', '1'),
    ( '0', '1', '1', '0'),
    ( '0', '1', '1', '1') );
```

The preceding declaration declares a two-dimensional array type *mem_data_md*. When constant *rom_data_md* is declared using this type, the initialization syntax remains the same, but the method of accessing an element of the array is different. In the following example, a single element of the array is accessed.

```
X := rom_data_md(3, 3);
```

This access will return the fourth element of the fourth row, which in this example is a '1'.

Unconstrained array types. An unconstrained array type is a type whose range or size is not completely specified when the type is declared. This allows multiple subtypes to share a common base type. Entities and subprograms can then operate on all of the different subtypes with a single subprogram, instead of a subprogram or entity per size.

An example of an unconstrained type declaration is as follows:

```
TYPE BIT_VECTOR IS ARRAY(NATURAL RANGE <>) OF BIT;
```

This is the type declaration for type BIT_VECTOR from the Standard package. This type declaration declares a type that is an array of type BIT. However, the number of elements of the array is not specified. The notation that depicts this is as follows:

```
RANGE <>
```

This notation specifies that the type being defined has an unconstrained range. The word NATURAL before the keyword RANGE, in the type declaration, specifies that the type is bounded only by the range of NATURAL. Type NATURAL is defined in the Standard package to have a range from 0 to integer'high (the largest integer value). Type BIT_VECTOR, then, can range in size from 0 elements to integer'high elements. Each element of the BIT_VECTOR type is of type BIT.

Unconstrained types are typically used as types of subprogram arguments, or entity ports. These entities or subprograms can be passed items of any size within the range of the unconstrained type.

For instance, let's assume that a designer wants a shift-right function, for type BIT_VECTOR. The function will use the unconstrained type BIT_VECTOR as the type of its ports, but it can be passed any type which is a subtype of type BIT_VECTOR. Let's walk through an example to illustrate how this works. The following is an example of an unconstrained shift-right function:

```
PACKAGE mypack IS
  SUBTYPE eightbit IS BIT_VECTOR(0 TO 7);
  SUBTYPE fourbit IS BIT_VECTOR(0 TO 3);
  FUNCTION shift_right(val : BIT_VECTOR)
    RETURN BIT_VECTOR;
END mypack;

PACKAGE BODY mypack IS
  FUNCTION shift_right(val : BIT_VECTOR) RETURN BIT_VECTOR IS
    VARIABLE result : BIT_VECTOR(0 TO (val'LENGTH - 1));
  BEGIN
    result := val;
    IF (val'LENGTH > 1) THEN
      FOR i IN 0 TO (val'LENGTH - 2) LOOP
        result(i) := result(i + 1);
      END LOOP;
      result(val'LENGTH - 1) := '0';
    ELSE
      result(0) := '0';
    END IF;
    RETURN result;
  END shift_right;
END mypack;
```

The package declaration (the first five lines of the model) declares two subtypes, *eightbit,* and *fourbit.* These two subtypes are subtypes of the unconstrained base type BIT_VECTOR. These two types constrain the base type to range 0 to 7 for type *eightbit* and range 0 to 3 for type *fourbit.*

In a typical hardware description language without unconstrained types, two different shift-right functions would need to be written to handle the two different-sized subtypes. One function would work with type *eightbit,* and the other would work with type *fourbit.* With unconstrained types in VHDL, a single function can be written that will handle both input types and return the correct type.

Based on the size of input argument *val,* the internal variable *result* is created to be of the same size. Variable *result* is then initialized to the value of input argument *val.* This is necessary because the value of input argument *val* can only be read in the function; it cannot have a value assigned to it in the function. If the size of input argument *val* is greater than 1, then the shift-right function will loop through the length of the subtype value passed into the function. Each loop will shift one of the bits of variable *result* one bit to the right. If the size of input argument *val* is less than 2, we will treat this as a special case and return a single bit whose value is '0'.

Record types

Record types group objects of many types together as a single object. Each element of the record can be accessed by its field name. Record elements can include elements of any type, including arrays and records. The elements of a record can be of the same type or different types. Like arrays, records are used to model abstract data elements.

An example of a record type declaration is as follows:

```
TYPE optype IS ( add, sub, mpy, div, jmp );
TYPE instruction IS
  RECORD
    opcode : optype;
    src  : INTEGER;
    dst  : INTEGER;
  END RECORD;
```

The first line declares the enumerated type *optype,* which will be used as one of the record field types. The second line starts the declaration of the record. The record type declaration begins with the keyword RECORD and ends with the clause END RECORD. All of the declarations between these two keywords are field declarations for the record.

Each field of the record represents a unique storage area which can be read from and assigned data of the appropriate type. This example declares three fields: *opcode* of type *optype,* and *src* and *dst* of type INTEGER. Each field can be referenced by using the name of the record, followed by a period, and the field name. An example of this type of access is as follows:

```
PROCESS(X)
  VARIABLE inst : instruction;
  VARIABLE source, dest : INTEGER;
  VARIABLE operator : optype;
BEGIN
  source := inst.src;      -- Ok line 1
  dest := inst.src;     -- Ok line 2

  source := inst.opcode;      -- error line 3
  operator := inst.opcode;     -- Ok line 4

  inst.src := dest;    -- Ok line 5
  inst.dst := dest;    -- Ok line 6

  inst := (add, dest, 2);   -- Ok line 7
  inst := (source);         -- error line 8
END PROCESS;
```

This example declares variable *inst,* which is of type *instruction.*
Also, variables matching the record field types are declared. Lines 1
and 2 show fields of the record being assigned to local process variables. The assignments are legal because the types match. Notice the
period after the name of the record to select the field.

Line 3 shows a case which is illegal. The type of field *opcode* does not
match the type of variable source. The compiler will flag this statement
as a type mismatch error. Line 4 shows the correct assignment occurring between the field *opcode* and a variable which matches its type.

Lines 5 and 6 show that not only can record fields be read from, but
they can be assigned to as well. In these two lines, two of the fields of
the record are assigned the values from variable *dest.*

Line 7 shows an example of an aggregate assignment. In this line, all
of the fields of the record are being assigned at once. The aggregate
assigned contains three entries: an *optype* value, an INTEGER variable value, and an INTEGER value. This is a legal assignment to variable record *inst.*

Line 8 shows an example of an illegal aggregate value for record *inst.*
There is only one value present in the aggregate, which is an illegal
type for the record.

In the examples so far, all of the elements of the records have been
scalars. Let's examine some examples of records that have more complex field types. A record for a data packet is as follows:

```
TYPE word IS ARRAY(0 TO 3) OF std_logic;
TYPE t_word_array IS ARRAY(0 TO 15) OF word;
TYPE addr_type IS
  RECORD
    source : INTEGER;
    key : INTEGER;
  END RECORD;

TYPE data_packet IS
  RECORD
    addr : addr_type;
    data : t_word_array;
    checksum : INTEGER;
    parity : BOOLEAN;
END RECORD;
```

The first two type declarations define type *word* and *addr_type,*
which are used in the record *data_packet.* Type *word* is a simple array
and type *addr_type* is a simple record. Record type *data_packet* contains four fields using these two types in combination with two VHDL
predefined types.

The following example shows how a variable of type *data_packet* would be accessed.

```
PROCESS(X)
  VARIABLE packet : data_packet;
BEGIN

  packet.addr.key := 5;    -- Ok line 1
  packet.addr := (10, 20);  -- Ok line 2

  packet.data(0) := ('0', '0', '0', '0'); -- Ok line 3

  packet.data(10)(4) := '1'; -- error line 4
  packet.data(10)(0) := '1'; -- Ok line 5

END PROCESS;
```

This example shows how complex record types are accessed. In line 1, a record field of a record is accessed. Field *key* is a record field of record *addr_type,* which is a field of record *data_packet.* This line assigns the value 5 to that field. Line 2 assigns an aggregate to the whole field called *addr* in record *data_packet.*

In line 3 the *data* field is assigned an aggregate for the 0 element of the array. Line 4 tries to assign to only one bit of the eleventh element of the data array field in record *data_packet,* but the second index value is *out of range.* Finally, line 5 shows how to assign to a single bit of the array correctly.

Composite types are very powerful tools for modeling complex and abstract data types. By using the right combination of records and arrays, you can make models easy to understand and efficient.

Access Types

Most hardware design engineers using VHDL will probably never use access types directly (a hardware designer may use the TextIO package, which uses access types, thereby an indirect use of access types), but access types provide very powerful programming language type operations. An access type in VHDL is very similar to a pointer in a language like Pascal or C. It is an address, or a handle, to a specific object.

Access types allow the designer to model objects of a dynamic nature. For instance, dynamic queues, fifos, etc., can be modeled easily using access types. Probably the most common operation using an access type would be creating and maintaining a linked list.

Only variables can be declared as access types. By the nature of access types, they can be used only in sequential processing. Access types are currently not synthesizable because they are usually used to model the behavior of dynamically sized structures such as a linked list.

When an object is declared to be of an access type, two predefined functions are automatically available to manipulate the object. These functions are named NEW and DEALLOCATE. Function NEW will allocate memory of the size of the object in bytes and return the access value. Function DEALLOCATE takes in the access value and returns the memory to the system. An example to show how this all works is as follows:

```
PROCESS(X)
  TYPE fifo_element_t IS ARRAY(0 TO 3)
    OF std_logic; -- line 1

  TYPE fifo_el_access IS
    ACCESS fifo_element_t; -- line 2

  VARIABLE fifo_ptr : fifo_el_access := NULL; -- line 3
  VARIABLE temp_ptr : fifo_el_access := NULL; -- line 4
BEGIN

  temp_ptr := new fifo_element_t; -- Ok line 5
  temp_ptr.ALL := ('0', '1', '0', '1');-- Ok line 6

  temp_ptr.ALL := ('0', '0', '0', '0');--Ok line 7
  temp_ptr.ALL(0) := '0';     -- Ok line 8

  fifo_ptr := temp_ptr;     -- Ok line 9
  fifo_ptr.ALL := temp_ptr.ALL; -- Ok line 10
END PROCESS;
```

In line 2, an access type is declared using the type declared in line 1. Lines 3 and 4 declare two access type variables of *fifo_el_access* type from line 2. This process now has two access variable objects that can be used to access objects of type *fifo_element_t*.

Line 5 calls the predefined function NEW, which allocates enough memory for a variable of type *fifo_element_t* and returns an access value to the memory allocated. The access value returned is then assigned to variable *temp_ptr*. Variable *temp_ptr* is now pointing to an object of type *fifo_element_t*. This value can be read from or assigned to using variable assignment statements.

In line 6, a value is assigned to the object pointed to by *temp_ptr*. Line 7 shows another way to assign a value using an access value. The keyword .ALL specifies that the entire object is being accessed. Subelements of the object can be assigned by using a subelement name after the access variable name. Line 8 shows how to reference a subelement of an array pointed to by an access value. In this example, the first element of the array will have a value assigned to it.

In the next few statements we will examine how access values can be copied among different objects. In line 9, the access value of *temp_ptr* is assigned to *fifo_ptr*. Now both *temp_ptr* and *fifo_ptr* are pointing to the same object. This is shown in Fig. 4.3.

Both *temp_ptr* and *fifo_ptr* can be used to read from and assign to the object being accessed.

Line 10 shows how one object value can be assigned to another using access types. The value of the object pointed to by *temp_ptr* will be assigned to the value pointed to by *fifo_ptr*.

Incomplete types

When implementing recursive structures such as linked lists, you need another VHDL language feature to complete the declarations. This feature is called the *incomplete type*. The incomplete type allows the declaration of a type to be defined later.

An example that demonstrates why this would be useful is as follows:

```
PACKAGE stack_types IS
  TYPE data_type IS ARRAY(0 TO 7) OF std_logic; -- line 1

  TYPE element_rec; -- incomplete type line 2

  TYPE element_ptr IS ACCESS element_rec; -- line 3
  TYPE element_rec IS  -- line 4
    RECORD   -- line 5
      data : data_type; -- line 6
      nxt : element_ptr;-- line 7
    END RECORD;      -- line 8
END stack_types;

USE WORK.stack_types.ALL;
ENTITY stack IS
  PORT(din : IN data_type;
     clk : IN std_logic;
     dout : OUT data_type;
     r_wb : IN std_logic);
END stack;

ARCHITECTURE stack OF stack IS
BEGIN
  PROCESS(clk)
```

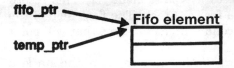

Figure 4.3 Multiple access type references.

```
      VARIABLE list_head : element_ptr := NULL;-- line 9
      VARIABLE temp_elem : element_ptr := NULL;-- line 10
      VARIABLE last_clk : std_logic := 'u'; -- line 11
  BEGIN
    IF (clk = '1') AND (last_clk = '0') THEN -- line 12
      IF (r_wb = '0') THEN -- line 13
          temp_elem := NEW element_rec; -- line 14
          temp_elem.data := din; -- line 15
          temp_elem.nxt := list_head; -- line 16
          list_head := temp_elem; -- line 17
          -- read mode     line 18
        ELSIF (r_wb = '1') THEN
          dout <= list_head.data; -- line 19
          temp_elem := list_head; -- line 20
          list_head := temp_elem.nxt; -- line 21
          DEALLOCATE(temp_elem); -- line 22
      ELSE
        ASSERT FALSE
        REPORT "read/write unknown while clock active"
        SEVERITY WARNING;       -- line 23
      END IF;
    END IF;
    last_clk := clk;        -- line 24
  END PROCESS;
END stack;
```

This example implements a stack using access types. The package
stack_types declares all of the types needed for the stack. In line 2 is a
declaration of the incomplete type *element_rec*. The name of the type is
specified, but no specification of the type is present. The purpose of this
declaration is to reserve the name of the type and allow other types to
gain access to the type when it is fully specified. The full specification
for this incomplete type appears in lines 4 through 8.

The fundamental reason for the incomplete type is to allow self-
referencing structures as linked lists. Notice that type *element_ptr* is
used in type *element_rec* in line 6. In order to use a type, it must first
be defined. Notice also that in the declaration for type *element_ptr*
in line 3, type *element_rec* is used. Since each type uses the other in
its respective declarations, neither type can be declared first without
a special way of handling this case. The incomplete type allows this
scenario to exist.

Lines 4 through 8 declare the record type *element_rec*. This record
type will be used to store the data for the stack. The first field of the
record is the data field, and the second is an access type that will point
to the next record in the stack.

The entity for stack declares port *din* for data input to the stack, a
clk input on which all operations are triggered, a *dout* port which

transfers data out of the stack, and finally a *r_wb* input which causes a read operation when high and a write operation when low. The process for the stack is triggered only when the *clk* input has an event occur. It is not affected by changes in *r_wb*.

Lines 9 through 11 declare some variables used to keep track of the data for the stack. Variable *list_head* will be the head of the linked list of data. It will always point to the first element of the list of items in the stack. Variable *temp_elem* will be used to hold a newly allocated element until it is connected into the stack list. Variable *last_clk* is used to hold the previous value of *clk* to enable transitions on the clock to be detected (this behavior can be duplicated with attributes, which are discussed in Chap. 7).

Line 12 checks to see if a 0 to 1 transition has occurred on the *clk* input. If so, then the stack needs to do a read or write depending on the *r_wb* input. Line 13 checks to see if *r_wb* is set up for a write to the stack. If so, lines 14 to 17 create a new data storage element and connect this element to the list.

Line 14 uses the predefined function NEW to allocate a record of type *element_rec* and return an access value to be assigned to variable *temp_elem*. This creates a structure that is shown graphically in Fig. 4.4.

Lines 15 and 16 fill in the newly allocated object with the data from input *din* and the access value to the head of the list. After line 16, the data structures appear as shown in Fig. 4.5.

Finally, in line 17, the new element is added to the head of the list. This is shown in Fig. 4.6.

Lines 18 to 22 of the model provide the behavior of the stack when an element is read from the stack. Line 19 copies the data from the stack element to the output port. Lines 20 to 22 disconnect the element from the stack list and return the memory to the system.

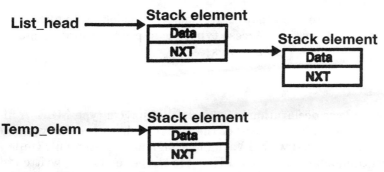

Figure 4.4 Allocate new stack element.

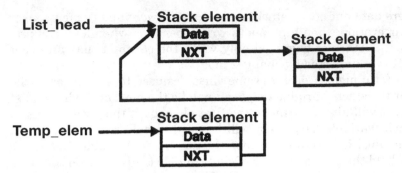

Figure 4.5   Point new element to head of list.

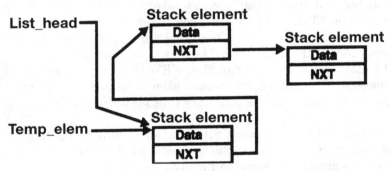

Figure 4.6   Point List_Head to new element.

Line 20 assigns the *temp_elem* access variable to point to the head of the list. This is shown in Fig. 4.7.

Line 21 moves the head of the list to the next element in the list. This is shown in Fig. 4.8.

Finally, in line 22, the element that had its data transferred out is deallocated and the memory returned to the memory pool. This is shown in Fig. 4.9.

Access types are very powerful tools for modeling complex and abstract types of systems. Access types bring programming language types of operations to VHDL processes.

File Types

A file type allows declarations of objects that have a type FILE. A file object type is actually a subset of the variable object type. A variable object can be assigned with a variable assignment statement, while a file object cannot be assigned. A file object can be read from, written to,

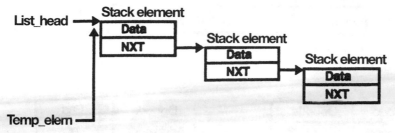

Figure 4.7   Point Temp_Elem to List_Head.

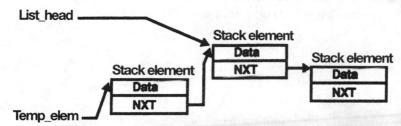

Figure 4.8   Move head pointer to next element.

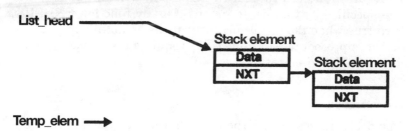

Figure 4.9   Deallocate element.

and checked for end of file only with special procedures and functions.

Files consist of sequential streams of a particular type. A file whose base object type is integer will consist of a sequential stream of integers. This is shown in Fig. 4.10.

A file whose object type is a complex record type will consist of a sequential stream of complex records. An example of how this might look is shown in Fig. 4.11.

At the end of the stream of data is an end-of-file mark. Two procedures and one function allow operations on file objects. They are as follows:

| Integer 1 | Integer 2 | .... | Integer N | End of file |

Figure 4.10   Pictorial representation of integer file.

Opcode	Opcode	....	Opcode	End
Addrmode	Addrmode	....	Addrmode	of
SRC	SRC	....	SRC	file
DST	DST	....	DST	mark

Figure 4.11   Complex file pictorial representation.

READ (file, data)—Procedure

WRITE (file, data)—Procedure

ENDFILE (file)—Function, returns boolean

Procedure READ will read an object from the file and return the object in argument *data*. Procedure WRITE will write argument *data* to the file specified by the file argument. Finally function ENDFILE will return true when the file is currently at the end-of-file mark.

To use these procedures and functions requires a file type declaration and a file object declaration.

File type declaration

A file type declaration specifies the name of the file type and the base type of the file. An example of a file type declaration is as follows:

```
TYPE integer_file IS FILE OF INTEGER;
```

This declaration specifies a file type whose name is *integer_file* and is of type INTEGER. This declaration corresponds to the file in Fig. 4.10.

File object declaration

A file object makes use of a file type and declares an object of type FILE. The file object declaration specifies the name of the file object, the mode of the file, and the physical disk path name. The file mode can be IN or OUT. If the mode is IN, then the file can be read with the

READ procedure. If the mode is OUT, then the file can be written with the WRITE procedure. An example is as follows:

```
FILE myfile : integer_file IS IN
    "/doug/test/examples/data_file";
```

This declaration declares a file object called *myfile* that is an input file of type *integer_file*. The last argument is the path name on the physical disk where the file is located (in most implementations this is true, but it is not necessarily so).

File type examples

To read the contents of a file, you can call the READ procedure within a loop statement. The loop statement can perform read operations until an end of file is reached, at which time the loop will be terminated. An example of a file read operation is as follows:

```
USE WORK.std_logic_1164.ALL;
ENTITY rom IS
  PORT(addr : IN INTEGER;
       cs : IN std_logic;
       data : OUT INTEGER);
END rom;

ARCHITECTURE rom OF rom IS
BEGIN
  PROCESS(addr, cs)
    VARIABLE rom_init : BOOLEAN := FALSE; -- line 1
    TYPE rom_data_file_t IS FILE OF INTEGER; -- line 2

    FILE rom_data_file : rom_data_file_t IS IN
        "/doug/dlp/test1.dat";        -- line 3

    TYPE dtype IS ARRAY(0 TO 63) OF INTEGER;

    VARIABLE rom_data : dtype; -- line 4
    VARIABLE i : INTEGER := 0; -- line 5
  BEGIN
    IF (rom_init = false) THEN -- line 6
      WHILE NOT ENDFILE(rom_data_file) -- line 7
          AND (i < 64) LOOP
        READ(rom_data_file, rom_data(i)); -- line 8
        i := i + 1;  -- line 9
      END LOOP;
      rom_init := true;   -- line 10
    END IF;
    IF (cs = '1') THEN   -- line 11
      data <= rom_data(addr); -- line 12
```

```
   ELSE
      data <= -1   -- line 13
   END IF;
  END PROCESS;
END rom;
```

This example shows how a *rom* can be initialized from a file the first time the model is executed and never again. A variable called *rom_init* is used to keep track of whether the *rom* has been initialized or not. If false, the *rom* has not been initialized; if true, the *rom* has already been initialized.

Line 2 of the example declares a file type *rom_data_file_t* that will be used to declare a file object. In line 3, a *rom_data_file* object is declared. In this example, the physical disk path name was hard-coded into the model, but a generic could have been used to pass a different path name for each instance of the *rom*.

Line 6 of the example tests variable *rom_init* for true or false. If false, the initialization loop is executed. Line 7 is the start of the initialization loop. The loop test makes use of the predefined function ENDFILE. The loop will execute until there is no more data in the file or when the *rom* storage area has been filled.

Each pass through the loop calls the predefined procedure READ. This procedure will read one integer at a time and place it in the element of *rom_data* that is currently being accessed. Each time through the loop, the index *i* is incremented to the next element position.

Finally, when the loop finishes the variable *rom_init* is set to true. The next time that the process is invoked, variable *rom_init* will be true, so the initialization loop will not be invoked again.

Writing a file is analogous to reading, except that the loop will not test every time through for an end-of-file condition. Each time a loop writing data is executed, the new object is appended to the end of the file. When the model is writing to a file, the file must have been declared with mode OUT.

File type caveats

In general, the file operations allowed are limited. Files cannot be opened, closed, or accessed in a random sequence. All that VHDL provides is a simple sequential capability. (VHDL is scheduled to be restandardized in 1992, and one of the items to be addressed is opening and closing of files.)

For textual input and output, there is another facility that VHDL provides, called TextIO. This facility provides for formatted textual input and output and is discussed in Chap. 8.

Subtypes

Subtype declarations are used to define subsets of a type. The subset can contain the entire range of the base type, but does not necessarily need to. A typical subtype adds a constraint(s) to an existing type.

The type integer encompasses the minimum range –2,147,483,647 to +2,147,483,647. In the Standard package (a designer should never redefine any of the types used in the Standard package; this can result in incompatible VHDL because of type mismatches), there is a subtype called NATURAL, whose range is from 0 to +2,147,483,647. This subtype is defined as follows:

```
TYPE INTEGER IS -2,147,483,647 TO +2,147,483,647;
SUBTYPE NATURAL IS INTEGER RANGE 0 TO +2,147,483,647;
```

After the keyword SUBTYPE is the name of the new subtype being created. The keyword IS is followed by the base type of the subtype. In this example, the base type is INTEGER. An optional constraint on the base type is also specified.

So, why would a designer want to create a subtype? There are two main reasons for doing so:

- To add constraints for selected signal assignment statements or case statements

- To create a resolved subtype (discussed along with resolution functions in Chap. 5)

When a subtype of the base type is used, the range of the base type can be constrained to be what is needed for a particular operation. Any functions that work with the base type will also work with the subtype.

Subtypes and base types also allow assignment between the two types. A subtype can always be assigned to the base type because the range of the subtype is always less than or equal to the range of the base type. The base type may or may not be able to be assigned to the subtype, depending on the value of the object of the base type. If the value is within the value of the subtype, then the assignment will succeed; otherwise, a range constraint error will result.

A typical example where a subtype is useful is adding a constraint to a numeric base type. In the preceding example, the NATURAL subtype constrained the integer base type to the positive values and zero. But what if this range is still too large? The constraint specified can be a user-defined expression that matches the type of the base type. In the example following, an 8-bit multiplexer is modeled with a much smaller constraint on the integer type.

```
PACKAGE mux_types IS
  SUBTYPE eightval IS INTEGER RANGE 0 TO 7; -- line 1
END mux_types;

USE WORK.mux_types.ALL;
USE WORK.std_logic_1164.ALL;
ENTITY mux8 IS
  PORT(I0, I1, I2, I3, I4, I5,
       I6, I7: IN std_logic;
       sel : IN eightval; -- line 2
       q : OUT std_logic);
END mux8;

ARCHITECTURE mux8 OF mux8 IS
BEGIN
  WITH sel SELECT -- line 3
    Q <= I0 AFTER 10 ns WHEN 0, -- line 4
         I1 AFTER 10 ns WHEN 1, -- line 5
         I2 AFTER 10 ns WHEN 2, -- line 6
         I3 AFTER 10 ns WHEN 3, -- line 7
         I4 AFTER 10 ns WHEN 4, -- line 8
         I5 AFTER 10 ns WHEN 5, -- line 9
         I6 AFTER 10 ns WHEN 6, -- line 10
         I7 AFTER 10 ns WHEN 7, -- line 11
END mux8;
```

The package *mux_types* declares a subtype *eightval,* which adds a constraint to base type INTEGER. The constraint allows an object of *eightval* to take on values from 0 to 7.

The package is included in entity *mux8,* which has one of its input ports, *sel,* declared using type *eightval.* In the architecture at line 3, a selected signal assignment statement uses the value of *sel* to determine which output is transferred to the output *Q.* If *sel* were not of the subtype *eightval,* but were strictly an integer type, then the selected signal assignment would need a value to assign for each value of the type, or an OTHERS clause. By adding the constraint to the integer type, all values of the type can be directly specified.

In this chapter we have examined the different types available in VHDL to the designer.

- Types can be used by three different types of objects: the *signal, variable,* and *constant.*

- Signals are the main mechanism for the connection of entities, and signals are used to pass information between entities.

- Variables are local to processes and subprograms and are used mainly as scratchpad areas for local calculations.

- Constants name a particular value of a type.

- Integers behave like mathematical integers, and real numbers behave like mathematical real numbers.

- Enumerated types can be used to describe user-defined operations, and they make a model much more readable.

- Physical types represent physical quantities such as distance, current, time, etc.

- Composite types consist of arrays and records. Arrays are a group of elements of the same type, and records are a group of elements of any type(s).

- Access types are like pointers in typical programming languages.

- File types are linear streams of data of a particular type that can be read and written from a model.

- Finally, subtypes can add constraints to a type.

In the next chapter, we will focus on another method of sequential statement modeling: the subprogram.

Subprograms and Packages

In this chapter, subprograms and packages will be discussed. Subprograms consist of procedures and functions used to perform common operations. Packages are mechanisms that allow sharing data among entities. Subprograms, types, and component declarations are the tools with which to build designs, and packages are the toolboxes.

Subprograms

Subprograms consist of procedures and functions. A procedure can return more than one argument, while a function always returns just one. In a function, all parameters are input parameters, while a procedure can have input parameters, output parameters, and inout parameters.

There are two versions of procedures and functions: a concurrent procedure and concurrent function, and a sequential procedure and sequential function. The concurrent procedure and function exist outside of a process statement or another subprogram, while the sequential function and procedure exist only in a process statement or another subprogram statement.

All statements inside of a subprogram are sequential. The same statements that exist in a process statement can be used in a subprogram, including WAIT statements.

A procedure exists as a separate statement in an architecture or process, while a function is usually used in an assignment statement or expression.

Function

In the following example is a function that takes in an array of the *std_logic* type (this is described in App. A) and returns an integer value. The integer value represents the numeric value of all of the bits treated as a binary number.

```
USE WORK.std_logic_1164.ALL;
PACKAGE num_types IS
  TYPE log8 IS ARRAY(0 TO 7) OF std_logic; -- line 1
END num_types;

USE WORK.std_logic_1164.ALL;
USE WORK.num_types.ALL;
ENTITY convert IS
  PORT(I1 : IN log8;  -- line 2
       O1 : OUT INTEGER); -- line 3
END convert;

ARCHITECTURE behave OF convert IS
  FUNCTION vector_to_int(S : log8) -- line 4
    RETURN INTEGER is              -- line 5
    VARIABLE result: INTEGER := 0; -- line 6
  BEGIN
    FOR i IN 0 TO 7 LOOP              -- line 7
      result :=result * 2;     -- line 8
      IF S(i) = '1' THEN          -- line 9
        result := result + 1; -- line 10
      END IF;
    END LOOP;
    RETURN result;                -- line 11
  END vector_to_int;

BEGIN
  O1 <= vector_to_int(I1);      -- line 12
END behave;
```

Line 1 of the example declares the array type used throughout the example. Lines 2 and 3 show the input and output ports of the *convert* entity, and their types. Lines 4 through 11 describe a function that is declared in the declaration region of the architecture *behave*. By declaring the function in the declaration region of the architecture, the function is visible to any region of the architecture.

Lines 4 and 5 declare the name of the function, the arguments to the function, and the type that the function returns. In line 6, a variable local to the function is declared. Functions have declaration regions very similar to process statements. Variables, constants, and types can be declared, but no signals.

Lines 7 through 10 declare a loop statement that will loop once for each value in the array type. The basic algorithm of the function is to do a shift and add for each bit position in the array. The result is first shifted (by multiplying by 2), and then if the bit position is a logical 1, a 1 value is added to the result.

At the end of the loop statement, variable *result* will contain the integer value of the array passed in. The value of the function is passed back via the RETURN statement. An example RETURN statement is shown in line 11.

Finally, line 12 shows how a function is called. The name of the function is followed by its arguments, enclosed in parentheses. The function will always return a value; therefore, the calling process, concurrent statement, etc., must have a place to which the function can return the value. In this example, the output of the function is assigned to an output port.

Parameters to a function are always *input only*. No assignment can be done to any of the parameters of the function. In the preceding example, the parameters were of a *constant* kind because no explicit kind was specified and the default is constant. The arguments are treated as if they were constants declared in the declaration area of the function.

The other kind of parameter that a function can have is a *signal* parameter. With a signal parameter, the attributes (attributes are discussed in Chap. 6) of the signal are passed in and are available for use in the function. The exception to this statement are attributes 'STABLE, 'QUIET, 'TRANSACTION, and 'DELAYED, which create special signals.

An example showing a function that contains signal parameters is as follows:

```
USE WORK.std_logic_1164.ALL;
ENTITY dff IS
  PORT(d, clk : IN std_logic;
       q : OUT std_logic);

  FUNCTION rising_edge(SIGNAL S : std_logic) -- line 1
    RETURN BOOLEAN IS                        -- line 2
  BEGIN
    -- this function makes use of attributes
    -- 'event and 'last_value discussed
    -- in Chapter 6
    IF (S'EVENT) AND (S = '1') AND       -- line 3
       (S'LAST_VALUE = '0') THEN         -- line 4
      RETURN TRUE;                -- line 5
    ELSE
      RETURN FALSE;               -- line 6
    END IF;
  END rising_edge;
END dff;

ARCHITECTURE behave OF dff IS
BEGIN
  PROCESS( clk)
```

```
  BEGIN
    IF rising_edge(clk) THEN        -- line 7
      q <= d;                  -- line 8
    END IF;
  END PROCESS;
END behave;
```

This example provides a rising edge detection facility for the D flip-flop being modeled. The function is declared in the entity declaration section and is therefore available to any architecture of the entity.

Lines 1 and 2 show the function declaration. There is only one parameter (*S*) to the function, and it is of a signal type. Lines 3 and 4 show an IF statement that determines whether the signal has just changed or not, if the current value is a '1', and whether the previous value was a '0'. If all of these conditions are true, then the IF statement will return a true value, signifying that a rising edge was found on the signal.

If any one of the conditions is not true, the value returned will be false, as shown in line 6. Line 7 shows an invocation of the function using the signal created by port *clk* of entity *dff*. If there is a rising edge on the signal *clk,* then the *d* value is transferred to the output *q*.

The most common use for a function is to return a value in an expression; however, there are two more classes of use available in VHDL. The first is a *conversion function* and the second is a *resolution function*. Conversion functions are used to convert from one type to another. Resolution functions are used to resolve bus contention on a multiply-driven signal.

Conversion functions

Conversion functions are used to convert an object of one type to another. They are used in component instantiation statements to allow mapping of signals and ports of different types. This type of situation usually arises when a designer wants to make use of an entity from another design that uses a different data type.

Assume that designer A was using a data type that had the following four values:

```
TYPE fourval IS (X, L, H, Z);
```

Designer B was using a data type that also contained four values, but the value identifiers were different, as shown here:

```
TYPE fourvalue IS ('X', '0', '1', 'Z');
```

Both of these types can be used to represent the states of a four-state value system for a VHDL model. If designer A wanted to use a model from designer B, but designer B used the values from type *four-value* as the interface ports to the model, then designer A cannot use the model without converting the types of the ports to the value system used by designer B. This problem can be solved through the use of conversion functions.

First, let's write the function that will convert between these two value systems. The values from the first type represent these distinct states:

X — unknown value

L — logical 0 value

H — logical 1 value

Z — high-impedance or open-collector value

The values from the second type represent these states:

'X' — unknown value

'0' — logical 0 value

'1' — logical 1 value

'Z' — high-impedance or open-collector value

From the description of the two value systems, the conversion function will be trivial. An example of one is shown here:

```
FUNCTION convert4val(S : fourval) RETURN fourvalue IS
BEGIN
  CASE S IS
    WHEN X =>
      RETURN 'X';
    WHEN L =>
      RETURN '0';
    WHEN H =>
      RETURN '1';
    WHEN Z =>
      RETURN 'Z';
  END CASE;
END convert4val;
```

This function will accept a value of type *fourval* and return a value of type *fourvalue*. The following example shows where such a function might be used.

```
PACKAGE my_std IS
  TYPE fourval IS (X, L, H, Z);
  TYPE fourvalue IS ('X', '0', '1', 'Z');

  TYPE fvector4 IS ARRAY(0 TO 3) OF fourval;
END my_std;

USE WORK.my_std.ALL;
ENTITY reg IS
  PORT(a : IN fvector4;
       clr: IN fourval;
       clk : IN fourval;
       q : OUT fvector4);

FUNCTION convert4val(S : fourval)
  RETURN fourvalue IS
BEGIN
  CASE S IS
    WHEN X =>
      RETURN 'X';
    WHEN L =>
      RETURN '0';
    WHEN H =>
      RETURN '1';
    WHEN Z =>
      RETURN 'Z';
  END CASE;
END convert4val;

FUNCTION convert4value(S : fourvalue)
    RETURN fourvalue IS
BEGIN
  CASE S IS
    WHEN X =>
      RETURN 'X';
     WHEN '0' =>
    RETURN L =>
    WHEN '1' =>
      RETURN H;
    WHEN 'Z' =>
      RETURN 'Z';
    END CASE;
  END convert4val;

END reg;

ARCHITECTURE structure OF reg IS
  COMPONENT dff
    PORT(d, clk, clr : IN fourvalue;
         q : OUT fourvalue);
  END COMPONENT;
```

```
BEGIN
  U1 : dff PORT MAP(convert4val(a(0)),
          convert4val(clk),
          convert4val(clr),
          convert4value(q) => q(0));

  U2 : dff PORT MAP(convert4val(a(1)),
          convert4val(clk),
          convert4val(clr),
          convert4value(q) => q(1));

  U3 : dff PORT MAP(convert4val(a(2)),
          convert4val(clk),
          convert4val(clr),
          convert4value(q) => q(2));

  U4 : dff PORT MAP(convert4val(a(3)),
          convert4val(clk),
          convert4val(clr),
          convert4value(q) => q(3));

END structure;
```

This example is a 4-bit register built out of flip-flops. The type used in the entity declaration for the register is a vector of type *fourval*. However, the flip-flops being instantiated have ports which are of type *fourvalue*. A type mismatch error will be generated if the ports of entity register are mapped directly to the component ports. Therefore, a conversion function is needed to convert between the two value systems.

If the ports are all of mode IN, then only one conversion is needed to map from the containing entity type to the contained entity type. In this example, if all of the ports were of mode input, then only function *convert4val* would be required.

If the component has output ports as well, then the output values of the contained entity need to be converted back to the containing entity type. In this example, the *q* port of component *dff* is an output port. The type of the output values will be *fourvalue*. These values cannot be mapped to the type *fourval* ports of entity *xregister*. Function *convert4value* will convert from a *fourvalue* type to a *fourval* type. Applying this function on the output ports will allow the port mapping to occur.

There are four component instantiations that use these conversion functions: components U1 through U4. Notice that the input ports use the *convert4val* conversion function, while the output ports use the *convert4value* conversion function.

Using the named association form of mapping for component instantiation, U1 would look like this:

```
U1: dff PORT MAP (
  d => convert4val( a(0) ),
  clk => convert4val( clk ),
  clr => convert4val( clr ),
  convert4value(q) => q(0) );
```

What this notation shows is that, for the input ports, the conversion functions are applied to the appropriate input signals (ports) before being mapped to the *dff* ports, and the output port value is converted with the conversion function before being mapped to the output port *q(0)*.

Conversion functions free the designer from generating a lot of temporary signals or variables to perform the conversion. The following example shows another method for performing conversion functions:

```
temp1 <= convert4val( a(0) );
temp2 <= convert4val( clk );
temp3 <= convert4val( clr );

U1 : dff PORT MAP (
  d => temp1,
  clk => temp2,
  clr => temp3,
  q => temp4);

q(0) <= convert4value(temp4);
```

This method is much more verbose, requiring an intermediate temporary signal for each port of the component being mapped. This clearly is not the preferred method.

If a port is of mode INOUT, conversion functions cannot be used with positional notation. The ports must use named association because two conversion functions must be associated with each inout port. One conversion function will be used for the input part of the inout port and the other will be used for the output part of the inout port.

In the following example, two bidirectional transfer devices are contained in an entity called *trans2*.

```
PACKAGE my_pack IS
  TYPE nineval IS (Z0, Z1, ZX,
                   R0, R1, RX,
                   F0, F1, FX);

  TYPE nvector2 IS ARRAY(0 TO 1) OF nineval;
  TYPE fourstate IS (X, L, H, Z);

  FUNCTION convert4state(a : fourstate)
    RETURN nineval;
```

```
  FUNCTION convert9val(a : nineval)
    RETURN fourstate;

END my_pack;
PACKAGE body my_pack IS
  FUNCTION convert4state(a : fourstate)
  RETURN nineval IS
BEGIN
  CASE a IS
    WHEN X =>
     RETURN FX;
    WHEN L =>
     RETURN FO;
    WHEN H =>
     RETURN F1;
    WHEN Z =>
     RETURN ZX;
  END CASE;
END convert4state;

FUNCTION convert9val(a : nineval)
  RETURN fourstate IS
BEGIN
  CASE a IS
    WHEN ZO =>
     RETURN Z;
    WHEN Z1 =>
     RETURN Z;
    WHEN ZX =>
     RETURN Z;
    WHEN RO =>
     RETURN L;
    WHEN R1 =>
     RETURN H;
    WHEN RX =>
     RETURN X;
    WHEN FO =>
     RETURN L;
    WHEN F1 =>
     RETURN H;
    WHEN FX =>
     RETURN X;
    END CASE;
  END convert9val;
END my_pack;

USE WORK.my_pack.ALL;
ENTITY trans2 IS
  PORT( a, b : INOUT nvector2;
```

```
        enable : IN nineval);
END trans2;

ARCHITECTURE struct OF trans2 IS
  COMPONENT trans
    PORT(x1, x2 : INOUT fourstate;
         en : IN fourstate);
  END COMPONENT;
BEGIN
  U1 : trans PORT MAP(
    convert4state(x1) => convert9val(a(0)),
    convert4state(x2) => convert9val(b(0)),
    en => convert9val(enable) );

  U2 : trans PORT MAP(
    convert4state(x1) => convert9val(a(1)),
    convert4state(x2) => convert9val(b(1)),
    en => convert9val(enable) );
END struct;
```

Each component is a bidirectional transfer device called *trans*. The *trans* device contains three ports. Ports *x1* and *x2* are inout ports and port *en* is an input port. When port *en* is an H value, *x1* is transferred to *x2,* and when port *en* is an L value, *x2* is transferred to *x1*.

The *trans* components use type *fourstate* for the port types, while the containing entity uses type *nineval*. Conversion functions are required to allow the instantiation of the *trans* components in architecture *struct* of entity *trans2*.

The first component instantiation statement for the *trans* component labeled U1 shows how conversion functions are used for inout ports. The first port mapping maps port *x1* to *a(0)*. Port *a(0)* is a *nineval* type; therefore, the signal created by the port is a *nineval* type. When this signal is mapped to port *x1* of component *trans,* it must be converted to a *fourstate* type. Conversion function *convert9val* must be called to complete the conversion. When data is transferred out to port *x1* for the out portion of the inout port, conversion function *convert4state* must be called.

The conversion functions are organized such that the side of the port mapping clause that changes contains the conversion function that must be called. When *x1* changes, function *convert4state* is called to convert the *fourstate* value to a *nineval* value before it is passed to the containing entity *trans2*. Conversely, when port *a(0)* changes, function *convert9val* is called to convert the *nineval* value to a *fourstate* value that can be used within the *trans* model.

Conversion functions are used to convert a value of one type to a value of another type. They can be called explicitly as part of execution or implicitly from a mapping in a component instantiation.

Resolution functions

A resolution function is used to return the value of a signal when the signal is driven by multiple drivers. It is illegal in VHDL to have a signal with multiple drivers without a resolution function attached to that signal.

A resolution function consists of a function that is called whenever one of the drivers for the signal has an event occur on it. The resolution function will be executed and will return a single value from all of the driver values; this value will be the new value of the signal.

In typical simulators, resolution functions are built in, or fixed. With VHDL the designer has the capability to define any type of resolution function desired, wired-or, wired-and, average signal value, etc.

A resolution function has a single-argument input and returns a single value. The single-input argument consists of an unconstrained array of driver values for the signal that the resolution function is attached to. If the signal has two drivers, the unconstrained array will be two elements long; if the signal has three drivers, the unconstrained array will be three elements long. The resolution function will examine the values of all of the drivers and return a single value called the *resolved value* of the signal.

Let's examine a resolution function for the type *fourval* that was used in the conversion function examples. The type declaration for *fourval* is as follows:

```
TYPE fourval IS (X, L, H, Z);
```

Four distinct values are declared that represent all of the possible values that the signal can obtain. The value L represents a logical 0; the value H represents a logical 1; the value Z represents a high-impedance or open-collector condition; and, finally, the value X represents an unknown condition in which the value can represent an L or an H, but we're not sure which. This condition can occur when two drivers are driving a signal—one driver driving with an H and the other driving with an L.

Listed by order of strength, with the weakest at the top, the values are as follows:

Z — weakest—H, L, or X can override

H,L — medium strength—only X can override

X — strong—no override

Using this information, a truth table for two inputs can be developed, as shown in Fig. 5.1.

	Z	L	H	X
Z	Z	L	H	X
L	L	L	X	X
H	H	X	H	X
X	X	X	X	X

Figure 5.1 Four-state truth table.

This truth table is for two input values; it can be expanded to more inputs by successively applying it to two values at a time. This can be done because the table is commutative and associative. An L and a Z, or a Z and an L will give the same results. An (L, Z) with H will give the same results as an (H, Z) with an L. These principles are very important, because the order of driver values within the input argument to the resolution function is nondeterministic from the designer's point of view. Any dependence on order can cause nondeterministic results from the resolution function.

Using all of this information, a designer can write a resolution function for this type. The resolution function will maintain the highest strength seen so far, and compare this value with new values a single element at a time, until all values have been exhausted. This algorithm will return the highest-strength value.

The following is an example of such a resolution function:

```
PACKAGE fourpack IS
  TYPE fourval IS (X, L, H, Z);
  TYPE fourval_vector IS ARRAY (natural RANGE <> ) OF fourval;

  FUNCTION resolve( s: fourval_vector) RETURN fourval;
END fourpack;

PACKAGE BODY fourpack IS
  FUNCTION resolve( s: fourval_vector) RETURN fourval IS
    VARIABLE result : fourval := Z;
  BEGIN
    FOR i IN s'RANGE LOOP
      CASE result IS
        WHEN Z =>
        CASE s(i) IS
          WHEN H =>
           result := H;
          WHEN L =>
           result := L;
          WHEN X =>
           result := X;
```

```
        WHEN OTHERS =>
         NULL;
        END CASE;

      WHEN L =>
       CASE s(i) IS
        WHEN H =>
         result := X;
        WHEN X =>
         result := X;
        WHEN OTHERS =>
         NULL;
        END CASE;

      WHEN H =>
       CASE s(i) IS
        WHEN L =>
         result := X;
        WHEN X =>
         result := X;
        WHEN OTHERS =>
         NULL;
        END CASE;

      WHEN X =>
       result := X;

      END CASE;
     END LOOP;
     RETURN result;
    END resolve;
  END fourpack;
```

The input argument is an unconstrained array of the driver-base type, *fourval.* The resolution function will examine all of the values of the drivers passed in argument *s,* one at a time, and return a single value of *fourval* type to be scheduled as the signal value.

Variable *result* is initialized to a Z value to take care of the case of zero drivers for the signal. In this case, the loop will never be executed, and the result value returned will be the initialization value. It is also a good idea to initialize the result value to the weakest value of the value system to allow overwriting by stronger values.

If a nonzero number of drivers exists for the signal being resolved, then the loop will be executed once for each driver value passed in argument *s.* Each driver value is compared with the current value stored in variable result. If the new value is stronger according to the rules outlined earlier, then the current result will be updated with the new value.

Let's look at some example driver values to see how this works. Assuming that argument *s* contained the driver values shown in Fig. 5.2, what would the result be?

Since there are two drivers, the loop will be executed twice. The first time through the loop variable *result* contains the initial value Z. The first driver value is also a Z value. Value Z compared with value Z will produce a resulting value Z.

The next iteration through the loop will retrieve the next driver value, which is H. The value H compared with value Z will return value H. The function will therefore return the value H as the resolved value of the signal.

Another case is shown in Fig. 5.3. In this example, there are three drivers, and the resolution function will execute the loop three times. The first iteration of the loop, the initial value of *result* (Z), will be compared with the first driver value (H). The value H will be assigned to *result*. In the next iteration *result* (H) will be compared with the second driver (Z). The value H will remain in *result* because the value Z is weaker. Finally, the last iteration *result* (H) will be compared with the last driver value (L). Since these values are of the same strength, the value X will be assigned to *result*. The value X will be returned from the function as the resolved value for the signal.

Nine-value resolution function. Some simulators use more complex types to represent the value of a signal. For instance, what might a resolution function look like for a nine-value system, typical of most workstation-based simulators in use currently. The nine values in the value system are as follows:

```
Z0, Z1, ZX, R0, R1, RX, F0, F1, FX
weakest---------------strongest
```

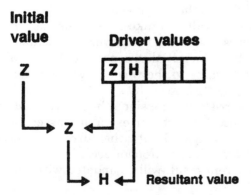

Initial value

Driver values

Z

Z H

Z

H   **Resultant value**

Figure 5.2 Four-state resolution with two values.

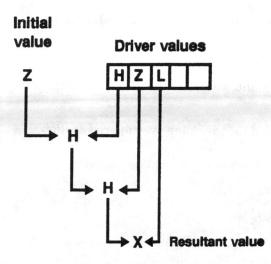

Figure 5.3 Four-state resolution with three values.

The system consists of three strengths and three logic values. The three strengths represent the following:

Z — high impedance strength, few hundred k of resistance

R — resistive, few k of resistance

F — forcing, few ohms of resistance

The three logic levels are represented as follows:

0 — logical 0 or false

1 — logical 1 or true

X — logical unknown

The nine states are described as follows:

Z0 — high-impedance 0

Z1 — high-impedance 1

ZX — high-impedance unknown

R0 — resistive 0

R1 — resistive 1

RX — resistive unknown

F0 — forcing 0

F1 — forcing 1

FX — forcing unknown

A few simple rules can be used to define how the resolution function should work.

- Strongest strength always wins.
- If strengths are the same and values are different, return same strength, but X value.

The type declarations needed for the value system are as follows:

```
PACKAGE ninepack IS
  TYPE strength IS (Z, R, F);
  TYPE nineval IS ( Z0, Z1, ZX,
                    R0, R1, RX,
                    F0, F1, FX );

  TYPE ninevalvec IS ARRAY(natural RANGE <>) OF nineval;

  TYPE ninevaltab IS ARRAY(nineval'LOW TO
      nineval'HIGH) OF strength;

  TYPE strengthtab IS ARRAY(strength'LOW TO
      strength'HIGH) OF nineval;

  FUNCTION resolve9( s: ninevalvec) RETURN nineval;

END ninepack;
```

The package body contains the resolution function (package bodies are discussed near the end of this chapter).

```
PACKAGE BODY ninepack IS
  FUNCTION resolve9( s: ninevalvec) RETURN nineval IS
    VARIABLE result: nineval;
    CONSTANT get_strength : ninevaltab :=
      (Z, --Z0
       Z, --Z1
       Z, --ZX
       R, --R0
       R, --R1
       R, --RX
       F, --F0
       F, --F1
       F); --FX

  CONSTANT x_tab : strengthtab :=
      (ZX, --Z
       RX, --R
       FX); --F
  BEGIN
    IF s'LENGTH = 0 THEN RETURN ZX; END IF;
    result := s(0);
```

```
FOR i IN s'RANGE LOOP
  IF get_strength(result) < get_strength(s(i)) THEN
    result := s(i);

  ELSIF get_strength(result) = get_strength(s(i)) THEN
    IF result/= s(i) THEN
        result := x_tab(get_strength(result));
      END IF;

    END IF;
  END LOOP;
  RETURN result;

END resolve9;
END ninepack;
```

The package *ninepack* declares a number of types used in this example, including some array types to make the resolution function easier to implement. The basic algorithm of the function is the same as the *fourval* resolution function; however, the operations with nine values are a little more complex. Function *resolve9* still does a pairwise comparison of the input values to determine the resultant value. With a nine-value system, the comparison operation is more complicated, and therefore some constant arrays were declared to make the job easier.

The constant *get_strength* returns the driving strength of the driver value. The constant *x_tab* will return the appropriate unknown nine-state value, given the strength of the input. These constants could have been implemented as IF statements or CASE statements, but constant arrays are much more efficient.

In the nine-value system there are three values at the lowest strength level, so the variable *result* has to be initialized more carefully to predict correct results. If there are no drivers, the range attribute of argument *s* will return 0 and the default value (ZX) will be returned.

Let's look at a few examples of driver-input arguments, and see what the resolution function will predict. An example of two drivers is shown in Fig. 5.4.

This example contains two driver values, Z1 and R0. Variable *result* is initialized to the first driver value, and the loop will execute as many times as there are drivers. The first time through the loop, *result* will equal Z1 and the first driver will equal Z1. Variable *result* will remain at Z1 because the values are equal. The next time through the loop, variable *result* contains Z1 and the second driver contains R0. The constant *get_strength* will return strength R. The constant *get_strength* for variable result will return strength Z. Strength R is lexically greater than strength Z. This is because value R has a higher position number than Z, because R is listed after Z in the type declaration for type *strength*. The fact that the new driver has a stronger strength value

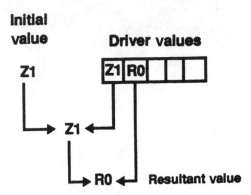

Figure 5.4 Nine-state resolution with two values.

than variable *result* will cause variable result to be updated with the stronger value, R0.

Another example will show how the constant x_tab is used to predict the correct value for conflicting inputs. The driver values are shown in the array in Fig. 5.5.

In this example, variable *result* is initialized to F0. The first iteration of the loop will do nothing because the first driver and the result-initialization value are the same value. The next iteration starts with variable *result* containing the value F0, and the next driver value as R0. Since the value in variable *result* is greater in strength than the value of the new driver, no action is implemented, except to advance the loop to the next driver.

The last driver contains the value F1. The strength of the value contained in variable *result* and the new driver value are the same.

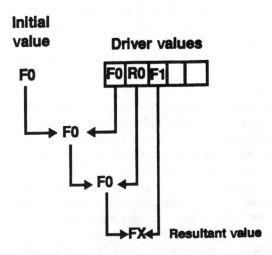

Figure 5.5 Nine-state resolution with three values.

Therefore, the IF statement checking this condition will be executed and will succeed. The next IF statement will check to see if the logical values are the same for both variable *result* and the new driver. Variable *result* contains an F0, and the new driver value contains an F1. The values are not the same, and the *x_tab* table will be used to return the correct unknown value for the strength of the driver values. The *x_tab* table will return the value FX, which will be returned as the resolved value.

A more efficient method to implement the loop would be to skip the first iteration where the first driver is compared to itself, because the value in variable *result* is initialized to the first driver value. It is left as an exercise to the reader to write this new loop iteration mechanism.

While VHDL simulators can support any type of resolution that can be legally written in the language, synthesis tools can support only a subset. The reason stems from the fact that the synthesis tools must build actual hardware from the VHDL description. If the resolution function maps into a common hardware behavior such as wired-or or wired-and, then most synthesis tools allow the user the capability to tag the resolution function appropriately. For instance, a resolution function that performs a wired-or function will be tagged with an attribute that tells the synthesis tools to connect the outputs together.

Composite type resolution. For simple signal values such as the *nineval* and *fourval* types, it is easy to see how to create the resolution function. But for signals of composite types it is not so obvious. How can one value of a composite type be stronger than another?

The answer is that one value must be designated as weaker than all of the other values. Then the principle is the same as any other type being resolved. In the *fourval* type, the value Z was considered the weakest state, and any of the other values could overwrite this value. In the *nineval* type, all values with a strength of Z could be overridden by values with a strength of R or F, and all values with strength R could be overridden by strength F.

To resolve a composite type, designate one value of the composite type as unusable except to indicate that the signal is not currently being driven. The resolution function will check how many drivers have this value and how many drivers have a driving value. If only one driving value exists, then the resolution function can return this value as the resolved value. If more than one driving value is present, then an error condition probably exists and the resolution function can announce the error.

A typical application for a composite type resolution function is shown in Fig. 5.6.

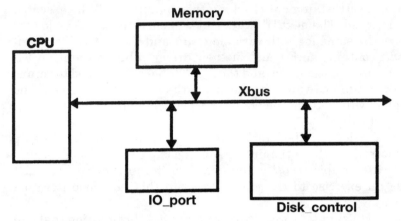

Figure 5.6 Block diagram of computer.

Signal XBUS can be driven from a number of sources but, hopefully, only one at a time. The resolution function must determine how many drivers are trying to drive XBUS and return the correct value for the signal.

Shown here are the type declarations and resolution function for a composite type used in such a circuit.

```
PACKAGE composite_res IS
 TYPE xtype IS
   RECORD
     addr : INTEGER;
     data : INTEGER;
   END RECORD;

   TYPE xtypevector IS ARRAY( natural RANGE <>) OF xtype;
   CONSTANT notdriven : xtype := (-1,-1);

   FUNCTION cresolve( t : xtypevector) RETURN xtype;
 END composite_res;

PACKAGE BODY composite_res IS
FUNCTION cresolve( t: xtypevector) RETURN xtype IS
 VARIABLE result : xtype := notdriven;
 VARIABLE drive_count : INTEGER := 0;
BEGIN
 IF t'LENGTH = 0 THEN RETURN notdriven;

 END IF;

 FOR i IN t'RANGE LOOP
   IF t(i) /= notdriven THEN
     drive_count := drive_count + 1;
```

```
      IF drive_count = 1 THEN
        result := t(i);
      ELSE
        result := notdriven;
        ASSERT FALSE
          REPORT "multiple drivers detected"
          SEVERITY ERROR;
      END IF;
    END IF;
  END LOOP;
  RETURN result;
 END cresolve;
END composite_res;
```

Type *xtype* declares the record type for signal *xbus*. Type *xtypevector* is an unconstrained array type of *xtype* values used for the resolution function input argument *t*. Constant *notdriven* declares the value of the record that will be used to signify that a signal driver is not driving. Negative number values were used to represent the *notdriven* state because, in this example, only positive values will be used in the *addr* and *data* fields. But what happens if all of the values must be used for a particular type? The easiest solution is probably to declare a new type which is a record, containing the original type as one field of the record, and a new field which is a boolean that determines whether the driver is driving or not driving.

In this example, resolution function *cresolve* first checks to make certain that at least one driver value is passed in argument *t* (drivers can be turned off using guarded signal assignment). If at least one driver is driving, the loop statement will loop through all driver values, looking for driving values. If a driving value is detected, and it is the first, then this value is assumed to be the output resolved value, until proven otherwise. If only one driving value occurs, that value will be returned as the resolved value.

If a second driving value appears, the output is set to the nondriven value, signifying that the outcome is uncertain, and the ASSERT statement will write out an error message to that effect.

In this example, the negative numbers of the integer type were not used except to indicate whether the signal was driving or not. We reserved one value to indicate this condition. Another value could be reserved to indicate the multiply-driven case such that when multiple drivers are detected on the signal, this value would be returned as the resolved value. An example might look like this:

```
CONSTANT multiple_drive : xtype := (-2,-2);
```

This constant provides the capability of distinguishing between a non-driven signal and a multiply-driven signal.

Resolved signals.   So far we have discussed how to write resolution functions that can resolve signals of multiple drivers, but we have not discussed how all of the appropriate declarations are structured to accomplish this.

Resolved signals are created using one of two methods. The first is to create a resolved subtype and declare a signal using this type. The second is to declare a signal specifying a resolution function as part of the signal declaration.

Let's discuss the resolved subtype method first. To create a resolved subtype, the designer declares the base type, then declares the subtype, specifying the resolution function to use for this type. An example would look like this:

```
TYPE fourval IS (X, L, H, Z);      -- won't compile
SUBTYPE resfour IS resolve fourval;      -- as is
```

The first declaration declares the enumerated type *fourval*. The second declaration is used to declare a subtype named *resfour*, that uses a resolution function named *resolve* to resolve the base type *fourval*. This syntax will not compile as is because the function *resolve* is not visible. To declare a resolved subtype requires a very specific combination of statements, in a very specific ordering.

A correct example of the resolved type is as follows:

```
PACKAGE fourpack IS
  TYPE fourval IS (X, L, H, Z); -- line 1
  TYPE fourvalvector IS ARRAY(natural RANGE <>)
       OF fourval;   -- line 2

  FUNCTION resolve( s: fourvalvector) RETURN fourval; -- line 3

  SUBTYPE resfour IS resolve fourval; -- line 4
END fourpack;
```

The statement in line 2 declares an unconstrained array of the base type that will be used to contain the driver values passed to the resolution function. The statement in line 3 declares the definition of the resolution function *resolve* so that the subtype declaration can make use of it. The body of the resolution function is implemented in the package body. Finally, the statement in line 4 declares the resolved subtype using the base type and the resolution function declaration.

The order of the statements is important, because each statement declares something that is used in the next statement. If the unconstrained array declaration is left out, the resolution function could not be declared, and if the resolution function was not declared, the subtype could not be declared.

The second method of obtaining a resolved signal is to specify the resolution function in the signal declaration. In the following example, a signal is declared using the resolution function *resolve*.

```
PACKAGE fourpack IS
  TYPE fourval IS (X, L, H, Z);
  TYPE fourvalvector IS ARRAY(natural RANGE <>)      OF
fourval;

  FUNCTION resolve( s: fourvalvector) RETURN fourval;
  SUBTYPE resfour IS resolve fourval;
END fourpack;

USE WORK.fourpack.ALL;
ENTITY mux2 IS
  PORT( i1, i2, a : IN fourval;
        q : OUT fourval);
END mux2;

ARCHITECTURE different OF mux2 IS
  COMPONENT and2
    PORT( a, b :IN fourval;
          c : OUT fourval);
END COMPONENT;
  COMPONENT inv
    PORT( a : IN fourval;
          b : OUT fourval);
  END COMPONENT;

  SIGNAL nota : fourval;

  -- resolved signal
  SIGNAL intq : resolve fourval := X;

BEGIN

  U1: inv PORT MAP(a, nota);

  U2: and2 PORT MAP(i1, a, intq);

  U3: and2 PORT MAP(i2, nota, intq);

  q <= intq;

END different;
```

The package *fourpack* declares all of the appropriate types and function declarations so that the resolution function *resolve* is visible in the entity. In the architecture declaration section signal *intq* is declared of type *fourval,* using the resolution function *resolve.* This signal is also given an initial value of X.

Signal *intq* is required to have a resolution function because it is the output signal for components U2 and U3. Each component provides a driver to signal *intq.* Resolution function *resolve* is used to determine the end result of the two driver values. Signal *nota* is not required to have a resolution function because it only has one driver, component U1.

Procedures

In the preceding section describing functions, we discussed how functions can have a number of input parameters and always return one value. In contrast, procedures can have any number of in, out, and inout parameters. A procedure call is considered a statement of its own, while a function usually exists as part of an expression. The most usual case of using a procedure is when more than one value is returned.

Procedures have basically the same syntax and rules as functions. A procedure declaration begins with the keyword PROCEDURE, followed by the procedure name, and then an argument list. The main difference between a function and a procedure is that the procedure argument list will most likely have a direction associated with each parameter, while the function argument list does not. In a procedure, some of the arguments can be mode IN, OUT, or INOUT, while in a function all arguments are of mode IN by default and can be only of mode IN.

A typical example where a procedure is very useful is during the conversion from an array of a multivalued type to an integer. A procedure showing an example of how to accomplish this is shown here:

```
USE WORK.std_logic_1164.ALL;
PROCEDURE vector_to_int (z : IN std_logic_vector;
        x_flag : OUT BOOLEAN; q : INOUT INTEGER) IS
BEGIN
  q := 0;
  x_flag := false;

  FOR i IN z'RANGE LOOP
    q := q * 2;

    IF z(i) = '1' THEN
      q := q + 1;
    ELSIF z(i) /= '0' THEN
```

```
    x_flag := TRUE;
   END IF;
  END LOOP;
END vector_to_int;
```

The behavior of this procedure is to convert the input argument z from an array of a type to an integer. However, if the input array has unknown values contained in it, an integer value cannot be generated from the array. When this condition occurs, output argument x_flag is set to true, indicating that the output integer value is unknown. A procedure was required to implement this behavior because more than one output value results from the procedure. Let's examine what the result from the procedure will be from the input array value shown here:

```
'0' '0' '1' '1'
```

The first step for the procedure is to initialize the output values to known conditions, in case a zero length input argument is passed in. Output argument x_flag is initialized to false, and will stay false until proven otherwise.

The loop statement will loop through the input vector z and progressively add each value of the vector until all values have been added. If the value is a '1', then it is added to the result. If the value is an '0', then no addition is done. If any other value is found in the vector, *the x_flag* result is set true, indicating that an unknown condition was found on one of the inputs. (Notice that parameter q is defined as an inout parameter. This is needed because the value is read in the procedure.)

Procedure with inout parameters

The examples we have discussed so far have dealt mostly with in and out parameters, but procedures can have inout parameters also. The following example shows a procedure that has an inout argument that is a record type. The record contains an array of eight integers, along with a field used to hold the average of all of the integers. The procedure will calculate the average of the integer values, write the average in the average field of the record, and return the updated record.

```
PACKAGE intpack IS
  TYPE bus_stat_vec IS ARRAY(0 to 7) OF INTEGER;
  TYPE bus_stat_t IS
    RECORD
      bus_val: bus_stat_vec;
      average_val : INTEGER;
    END RECORD;

  PROCEDURE bus_average( x : inout bus_stat_t );
```

```
END intpack;
PACKAGE BODY intpack IS
  PROCEDURE bus_average( x : inout bus_stat_t) IS
    VARIABLE total : INTEGER := 0;
  BEGIN
    FOR i IN 0 TO 7 LOOP
      total := total + x.bus_val(i);
    END LOOP;
    x.average_val := total/ 8;
  END bus_average;
END intpack;
```

A process calling the procedure might look as shown below:

```
PROCESS( mem_update )
  VARIABLE bus_statistics : bus_stat_t;
BEGIN
  bus_statistics.bus_val :=
    (50, 40, 30, 35, 45, 55, 65, 85 );
  bus_average(bus_statistics);
  average <= bus_statistics.average_val;

END PROCESS;
```

The variable assignment to *bus_statistics.bus_val,* fills in the appropriate bus utilization values to be used for the calculation. The next line is the call to the *bus_average* procedure, which will perform the averaging calculation. Initially, the argument to the *bus_average* procedure is an input value, but after the procedure has finished, the argument becomes an output value that can be used inside the calling process. The output value from the procedure is assigned to an output signal in the last line of the process.

Side effects

Procedures have an interesting problem that is not shared by their function counterparts. Procedures can cause side effects to occur. A side effect is the result of changing the value of an object inside a procedure when that object was not an argument to the procedure. For instance, a signal of an architecture can be assigned a value from within a procedure, without that signal being an argument passed into the procedure. For instance, if two signals are not declared in the argument list of a procedure, but are assigned from the current procedure, any assignments to these signals are side effects.

This is not a recommended method for writing a model. The debugging and maintenance of a model of this type can be very difficult. This feature was presented so that the reader would understand the behavior if such a model were examined.

Packages

The primary purpose of a package is to encapsulate elements that can be shared (globally) among two or more design units. A package is a common storage area used to hold data to be shared among a number of entities. Declaring data inside of a package allows the data to be referenced by other entities; thus, the data can be shared.

A package consists of two parts: a package declaration section and a package body. The package declaration defines the interface for the package, much the same way that the entity defines the interface for a model. The package body specifies the actual behavior of the package in the same method that the architecture statement does for a model.

Package declaration

The package declaration section can contain the following declarations:

- Subprogram declaration
- Type, subtype declaration
- Constant, deferred constant declaration
- Signal declaration, creates a global signal
- File declaration
- Alias declaration
- Component declaration
- Attribute declaration, a user-defined attribute (Chap. 8)
- Attribute specification
- Disconnection specification
- Use clause

All of the items declared in the package declaration section are visible to any design unit that uses the package with a USE clause. The interface to a package consists of any subprograms or deferred constants declared in the package declaration. The subprogram and deferred constant declarations must have a corresponding subprogram body and deferred constant value in the package body or an error will result.

Deferred constants

Deferred constants are constants which have their name and type declared in the package declaration section but have the actual value specified in the package body section. An example of a deferred constant in the package declaration is as follows:

```
PACKAGE tpack IS
  CONSTANT timing_mode : t_mode;
END tpack;
```

This example shows a deferred constant called *timing_mode* being defined as type *t_mode*. The actual value of the constant will be specified when the package body for package *tpack* is compiled. This feature allows late binding of the value of a constant so that the value of the constant can be specified at the last possible moment and can be changed easily. Any design unit that uses a deferred constant from the package declaration need not be recompiled if the value of the constant is changed in the package body. Only the package body needs to be recompiled.

Subprogram declaration

The other item that forms the interface to the package is the subprogram declaration. A subprogram declaration allows the designer to specify the interface to a subprogram separately from the subprogram body. This functionality allows any designers using the subprogram to start or continue with the design, while the specification of the internals of the subprograms are detailed. It also gives the designer of the subprogram bodies freedom to change the internal workings of the subprograms, without affecting any designs that use the subprograms. An example of a subprogram declaration is as follows:

```
PACKAGE cluspack IS
  TYPE nineval IS (Z0, Z1, ZX,
                   R0, R1, RX,
                   F0, F1, FX );
  TYPE t_cluster IS ARRAY(0 to 15) OF nineval;
  TYPE t_clus_vec IS ARRAY(natural range <>) OF t_cluster;

  FUNCTION resolve_cluster( s: t_clus_vec ) RETURN t_cluster;
  SUBTYPE t_wclus IS resolve_cluster t_cluster;
  CONSTANT undriven : t_wclus;

END cluspack;
```

The subprogram declaration for *resolve_cluster* specifies the name of the subprogram, any arguments to the subprogram, their types and modes, and the return type if the subprogram is a function. This declaration can be used to compile any models that intend to use it, without the actual subprogram body specified yet. The subprogram body must exist before the simulator is built, during elaboration.

Package body

The main purpose of the package body is to define the values for deferred constants and specify the subprogram bodies for any subprogram declarations from the package declaration. However, the package body can also contain the following declarations:

- Subprogram declaration
- Subprogram body
- Type, subtype declaration
- Constant declaration, which fills in the value for the deferred constant
- File declaration
- Alias declaration
- Use clause

All of the declarations in the package body, except for the constant declaration that is specifying the value of a deferred constant and the subprogram body declaration, will be local to the package body.

Let's examine a package body for the package declaration that was discussed in the last section:

```
PACKAGE BODY cluspack IS
  CONSTANT undriven : t_wclus :=
              (ZX, ZX, ZX, ZX,
               ZX, ZX, ZX, ZX,
               ZX, ZX, ZX, ZX,
               ZX, ZX, ZX, ZX);

  FUNCTION resolve_cluster ( s: t_clus_vec ) return t_cluster
IS
    VARIABLE result : t_cluster;
    VARIABLE drive_count : INTEGER;
  BEGIN
    IF s'LENGTH = 0 THEN RETURN undriven;
    END IF;
    FOR i in s'RANGE LOOP
      IF s(i) /= undriven THEN
        drive_count := drive_count + 1;
```

```
        IF drive_count = 1 THEN
          result := s(i);
        ELSE
          result := undriven;
          ASSERT FALSE
            REPORT "multiple drivers detected"
            SEVERITY ERROR;
        END IF;
      END IF;
    END LOOP;
    RETURN result;
  END resolve_cluster;
END cluspack;
```

The package body statement is very similar to the package declaration except for the keyword BODY after package. The contents of the two design units are very different, however. This package body example contains only two items, the deferred constant value for deferred constant *undriven,* and the subprogram body for subprogram *resolve_cluster.* Notice how the deferred constant value specification matches the deferred constant declaration in the package declaration, and the subprogram body matches the subprogram declaration in the package declaration. The subprogram body must match the subprogram declaration exactly, in the number of parameters, the type of parameters, and the return type.

A package body can also contain local declarations that are used only within the package body to create other subprogram bodies, or deferred constant values. These declarations are not visible outside of the package body but can be very useful within the package body. An example of a complete package making use of this feature is as follows:

```
USE WORK.std_logic_1164.ALL;
PACKAGE math IS
  TYPE st16 IS ARRAY(0 TO 15) OF std_logic;

  FUNCTION add(a, b: IN st16) RETURN st16;
  FUNCTION sub(a, b: IN st16) RETURN st16;

END math;
PACKAGE BODY math IS

  FUNCTION vect_to_int(S : st16) RETURN INTEGER IS
    VARIABLE result : INTEGER := 0;
  BEGIN
    FOR i IN 0 TO 7 LOOP
      result := result * 2;

      IF S(i) = '1' THEN
```

```
        result := result + 1;
      END IF;
    END LOOP;

  RETURN result;
END vect_to_int;

FUNCTION int_to_st16(s : INTEGER) RETURN st16 IS
  VARIABLE result : st16;
  VARIABLE digit : INTEGER :_ 2**15;
  VARIABLE local : INTEGER;
BEGIN
  local := s;
  FOR i IN 15 DOWNTO 0 LOOP
    IF local/digit >= 1 THEN
      result(i) := '1';
      local := local - digit;
    ELSE
      result(i) := '0';
    END IF;

    digit := digit/2;

  END LOOP;
  RETURN result;
END int_to_st16;

FUNCTION add(a, b: IN st16) RETURN st16 IS
  VARIABLE result : INTEGER;
BEGIN
  result := vect_to_int(a) + vect_to_int(b);
  RETURN int_to_st16(result);
END add;

FUNCTION sub(a, b: IN st16) RETURN st16 IS
  VARIABLE result : INTEGER;
BEGIN
  result := vect_to_int(a) - vect_to_int(b);
  RETURN int_to_st16(result);
END sub;

END math;
```

The package declaration declares a type, *st16,* and two functions, *add* and *sub,* that work with this type. The package body has function bodies for function declarations *add* and *sub,* and also includes two functions that are used only in the package body. These functions are *int_to_st16* and *vect_to_int.* These functions are not visible outside of the package body. To make these functions visible, a function declaration would need to be added to the package declaration, for each function.

Functions *vect_to_int* and *int_to_st16* must be declared ahead of function *add* to compile correctly. All functions must be declared before they are used to compile correctly.

In this chapter, we discussed the different kinds of subprograms and some of the uses for them.

- Subprograms consist of functions and procedures. Functions have only input parameters and a single return value, while procedures can have any number of in, out, and inout parameters.

- Functions can be used as conversion functions to convert from one type to another.

- Functions can be used as resolution functions to calculate the proper value on a multiply-driven network.

- Procedures are considered statements, while functions are usually part of an expression. Procedures can exist alone, while functions are usually called as part of a statement.

- Packages are used to encapsulate information that is to be shared among multiple design units.

- Packages consist of a package declaration in which all of the type, subprogram, and other declarations exist, and a package body in which subprogram bodies and deferred constants exist.

In the next chapter we will discuss how attributes can make some descriptions easier to read, and more compact.

6

Predefined Attributes

This chapter will discuss VHDL predefined attributes, and the way that concise readable models can be written using attributes. Predefined attributes are data that can be obtained from blocks, signals, and types or subtypes. The data obtained will fall into one of the categories shown below:

Value kind.   A simple value is returned.

Function kind.   A function call is performed to return a value.

Signal kind.   A new signal is created whose value is derived from another signal.

Type kind.   A type mark is returned.

Range kind.   A range value is returned.

Predefined attributes have a number of very important applications. Attributes can be used to detect clock edges, perform timing checks in concert with ASSERT statements, return range information about unconstrained types, and much more. All of these applications will be examined in this chapter. First, we will discuss each of the predefined attribute kinds and the ways that these attributes can be applied to modeling.

Value Kind Attributes

Value attributes are used to return a particular value about an array of a type, a block, or a type in general. Value attributes can be used to return the length of an array or the lowest bound of a type. Value attributes can be further broken down into three subclasses:

1. Value type attributes, which return the bounds of a type

2. Value array attributes, which return the length of an array

3. Value block attributes, which return block information

Value type attributes

Value type attributes are used to return the bounds of a type. For instance, a type defined as follows would have a low bound of 0 and a high bound of 7.

```
TYPE state IS (0 TO 7);
```

There are four predefined attributes in the value type attribute category. They are:

T'LEFT   returns the left bound of a type or subtype
T'RIGHT   returns the right bound of a type or subtype
T'HIGH   returns the upper bound of a type or subtype
T'LOW   returns the lower bound of a type or subtype

Attributes are specified by the character ' and then the attribute name. The object preceding the ' is the object to which the attribute is attached. The capital T in the preceding description means that the object to which the attribute is attached is a type. The ' character is pronounced *tick* among VHDL hackers. Therefore, the first of the preceding attributes is specified by T *tick* left.

The left bound of a type or subtype is the leftmost entry of the range constraint. The right bound is the rightmost entry of the type or subtype. In the following example, the left bound is –32,767 and the right bound is 32,767.

```
TYPE smallint IS -32767 TO 32767;
```

The upper bound of a type or subtype is the bound with the largest value, and the lower bound is the bound with the lowest value. For the type *smallint* shown here, the upper bound is 32,767 and the lower bound is –32,767.

To use one of these value attributes, the type mark name is followed by the attribute desired. For example, this is the syntax to return the left bound of a type.

```
PROCESS(x)
  SUBTYPE smallreal IS REAL RANGE -1.0E6 TO 1.0E6;
  VARIABLE q : real;
```

```
BEGIN
  q := smallreal'LEFT;
  --use of 'left returns
  -- -1.0E6
END PROCESS;
```

In this example, variable q is assigned the left bound of type *small-real*. Variable q must have the same type as the bounds of the type for the assignment to occur. (The assignment could also occur if variable q was cast into the appropriate type.) After the assignment has occurred, variable q will contain −1.0E6, which is the left bound of type *small-real*.

In the next example, all of the attributes are used to show what happens when a DOWNTO range is used for a type.

```
PROCESS(a)
  TYPE bit_range IS ARRAY(31 DOWNTO 0) OF BIT;
  VARIABLE left_range, right_range, uprange, lowrange :
integer;
BEGIN
  left_range := bit_range'LEFT;
  -- returns 31

  right_range := bit_range'RIGHT;
  -- returns 0

  uprange := bit_range'HIGH;
  --returns 31

  lowrange := bit_range'LOW;
  -- returns 0
END PROCESS;
```

This example shows how the different attributes can be used to return information about a type. When ranges of a type are defined using (a TO b) where $b > a$, the 'LEFT attribute will always equal the 'LOW attribute, but when a range specification using (b DOWNTO a) where $b > a$ is used, the 'HIGH and 'LOW can be used to determine the upper and lower bounds of the type.

Value type attributes are not restricted to numeric types. These attributes can also be used with any scalar type. An example using enumerated types is as follows:

```
ARCHITECTURE b OF a IS
  TYPE color IS (blue, cyan, green, yellow, red, magenta);
  SUBTYPE reverse_color IS color RANGE red DOWNTO green;
  SIGNAL color1, color2, color3,
```

```
        color4, color5, color6,
        color7, color8 : color;
BEGIN

  color1 <= color'LEFT; -- returns blue
  color2 <= color'RIGHT; -- returns magenta

  color3 <= color'HIGH; -- returns magenta
  color4 <= color'LOW; -- returns blue

  color5 <= reverse_color'LEFT;
  -- returns red

  color6 <= reverse_color'RIGHT;
  --returns green

  color7 <= reverse_color'HIGH;
  -- returns red

  color8 <= reverse_color'LOW;
  --returns green
END b;
```

This example illustrates how value type attributes can be used with enumerated types to return information about the type. Signals *color1* and *color2* are assigned *blue* and *magenta,* respectively, the left and right bounds of the type. It is easy to see how these values are obtained by examining the declaration of the type. The left bound of the type is *blue* and the right bound is *magenta.* What will be returned for the 'HIGH and 'LOW attributes of an enumerated type? The answer relates to the position numbers of the type. For an integer and real type, the position numbers of a value are equal to the value itself, but for an enumerated type, the position numbers of a value are determined by the declaration of the type. Values declared earlier will have lower position numbers than values declared later. Value *blue* from the preceding example will have a position number of 0, because it is the first value of the type. Value *cyan* will have a position number 1, *green* has 2, etc. From these position numbers, the high and low bounds of the type can be found.

Signals *color5* through *color8* are assigned attributes of the type *reverse_color.* This type has a DOWNTO range specification. Attributes 'HIGH and 'RIGHT will not return the same value because the range is reversed. Value *red* has a higher position number than value *green* and, therefore, a DOWNTO is needed for the range specification.

Value array attributes

There is only one value array attribute, 'LENGTH. Given an array type, this attribute will return the total length of the array range specified. This attribute works with array ranges of any scalar type and with multidimensional arrays of scalar-type ranges. A simple example is as follows:

```
PROCESS(a)
  TYPE bit4 IS ARRAY(0 TO 3) of BIT;
  TYPE bit_strange IS ARRAY(10 TO 20) OF BIT;
  VARIABLE len1, len2 : INTEGER;
BEGIN
  len1 := bit4'LENGTH;   -- returns 4
  len2 := bit_strange'LENGTH; -- returns 11
END PROCESS;
```

The assignment to *len1* will assign the value of the number of elements in array type *bit4*. The assignment to *len2* will assign the value of the number of elements of type *bit_strange*.

This attribute also works with enumerated-type ranges, as shown by the following example:

```
PACKAGE p_4val IS
    TYPE t_4val IS ('X', '0', '1', 'Z');
  TYPE t_4valX1 IS ARRAY(t_4val'LOW TO t_4val'HIGH) OF
  t_4val;

  TYPE t_4valX2 IS ARRAY(t_4val'LOW TO t_4val'HIGH) OF
  t_4valX1;
  TYPE t_4valmd IS ARRAY(t_4val'LOW TO t_4val'HIGH,
                 t_4val'LOW TO t_4val'HIGH) OF t_4val;

  CONSTANT andsd : t_4valX2 :=
      (('X',   -- XX
       t'0',   -- X0
        'X',   -- X1  (Notice this is an
        'X'),  -- XZ  array of arrays.)
       ('0',   -- 0X
        '0',   --00
        '0',   -- 01
        '0'),  -- 0Z
       ('X',   -- 1X
        '0',   -- 10
        '1',   -- 11
        'X'),  -- 1Z
       ('X',   -- ZX
        '0',   -- Z0
        'X',   -- Z1
        'X')); -- ZZ

  CONSTANT andmd : t_4valmd :=
```

```
      (('X',   -- XX
        '0',   -- X0
        'X',   -- X1
        'X'),  -- XZ  (Notice this example
       ('0',   -- 0X  is a multidimensional
        '0',   -- 00  array.)
        '0',   -- 01
        '0'),  -- 0Z
       ('X',   -- 1X
        '0',   -- 10
        '1',   -- 11
        'X'),  --1Z
       ('X',   -- ZX
        '0',   -- Z0
        'X',   -- Z1
        'X')); -- ZZ
END p_4val;
```

The two composite type constants, *andsd* and *andmd,* provide a lookup table for an AND function of type *t_4val.* The first constant, *andsd,* uses an array of array values, while the second constant, *andmd,* uses a multidimensional array to store the values. The initialization of both constants is specified by the same syntax. If the 'LENGTH attribute is applied to these types as follows, the results shown in the VHDL comments are obtained:

```
PROCESS(a)
  VARIABLE len1, len2, len3, len4 : INTEGER;

BEGIN
  len1 := t_4valX1'LENGTH;  -- returns 4
  len2 := t_4valX2'LENGTH;  -- returns 4

  len3 := t_4valmd'LENGTH(1); -- returns 4
  len4 := t_4valmd'LENGTH(2); -- returns 4
END PROCESS;
```

Type *t_4valX1* is a four-element array of type *t_4val.* The range of the array is specified using the predefined attributes 'LOW and 'HIGH of the *t_4val* type. Assigning the length of type *t_4valX1* to *len1* will return the value 4, the number of elements in array type *t_4valX1.* The assignment to *len2* will also return the value 4, because the range of type *t_valX2* is from 'LOW to 'HIGH of element type *t_4valX1.*

The assignments to *len3* and *len4* make use of a multidimensional array type, *t_4valmd.* Since a multidimensional array has more than one range, an argument is used to specify a particular range. The range will default to the first range, if none is specified. In the type *t_4valmd* example, the designer can pick the first or second range, because there are only two to choose from. To pick a range, the argument passed to the attribute specifies the number of the range, starting at 1. An argument value of 1 picks the first range, an argument value of 2 picks the second range, and so on.

The assignment to *len3* in the preceding example passed in the value 1 to pick the first range. The first range is from *t_4val*'LOW to *t_4val*'HIGH, or four entries. The second range is exactly the same as the first; therefore, both assignments will return 4 as the length of the array.

If the argument to 'LENGTH is not specified, it will default to 1. This was the case in the first examples of 'LENGTH, when no argument was specified. There was only one range, so the correct range was selected.

Value block attributes

There are two attributes that form the set of attributes that work with blocks and architectures. Attributes 'STRUCTURE and 'BEHAVIOR return information about how a block in a design is modeled. Attribute 'BEHAVIOR will return true if the block specified by the block label, or architecture specified by the architecture name, contains no component instantiation statements. Attribute 'STRUCTURE will return true if the block or architecture contains only component instantiation statements and/or passive processes.

The two examples that follow will illustrate how these attributes work. The first example contains only structural VHDL.

```
USE WORK.std_logic_1164.ALL;
ENTITY shifter IS
PORT(   clk, left : IN std_logic;
        right    : OUT std_logic;
END shifter;

ARCHITECTURE structural OF shifter IS
  COMPONENT dff
    PORT(   d, clk : IN std_logic;
            q : OUT   std_logic);
  END COMPONENT;
  SIGNAL i1, i2, i3: std_logic;
BEGIN
  u1: dff PORT MAP(d => left, clk => clk, q => i1);
  u2: dff PORT MAP(d => i1, clk => clk, q => i2);
  u3: dff PORT MAP(d => i2, clk => clk, q => i3);
  u4: dff PORT MAP(d => i3, clk => clk, q => right);
  checktime: PROCESS(clk)
    VARIABLE last_time : time := time'left;
  BEGIN
    ASSERT (NOW - last_time = 20 ns)
```

```
    REPORT "spike on clock"
    SEVERITY WARNING;
  last_time := now;
END PROCESS checktime;
END structural;
```

The preceding example is a shift register modeled using four *dff* components connected in series. A passive process statement exists in the architecture for entity *shifter,* used to detect spikes on the *clk* input. In the following example are the results of the attributes for the architecture *structural.*

structural'BEHAVIOR   returns false

structural'STRUCTURE   returns true

The passive process, *checktime,* will have no effect on the fact that the architecture is structural. If the process contained signal assignment statements, then the process would no longer be considered passive, and attribute 'STRUCTURE would also return false.

For any block or architecture that does not contain any component instantiation statements, attribute 'BEHAVIOR will be true, and attribute 'STRUCTURE will be false. For blocks or architectures that mix structure and behavior, both attributes will return false.

Function Kind Attributes

Function attributes return information to the designer about types, arrays, and signals. When a function kind attribute is used in an expression, a function call occurs that uses the value of the input argument to return a value. The value returned can be a position number of an enumerated value, an indication of whether a signal has changed this delta, or one of the bounds of an array.

Function attributes can be subdivided into three general classifications. These are:

1. Function type attributes, which return type values

2. Function array attributes, which return array bounds

3. Function signal attributes, which return signal history information

Function type attributes

Function type attributes return particular information about a type. Given the position number of a value within a type, the value can be returned. Also, values to the left or right of an input value of a particular type can be returned.

Function type attributes are one of the following:

'POS (value)	returns position number of value passed in
'VAL (value)	returns value from position number passed in
'SUCC (value)	returns next value in type after input value
'PRED (value)	returns previous value in type before input value
'LEFTOF (value)	returns value immediately to the left of the input value
'RIGHTOF (value)	returns value immediately to the right of the input value

A typical use of a function type attribute is to convert from an enumerated or physical type to an integer type. An example of conversion from a physical type to an integer type is as follows:

```
PACKAGE ohms_law IS
  TYPE current IS RANGE 0 TO 1000000
    UNITS
      ua;      -- micro amps
      ma = 1000 ua;  -- milli amps
      a = 1000 ma;  -- amps
    END UNITS;

  TYPE voltage IS RANGE 0 TO 1000000
    UNITS
      uv;      -- micro volts
      mv = 1000 uv;  -- milli volts
      v = 1000 mv;  --volts
    END UNITS;

  TYPE resistance IS RANGE 0 TO 100000000
    UNITS
      ohm;     -- ohms
      Kohm = 1000 ohm;  -- kilo ohms
      Mohm = 1000 Kohm;  -- mega ohms
    END UNITS;
END ohms_law;

USE WORK.ohms_law.ALL;
ENTITY calc_resistance IS
  PORT( i : IN current; e : IN voltage;
        r : OUT resistance);
END calc_resistance;

ARCHITECTURE behave OF calc_resistance IS
BEGIN
  ohm_proc: PROCESS( i, e )
    VARIABLE convi, conve, int_r : integer;
```

```
BEGIN
  convi := current'POS(i);  -- current in ua
  conve := voltage'POS(e);  -- voltage in uv
  -- resistance in ohms
  int_r := conve \ convi;

  r <= resistance'VAL(int_r);

  -- another way to write this example
  -- is shown below
  -- r <=resistance'VAL(current'POS(i)
  -- \ voltage'POS(e));

 END PROCESS;
END behave;
```

Package *ohms_law* declares three physical types used in this example. Types *current, voltage,* and *resistance* will be used to show how physical types can be converted to type INTEGER and back to a physical type.

Whenever ports *i* or *e* have an event occur on them, process *ohm_proc* is invoked and will calculate a new value of resistance (*r*) from the current (*i*) and the voltage (*e*). Variables *conve, convi,* and *int_r* were not necessary in this example but were added for ease of understanding. The commented-out assignment to output *r* shows an example where the internal variables are not needed.

The first statement of the process will assign the position number of the input value to variable *convi.* If the input value is 10 ua, then 10 will be assigned to variable *convi.*

The second statement will assign the position number of the value of input *e,* to variable *conve.* The base unit of type voltage is uv (microvolts); therefore, the position number of any voltage value will be determined based on how many uv the input value is equal to.

The last line in the process converts the resistance value calculated from the previous line to the appropriate ohms value in type *resistance.* The 'VAL attribute is used to convert a position number to a physical type value of type *resistance.*

This example illustrated how 'POS and 'VAL worked, but not 'SUCC, 'PRED, 'RIGHTOF, and 'LEFTOF. A very simple example using these attributes is shown here:

```
PACKAGE p_color IS
  TYPE color IS ( red, yellow, green, blue, purple, orange );
  SUBTYPE reverse_color is color RANGE orange downto red ;

END p_color;
```

Assuming the foregoing types, the following results are obtained:

color ' SUCC (blue)	returns purple
color ' PRED (green)	returns yellow
reverse_color ' SUCC (blue)	returns green
reverse_color ' PRED (green)	returns blue
color ' RIGHTOF (blue)	returns purple
color ' LEFTOF (green)	returns yellow
reverse_color ' RIGHTOF (blue)	returns green
reverse_color ' LEFTOF (green)	returns blue

For ascending ranges, the following is true:

```
'SUCC(x) = 'RIGHTOF(x);
'PRED(x) = 'LEFTOF(x);
```

For descending ranges, the opposite is true:

```
'SUCC(x) = 'LEFTOF(x);
'PRED(x) = 'RIGHTOF(x);
```

What happens if the value passed to 'SUCC, 'PRED, etc., is at the limit of the type? For instance, for type *color*, what is the value of the following expression?

```
y := red;
x := color'PRED(y);
```

The second expression will cause a runtime error to be reported, because a range constraint has been violated.

Function array attributes

Function array attributes return the bounds of array types. An operation that requires accessing every location of an array can use these attributes to find the bounds of the array.

The four kinds of function array attributes are:

array ' LEFT (*n*)	returns the left bound of index range *n*
array ' RIGHT (*n*)	returns the right bound of index range *n*
array ' HIGH (*n*)	returns the upper bound of index range *n*
array ' LOW (*n*)	returns the lower bound of index range *n*

These attributes are exactly like the value type attributes that were discussed earlier, except that these attributes work with arrays.

For ascending ranges, the following is true:

array'LEFT = array'LOW

array'RIGHT = array'HIGH

For descending ranges, the opposite is true:

array'LEFT = array'HIGH

array'RIGHT = array'LOW

An example where these attributes are very useful is as follows:

```
PACKAGE p_ram IS
  TYPE t_ram_data IS ARRAY(0 TO 511) OF INTEGER;

  CONSTANT x_val : INTEGER := -1;
  CONSTANT z_val : INTEGER := -2;
END p_ram;

USE WORK.p_ram.ALL;
USE WORK.std_logic_1164.ALL;
ENTITY ram IS
  PORT( data_in : IN INTEGER;
        addr : IN INTEGER;
        data : OUT INTEGER;
        cs : IN std_logic;
        r_wb: in std_logic);
END ram;

ARCHITECTURE behave_ram OF ram IS
BEGIN
  main_proc: PROCESS( cs, addr, r_wb )
    VARIABLE ram_data : t_ram_data;
    VARIABLE ram_init : boolean := false;
  BEGIN
    IF NOT(ram_init) THEN
      FOR i IN ram_data'LOW TO ram_data'HIGH LOOP
        ram_data(i) := 0;
      END LOOP;

      ram_init := TRUE;
    END IF;

    IF (cs = 'X') OR (r_wb = 'X')THEN
      data <= x_val;

    ELSIF ( cs = '0' ) THEN
      data <=z_val;

    ELSIF (r_wb = '1') THEN
      IF (addr = x_val) OR (addr = z_val) THEN
        data <=x_val;
```

```
      ELSE
        data <=ram_data(addr);
      END IF;
    ELSE
      IF (addr = x_val) OR (addr = z_val) THEN
        ASSERT FALSE
          REPORT " writing to unknown address"
          SEVERITY ERROR;
        data <= x_val;
      ELSE
        ram_data(addr) :=data_in;
        data <= ram_data(addr);
      END IF;

    END IF;
  END PROCESS;
END behave_ram;
```

This example implements an integer-based RAM device. There are 512 integer locations in the RAM, which is controlled by two control lines. The first is *cs* (chip select), and the second is *r_wb* (read/write bar). The model contains an IF statement that initializes the contents of the RAM to a known value. A boolean variable (*ram_init*) is declared to keep track of whether the RAM has been initialized or not. If this variable is false, the RAM has not yet been initialized. If true, initialization has been performed.

The first time the process is executed, variable *ram_init* will be false, and the IF statement will be executed. Inside the IF statement is a loop statement that will loop through every location of the RAM and set the location to a known value. This process is necessary because the starting value of type INTEGER is the value integer'LEFT, or –2,147,483,647. Notice the use of function array attributes 'LOW and 'HIGH to control the range of the initialization loop.

Once the loop has been executed and all RAM locations have been initialized, the *ram_init* variable is set to true. Setting the variable *ram_init* to true will prevent the initialization loop from executing again.

The rest of the model implements the read and write functions based on the values of *addr, data_in, r_wb,* and *cs.* This model performs a lot of error checking for unknown values on input ports. The model will try to intelligently handle these unknown input values.

Function signal attributes

Function signal attributes are used to return information about the behavior of signals. These attributes can be used to report whether a signal has just changed value, how much time has passed since the last event transition, or what the previous value of the signal was. There are five attributes that fall into this category, and a brief description is shown below:

S'EVENT	returns true if an event occurred during the current delta, and otherwise returns false
S'ACTIVE	returns true if a transaction occurred during the current delta, and otherwise returns false
S'LAST_EVENT	returns time elapsed since the previous event transition of signal
S'LAST_VALUE	returns previous value of S before the last event
S'LAST_ACTIVE	returns time elapsed since the previous transaction of signal

Attributes 'EVENT and 'LAST_VALUE. Attribute 'EVENT is very useful for determining clock edges. By checking if a signal is at a particular value and if the signal has just changed, it can be deduced that an edge has occurred on the signal. An example of a rising edge detector is as follows:

```
USE WORK.std_logic_1164.ALL;
ENTITY dff IS
  PORT( d, clk : IN std_logic;
        q : OUT std_logic);
END dff;

ARCHITECTURE dff OF dff IS
BEGIN
  PROCESS(clk)
  BEGIN
    IF ( clk = '1') AND ( clk'EVENT ) THEN
      q <= d;
    END IF;
  END PROCESS;
END dff;
```

This example shows a very simple *dff* model. The *clk* input is used to transfer the *d* input to the *q* output, on a rising edge of the *clk*. To detect the rising edge of the *clk* input, this model makes use of the 'EVENT attribute. If the value of the *clk* input is a '1', and the value has just changed, then a rising edge must have occurred. (When a synthesis tool is applied to the preceding example, a flip-flop will result.)

What the preceding example ignores is the fact that an 'X' value to a '1' value will also look like a rising edge when it is not. The next example will show how to correct this problem using the 'LAST_VALUE attribute. The IF statement from the preceding example is rewritten as shown here:

```
IF ( clk = '1' ) AND ( clk'EVENT )
     and ( clk'LAST_VALUE = '0') THEN
  q <= d;
END IF;
```

In this example, one more check is made to make certain that the last value of the *clk* input was a '0' before the new event occurred.

In both examples, the 'EVENT attribute was not really needed, because the process statement had only *clk* as its sensitivity list. The only way that the process statement could be executed would be because of an event on signal *clk*. This is a true statement, but it is a good modeling practice to check for the event anyway. Sometime in the future, the model may be modified to include an asynchronous preset or clear, and these signals will be added to the sensitivity list for the process statement. Now when an event occurs on any of the inputs, the process will be invoked. Using the 'EVENT attribute, the process can determine which input caused the process to be invoked.

Attribute 'LAST_EVENT. Attribute 'LAST_EVENT returns the time since the previous event occurred on the signal. This attribute is very useful for implementing timing checks, such as setup checks, hold checks, and pulse-width checks. An example of a setup time and a hold time are shown in Fig. 6.1.

The rising edge of signal *clk* is the reference edge to which all checks are performed. A setup-time check will guarantee that the data input does not change during the setup time, and the hold-time check will

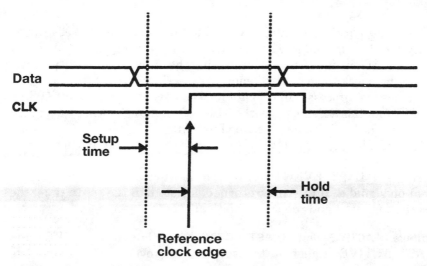

Figure 6.1 Setup and hold time waveform description.

guarantee that the data input does not change during the time equal to the hold time after the reference edge. This will ensure correct operation of the device.

An example of the setup-time check using the 'LAST_EVENT attribute is as follows:

```
USE WORK.std_logic_1164.ALL;
ENTITY dff IS
  GENERIC ( setup_time, hold_time : TIME );
  PORT( d, clk : IN std_logic;
        q : OUT std_logic);
BEGIN
  setup_check : PROCESS ( clk )
  BEGIN
    IF ( clk = '1' ) and ( clk'EVENT ) THEN
      ASSERT ( d'LAST_EVENT >= setup_time )
      REPORT "setup violation"
      SEVERITY ERROR;
    END IF;
  END PROCESS setup_check;
END dff;

ARCHITECTURE dff_behave OF dff IS
BEGIN
  dff_process : PROCESS ( clk )
  BEGIN
    IF ( clk = '1' ) AND ( clk'EVENT ) THEN
      q <= d;
    END IF;
  END PROCESS dff_process;
END dff_behave;
```

The *setup_check* procedure is contained in a passive process in the entity for the *dff* model. The check could have been included in the architecture for the *dff* model, but having the check in the entity allows the timing check to be shared among any architecture of the entity.

The passive process will execute for each event on signal *clk*. When the *clk* input has a rising edge, the ASSERT statement will be executed and perform the check for a setup violation.

The ASSERT statement will check to see that input *d* has not had an event during the setup time passed in by the generic *setup_time*. Attribute *d*'LAST_EVENT will return the time since the most recent event on signal *d*. If the time returned is less than the setup time, the assertion will fail and report a violation.

Attribute 'ACTIVE and 'LAST_ACTIVE. Attributes 'ACTIVE and 'LAST_ACTIVE trigger on transactions and events of the signal to which they are attached. A transaction on a signal occurs when a model in or inout port has an event occur which triggers the execution of the model. The model is executed, but the result of the execution produces the same output values. For instance, if an AND gate has a ' 1 ' value on one input and a ' 0 ' on the other, the output value will be ' 0 '. If the input with a ' 1 ' value now changes to a ' 0 ' value, the output will remain ' 0 ', no event will be generated, but a transaction will have been generated on the output of the AND gate.

Attribute ' ACTIVE will return true when a transaction or event occurs on a signal, and attribute ' LAST_ACTIVE will return the time since a previous transaction or event occurred on the signal it is attached to. Both of these attributes are counterparts for attributes ' EVENT and ' LAST_EVENT, which provide the same behavior for events.

Signal Kind Attributes

Signal kind attributes are used to create special signals, based on other signals. These special signals return information to the designer about the signal that the attribute is attached to. The information returned is very similar to some of the functionality provided by some of the function attributes. The difference is that these special signals can be used anywhere that a normal signal can be used, including sensitivity lists.

Signal attributes return information such as whether a signal has been stable for a specified amount of time, and when a transaction has occurred on a signal. Signal attributes can also create a delayed version of the signal.

One restriction on the use of these attributes is that they cannot be used within a subprogram. A compiler error message will result if a signal kind attribute is used within a subprogram.

There are four attributes in the signal kind category. They are as follows:

s ' DELAYED [(time)]	creates a signal of the same type as the reference signal that follows the reference signal, delayed by the time of the optional time expression
s ' STABLE [(time)]	creates a boolean signal that is true whenever the reference signal has had no events for the time specified by the optional time expression
s ' QUIET [(time)]	creates a boolean signal that is true whenever the reference signal has had no transactions or events for the time specified by the optional time expression
s ' TRANSACTION	creates a signal of type BIT that toggles its value for every transaction or event that occurs on *s*

Attribute ' DELAYED.   Attribute ' DELAYED creates a delayed version of the signal that it is attached to. The same functionality can be obtained using a transport-delayed signal assignment. The difference between a transport delay assignment and the ' DELAYED attribute is that the designer has to do more bookkeeping with the transport signal assignment method. With a transport signal assignment, a new signal must be declared.

Let's look at one use for the ' DELAYED attribute. One method for modeling ASIC devices is to place path-related delays on the input pins of the ASIC library part. An example of this method is shown in Fig. 6.2.

Typically, before the layout process, educated guesses are made for the delays of each input. After layout, the real delay values are back-annotated to the model, and the simulation is run again with the real delays. One method to provide for back annotation of the delay values is to use generic values specified in the configuration for the device (configurations are discussed in Chap. 7). A typical model for one of the *and2* gates shown in Fig. 6.2 might look like this:

```
USE WORK.std_logic_1164.ALL;
ENTITY and2 IS
  GENERIC ( a_ipd, b_ipd, c_opd : TIME );
  PORT ( a, b : IN std_logic;
         c: OUT std_logic);
END and2;

ARCHITECTURE int_signals OF and2 IS
  SIGNAL inta, intb : std_logic;
```

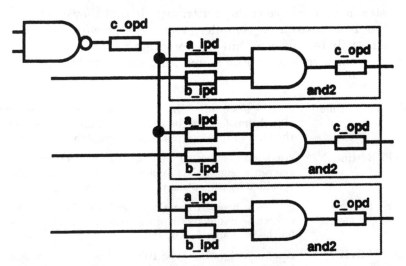

Figure 6.2   Gate array logic with input and output delays.

```
BEGIN
  inta <= TRANSPORT a AFTER a_ipd;
  intb <=TRANSPORT b AFTER b_ipd;

  c <= inta AND intb AFTER c_opd;
END int_signals;

ARCHITECTURE attr OF and2 IS
BEGIN
  c <= a'DELAYED(a_ipd) AND b'DELAYED(b_ipd) AFTER c_opd;
END attr;
```

In the preceding example, two architectures for entity *and2* show two different methods of delaying the input signals by the path delay. The first method uses transport-delayed internal signals to delay the input signals. These delayed signals are then ANDed together and assigned to output port *c*.

The second method makes use of the predefined signal attribute 'DELAYED. Input signals *a* and *b* are delayed by the path delay generic value *a_ipd* (*a* input path delay) and *b_ipd* (*b* input path delay). The values of the delayed signals are ANDed together and assigned to output port *c*.

If the optional time expression for attribute 'DELAYED is not specified, 0 ns is assumed. A signal delayed by 0 ns is delayed by one delta (delta delay is discussed in Chap. 2).

Another application for the 'DELAYED attribute is to perform a hold check. Earlier in this chapter we discussed what setup and hold times were, and how to implement the setup check using 'LAST_EVENT. To implement the hold check requires the use of a delayed version of the *clk* signal. The previous example has been modified to include the hold check function as follows:

```
USE WORK.std_logic_1164.ALL;
ENTITY dff IS
  GENERIC ( setup_time, hold_time : TIME );
  PORT( d, clk : IN std_logic;
        q : OUT std_logic);
BEGIN
  setup_check : PROCESS ( clk )
  BEGIN
    IF ( clk = '1' ) and ( clk'EVENT ) THEN
      ASSERT ( d'LAST_EVENT >= setup_time )
        REPORT "setup violation"
        SEVERITY ERROR;
    END IF;
  END PROCESS setup_check;
```

```
   hold_check : PROCESS (clk'DELAYED(hold_time))
   BEGIN
     IF ( clk'DELAYED(hold_time) = '1' ) and
            ( clk'DELAYED(hold_time)'EVENT ) THEN

       ASSERT ( d'LAST_EVENT = 0 ns ) OR ( d'LAST_EVENT >
hold_time )
         REPORT "hold violation"
         SEVERITY ERROR;

     END IF;
   END PROCESS hold_check;
END dff;

ARCHITECTURE dff_behave OF dff IS
BEGIN
  dff_process : PROCESS ( clk )
  BEGIN
    IF ( clk = '1' ) AND ( clk'EVENT ) THEN
      q <= d;
    END IF;

  END PROCESS dff_process;
END dff_behave;
```

A delayed version of the *clk* input is used to trigger the hold check. The *clk* input is delayed by the amount of the hold check. If the data input changes within the hold time, d'LAST_EVENT will return a value that is less than the hold time. When d changes exactly at the same time as the delayed *clk* input, d'LAST_EVENT will return 0 ns. This is a special case, and is legal, so it must be handled specially.

An alternative method for checking the hold time of a device is to trigger the hold check process when the d input changes, and then look back at the last change on the *clk* input. However, this is more complicated and requires the designer to manually keep track of the last reference edge on the *clk* input.

Another interesting feature of attributes that this model pointed out is the cascading of attributes. In the preceding example, the delayed version of the *clk* signal was checked for an event. This necessitated the use of *clk*'DELAYED (hold_time) 'EVENT. The return value from this attribute will be true whenever the signal created by the 'DELAYED attribute has an event during the current delta time point. In general, attributes can be cascaded any level if the values returned from the previous attribute are appropriate for the next attribute.

Attribute 'STABLE.   Attribute 'STABLE is used to determine the relative activity level of a signal. It can be used to determine if the signal just changed or has not changed in a specified period of time. The resulting value output is itself a signal that can be used to trigger other processes.

The following is an example of how attribute 'STABLE works:

```
USE WORK.std_logic_1164.ALL;
ENTITY pulse_gen IS
  PORT( a : IN std_logic;
        b : OUT BOOLEAN);
END pulse_gen;

ARCHITECTURE pulse_gen OF pulse_gen IS
BEGIN
  b <= a'STABLE( 10 ns );
END pulse_gen;
```

Shown in Fig. 6.3 is the resulting waveform b when waveform a is presented to the model.

At the first two changes in signal a (10 and 30 ns), signal b will immediately change to false (actually at the next delta). Then, when signal a has been stable for 10 ns, signal b will change to true. At time 55 ns, signal a changes value again, so signal b will change to false. Because signal a changes 5 ns later (60 ns), signal a will not have been stable long enough to allow output b to go to a true value. Only 10 ns after the last change on signal a (60 ns) will the input signal a have been stable long enough to allow signal b to change to true.

If the time value specified for the 'STABLE attribute is 0 ns, or not specified, then the 'STABLE attribute will be false for 1 delta whenever the signal that the attribute is attached to changes. An example of this scenario is shown in Fig. 6.4.

When used in this method, the resulting signal value has the same timing but opposite value as function attribute 'EVENT. A statement to detect the rising edge of a clock could be written in two ways, as shown here:

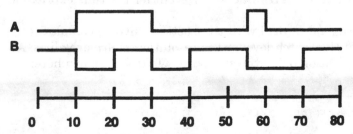

Figure 6.3 Example showing 'DELAYED (10 ns).

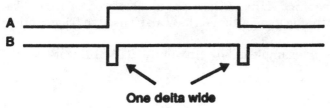

One delta wide

Figure 6.4   Example showing 'DELAYED (0 ns).

```
IF (( clk'EVENT ) AND ( clk = '1' ) AND
            ( clk'LAST_VALUE = '0' )) THEN
.
. -- DO PROCESSING
.
END IF;
IF (( NOT( clk'STABLE) ) AND ( clk = '1' ) AND
            clk'LAST_VALUE = '0' )) THEN
.
. --- DO PROCESSING
.
END IF;
```

In both cases, the IF statement will detect the rising edge, but the IF statement using 'EVENT will be more efficient in memory space and speed. The reason for this is that attribute 'STABLE creates an extra signal in the design which will use more memory to store and, whenever the value for the new signal needs to be updated, it must be scheduled. Keeping track of signal events costs memory and time.

Attribute 'QUIET.   Attribute 'QUIET has the same functionality as 'STABLE, except that 'QUIET is triggered by transactions on the signal to which it is attached, in addition to events. Attribute 'QUIET will create a BOOLEAN signal that is true whenever the signal it is attached to has not had a transaction or event for the time expression specified.

Typically, models that deal with transactions involve complex models of devices at the switch level or the resolution of driver values. An interesting application using the attribute 'QUIET is shown here:

```
ARCHITECTURE test OF test IS
  TYPE t_int is (int1, int2, int3, int4, int5 );
  SIGNAL int, intsig1, intsig2, intsig3 : t_int;
  SIGNAL lock_out : BOOLEAN;
```

```
BEGIN
  int1_proc: PROCESS
  BEGIN
    .
    .
    .
    WAIT ON trigger1; -- outside trigger signal
    WAIT UNTIL clk = '1';
     IF NOT(lock_out) THEN
      intsig1 <= int1;
     END IF;
END PROCESS int1_proc;

  int2_proc: PROCESS
  BEGIN
    .
    .
    .
    WAIT ON trigger2;-- outside trigger signal
    WAIT UNTIL clk = '1';
     IF NOT(lock_out) THEN
      intsig2 <=int2;
     END IF;
  END PROCESS int2_proc;

  int3 proc: PROCESS
  BEGIN
  .
  .
  .
 WAIT ON trigger3;-- outside trigger signal
    WAIT UNTIL clk = '1';
     IF NOT(lock_out) THEN
      intsig3 <=int3;
     END IF;
  END PROCESS int3_proc;

int <=intsig1 WHEN NOT(intsig1'QUIET) ELSE
     intsig2 WHEN NOT(intsig2'QUIET) ELSE
     intsig3 WHEN NOT(intsig3'QUIET) ELSE
     int;

int_handle : PROCESS
BEGIN
  WAIT ON int'TRANSACTION;-- described next
  lock_out <= TRUE;
  WAIT FOR 10 ns;
  CASE int IS
    WHEN int1 =>
      .
      .
```

```
    WHEN int2 =>
      .
      .
    WHEN int3 =>
      .
      .
    WHEN int4 =>
      .
      .
    WHEN int5 =>
      .
      .
    END CASE;
    lock_out <= false;
  END PROCESS;
END test;
```

This example shows how a priority mechanism could be modeled for an interrupt handler. Process *int1_proc* has the highest priority, and process *int3_proc* has the lowest. Whenever one of the processes is triggered, the appropriate interrupt handler is placed on signal *int*, and the interrupt handler for that interrupt is called.

The model consists of three processes that drive the interrupt signal *int*, and another process to call the appropriate interrupt handling function. Signal *int* is not a resolved signal and therefore cannot have multiple drivers. If a resolution function is written for signal *int*, the order of the drivers cannot be used to determine priority. Therefore, the preceding approach was taken.

In this approach, three internal signals *intsig1, intsig2,* and *intsig3* are driven by each of the processes, respectively. These signals are then combined, using a conditional signal assignment statement. The conditional signal assignment statement makes use of the predefined attribute 'QUIET to determine when a transaction has been assigned to a driver of a signal. It is required that transactions are detected on the internal signals, because the process will always assign the same value, so an event will occur only on the first assignment.

The priority mechanism is controlled by the conditional signal assignment statement. When a transaction occurs on *intsig1, intsig2,* or *intsig3,* the assignment statement will evaluate and assign the appropriate value to signal *int* based on the signal(s) that had a transaction. If a transaction occurred only on *intsig2, intsig2* 'QUIET would be false, causing the conditional signal assignment statement to place the value of *intsig2* on signal *int*. But what happens if *intsig3* and *intsig2* occur at the same time? The conditional signal assignment statement will evaluate, and the first clause that has a WHEN expression return true will do the assignment and then exit the rest of the statement. For this example, the value for *intsig2* will be returned, because it is first in the conditional signal assignment statement. The priority of the inputs is determined by the order of the WHEN clauses in the conditional signal assignment statement.

Attribute 'TRANSACTION. The process that implemented the interrupt handling for the previous example uses the 'TRANSACTION attribute in a WAIT statement. This attribute is another of the attributes that creates a signal where it is used. Attribute 'TRANSACTION creates a signal of type BIT that toggles from '1' or '0' for every transaction of the signal that it is attached to. This attribute is useful for invoking processes when transactions occur on signals.

In the preceding example, the interrupt handler process needs to be executed whenever a transaction occurs on signal *int*. This is true because the same interrupt could happen twice or more in sequence. If this occurred, a transaction, not an event, would be generated on signal *int*. Without the attribute 'TRANSACTION, WAIT statements are sensitive to events. By using the attribute 'TRANSACTION, the value of *int*'TRANSACTION will toggle for every transaction causing an event to occur, thus activating the WAIT statement.

Type Kind Attributes

Type attributes return values of kind type. There is only one type attribute, and it must be used with another value or function type attribute. The only type attribute available in VHDL is the attribute

```
t'BASE.
```

This attribute will return the base type of a type or subtype. This attribute can be used only as the prefix of another attribute, as shown by the following example:

```
do_nothing : PROCESS(x)
  TYPE color IS (red, blue, green, yellow, brown, black);
  SUBTYPE color_gun IS color RANGE red TO green;

  VARIABLE a : color;
BEGIN
  a := color_gun'BASE'RIGHT;    -- a = black
  a := color'BASE'LEFT;         -- a = red

  -- a = yellow
  a := color_gun'BASE'SUCC(green);

END PROCESS do_nothing;
```

In the first assignment to variable *a*, *color_gun*'BASE will return type *color*, the base type of *color_gun*. The statement *color*'RIGHT will then return the value *black*. In the second assignment statement, the base type of type *color* is type *color*. The statement *color*'LEFT will return the value *red*. In the last assignment, *color_gun*'BASE returns type *color*, and *color*'SUCC(green) returns *yellow*.

Range Kind Attributes

The last two predefined attributes in VHDL return a value kind of range. These attributes work only with constrained array types, and return the index range specified by the optional input parameter. The attribute notations are as follows:

a'RANGE[(n)]

a'REVERSE_RANGE[(n)]

Attributes 'RANGE will return the nth range denoted by the value of parameter n. Attribute 'RANGE will return the range in the order specified, and 'REVERSE_RANGE will return the range in reverse order.

Attributes 'RANGE and 'REVERSE_RANGE can be used to control the number of times that a loop statement will loop. The following is an example:

```
FUNCTION vector_to_int(vect: std_logic_vector) RETURN INTEGER
IS
  VARIABLE result : INTEGER := 0;
BEGIN
  FOR i IN vect'RANGE LOOP

    result := result * 2;

    IF vect(i) = '1' THEN
      result := result + 1;
    END IF;

  END LOOP;

  RETURN result;
END vector_to_int;
```

This function converts an array of bits into an integer value. The number of times that the loop needs to be executed is determined by the number of bits in the input argument *vect*. When the function call is made, the input argument cannot be an unconstrained value; therefore, the attribute 'RANGE can be used to determine the range of the input vector. The range can then be used in the loop statement to determine the number of times to execute the loop and finish the conversion.

The 'REVERSE_RANGE attribute works similarly to the 'RANGE attribute, except that the range will be returned in the reverse order. For the following type, the 'RANGE attribute will return 0 TO 15, and the 'REVERSE_RANGE attribute will return 15 DOWNTO 0.

```
TYPE array 16 IS ARRAY(0 TO 15) OF BIT;
```

In this chapter, we discussed how VHDL attributes extend the language to provide some very useful functionality. They make models much easier to read and maintain. To recap:

- Some kinds of attributes simply return values, while others create new signals.
- 'LEFT, 'RIGHT, 'LENGTH, 'HIGH, and 'LOW can be used to get the bounds of a type or array.
- 'POS, 'VAL, 'SUCC, 'PRED, 'LEFTOF, and 'RIGHTOF can be used to manipulate enumerated types.
- 'ACTIVE, 'EVENT, 'LAST_ACTIVE, 'LAST_EVENT, and 'LAST_VALUE can be used to return information about when events occur.
- 'DELAYED, 'STABLE, 'QUIET, and 'TRANSACTION create new signals that return information about other signals.
- range attributes 'RANGE and 'REVERSE_RANGE can be used to control statements over the exact range of a type.

In the next chapter, we will examine configurations—the method of binding architectures to entities.

Configurations

Configurations are a primary design unit used to bind component instances to entities. For structural models, configurations can be thought of as the parts list for the model. For component instances, the configuration will specify from many architectures for an entity which architecture to use for a specific instance. When the configuration for an entity-architecture combination is compiled into the library, a simulatable object is created.

Configurations can also be used to specify generic values for components instantiated in the architecture configured by the configuration. This mechanism, for example, provides a late-binding capability for delay values. Delay values calculated from a physical layout tool, such as a printed circuit board design system or a gate array layout system, can be inserted in a configuration to provide a simulation model with actual delays in the design.

If the designer wants to use a component in an architecture that has different port names from the architecture component declaration, the new component can have its ports mapped to the appropriate signals. With this functionality, libraries of components can be mixed and matched easily.

The configuration can also be used to provide a very fast substitution capability. Multiple architectures can exist for a single entity. One architecture might be a behavioral model for the entity, while another architecture might be a structural model for the entity. The architecture used in the containing model can be selected by specifying which architecture to use in the configuration, and recompiling only the configuration. After compilation, the simulatable model will use the specified architecture.

Default Configurations

The simplest form of explicit configuration is the default configuration (the simplest configuration is none at all, in which the last architecture compiled is used for an entity). This configuration can be used for models that do not contain any blocks or components to configure. The default configuration will specify the configuration name, the entity being configured, and the architecture to be used for the entity. An example of two default configurations is shown by configurations *big_count* and *small_count,* as follows:

```
USE WORK.std_logic_1164.ALL;
ENTITY counter IS
  PORT(load, clear, clk : IN std_logic;
       data_in : IN INTEGER;
       data_out : OUT INTEGER);
END counter;

ARCHITECTURE count_255 OF counter IS
BEGIN
  PROCESS(clk)
    VARIABLE count : INTEGER :=0;
  BEGIN
    IF clear = '1' THEN
     count := 0;
    ELSIF load = '1' THEN
     count := data_in;
    ELSE
      IF (clk'EVENT) AND (clk = '1') AND
         (clk'LAST_VALUE = '0') THEN
        IF (count = 255) THEN
          count := 0;
        ELSE
          count := count + 1;
        END IF;
      END IF;
    END IF;
    data_out <= count;
  END PROCESS;
END count_255;

ARCHITECTURE count_64k OF counter IS
BEGIN
  PROCESS(clk)
    VARIABLE count : INTEGER := 0;
  BEGIN
    IF clear = '1' THEN
      count := 0;
```

```
    ELSIF load = '1' THEN
     count := data_in;
    ELSE
      IF (clk'EVENT) AND (clk = '1') AND
         (clk'LAST_VALUE = '0') THEN
        IF (count = 65535) THEN
          count := 0;
        ELSE
          count :- count + 1;
        END IF;
      END IF;
    END IF;
    data_out <= count;
  END PROCESS;
END count_64k;

CONFIGURATION small_count OF counter IS
  FOR count_255
  END FOR;
END small_count;

CONFIGURATION big_count OF counter IS
  FOR count_64k
  END FOR;
END big_count;
```

This example shows how two different architectures for a counter
entity can be configured using two default configurations. The entity
for the counter does not specify any bit width for the data to be loaded
into the counter or data from the counter. The data type for the input
and output data is INTEGER. With a data type of integer, multiple
types of counters can be supported up to the integer representation
limit of the host computer for the VHDL simulator.

The two architectures of entity counter specify two different-sized
counters that can be used for the entity. The first architecture,
count_255, specifies an 8-bit counter. The second architecture,
count_64k, specifies a 16-bit counter. The architectures specify a synchronous counter with a synchronous load and clear. All operations for
the device occur with respect to the clock.

Each of the two configurations for the entity specifies a different
architecture for the *counter* entity. Let's examine the first configuration in more detail. The configuration design unit begins with the keyword CONFIGURATION and is followed by the name of the
configuration. In this example, the name of the configuration is
small_count. The keyword OF precedes the name of the entity begin
configured (*counter*). The next line of the configuration starts the block
configuration section. The keyword FOR is followed by a name of the

architecture to use for the entity being configured or the name of the block of the architecture that will be configured. Any component or block configuration information will then exist between the FOR ARCHITECTURE clause and the matching END FOR.

In this architecture, there are no blocks or components to configure; therefore, the block configuration area from the FOR clause to the END FOR clause will be empty, and the default will be used. The configuration is called the default configuration because the default will be used for all objects in the configuration.

The first configuration is called *small_count* and binds architecture *count_255* with entity *counter* to form a simulatable object. The second configuration binds architecture *count_64k* with entity *counter* and forms a simulatable object called *big_count*.

Component Configurations

In this section we will discuss how architectures that contain instantiated components can be configured. Architectures that contain other components are called *structural architectures*. These components are configured through component configuration statements.

Let's first look at some very simple examples of component configurations, and then at some progressively more complex examples. The first example is a simple 2-to-4 decoder device. Figure 7.1 shows the symbol for the decoder, and Fig. 7.2 shows the schematic.

The components used in the design are defined using the following VHDL description:

```
USE WORK.std_logic_1164.ALL;
ENTITY inv IS
  PORT( a : IN std_logic;
        b : OUT std_logic);
END inv;
```

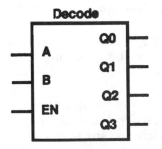

Figure 7.1 Symbol for decoder example.

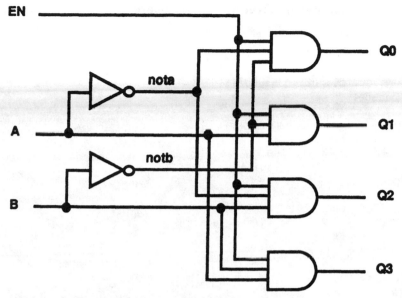

Figure 7.2   Gate-level schematic for decoder.

```
ARCHITECTURE behave OF inv IS
BEGIN
  b <= NOT(a) AFTER 5 ns;
END behave;

CONFIGURATION invcon OF inv IS
  FOR behave
  END FOR;
END invcon;

USE WORK.std_logic_1164.ALL;
ENTITY and3 IS
  PORT( a1, a2, a3 : IN std_logic;
        o1 : OUT std_logic);
END and3;

ARCHITECTURE behave OF and3 IS
BEGIN
  o1 <= a1 AND a2 AND a3 AFTER 5 ns;
END behave;

CONFIGURATION and3con OF and3 IS
  FOR behave
  END FOR;
END and3con;
```

Next, the entity and architecture for *decode* are shown:

```
USE WORK.std_logic_1164.ALL;
ENTITY decode IS
  PORT( a, b, en : IN std_logic;
        q0, q1, q2, q3 : OUT std_logic);
END decode;

ARCHITECTURE structural OF decode IS
  COMPONENT inv
    PORT( a : IN std_logic;
          b : OUT std_logic);
  END COMPONENT;

  COMPONENT and3
    PORT( a1, a2, a3 : IN std_logic;
          o1 : OUT std_logic);
  END COMPONENT;

  SIGNAL nota, notb : std_logic;
BEGIN
  I1 : inv
    PORT MAP(a, nota);

  I2 : inv
    PORT MAP(b, notb);

  A1 : and3
    PORT MAP(nota, en, notb, Q0);

  A2 : and3
    PORT MAP(a, en, notb, Q1);

  A3 : and3
    PORT MAP(nota, en, b, Q2);

  A4 : and3
    PORT MAP(a, en, b, Q3);

END structural;
```

When all of the entities and architectures have been compiled into the working library, the circuit can be simulated. The simulator will use the last compiled architecture to build the executable design for the simulator because it is the default. Using the last compiled architecture for an entity to build the simulator will work fine in a typical system, until more than one architecture exists for an entity. Then it can become confusing as to which architecture was compiled last. A better method is to specify exactly which architecture to use for each entity. The component configuration binds architectures to entities.

Two different styles can be used for writing a component configuration for an entity. The lower-level configuration style specifies lower-level configurations for each component, and the entity-architecture style specifies entity-architecture pairs for each component. The word *style* is used to describe these two different configurations because there is no hard-and-fast rule about how to use them. Lower-level configurations can be mixed with entity-architecture pairs, creating a mixed-style configuration.

Lower-level configurations

Let's examine the configuration for the lower-level configuration style first. An example of such a configuration for the decode entity is as follows:

```
CONFIGURATION decode_llcon OF decode IS
  FOR structural
    FOR I1 : inv USE CONFIGURATION WORK.invcon;
    END FOR;

    FOR I2 : inv USE CONFIGURATION WORK.invcon;
    END FOR;

    FOR ALL : and3 USE CONFIGURATION WORK.and3con;
    END FOR;

  END FOR;
END decode_llcon;
```

This configuration specifies which configuration to use for each component in architecture *structural* of entity *decode*. The specified lower-level configuration must already exist in the library for the current configuration to compile. Each component being configured has a FOR clause to begin the configuration, and an END FOR clause to end the configuration specification for the component. Each component can be specified with the component instantiation label directly, as shown for component I1, or with an ALL or OTHERS clause as shown by the *and3* components.

Once the component is uniquely specified by label or otherwise, the USE CONFIGURATION clause specifies which configuration to use for this instance of the component. In the preceding example, the configuration specification for component I1 will use the configuration called *invcon,* from the working library. In order for configuration *decode_llcon* to compile, configuration *invcon* must have been already compiled into library WORK.

Notice that the names of the entities, architectures, and configurations reflect a naming convention. In general, this is a good practice. It will help distinguish the different types of design units from one another when they all exist in a library.

The advantage of this style of configurations is that most configurations are easy to write and understand. The disadvantage is not being able to change the configuration of a lower-level component without implementing a two-step or more process of recompilation when hierarchy levels increase.

Entity-architecture pair configuration

The other style of component configurations is the entity-architecture pair style. An example of a configuration that uses the same entity and architectures as the previous example is as follows:

```
CONFIGURATION decode_eacon OF decode IS
  FOR structural
    FOR I1 : inv USE ENTITY WORK.inv(behave);
    END FOR;

    FOR OTHERS : inv USE ENTITY WORK.inv(behave);
    END FOR;

    FOR A1 : and3 USE ENTITY WORK.and3(behave);
    END FOR;

    FOR OTHERS : and3 USE ENTITY WORK.and3(behave);
    END FOR;

  END FOR;
END decode_eacon;
```

This configuration looks very similar to the lower-level configuration style except for the USE clause in the component specification. In the previous example, a configuration was specified, but in this style, an entity-architecture pair is specified. The architecture is actually optional. If no architecture is specified, the last compiled architecture for the entity is used.

Let's take another look at the FOR clause for the first inverter, I1. In the preceding example, the component is still specified by the label or by an ALL or OTHERS clause. In this example, a USE ENTITY clause follows. This clause specifies the name of the entity to use for this component. The entity can have a completely different name than the component being specified. The component name comes from the component declaration in the architecture, while the entity name comes from the actual entity that has been compiled in the library specified. Following the entity is an optional architecture name that specifies which architecture to use for the entity.

Notice that the OTHERS clause is used for the second inverter in this example. The first inverter is configured from its label, I1, and all components that have not yet been configured will be configured by the OTHERS clause. This capability allows component I1 to use an architecture that is different from the other components to describe its behavior. This concept allows mixed-level modeling to exist. One component can be modeled at the switch or gate level, and the other can be modeled at the behavior level.

To change the architecture used for a component with the first configuration *decode_llcon* requires modifying the lower-level configuration and recompiling, then recompiling any higher-level configurations that depend on it. With the second configuration *decode_eacon,* to change the architecture for a component involves modifying configuration *decode_eacon* and recompiling. No other configurations need be recompiled.

Port maps

In the last two examples of component configurations, default mapping of entity ports and component ports was used. When the port names for an entity being configured to a component match the component port names, no other mapping need take place. The default mapping will cause the ports to match. What happens when the component ports do not match the entity being mapped to the component instance? Without any further information, the compiler cannot figure out which ports to map to which and will produce an error. However, more information can be passed to the compiler with the configuration port map clause.

The configuration port map clause looks exactly like the component instantiation port map clause used in an architecture. The configuration port map clause specifies which of the component ports map to the actual ports of the entity. If the port names are different, then the port map clause will specify the mapping.

Let's change the port names of the *inv* component used in the previous example and see what the effect will be in the configuration.

```
USE WORK.std_logic_1164.ALL;
ENTITY inv IS
   PORT( x : IN std_logic;
         y : OUT std_logic);
END inv;

ARCHITECTURE behave OF inv IS
BEGIN
   y <= NOT(x) AFTER 5 ns;
END behave;
```

```
CONFIGURATION invcon OF inv IS
  FOR behave
  END FOR;
END invcon;
```

The entity and architecture for *decode* will stay exactly the same, including the component declaration. The configuration, however, will need to add the port map clause, as shown in the following example:

```
CONFIGURATION decode_map_con OF decode IS
  FOR structural
    FOR I1 : inv USE ENTITY WORK.inv(behave)
      PORT MAP( a => x, b => y );
    END FOR;

    FOR I2 : inv USE ENTITY WORK.inv(behave)
      PORT MAP( a => x, b => y );
    END FOR;

    FOR ALL : and3 USE ENTITY WORK.and3(behave);
    END FOR;

  END FOR;
END decode_map_con;
```

The port map clause will map the port names of the component declarations, called the *formal ports,* to the port names of the entities from the library. The ports of the entities from the library being mapped are called *actuals.* The ports are mapped using named association. The rules for mapping ports using named association in the configuration port map clause are the same rules as those used in the component instantiation port map clause.

In the preceding example, component declaration *inv*, port *a*, is mapped to entity *inv*, port *x*, of the actual entity. Component declaration *inv*, port *b*, is mapped to entity *inv*, port *y*, of the actual entity. Using the configuration port map clause can allow entities with completely different port names to be mapped into existing architectures.

Mapping Library Entities

Not only can the ports be mapped with the configuration statement, but entities from libraries can be mapped to components as well. This capability allows the names of components to differ from the actual entities being mapped to them. The designer can easily switch the entity used for each component in the architecture from one entity to another. This feature allows the designer to map component instances to different entities.

Let's look again at the decoder example from the beginning of this chapter. The inverter, *inv*, for the decoder could be modeled using NMOS transistors as shown in Fig. 7.3.

Component X1 is an NMOS depletion transistor, which for all intents and purposes in digital simulation acts like a resistor. Component X2 is a unidirectional pass transistor that transfers ground from the triangular-shaped component X3 to signal 01. Components X3 and X4 are ground and VCC, respectively. The model that represents this circuit is shown below:

```
USE WORK.std_logic_1164.ALL;
ENTITY ground IS
  PORT( x : OUT std_logic );
END ground;

ARCHITECTURE dirt OF ground IS
BEGIN
  X <= '0';
END dirt;
```

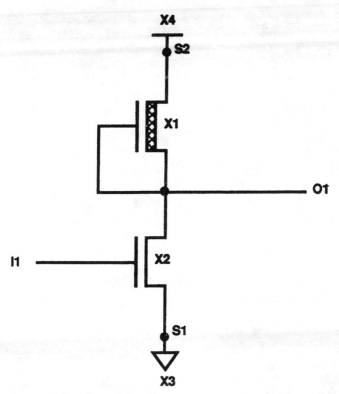

Figure 7.3   Transistor-level schematic for inverter.

```
CONFIGURATION groundcon OF ground IS
  FOR dirt
  END FOR;
END groundcon;

USE WORK.std_logic_1164.ALL;
ENTITY vcc IS
  PORT( x : OUT std_logic);
END vcc;

ARCHITECTURE plus5 OF vcc IS
BEGIN
  x <= '1';
END plus5;

CONFIGURATION vcccon OF vcc IS
  FOR plus5
  END FOR;
END vcccon;
```

The two transistor devices are shown below:

```
USE WORK.std_logic_1164.ALL;
ENTITY dep IS
  PORT( top : IN std_logic;
        bottom : OUT std_logic);
END dep;

ARCHITECTURE behave OF dep IS
BEGIN
  bottom <= R1 WHEN top = '1' ELSE
            R0 WHEN top = '0' ELSE
            RX WHEN top = 'X' ELSE
            top;
END behave;

CONFIGURATION depcon OF dep IS
  FOR behave
  END FOR;
END depcon;

USE WORK.std_logic_1164.ALL;
ENTITY uxfr IS
  PORT( left, sw : IN std_logic;
        right : out std_logic);
END uxfr;

ARCHITECTURE behave OF uxfr IS
BEGIN
  uxfr_proc: PROCESS(left, sw)
  BEGIN
```

```
      CASE sw is
        WHEN '1'|'H' =>
          right <= left;
        WHEN '0'|'L' =>
          right <= 'z';
        WHEN OTHERS =>
          right <= 'X';
      END CASE;
    END PROCESS uxfr_proc;
END behave;

CONFIGURATION uxfrcon OF uxfr IS
  FOR behave
  END FOR;
END uxfrcon;
```

These parts can be connected together, with the entity-architecture
that follows, to form a structural representation of the inverter.

```
USE WORK.std_logic_1164.ALL;
ENTITY struc_inv IS
  PORT( I1 : IN std_logic;
        O1 : OUT std_logic);
END struc_inv;

ARCHITECTURE structural OF struc_inv IS
  COMPONENT ground
    PORT( X : OUT std_logic);
  END COMPONENT;

  COMPONENT vcc
    PORT( X : OUT std_logic);
  END COMPONENT;

  COMPONENT dep
    PORT( top : IN std_logic;
          bottom : OUT std_logic);
  END COMPONENT;

  COMPONENT uxfr
    PORT( left, sw : IN std_logic;
          right : OUT std_logic);
  END COMPONENT;

  SIGNAL s1, s2 : std_logic;

BEGIN

  x1 : dep
    PORT MAP( top => s2, bottom => O1 );

  x2 : uxfr
    PORT MAP( left => s1, sw => I1, right => O1 );
```

```
  x3 : ground
    PORT MAP( x => s1 );

  x4 : vcc
    PORT MAP( x => s2 );

END structural;
```

This architecture can then be configured with the following configuration:

```
CONFIGURATION inv_transcon OF struc_inv IS
  FOR structural
    FOR x1 : dep USE CONFIGURATION WORK.depcon;
    END FOR;

    FOR x2 : uxfr USE CONFIGURATION WORK.uxfrcon;
    END FOR;

    FOR x3 : ground USE CONFIGURATION WORK.groundcon;
    END FOR;

    FOR x4 : vcc USE CONFIGURATION WORK.vcccon;
    END FOR;
  END FOR;
END inv_transcon;
```

Now configuration *decode_map_con* of entity *decode,* described earlier, can be modified as follows:

```
CONFIGURATION decode_map_con OF decode IS
  FOR structural
    FOR I1 : inv USE ENTITY WORK.inv(behave)
      PORT MAP( a => x, b => y );
    END FOR;

    FOR I2 : struc_inv USE CONFIGURATION WORK.inv_transcon
      PORT MAP( a => I1, b => O1 );
    END FOR;
    FOR ALL : and3 USE ENTITY WORK.and3(behave);
    END FOR;
  END FOR;
END decode_map_con;
```

This configuration maps the first inverter, I1, to entity *inv,* and the second inverter, I2, to the structural inverter, *struc_inv.* Also, the I1 and O1 ports of *struc_inv* are mapped to ports *a* and *b* of the component declaration for component *inv.*

Generics in Configurations

Generics are parameters that are used to pass information into entities. Typical applications include passing in a generic value for the rise and fall delay of output signals of the entity. Other applications include passing in temperature, voltage, and loading to calculate delay values in the model (for modeling efficiency, delay calculations should be done prior to simulation, and the calculated delay values can then be passed back into the model through generics). A description of generics can be found in Chap. 3. This section will concentrate on how configurations can be used to specify the value of generics.

Generics can be declared in entities, but can have a value specified in a number of places.

- A default value can be specified in the generic declaration.
- A value can be mapped in the architecture, in the component instantiation.
- A default value can be specified in the component declaration.
- A value can be mapped in the configuration for the component.

Default values specified in the generic declaration, or the component declaration, can be overridden by mapped values in the architecture or configuration sections. If no overriding values are present, the default values will be used, but if a value is mapped to the generic with a generic map, the default value will be overridden.

To see an example of this, let's modify the decoder example, used previously in this chapter, to include two generics. The first will specify a timing mode to run the simulation, and the second is a composite type containing the delay values for the device. These two types are declared in the package *p_time_pack,* as follows:

```
USE WORK.std_logic_1164.ALL;
PACKAGE p_time_pack IS
  TYPE t_time_mode IS (minimum, typical, maximum);
  TYPE t_rise_fall IS
    RECORD
      rise : TIME;
      fall : TIME;
    END RECORD;

  TYPE t_time_rec IS ARRAY(t_time_mode'LOW TO
            t_time_mode'HIGH) OF t_rise_fall;

  FUNCTION calc_delay(newstate : IN std_logic; mode : IN t_time_mode;
            delay_tab : IN t_time_rec ) return time;

END p_time_pack;
```

```
PACKAGE BODY p_time_pack IS
  FUNCTION calc_delay(newstate : IN std_logic; mode : IN t_time_mode;
             delay_tab : IN t_time_rec ) return time IS
  BEGIN
    CASE newstate IS
       WHEN '0' =>
         RETURN delay_tab(mode).fall;
       WHEN '1' =>
         RETURN delay_tab(mode).rise;
       WHEN OTHERS =>
         IF (delay_tab(mode).rise <= delay_tab(mode).fall) THEN
           RETURN delay_tab(mode).rise;
         ELSE
           RETURN delay_tab(mode).fall;
         END IF;
    END CASE;
  END calc_delay;
END p_time_pack;
```

This package declares types *t_time_mode* and *t_time_rec,* which will be used for the generics of the inverter and three input AND gates. It also includes a new function, *calc_delay,* which will be used to retrieve the proper delay value from the delay table, depending on the type of transition occurring.

The *and3* and *inv* gates of the decoder example have been rewritten to include the generics discussed previously, as well as the delay calculation function. The new models are as follows:

```
USE WORK.std_logic_1164.ALL;
USE WORK.p_time_pack.ALL;
ENTITY inv IS
  GENERIC( mode : t_time_mode;
       delay_tab : t_time_rec :=
          (( 1 ns, 2 ns), -- min
           ( 2 ns, 3 ns), -- typ
           ( 3 ns, 4 ns)));      -- max

  PORT( a : IN std_logic;
        b : OUT std_logic);
END inv;

ARCHITECTURE inv_gen OF inv IS
BEGIN
  inv_proc : PROCESS(a)
    VARIABLE state : std_logic;
  BEGIN
    state := NOT(a);
    b <= state after calc_delay( state, mode, delay_tab);
  END PROCESS inv_proc;
END inv_gen;
```

```
USE WORK.std_logic_1164.ALL;
USE WORK.p_time_pack.ALL;
ENTITY and3 IS
  GENERIC( mode : t_time_mode;
    delay_tab : t_time_rec :=
      (( 2 ns, 3 ns), -- min
       ( 3 ns, 4 ns), -- typ
       ( 4 ns, 5 ns))); -- max

  PORT( a1, a2, a3 : IN std_logic;
        o1 : OUT std_logic);
END and3;

ARCHITECTURE and3_gen OF and3 IS
BEGIN
  and3_proc : PROCESS( a1, a2, a3 )
    VARIABLE state : std_logic;
  BEGIN
    state := a1 AND a2 AND a3;
    o1 <= state after calc_delay( state, mode, delay_tab);
  END PROCESS and3_proc;
END and3_gen;
```

After the entities and architectures for the gates have been defined, configurations that will provide specific values for the generics will be defined.

These models can have their generic values specified by two methods. The first method is to specify the generic values in the architecture where the components are being instantiated. The second method is to specify the generic values in the configuration for the model, where the components are instantiated.

Generic Value Specification in Architecture

Specifying the generic values in the architecture of an entity allows the designer to delay the specification of the generic values until the architecture of the entity is created. Different generic values can be specified for each instance of an entity, allowing one entity to represent many different physical devices. An example of an architecture with the generic values specified in it is as follows:

```
ARCHITECTURE structural OF decode IS
  COMPONENT inv
    GENERIC( mode : t_time_mode;
             delay_tab : t_time_rec);
    PORT( a : IN std_logic;
          b : OUT std_logic);
  END COMPONENT;
```

```
    COMPONENT and3
      GENERIC( mode : t_time_mode;
            delay_tab : t_time_rec);
      PORT( a1, a2, a3 : IN std_logic;
            o1 : OUT std_logic);
    END COMPONENT;

    SIGNAL nota, notb : std_logic;
  BEGIN
    I1 : inv
      GENERIC MAP( mode => maximum,
              delay_tab => ((1.3 ns, 1.9 ns),
                            (2.1 ns, 2.9 ns),
                            (3.2 ns, 4.1 ns)))
      PORT MAP( a, nota );

    I2 : inv
      GENERIC MAP( mode => minimum,
              delay_tab => ((1.3 ns, 1.9 ns),
                            (2.1 ns, 2.9 ns),
                            (3.2 ns, 4.1 ns)))
      PORT MAP( b, notb );

    A1 : and3
      GENERIC MAP( mode => typical,
              delay_tab => ((1.3 ns, 1.9 ns),
                            (2.1 ns, 2.9 ns),
                            (3.2 ns, 4.1 ns)))
      PORT MAP( nota, en, notb, q0 );

    A2 : and3
      GENERIC MAP( mode => minimum,
              delay_tab => ((1.3 ns, 1.9 ns),
                            (2.1 ns, 2.9 ns),
                            (3.2 ns, 4.1 ns)))

      PORT MAP( a, en, notb, q1 );

    A3 : and3
      GENERIC MAP( mode => maximum,
              delay_tab => ((1.3 ns, 1.9 ns),
                            (2.1 ns, 2.9 ns),
                            (3.2 ns, 4.1 ns)))
      PORT MAP( nota, en, b, q2 );

    A4 : and3
      GENERIC MAP( mode => maximum,
              delay_tab => ((2.3 ns, 2.9 ns),
                            (3.1 ns, 3.9 ns),
                            (4.2 ns, 5.1 ns)))
      PORT MAP( a, en, b, q3 );
  END structural;
```

Generics are treated in the same manner as ports with respect to how they are mapped. If a component port in a component declaration has a different name than the actual entity compiled into the library, then a port map clause is needed in the configuration specification for the containing entity. The same is true for a generic. If a generic declaration in a component declaration has a different name than the actual generic for the component, then a generic map clause is needed to make the appropriate mapping.

In the preceding example, the generic names are the same in the entity declaration and the component declaration, and therefore the default mapping will provide the appropriate connection between the two.

The configuration for the preceding example needs only to specify which actual entities will be used for the component instantiations in the architecture. No generic information needs to be provided, because the generics have been mapped in the architecture. The configuration can be specified as follows:

```
CONFIGURATION decode_gen_con2 OF decode IS
  FOR structural
    FOR i1, i2 : inv USE ENTITY WORK.inv(inv_gen);
    END FOR;
    FOR a1, a2, a3, a4 : and3 USE ENTITY WORK.and3(and3_gen);
    END FOR;
  END FOR;
END decode_gen_con2;
```

The lower-level configuration cannot specify values for the generics if the architecture has mapped values to the generics in the architecture.

Generic Specifications in Configurations

The method of specifying generic values with the most flexibility is to specify generic values in the configuration for the entity. This method allows the latest binding of all the methods for specifying the values for generics. Usually, the later the values are specified, the better. Late binding allows back annotation of path-delay generics to occur in the configuration.

For instance, there are a number of steps involved in the design of an ASIC:

- Create the logic design model of a device.
- Simulate the model.
- Add estimated delays to device model.
- Simulate model.

- Create physical layout of the model.
- Calculate physical delays from the layout.
- Feed back physical delays to the device model.
- Resimulate using actual delays.

The process of feeding back the physical delays into the model can be accomplished by modifying the architecture or by creating a configuration to map the delays back to the model. Modifying the architecture would involve changing the values in all of the generic map clauses used to map the delays in the architecture. This method has a big drawback. Modifying the architecture that contains the component instantiation statements requires recompilation of the architecture and the configuration for the design unit. This can be an expensive proposition in a very large design.

The second method, which creates a configuration that maps all of the delays to the generics of the entity, is much more efficient. A configuration of this type would contain a generic map value for each generic to be specified in the configuration. Any generics not specified in the configuration would be mapped in the architecture or defaulted.

Let's use the decoder example again, but now assume that it represents part of an ASIC that will have delays back-annotated to it. The *inv* and *and3* devices will have an intrinsic propagation delay through the device that is based on the internal characteristics of the device, and these devices will have an external delay that is dependent on the driver path and device loading. The intrinsic and external delays will be passed into the model as generic values. The intrinsic delay is passed into the model to allow a single model to be used for model processes. The external delay is passed to the model, because it may vary for every instance, as loading may be different for each instance (a more accurate model of delays is obtained using input delays).

The entity and architecture for the *inv* and *and3* gates look like this:

```
USE WORK.std_logic_1164.ALL;
ENTITY inv IS
  GENERIC(int_rise, int_fall, ext_rise,
      ext_fall : time);
  PORT( a: IN std_logic; b: OUT std_logic);
END inv;

ARCHITECTURE inv_gen 1 OF inv IS
BEGIN
  inv_proc : PROCESS(a)
    VARIABLE state : std_logic;
```

```
  BEGIN
    state := NOT(a);
    IF state = '1' THEN
      b <= state AFTER (int_rise + ext_rise);
    ELSIF state = '0' THEN
      b <=state AFTER (int_fall + ext_fall);
    ELSE
      b <= state AFTER (int_fall + ext_fall);
    END IF;
  END PROCESS inv_proc;
END inv_gen1;
------------------------------------------------------
USE WORK.std_logic_1164.ALL;
ENTITY and3 IS
  GENERIC(int_rise, int_fall, ext_rise, ext_fall : time);
  PORT( a1, a2, a3: IN std_logic;
        o1: OUT std_logic);
END and3;

ARCHITECTURE and3_gen1 OF and3 IS
BEGIN
  and3_proc : PROCESS(a1, a2, a3)
    VARIABLE state : std_logic;
  BEGIN
    state := a1 AND a2 AND a3;

    IF state = '1' THEN
      o1 <= state AFTER (int_rise + ext_rise);
    ELSIF state = '0' THEN
      o1 <= state AFTER (int_fall + ext_fall);
    ELSE
      o1 <= state AFTER (int_fall + ext_fall);
    END IF;

  END PROCESS and3_proc;
END and3_gen1;
```

There are no local configurations specified at this level in the design, because this has nearly the same effect of mapping the generic values in the architecture. Instead, a full configuration for entity *decode* will be specified that will map the generics at all levels of the decoder. The entity and architecture for the decoder, as shown here, are very similar to the original example used earlier.

```
USE WORK.std_logic_1164.ALL;
ENTITY decode IS
  PORT( a, b, en : IN std_logic;
        q0, q1, q2, q3 : OUT std_logic);
END decode;
```

```
ARCHITECTURE structural OF decode IS
  COMPONENT inv
    PORT( a : IN std_logic;
          b : OUT std_logic);
  END COMPONENT;

  COMPONENT and3
    PORT( a1, a2, a3 : IN std_logic;
          o1 : OUT std_logic);
  END COMPONENT;

  SIGNAL nota, notb : std_logic;
BEGIN
  I1 : inv
    PORT MAP( a, nota);

  I2 : inv
    PORT MAP( b, notb);

  AN1 : and3
    PORT MAP( nota, en, notb, q0);

  AN2 : and3
    PORT MAP( a, en, notb, q1);

  AN3 : and3
    PORT MAP( nota, en, b, q2);

  AN4 : and3
    PORT MAP( a, en, b, q3);
END structural;
```

Notice that the component declarations for components *inv* and *and3* in the architecture declaration section do not contain the generics declared in the entity declarations for entities *inv* and *and3*. Since the generics are not being mapped in the architecture, there is no need to declare the generics for the components in the architecture.

The configuration to bind all of these parts together into an executable model is as follows:

```
CONFIGURATION decode_gen1_con OF decode IS
  FOR structural
    FOR I1 : inv USE ENTITY WORK.inv(inv_gen1)
      GENERIC MAP( int_rise => 1.2 ns,
                   int_fall => 1.7 ns,
                   ext_rise => 2.6 ns,
                   ext_fall => 2.5 ns);
    END FOR;
```

```
FOR I2 : inv USE ENTITY WORK.inv(inv_gen1)
  GENERIC MAP( int_rise => 1.3 ns,
               int_fall => 1.4 ns,
               ext_rise => 2.8 ns,
               ext_fall => 2.9 ns);
END FOR;

FOR AN1 : and3 USE ENTITY WORK.and3(and3_gen1)
  GENERIC MAP( int_rise => 2.2 ns,
               int_fall => 2.7 ns,
               ext_rise => 3.6 ns,
               ext_fall => 3.5 ns);
END FOR;

FOR AN2 : and3 USE ENTITY WORK.and3(and3_gen1)
  GENERIC MAP( int_rise => 2.2 ns,
               int_fall => 2.7 ns,
               ext_rise => 3.1 ns,
               ext_fall => 3.2 ns);
END FOR;

FOR AN3 : and3 USE ENTITY WORK.and3(and3_gen1)
  GENERIC MAP( int_rise => 2.2 ns,
               int_fall => 2.7 ns,
               ext_rise => 3.3 ns,
               ext_fall => 3.4 ns);
END FOR;

FOR AN4 : and3 USE ENTITY WORK.and3(and3_gen1)
  GENERIC MAP( int_rise => 2.2 ns,
               int_fall => 2.7 ns,
               ext_rise => 3.0 ns,
               ext_fall => 3.1 ns);
  END FOR;
 END FOR;
END decode_gen1_con;
```

Each component instance is configured to the correct entity and architecture, and the generics of the entity are mapped with a generic map clause. Using this type of configuration allows each instance to have unique delay characteristics. Of course, the generics passed into the device can represent any type of data that the designer wishes, but typically the generics are used to represent delay information.

The power of this type of configuration is realized when the delay values are updated. For instance, in the ASIC example, the estimated delays are included in the configuration initially, but after the ASIC device has been through the physical layout process, the actual delay information can be determined. This information can be fed back into the configuration so that the configuration has the actual delay information calculated from the layout tool. To build a new simulatable device, including the new delay information, requires only a recompile of the configuration. The entities and architectures do not need to be recompiled.

If the delay information was included in the architecture for the device, then a lot more of the model would need to be recompiled in order to build the simulatable entity. All of the architectures that included the generics would need to be recompiled, and so would the configuration for the entity. A lot of extra code would be recompiled unnecessarily.

The information in this section on generics can be summarized by the charts shown in Figs. 7.4 and Fig. 7.5 (these charts were originally created by Paul Krol).

These charts show the effect of the declarations and mapping of generics on the values actually obtained in the model. The first four columns of Fig. 7.4 describe where a particular generic, G, can be declared and mapped to a value. The next column describes the error/warning number returned from a particular combination of declaration and mapping. The next two columns describe the values obtained by the generic, G, and any other generics for the entity for a particular declaration and mapping combination. At the bottom of Fig. 7.4 and in Fig. 7.5 are the tables of translations used to translate the character values used to the appropriate action taken.

Declaration		Mapping		Error/warning	Generic values	
Entity	Component	Instance	Configuration		Same	Other
D	D	A			I	E
D	N	A			I	E
D	N		A		C	E
N	D	A			I	M
N	D		A		C	M
X	D/N		A	1		
X	D/N			2		
X	D/N	A		2		•
D/N	X	A		3		
D/N	X		A		C	E
		A	A	4		
		X	X	5		

Figure 7.4   Configuration generic table.

Declarations/mapping	
D	Declared, with default value
N	Declared, with no default value
X	Not declared
A	Actual mapped

Errors/warnings	
1	Can only map generic in configuration if declared in the entity
2	Generic declared in component but not in entity, hence it is not used
3	Can only map generic in component instance if declared in component declarations
4	Can't map a generic in the component instance and the configuration
5	Must map at least one generic to get the default value for other generics

Generic values	
E	Default taken from entity
M	Default taken from configuration
I	Actual taken from component instance
C	Actual taken from configuration

Figure 7.5   Configuration generic table translations.

Board-Socket-Chip Analogy

A good analogy for describing how entity declarations, architectures, component declarations, and configuration specifications all interact is the board-socket-chip analogy (this analogy was originally presented to the author by Dr. Alec Stanculescu). In this analogy, the architecture of the top-level entity represents the board being modeled. The component instance represents a socket on the board, and the lower-level entity being instantiated in the architecture represents the chip.

This analogy helps describe how the ports and generics are mapped at each level. At the board (architecture) level, component socket pins are interconnected with signals. The chip pins are then connected to socket pins when the chip is plugged into the socket. The following is an example of how this works:

```
USE WORK.std_logic_1164.ALL;
ENTITY board IS
  GENERIC (qdelay, qbdelay : time);
  PORT( clk, reset, data_in : IN std_logic;
        data_out : OUT std_logic);
END board;

ARCHITECTURE structural OF board IS
  COMPONENT dff
    GENERIC( g1, g2 : time);
    PORT( p1, p2, p3, p4 : IN std_logic;
          p5, p6 : OUT std_logic);
END COMPONENT;

SIGNAL ground : std_logic := '1';
SIGNAL int1, nc : std_logic;

BEGIN
  U1 : dff
    GENERIC MAP( g1 => qdelay,
                 g2 => qbdelay)
    PORT MAP( p1 => clk,
              p2 => data_in,
              p3 => reset,
              p4 => ground,
              p5 => int1,
              p6 => nc);

  U2 : dff
    GENERIC MAP( g1 => qdelay,
                 g2 => qbdelay)
    PORT MAP( p1 => clk,
              p2 => int1,
              p3 => reset,
              p4 => ground,
              p5 => data_out,
              p6 => nc);
END structural;
```

The entity and architecture shown are a simple 2-bit shift register made from two D flip-flop (DFF) component instantiations. This example, though relatively simple, will show how ports and generics are mapped at different levels.

The component instance for component DFF in the architecture statement part acts like a socket in the architecture for the board. When a component instance is placed in the architecture, signals are used to connect the component to the board, which is the architecture. The actual chip is not connected to the socket until a configuration is specified for the board entity. If all of the names of the socket ports and generics match the names of the actual entity being used, then no mapping is needed. The default mapping will connect the chip to the socket. If the names are different or the number of ports are not the same for the component instantiation and the actual entity, then a mapping between the socket (component instantiation) and the chip (actual entity) is needed.

The actual chip to be mapped is described by the following entity and architecture:

```
USE WORK.std_logic_1164.ALL;
ENTITY dff IS
  GENERIC( q_out, qb_out : time);
  PORT( preset, clear, din,
        clock : IN std_logic;
        q, qb : OUT std_logic);
END dff;

ARCHITECTURE behave OF dff IS
BEGIN
  dff_proc : PROCESS(preset, clear, clock)
    VARIABLE int_q : std_logic;
  BEGIN
    IF preset = '0' and clear = '0' THEN
      IF (clock'EVENT) AND (clock = '1') THEN
        int_q := din;
      END IF;

    ELSIF preset = '1' AND clear = '0' THEN
      int_q := '1';

    ELSIF clear = '1' AND preset = '0' THEN
      int_q := '0';

    ELSE
      int_q := 'X';

    END IF;

    q <= int_q after q_out;

    int_q := not(int_q);
    qb <= int_q after qb_out;

  END PROCESS dff_proc;
END behave;
```

The names of the ports and generics are completely different than the component declaration; therefore, mapping is required. A configuration that will place the actual chip in the socket (map the ports and generics) is as follows:

```
CONFIGURATION board_con OF board IS
  FOR structural
    FOR U1,U2: dff USE ENTITY WORK.dff(behave)
      GENERIC MAP( q_out => g1, qb_out => g2)
      PORT MAP( preset => ground, clear => p3,
            din => p2, clock => p1,
            q => p5, qb => p6);
    END FOR;
  END FOR;
END board_con;
```

Block Configurations

When an architecture contains block statements, the configuration must reflect this fact (block statements are discussed in Chap. 2). Blocks act like another level of hierarchy between the containing architecture and any components being configured. The configuration must specify which block of a configuration is being configured when the architecture is being configured.

The following is an architecture fragment that contains three blocks:

```
USE WORK.std_logic_1164.ALL;
ENTITY cpu IS
  PORT( clock : IN std_logic;
        addr : OUT std_logic_vector(0 to 3);
        data : INOUT std_logic_vector(0 to 3);
        interrupt : IN std_logic;
        reset : IN std_logic);
END cpu;

ARCHITECTURE fragment OF cpu IS
  COMPONENT int_reg
    PORT( data : IN std_logic;
          regclock : IN std_logic;
          data_out : OUT std_logic);
  END COMPONENT;

  COMPONENT alu
    PORT( a, b : IN std_logic;
          c, carry : OUT std_logic);
  END COMPONENT;

  SIGNAL a, b c, carry : std_logic_vector(0 TO 3);
BEGIN
  reg_array : BLOCK
  BEGIN
    R1 : int_reg
      PORT MAP( data(0), clock, data(0));
```

```
   R2 : int_reg
     PORT MAP( data(1), clock, data(1));

   R3 : int_reg
     PORT MAP( data(2), clock, data(2));

   R4 : int_reg
     PORT MAP( data(3), clock, data(3));
  END BLOCK reg_array;

  shifter : BLOCK
  BEGIN
    A1 : alu
      PORT MAP( a(0), data(0), c(0), carry(0));

    A2 : alu
      PORT MAP( a(1), data(1), c(1), carry(1));

    A3 : alu
      PORT MAP( a(2), data(2), c(2), carry(2));

    A4 : alu
      PORT MAP( a(3), data(3), c(3), carry(3));

    shift_reg : BLOCK
    BEGIN
      R1 : int_reg
        PORT MAP( b(0), clock, b(1));

    END BLOCK shift_reg;
  END BLOCK shifter;
END fragment;
```

The architecture consists of three blocks, each of which contains component instantiations. The first block contains four *int_reg* components, and the second contains an *alu* component plus another BLOCK statement. The last block contains a single *int_reg* component.

The configuration for this architecture must take into account the fact that BLOCK statements exist in the architecture. A simple configuration for the architecture is as follows:

```
CONFIGURATION cpu_con OF cpu IS
  FOR fragment
    FOR reg_array
      FOR ALL: int_reg USE CONFIGURATION WORK.int_reg_con;
      END FOR;
    END FOR;
    FOR shifter
      FOR ALL : alu USE CONFIGURATION WORK.alu_con;
      END FOR;
```

```
    FOR shift_reg
      FOR R1 : int_reg USE CONFIGURATION WORK.int_reg_con;
      END FOR;
     END FOR;
   END FOR;
  END FOR;
 END cpu_con;
```

In the configuration *cpu_con* of entity *cpu,* architecture *fragment* will be used for the entity. Inside of block *reg_array,* all (R1–R4) of the *int_reg* components will use configuration *int_reg_con.* In block *shifter,* the *alu* component (A1) will use configuration *alu_con.* For block *shift_reg* inside of block *shifter,* the *int_reg* component will use configuration *int_reg_con.*

Architecture Configurations

The last type of configuration that will be discussed is the architecture configuration. This configuration exists in the architecture declarative region and specifies the configurations of parts used in the architecture. If this type of configuration is used, a separate configuration declaration is not needed to configure the components used in the architecture.

The example configuration shown will be for a very high-level description of an autopilot. The autopilot block diagram is shown in Fig. 7.6. The following is an example of this type of configuration:

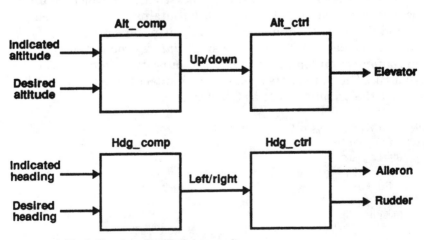

Figure 7.6   Block diagram of autopilot example.

```
PACKAGE ap IS
  SUB TYPE alt IS INTEGER RANGE 0 TO 50000;
  SUB TYPE hdg IS INTEGER RANGE 0 TO 359;
  SUB TYPE vdir IS INTEGER RANGE 0 TO 9;
  SUB TYPE hdir IS INTEGER RANGE 0 TO 9;
  SUB TYPE control IS INTEGER RANGE 0 TO 9;
END ap;

USE WORK.ap.ALL;
ENTITY autopilot IS
  PORT( altitude : IN alt;
        altitude_set : IN alt;
        heading : IN hdg;
        heading_set : IN hdg;
        rudder : OUT control;
        aileron : OUT control;
        elevator : OUT control);
END autopilot;

ARCHITECTURE block_level OF autopilot IS
  COMPONENT alt_compare
    PORT( alt_ref : IN alt;
          alt_ind : IN alt;
          up_down : OUT vdir);
  END COMPONENT;

  COMPONENT hdg_compare
    PORT( hdg_ref : IN hdg;
          hdg_ind : IN hdg;
          left_right : OUT hdir);
  END COMPONENT;

  COMPONENT hdg_ctrl
    PORT( left_right : IN hdir;
          rdr : OUT control;
          alrn : OUT control);
  END COMPONENT;

  COMPONENT alt_ctrl
    PORT( up_down : IN vdir;
          elevator : OUT control);
  END COMPONENT;

  SIGNAL up_down : vdir;
  SIGNAL left_right : hdir;

  FOR M1 : alt_compare USE CONFIGURATION WORK.alt_comp_con;

  FOR M2 : hdg_compare USE CONFIGURATION WORK.hdg_comp_con;

  FOR M3 : hdg_ctrl USE ENTITY WORK.hdg_ctrl(behave);

  FOR M4 : alt_ctrl USE ENTITY WORK.alt_ctrl(behave);
```

```
BEGIN
  M1 : alt_compare
    PORT MAP( alt_ref => altitude,
              alt_ind => alt_set,
              up_down => up_down);

  M2 : hdg_compare
    PORT MAP( hdg_ref => heading,
              hdg_ind => hdg_set,
              left_right => left_right);

  M3 : hdg_ctrl
    PORT MAP( left_right => left_right,
              rdr => rudder,
              alrn => aileron);

  M4 : alt_ctrl
    PORT MAP( up_down => up_down,
              elevator => elevator);

END block_level;
```

This model is a top-level description of an autopilot. There are four instantiated components that provide the necessary functionality of the autopilot. This model demonstrates how component instantiations can be configured in the architecture declaration section of an architecture. Notice that, after the component declarations in the architecture declaration section of architecture *block_level*, there are four statements similar to the following:

```
FOR M1 : alt_compare USE CONFIGURATION WORK.alt_comp_con;
```

These statements allow the designer to specify either the configuration or the entity-architecture pair to use for a particular component type. This type of configuration does not provide the same flexibility to the designer as the separate configuration declaration, but it is useful for small designs.

Configurations are a useful tool for managing large designs. With proper use of configurations, a top-down design approach can be implemented that allows all levels of description of the design to be used for the most efficient model needed at any point in the design process.

In this chapter, we discussed the following points:

- Default configurations can be used to bind architectures to entities.

- Component configurations can be used to specify which entity to use for each component instantiation.

- Port maps within configurations allow mapping entities with different names to component instances.

- Generics can be specified in configurations to allow late binding of generic information.

- Block configurations can be used to configure architectures with block statements in them.

- Architecture configurations allow specification of configurations for component instantiations in the architecture declaration section.

The reader has now been introduced to the basic features of VHDL. In the next chapter, we will examine some of the more esoteric but useful features that exist in VHDL.

Chapter

8

Advanced Topics

In this chapter some of the more esoteric features of VHDL will be discussed. Some of the features may be useful for certain types of designs, and not for others. Typical usage examples will be presented to show how these features might be taken advantage of.

Some of the features discussed will be overloading, qualified expressions, user-defined attributes, generate statements, aliases, and TextIO. All of these features provide the user with an advanced environment with which to do modeling.

Overloading

Overloading allows the designer to write much more readable code. An object is overloaded when the same object name exists for multiple subprograms or type values. The VHDL compiler will select the appropriate object to use in each instance.

In VHDL, a number of types of overloading are possible. Subprograms can be overloaded, operators can be overloaded, and enumeration types can be overloaded. Overloading subprograms allows subprograms to operate on objects of different types. Overloading an operator allows the operator to perform the same operation on multiple types. Overloading frees the designer from the necessity of generating countless unique names for subprograms that do virtually the same operation. The result of using overloaded subprograms and operators is models that are easier to read and maintain.

Subprogram overloading

Subprogram overloading allows the designer to write multiple subprograms with the same name, but the number of arguments, the type of arguments, and return value (if any) can be different. The VHDL compiler, at compile time, will select the subprogram that matches the subprogram call. If no subprogram matches the call, an error is generated.

The following example illustrates how a subprogram can be overloaded by the argument type.

```
USE WORK.std_logic_1164.ALL;
PACKAGE p_shift IS
  TYPE s_int IS RANGE 0 TO 255;
  TYPE s_array IS ARRAY(0 TO 7) OF std_logic;

  FUNCTION shiftr( a : s_array) return s_array;
  FUNCTION shiftr( a : s_int) return s_int;
END p_shift;
PACKAGE BODY p_shift IS
  FUNCTION shiftr( a : s_array) return s_array IS
    VARIABLE result : s_array;
  BEGIN
    FOR i IN a'RANGE LOOP
      IF i = a'HIGH THEN
        result(i) := '0';
      ELSE
        result(i) := a(i + 1);
      END IF;
    END LOOP;

    RETURN result;
  END shiftr;

  FUNCTION shiftr( a : s_int) return s_int IS
  BEGIN
    RETURN (a/2);
  END shiftr;
END p_shift;
```

The package *p_shift* contains two functions, both named *shiftr.* Both functions provide a right-shift capability, but each function operates on a specific type. One function works only with type *s_int,* and the other works only with type *s_array.* The compiler will pick the appropriate function, based on the calling argument(s) and return argument.

In the following example, different types of function calls are shown, as well as the results obtained with each call.

```
USE WORK.p_shift.ALL;
ENTITY shift_example IS
END shift_example;
```

```
ARCHITECTURE test OF shift_example IS
  SIGNAL int_signal : s_int;
  SIGNAL array_signal : s_array;
BEGIN
  -- picks function that works with s_int type
  int_signal <= shiftr(int_signal);

  -- picks function that works with
  --s_array type
  array_signal <= shiftr(array_signal);

  -- produces error because no function
  -- will match
  array_signal <= shiftr(int_signal);
END test;
```

The architecture *test* contains three calls to function *shiftr*. The first calls *shiftr* with an argument type of *s_int*, and a return type of *s_int*. This call will use the second function described in package body *p_shift*, the function with input arguments, and return type of *s_int*.

The second call to *shiftr* uses the array type *s_array*, and therefore will pick the first function defined in package *p_shift*. Both the input argument(s) type(s) and return type must match in order for the function to match the call.

The third call to function *shiftr* shows an example of a call where the input argument matches the *s_int* type function, but the return type of the function does not match the target signal. With the functions currently described in package *p_shift*, no function matches exactly, and therefore the compilation of the third line will produce an error.

To make the third call legal, all that is needed is to define a function that matches the types of the third call. An example of the function declaration follows. The function body for this function is left as an exercise for the reader.

```
FUNCTION shiftr( a : s_int) return s_array;
```

Overloading subprogram argument types. In order to overload argument types, the base type of the subprogram parameters or return value must differ. For example, base types do not differ when two subtypes are of the same type. Two functions that try to overload these subtypes will produce a compile error. An example is as follows:

```
PACKAGE type_error IS
  SUBTYPE log4 IS BIT_VECTOR( 0 TO 3);
  SUBTYPE log8 IS BIT_VECTOR( 0 TO 7);
```

```
-- this function is Ok
FUNCTION "not"( a : log4) return integer;
-- this function declaration will cause an
-- error
FUNCTION "not"( a : log8) return integer;

END type_error;
```

This package declares two subtypes, *log4* and *log8,* of the uncon-strained BIT_VECTOR type. Two functions named *not* are then declared using these subtypes. The first function declaration is legal, but the sec-ond function declaration will cause an error. The error is that two func-tions have been declared for the same base type. The two types *log4* and *log8* are not distinct, because they both belong to the same base type.

All of the examples shown so far have been overloading of functions. Overloading of procedures works in the same manner.

Subprogram parameter overloading.   Two or more subprograms with the same name can have a different number of parameters. The types of the parameters could be the same, but the number of parameters can be different. This is shown by the following example:

```
USE WORK.std_logic_1164.ALL;
PACKAGE p_addr_convert IS

    FUNCTION convert_addr(a0, a1 : std_logic) return integer;

    FUNCTION convert_addr(a0, a1, a2 : std_logic) return integer;

    FUNCTION convert_addr(a0, a1, a2, a3 : std_logic) return integer;

END p_addr_convert;

PACKAGE BODY p_addr_convert IS
    FUNCTION convert_addr(a0, a1 : std_logic) RETURN INTEGER IS
      VARIABLE result : INTEGER := 0;
    BEGIN
      IF (a0 = '1') THEN
        result := result + 1;
      END IF;

      IF (a1 = '1') THEN
        result := result + 2;
      END IF;

      RETURN result;
    END convert_addr;

    FUNCTION convert_addr(a0, a1, a2 : std_logic) RETURN INTEGER IS
      VARIABLE result : INTEGER := 0;
    BEGIN
```

```
      result := convert_addr(a0, a1);

    IF (a2 = '1') THEN
      result := result + 4;
    END IF;
    RETURN result;
  END convert_addr;

  FUNCTION convert_addr(a0, a1, a2, a3 : std_logic) RETURN INTEGER IS
    VARIABLE result : INTEGER := 0;
  BEGIN

    result := convert_addr(a0, a1, a2);

    IF (a3 = '1') THEN
      result := result + 8;
    END IF;
    RETURN result;
  END convert_addr;

END p_addr_convert;
```

This package declares three functions that convert 2, 3, or 4 input bits into integer representation. Each function is named the same, but the appropriate function will be called depending on the number of input arguments that are passed to the function. If 2 bits are passed to the function, then the function with two arguments is called. If 3 bits are passed, the function with three arguments is called, and so on.

An example using these functions is as follows:

```
USE WORK.std_logic_1164.ALL;
USE WORK.p_addr_convert.ALL;
ENTITY test IS
  PORT(i0, i1, i2, i3 : in std_logic);
END test;

ARCHITECTURE test1 OF test IS
  SIGNAL int1, int2, int3 : INTEGER;
BEGIN
  -- uses first function
  int1 <= convert_addr(i0, i1);

  -- uses second function
  int2 <= convert_addr(i0, i1, i2);

  -- uses third function
  int3 <= convert_addr(i0, i1, i2, i3);
END test1;
```

The first call to the *convert_addr* function has only two arguments in the argument list, and therefore the first function in package *p_addr_convert* will be used. The second call has three arguments in its argument list, and will call the second function. The last call matches the third function from package *p_addr_convert*.

Overloading operators

One of the most useful applications of overloading is the overloading of operators. The need for overloading operators arises because the operators supplied in VHDL work only with specific types. For instance, the + operator works only with integer, real, and physical types, while the & (concatenation) operator works only with array types. If a designer wants to use a particular operator on a user-defined type, then the operator must be overloaded to handle the user type. A complete listing of the operators and the types supported by them can be found in chapter 7 of the LRM.

An example of a typical overloaded operator is the + operator. The + operator is defined for the numeric types, but if the designer wants to add two BIT_VECTOR objects, the + operator will not work. The designer must write a function that overloads the operator to accomplish this operation. The package below shows an overloaded function for operator + that will allow addition of two objects of BIT_VECTOR types.

```
PACKAGE math IS
  FUNCTION "+"( 1,r : BIT_VECTOR) RETURN INTEGER;
END math;

PACKAGE BODY math IS
  FUNCTION vector_to_int( S : BIT_VECTOR) RETURN INTEGER IS
    VARIABLE result : INTEGER := 0;
    VARIABLE prod : INTEGER := 1;
  BEGIN
    FOR i IN s'RANGE LOOP
      IF s(i) = '1' THEN
        result := result + prod;
      END IF;
      prod := prod * 2;
    END LOOP;

    RETURN result;
  END vector_to_int;

  FUNCTION "+"(1,r : BIT_VECTOR) RETURN INTEGER IS
  BEGIN
    RETURN ( vector_to_int(1) + vector_to_int(r));
  END;
END math;
```

Whenever the + operator is used in an expression, the compiler will call the + operator function that matches the types of the operands. When the operands are of type INTEGER, the built-in + operator function will be called. If the operands are of type BIT_VECTOR, then the function from package *math* will be called. The following example shows uses for both functions:

```
USE WORK.math.ALL;
ENTITY adder IS
  PORT( a, b : IN BIT_VECTOR(0 TO 7);
        c : IN INTEGER;
        dout : OUT INTEGER);
END adder;

ARCHITECTURE test OF adder IS
  SIGNAL internal : INTEGER;
BEGIN
  internal <= a + b;
  dout <= c + internal;
END test;
```

This example illustrates how overloading can be used to make very readable models. The value assigned to signal *internal* is the sum of inputs *a* and *b*. Since *a* and *b* are of type BIT_VECTOR, the overloaded operator function that has two BIT_VECTOR arguments is called. This function will add the values of *a* and *b* together and return an integer value to be assigned to signal *internal*.

The second addition uses the standard built-in addition function that is standard in VHDL because both operands are of type INTEGER. This model could have been written as shown here, but would still function in the same manner.

```
PACKAGE math IS
  FUNCTION addvec( l,r : bit_vector) RETURN INTEGER;
END math;

PACKAGE BODY math IS
  FUNCTION vector_to_int( S : bit_vector) RETURN INTEGER IS
    VARIABLE result : INTEGER := 0;
    VARIABLE prod : INTEGER := 1;
  BEGIN
    FOR i IN s'RANGE LOOP
      IF s(i) = '1' THEN
        result := result + prod;
      END IF;
      prod := prod * 2;
    END LOOP;
```

```
   RETURN result;
 END vector_to_int;

 FUNCTION addvec(1,r : bit_vector) RETURN INTEGER IS
 BEGIN
   RETURN ( vector_to_int(1) + vector_to_int(r));
 END addvec;
END math;
USE WORK.math.ALL;
ENTITY adder IS
  PORT( a, b : IN BIT_VECTOR(0 TO 7);
        c : IN INTEGER;
        dout : OUT INTEGER);
END adder;

ARCHITECTURE test2 OF adder IS
  SIGNAL internal : INTEGER;
BEGIN
  internal <= addvec(a,b);
  dout <= c + internal;
END test2;
```

In this example, a function called *advec* is used to add *a* and *b*. Both coding styles give exactly the same results, but the first example using the overloaded + operator is much more readable, and easier to maintain. If another person besides the designer of a model takes over the maintenance of the model, it will be much easier for the new person to understand the model if overloading was used.

Operator argument type overloading.   Arguments to overloaded operator functions do not have to be of the same type, as the previous two examples have shown. The parameters to an overloaded operator function can be of any type. In some cases, it is preferable to write two functions so that the order of the arguments is not important.

Let's examine the functions for an overloaded logical operator that mixes signals of type BIT, and signals of a nine-state value system.

```
PACKAGE p_logic_pack IS
  TYPE t_nine_val IS (Z0, Z1, ZX,
                      R0, R1, RX,
                      F0, F1, FX);

  FUNCTION "AND"( 1, r : t_nine_val) RETURN BIT;

  FUNCTION "AND"( 1 : BIT; r : t_nine_val) RETURN BIT;

  FUNCTION "AND"( 1 : t_nine_val; r : BIT) RETURN BIT;
```

```
END p_logic_pack;

PACKAGE BODY p_logic_pack IS
  FUNCTION nine_val_2_bit( t : IN t_nine_val) RETURN BIT IS
  TYPE t_nine_val_conv IS ARRAY(t_nine_val) OF BIT;
  CONSTANT nine_2_bit : t_nine_val_conv :=
         ('0',  -- Z0
          '1',  -- Z1
          '1',  -- ZX
          '0',  -- R0
          '1',  -- R1
          '1',  -- RX
          '0',  -- F0
          '1',  -- F1
          '1'); -- FX
BEGIN
  RETURN nine_2_bit(t);
END nine_val_2_bit;

  FUNCTION "AND"(1,r : t_nine_val) RETURN BIT IS
  BEGIN
    RETURN (nine_val_2_bit(1) AND nine_val_2_bit(r));
  END;

  FUNCTION "AND"(1 :BIT; r : t_nine_val) RETURN BIT IS
  BEGIN
    RETURN ( 1 AND nine_val_2_bit(r));
  END;

  FUNCTION "AND"(1 : t_nine_val; r : BIT) RETURN BIT IS
  BEGIN
    RETURN (nine_val_2_bit(1) AND r);
  END;
END p_logic_pack;
```

The package *p_logic_pack* declares three overloaded functions for the AND operator. In one function, both input types are type *t_nine_val.* In the other two functions, only one input is type *t_nine_val,* and the other input is type BIT. All functions return a result of type BIT. Notice that to overload the AND operator, the syntax is the same as overloading the + operator from the previous example.

When the AND operator is used in a model, the appropriate function will be called, based on the types of the operands. In the code fragments that follow, we can see the differences.

```
SIGNAL a, b : t_nine_val;
SIGNAL c,e1, e2, e3 : bit;
```

```
e1 <= a AND b;
-- calls first function

e2 <= a AND c;
-- calls third function

e3 <= c AND b;
-- calls second function
```

By having three functions called AND, we do not need to worry about which side of the operator an expression resides on. All of the possible combinations of operator order will be covered with three functions, because the function for two inputs of type BIT are built in.

Aliases

An alias creates a new name for all or part of the range of an array type. It is very useful for naming parts of a range as if they were subfields. For example, in a CPU model an instruction is fetched from memory. The instruction may be an array of 32 bits that is interpreted as a number of smaller fields to represent the instruction opcode, source register 1, source register 2, etc. Aliases provide a mechanism to name each of the subfields of the instruction and to reference these fields directly by the alias names. This is shown by the following example:

```
SIGNAL instruction : BIT_VECTOR(31 DOWNTO 0);

ALIAS opcode : BIT_VECTOR(3 DOWNTO 0) IS instruction(31 DOWNTO 28);
ALIAS src_reg : BIT_VECTOR(4 DOWNTO 0) IS instruction(27 DOWNTO 23);

ALIAS dst_reg : BIT_VECTOR(4 DOWNTO 0) IS instruction(22 DOWNTO 18);
```

In this example, the aliases have been created for a signal object. Using the alias name in an assignment or referencing operation is the same as using the piece of the instruction object being aliased, but much more convenient.

Remember that the semantics in place for the object being aliased are applied to the alias as well. If an alias is created for a constant object, the alias cannot have an assignment for the same reasons that a constant cannot have an assignment.

Qualified Expressions

One of the side effects of overloading is that multiple functions or procedures may match in a particular instance because the types are ambiguous. In order for the compiler to figure out which subprogram to use, a qualified expression may be required. A qualified expression states the exact type that the expression should attain. For instance, when evaluating an expression containing a mixture of overloaded subprograms and constant values, the designer may need to qualify an expression to produce correct results. An example of such a situation is as follows:

```
PACKAGE p_qual IS
  TYPE int_vector IS ARRAY(NATURAL RANGE <>) OF INTEGER;

  FUNCTION average( a : int_vector) RETURN INTEGER;

  FUNCTION average( a : int_vector) RETURN REAL;

END p_qual;

USE WORK.p_qual.ALL;
ENTITY normalize IS
  PORT( factor : IN REAL;
        points : IN int_vector;
        result : OUT REAL);
END normalize;

ARCHITECTURE qual_exp OF normalize IS
BEGIN
  result <= REAL'(average(points)) * factor;
END qual_exp;
```

Package *p_qual* defines two overloaded functions named *average* and an unconstrained type, *int_vector.* The package body is left as an exercise for the reader.

Architecture *qual_exp* has a single concurrent signal assignment statement that calls function *average.* Since there are two functions named *average,* there are two possible functions that can be used by this call. In order to clarify which function to use, the expression has been qualified to return a REAL type. The keyword REAL followed by a ' mark specifies that the expression inside the parentheses will return a type REAL.

The expression was qualified to make sure that the *average* function returning a REAL number was called instead of the *average* function that returns an INTEGER. In this example, the expression required a qualified expression to allow the architecture to compile. The compiler will not make any random guesses about which function to use. The designer must specify exactly which one to use in cases where more than one function can match; otherwise, an error is generated.

Another use for a qualified expression is to build the source value for an assignment statement. Based on the type of the signal assignment target, the source value can be built. An example is as follows:

```
PACKAGE p_qual_2 IS
  TYPE vector8 IS ARRAY( 0 TO 7) OF BIT;
END p_qual_2;

USE WORK.p_qual_2.ALL;
ENTITY latch IS
  PORT( reset, clock : IN BIT;
        data_in : IN vector8;
        data_out : OUT vector8);
END latch;

ARCHITECTURE behave OF latch IS
BEGIN
  PROCESS(clock)
  BEGIN
    IF (clock = '1') THEN
      IF (reset = '1') THEN
        data_out <= vector8'(others => '0');
      ELSE
        data_out <= data_in;
      END IF;
    END IF;
  END PROCESS;
END behave;
```

This example is an 8-bit transparent latch, with a reset line to set the latch to zero. When the *clock* input is a '1' value, the latch is transparent, and input values are reflected on the output. When the *clock* input is '0', the *data_in* value is latched. When reset is a '1' value while clock input is a '1', the latch will be reset. This is accomplished by assigning all '0's to *data_out*. One method to assign all '0's to *data_out* is to use an aggregate assignment. Since *data_out* is 8 bits, the aggregate assignment shown here will set *data_out* to all '0's.

```
data_out <= ('0', '0', '0', '0', '0', '0', '0', '0');
```

This aggregate will work fine unless the type of *data_out* changes. If the type of output *data_out* were suddenly changed to 16 bits instead of 8, the aggregate could no longer be used.

Another method to accomplish the assignment to output *data_out* is to use a qualified expression. The assignment to *data_out* when reset = '1' in the preceding example shows how this might be done. The expression

```
(others => '0')
```

can be qualified with the type of the target signal (*data_out*). This allows the compiler to determine how large the target signal is and how large to make the source being assigned to the signal. Now whenever the target signal type is changed, the source will change to match.

User-Defined Attributes

VHDL user-defined attributes are a mechanism for attaching data to VHDL objects. The data attached can be used during simulation or by another tool that reads the VHDL description. Data such as the disk file name of the model, loading information, driving capability, resistance, capacitance, physical location, etc., can be attached to objects. The type and value of the data is completely user-definable. The value, once specified, is constant throughout the simulation.

User-defined attributes can behave similarly to entity generic values, with one exception. Generics are legal only on entities, but user-defined attributes can be assigned to the following list of objects.

- Entity
- Architecture
- Configuration
- Procedure
- Function
- Package
- Type and subtype
- Constant
- Signal
- Variable
- Component
- Label

To see how user-defined attributes operate, let's examine the following description:

```
PACKAGE p_attr IS
  TYPE t_package_type IS ( leadless,
                           pin_grid,
                           dip);

  ATTRIBUTE package_type : t_package_type;
  ATTRIBUTE location : INTEGER;

END p_attr;

USE WORK.p_attr.ALL;
ENTITY board IS
  PORT(

     .
     .
     .
     );
END board;

ARCHITECTURE cpu_board OF board IS
  COMPONENT mc68040
    GENERIC( ...... );
    PORT(

     .
     .
     .
     );
  END COMPONENT;
  SIGNAL a : INTEGER;
  SIGNAL b : t_package_type;

  ATTRIBUTE package_type OF mc68040 : COMPONENT IS pin_grid;

  ATTRIBUTE location OF mc68040 : COMPONENT IS 20;
BEGIN
  a <= mc68040'location;
  -- returns 20

  b <= mc68040'package_type;
  -- returns pin_grid

END cpu_board;
```

This is a very simple example of how attributes can be attached to objects. Much more complicated types and attributes can be created. What this example shows is a code fragment of a CPU board design in which the package type and location information are specified as attributes of the single microprocessor used in the design.

The *package_type* attribute is used to hold the kind of packaging used for the microprocessor. Attributes that have values specified do not have to be used in the simulation. Other tools, such as physical layout tools or fault simulation, can make use of attributes that a logic simulator cannot.

In this example, a physical layout tool could read the package type information from the *package_type* attribute and, based on the value assigned to the attribute, fill in the value for the location attribute.

The package *p_attr* defines the type used for one of the attributes, and contains the attribute declarations for two attributes. The attribute declarations make the name and type of the attribute visible to any object for use if needed.

In the architecture *cpu_board* of entity *board* are the attribute specifications. The attribute specification describes the attribute name to be used, the name of the object to which the attribute is attached, the object kind, and finally the value of the attribute.

To access the value of a user-defined attribute, use the same syntax for a predefined attribute. In the signal assignment statements of architecture *cpu_board*, the attribute value is retrieved by specifying the name of the object, followed by a ', and finally the attribute name.

Generate Statements

Generate statements provide the designer with the capability of creating replicated structures, or selecting between multiple representations of a model. Generate statements can contain IF THEN and looping constructs, nested to any level, that will create concurrent statements.

Typical applications include memory arrays, registers, etc. Another application is to emulate a conditional compilation mechanism found in other languages such as C.

The following is a simple example showing the basics of generate statements:

```
USE WORK.std_logic_1164.ALL;
ENTITY shift IS
    PORT( a, clk : IN std_logic;
          b : OUT std_logic);
END shift;

ARCHITECTURE gen_shift OF shift IS
  COMPONENT dff
    PORT( d, clk : IN std_logic;
          q : OUT std_logic);
  END COMPONENT;

  SIGNAL z : std_logic_vector( 0 TO 4 );
BEGIN
  z(0) <= a;
```

```
g1 : FOR i IN 0 TO 3 GENERATE
  dffx : dff PORT MAP( z(i), clk, z(i + 1));
END GENERATE;

b <= z(4);
END gen_shift;
```

This example represents the behavior of a 4-bit shift register. Port *a* is the input to the shift register, and port *b* is the output. Port *clk* will shift the data from *a* to *b*.

Architecture *gen_shift* of entity *shift* contains two concurrent signal assignment statements, and one GENERATE statement. The signal assignment statements connect the internal signal *z* to input port *a* and output port *b*. The generate statement in this example uses a FOR scheme to generate four DFF components. The resultant schematic for this architecture is shown in Fig. 8.1.

The FOR in the generate statement acts exactly like the FOR loop sequential statement, in that variable *i* need not be declared previously, *i* is not visible outside the generate statement, and *i* cannot be assigned inside the generate statement.

The result of the generate statement is functionally equivalent to the following architecture:

```
ARCHITECTURE long_way_shift OF shift IS
  COMPONENT dff
    PORT( d, clk : IN std_logic;
          q : OUT std_logic);
  END COMPONENT;

  SIGNAL z : std_logic_vector( 0 TO 4 );
BEGIN
  z(0) <= a;

  dff1: dff PORT MAP( z(0), clk, z(1) );
  dff2: dff PORT MAP( z(1), clk, z(2) );
  dff3: dff PORT MAP( z(2), clk, z(3) );
  dff4: dff PORT MAP( z(3), clk, z(4) );
```

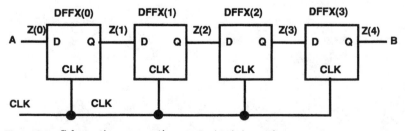

Figure 8.1 Schematic representing generate statement.

```
  b <= z(4);
END long_way_shift;
```

The difference between the two architectures is that architecture *gen_shift* could be specified with generic parameters such that different size shift registers could be generated based on the value of the generic parameters. Architecture *long_way_shift* is fixed in size and cannot be changed.

Irregular generate statement

The last example showed how a regular structure could be generated, but in practice most structures are not completely regular. Most regular structures have irregularities at the edges. This is shown by Fig. 8.2.

In the last example, the irregularities were handled by the two concurrent signal assignment statements. Another way to handle the irregularities is shown by the following example:

```
USE WORK.std_logic_1164.ALL;
ENTITY shift IS
  GENERIC ( len : INTEGER);
  PORT( a, clk : IN std_logic;
        b : OUT std_logic);
END shift;

ARCHITECTURE if_shift OF shift IS
  COMPONENT dff
    PORT( d, clk : IN std_logic;
          q : OUT std_logic);
  END COMPONENT;

  SIGNAL z : std_logic_vector( 1 TO (len -1) );
BEGIN
  g1 : FOR i IN 0 TO (len -1) GENERATE
  g2 : IF i = 0 GENERATE
```

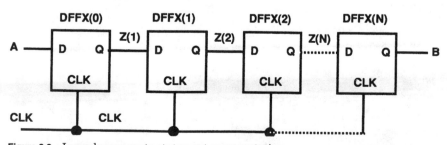

Figure 8.2 Irregular generate statement representation.

```
      dffx : dff PORT MAP( a, clk, z(i + 1));
    END GENERATE;

    g3 : IF i = (len -1) GENERATE
      dffx : dff PORT MAP( z(i), clk, b );
    END GENERATE;
    g4 : IF (i > 0) AND i < (len -1) GENERATE
      dffx : dff PORT MAP( z(i), clk, Z(i + 1) );
    END GENERATE;

  END GENERATE;
END if_shift;
```

This example uses a shift register that has a configurable size. Generic *len* passed in specifies the length of the shift register (generic *len* must be at least 2 for the shift register to work properly). Generic *len* is used in the specification of the length of signal array *z*. This type of array is known as a *generically constrained array* because the size of the array is specified through one or more generics.

The FOR clause of the generate also uses generic *len* to specify the maximum number of DFF components to be generated. Notice that this generate statement uses the conditional form of the generate statement. If the condition is true, the concurrent statements inside the generate statement are generated; otherwise, nothing is generated.

The first IF-THEN condition checks for the first flip-flop in the shift register. If this is the first flip-flop, notice that the port map clause will map the input signal *a* directly to the flip-flop instead of through an intermediate signal. The same is true of the next IF-THEN condition. It checks for the last flip-flop of the shift register and maps the last output to output port *b*. Any other flip-flops in the shift register are generated by the third conditional generate statement.

Another interesting example using the conditional generate statement is as follows:

```
PACKAGE gen_cond IS
  TYPE t_checks IS ( onn, off);
END gen_cond;

USE WORK.gen_cond.ALL;
USE WORK.std_logic_1164.ALL;
ENTITY dff IS
  GENERIC( timing_checks : t_checks;
           setup, qrise, qfall, qbrise, qbfall : time);
  PORT( din, clk : IN std_logic;
        q, qb : OUT std_logic);
END dff;
```

```
ARCHITECTURE condition OF dff IS
BEGIN
  G1 : IF (timing_checks = onn) GENERATE
     ASSERT ( din'LAST_EVENT >setup)
        REPORT "setup violation"
        SEVERITY ERROR;
   END GENERATE;

   PROCESS(clk)
     VARIABLE int_qb : std_logic;
   BEGIN
     IF (clk = '1') AND (clk'EVENT) AND (clk'LAST_VALUE = '0') THEN
        int_qb := not din;

        q <= din AFTER calc_delay( din, qrise, qfall);

        qb <= int_qb AFTER calc_delay( int_qb, qbrise, qbfall);
     END IF;
   END PROCESS;
END condition;
```

In this example, a DFF component is modeled using a generate statement to control whether or not a timing check statement is generated for the architecture. The generic, *timing_checks,* can be passed a value of *onn* or *off* (we cannot use a value of *on* because it is a reserved word). If the value is *onn,* then the generate statement will generate a concurrent assertion statement. If the value of generic *timing_checks* is *off,* then no assertion statement is generated. This functionality emulates the conditional compilation capability of some programming languages, such as C and Pascal.

TextIO

One of the predefined packages that is supplied with VHDL is the Textual Input and Output (TextIO) package. The TextIO package contains procedures and functions that allow the designer the capability of reading from, and writing to, formatted text files. These text files are ASCII files of any format that the designer desires (VHDL does not impose any limits of format, but the host machine might impose limits). TextIO treats these ASCII files as files of lines, where a line is a string, terminated by a carriage return. There are procedures to read a line, write a line, and a function that checks for end of file.

The TextIO package also declares a number of types that are used while processing text files. Type *line* is declared in the TextIO package and is used to hold a line to write to a file or a line that has just been read from the file. The *line* structure is the basic unit upon which all

TextIO operations are performed. For instance, when reading from a file, the first step is to read a line from the file into a structure of type *line*. Then the *line* structure is processed field by field.

The opposite is true for writing to a file. First the *line* structure is built field-by-field in a temporary line data structure, then the *line* is written to the file.

A very simple example of a TextIO behavior is as follows:

```
USE STD.TEXTIO.ALL;
USE WORK.std_logic_1164.ALL;
ENTITY square IS
  PORT( go : IN std_logic);
END square;

ARCHITECTURE simple OF square IS
BEGIN
  PROCESS(go)
    FILE infile : TEXT IS IN "/doug/test/example1";

    FILE outfile : TEXT IS OUT "/doug/test/outfile1";

    VARIABLE out_line, my_line : LINE;
    VARIABLE int_val : INTEGER;
  BEGIN
    WHILE NOT( ENDFILE(infile)) LOOP
      -- read a line from the input file
      READLINE( infile, my_line);

      -- read a value from the line
      READ( my_line, int_val);

      -- square the value
      int_val := int_val **2;

      -- write the squared value to the line
      WRITE( out_line, int_val);

      -- write the line to the output file
      WRITELINE( outfile, out_line);
    END LOOP;
  END PROCESS;
END simple;
```

This example shows how to read a single integer value from a line, square the value, and write the squared value to another file. It illustrates how TextIO can be used to read values from files and write values to files.

The process statement is executed whenever signal *go* has an event occur. The process will then loop until an end-of-file condition occurs on the input file *infile*. The READLINE statement reads a line from the file and places the line in variable *my_line*. The next executable line contains a READ procedure call that will read a single integer value from *my_line* into variable *int_val*. Procedure READ is an overloaded procedure that will read different type values from the line, depending on the type of the argument passed to it.

Once the value from the file has been read into variable *int_val*, the variable is squared, and the squared value is written to another variable of type *line*, called *out_line*. Procedure WRITE is also an overloaded procedure that will write a number of different value types, depending on the type of the argument passed to it.

The last TextIO procedure call made is the WRITELINE procedure call. This procedure will write out the line variable *out_line* to the output file *outfile*.

If the following input file is used as input to this architecture, the second file shown will reflect the output generated.

```
10
20
50
16#A#       <-- hex input
1_2_3       <-- underscores ignored
87     52  <-- second argument ignored
```

The output from the input file would look like this:

```
100
400
2500
100
15129
7569
```

The first value in the input file is 10. It is squared to result in 100 and written to the output file. The same is true for the values 20 and 50. The next value in the file is specified in hexadecimal notation. A hexadecimal A value is 10 base ten, which squared results in 100.

The next example in the file shows a number with embedded underscore characters. The underscores are used to separate fields of a number and are ignored in the value of the number. The number 1_2_3 is the same as 123.

The last entry in the input file shows a line with two input values on the line. When the line is read into the *my_line* variable, both values will exist in the line but, because there is only one READ procedure call, only the first value will be read from the line.

More than one data item can be read from a single line, as well as data items of any types. For instance, a TextIO file could be a list of instructions for a microprocessor. The input file could contain the type of instruction, a source address, and a destination address. This is shown by the simple example here:

```
USE WORK.TEXTIO.ALL;
PACKAGE p_cpu IS
  TYPE t_instr IS (jump, load,
                   store, addd,
                   subb, test, noop);

  FUNCTION convertstring( s : STRING) RETURN t_instr;

END p_cpu;

PACKAGE BODY p_cpu IS
  FUNCTION convertstring( s : STRING) RETURN t_instr IS
    SUBTYPE twochar IS string(1 to 2);
    VARIABLE val : twochar;
  BEGIN
    val := s(1 to 2);
    CASE val IS

      WHEN "ju" =>
       RETURN jump;
      WHEN "lo" =>
       RETURN load;
      WHEN "st" =>
       RETURN store;
      WHEN "ad" =>
       RETURN addd;
      WHEN "su" =>
       RETURN subb;
      WHEN "te" =>
       RETURN test;
      WHEN "no" =>
       RETURN noop;
      WHEN others =>
       RETURN noop;
    END CASE;
  END convertstring;
END p_cpu;

USE WORK.p_cpu.ALL;
USE WORK.TEXTIO.ALL;
  ENTITY cpu_driver IS
    PORT( next_instr : IN BOOLEAN;
      instr : OUT t_instr;
      src : OUT INTEGER;
```

```
      dst : OUT INTEGER);
  END cpu_driver;

  ARCHITECTURE a_cpu_driver OF cpu_driver IS
    FILE instr_file : TEXT IS IN "instfile";
  BEGIN
    read_instr : PROCESS( next_instr)
      VARIABLE aline : LINE;
      VARIABLE a_instr : STRING(1 to 4);
      VARIABLE asrc, adst : INTEGER;
    BEGIN
      IF next_instr THEN
        IF ENDFILE(instr_file) THEN
          ASSERT FALSE
            REPORT "end of instructions"
            SEVERITY WARNING;
        ELSE
          READLINE( instr_file, aline);
          READ( aline, a_instr);
          READ( aline, asrc);
          READ( aline, adst);
        END IF;

        instr <= convertstring(a_instr);
        src <= asrc;
        dst <= adst;

      END IF;
    END PROCESS read_instr;
  END a_cpu_driver;
```

Package *p_cpu* defines type *t_instr,* the enumerated type that represents CPU instructions to be executed. The package also defines a function, *convert_string,* that will be used to convert the string value read in using TextIO procedures into a *t_instr type.* The conversion is necessary because the TextIO package does not contain any procedures for reading in user-defined types (however, a designer can write a user-defined overloaded procedure that has the same basic interface as the procedures in the TextIO package). This process is usually very straightforward, as seen by the *convert_string* procedure.

Entity *cpu_driver* is the entity that will be reading in the file of instructions. It has a single input port called *next_instr* which is used to signal the entity to read in the next instruction. When a true event occurs on input port *next_instr,* process *read_instr* will execute. If the file is at the end already, the assert statement will be called, and a warning message will be issued. If we are not at the end of the file, the process will read in a line from the file into variable *aline.*

Successive reads on variable *aline* will retrieve the appropriate fields from the line. All of the reads return the value into internal variables, but variables *asrc* and *adst* were not really needed because there exists a TextIO procedure for reading integer values. Variable *ainstr* was used to allow the string read in to be converted into the enumerated type *t_instr* before being assigned to the output port *instr.*

This chapter showed some of the more esoteric features of VHDL, and concludes the discussion of VHDL features. The next two chapters will concentrate on the synthesis process and how to write VHDL for synthesis. The following few chapters will then guide the reader through a top-down description of a device.

Synthesis

One of the most useful applications of VHDL today is for synthesizing ASIC descriptions. This chapter and the next will focus on how to write VHDL for synthesis.

Synthesis is an automatic method of converting a higher level of abstraction to a lower level of abstraction. There are several synthesis tools available currently, including commercial as well as university-developed tools. In this discussion, the examples will use the commercially available Synopsys VHDL Compiler and Synopsys Design Compiler™ tools.

The current Synthesis tools available today convert Register Transfer Level (RTL) descriptions to gate-level netlists. These gate-level netlists consist of interconnected gate-level macro cells. Models for the gate-level cells are contained in technology libraries for each type of technology supported. These gate-level netlists currently can be optimized for area, speed, testability, etc. The synthesis process is shown in Fig. 9.1.

The inputs to the synthesis process are an RTL (Register Transfer Level) VHDL description, circuit constraints and attributes for the design, and a technology library. The synthesis process produces an optimized gate-level netlist from all of these inputs. In the next few sections, each of these inputs will be described, and we will discuss the synthesis process in more detail.

Register Transfer-Level Description

A register transfer-level description is characterized by a style that specifies all of the registers in a design, and the combinational logic between. This is shown by the "register and cloud" diagram in Fig. 9.2.

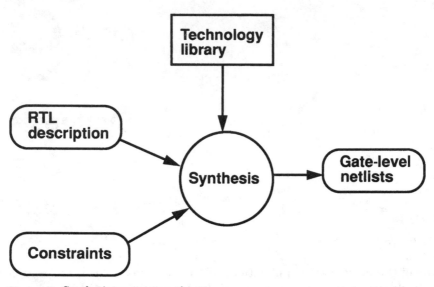

Figure 9.1 Synthesis process overview.

The registers are described either explicitly, through component instantiation, or implicitly, through inference. The registers are shown as the rectangular objects connected to the clock signal. The combinational logic is described either by logical equations, sequential control statements (CASE, IF then ELSE, etc.), subprograms, or through concurrent statements, and are represented by the "cloud" objects between registers.

RTL descriptions are used for synchronous designs and describe the clock-by-clock behavior of the design. An example of an RTL description that uses component instantiation is as follows:

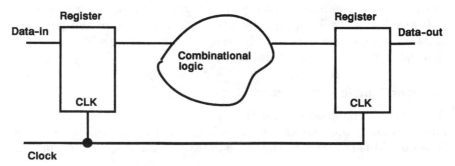

Figure 9.2 Register and cloud diagram.

```
ENTITY datadelay IS
  PORT( clk, din, en : IN BIT;
        dout : OUT BIT);
END datadelay;

ARCHITECTURE synthesis OF datadelay IS
  COMPONENT dff
      PORT(clk, din : IN BIT;
           q,qb : OUT BIT);
  END COMPONENT;
    SIGNAL q1, q2, qb1, qb2 : BIT;
BEGIN

    r1 : dff PORT MAP(clk, din, q1, qb1);
    r2 : dff PORT MAP(clk, q1, q2, qb2);

    dout <= q1 WHEN en = '1' ELSE
             q2;

END synthesis;
```

This example is the circuit for a selectable data delay circuit. The circuit will delay the input signal *din* by 1 or 2 clocks, depending on the value of *en*. If *en* is a 1, then input *din* will be delayed by 1 clock. If *en* is a 0, input *din* will be delayed by 2 clocks.

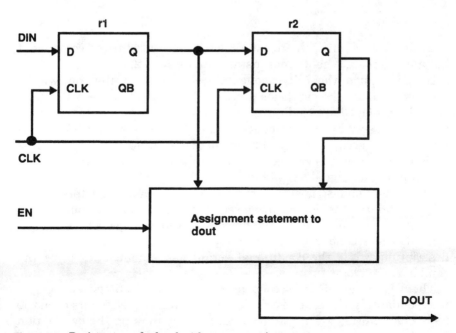

Figure 9.3   Register transfer level with component instances.

Figure 9.3 shows a schematic representation of this circuit. The clock signal connects to the *clk* input of both flip-flops, while the *din* signal connects only to the first flip-flop. The *q* output of the first flip-flop is then connected to the *d* input of the next flip-flop. The selected signal assignment to signal *dout* forms a mux operation that selects between the two flip-flop outputs.

This example could be rewritten as follows, using register inference:

```
ENTITY datadelay IS
  PORT( clk, din, en : IN BIT;
        dout : OUT BIT);
END datadelay;

ARCHITECTURE inference OF datadelay IS
  SIGNAL q1, q2 : BIT;
BEGIN
  reg_proc: PROCESS
  BEGIN

    WAIT UNTIL clk'EVENT and clk = '1';

    q1 <= din;
    q2 <= q1;

  END PROCESS;

    dout <= q1 WHEN en = '1' ELSE
            q2;

END inference;
```

In the first version, the registers are instantiated using component instantiation statements that instantiate *r1* and *r2*.

In this version, the *dff* components are not instantiated, but will be inferred through the synthesis process. Register inference will be discussed more in Chap. 10. Process *reg_proc* has a WAIT statement that will be triggered by positive edges on the clock. When the WAIT statement is triggered, signal *q1* is assigned the value of *din,* and *q2* is assigned the previous value of *q1*. This, in effect, creates two flip-flops. One flip-flop for signal *q1*, and the other for signal *q2*.

This is a register transfer-level description because registers *r1* and *r2* from the first version form the registers, and the conditional signal assignment for port *dout* forms the combinational logic between registers. In the second version, the inferred registers form the register description, while the conditional signal assignment still forms the combinational logic.

The advantage of the second description is that it is technology-independent. In the first description, actual flip-flop elements from the technology library were instantiated, thereby making the description technology-dependent. If the designer should decide to change technologies, all of the instances of the flip-flops would need to be changed to the flip-flops from the new technology. In the second version of the design, the designer did not specify particular technology library components, and the synthesis tools are free to select flip-flops from whatever technology library the designer is currently using, as long as these flip-flops match the functionality required.

After synthesis, both of these descriptions produce a gate-level description as shown in Fig. 9.4.

Notice that the gate-level description has two registers, with mux logic controlling the output signal from each register. Depending on the technology library selected and the constraints, the mux logic will vary widely from and-or-invert gates to instantiated two-input multiplexers.

The netlist generated by the Synopsys Design Compiler for the same design is as follows:

```
entity datadelay is

   port( clk, din, en : in BIT; dout : out BIT);

end datadelay;

architecture STRUCTURAL_VIEW of datadelay is

  component MUX21L
    port( A, B, S : in BIT; Z : out BIT);
  end component;

  component FD1
    port( D, CP : in BIT; Q, QN : out BIT);
  end component;

  signal q1, net18, net17 : BIT;

  begin
```

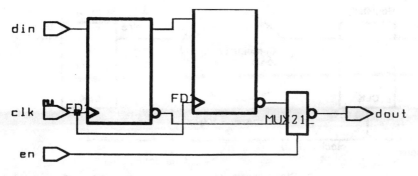

Figure 9.4 Data delay design after mapping.

```
q2_reg : FD1 port map( D => q1, CP => clk, Q => open, QN => net18);
q1_reg : FD1 port map( D => din, CP => clk, Q => q1, QN => net17);
U10 : MUX21L port map( A => net18, B => net17, S => en, Z => dout);
end STRUCTURAL_VIEW;
```

It produces the logic one would expect to see from the description entered.

Constraints

Constraints are used to control the output of the optimization and mapping process. They provide goals that the optimization and mapping processes try to meet, and they control the structural implementation of the design. The constraints available in synthesis tools today include area, timing, power, and testability constraints. In the future, we will probably see packaging constraints, layout constraints, etc. However, the most common constraints in use today are the area and timing constraints.

A block diagram of a design with some possible contraints is shown in Fig. 9.5. Again, the design is shown using the "register and cloud" notation. The combinational logic between registers is represented as clouds, with wires going in and out representing the interconnection to the registers.

There are a number of constraints shown on the diagram, including maximum delay constraints, late arrival constraints, clock constraints, and area constraints for the entire design.

Maximum delay constraints specify the latest time that a signal can occur. Clock constraints are used to specify the operating frequency of

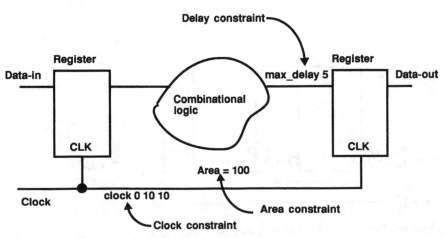

Figure 9.5   Register and cloud diagram with constraints.

the clock. From the clock constraint, maximum delay constraints of each signal feeding a clocked register can be calculated. The area constraint specifies the largest area that the design should take. These constraints are discussed in the sections that follow.

Area constraints

Area constraints are used to specify an area goal within which the designer wishes the circuit to stay. Most synthesis tools allow the designer to specify the area goal in the units used to describe the gate-level macro cells in the technology library. For instance, if the technology library used gate equivalents as the unit of measure for each cell, the area goal would be specified in terms of gate equivalents. A typical area constraint in Synopsys Design Compiler format is as follows:

```
max_area 1200
```

This constraint tells the synthesis tool to optimize the design until the design is less than or equal to 1200 library units.

Synthesis tools usually allow the designer to specify a nonzero value for the area such that, when the synthesis tool meets that area constraint, it stops optimizing. Alternately, if the value 0 is specified, the synthesis tool will try all possible rules and algorithms to get the design as small as possible.

Specifying a 0 delay can backfire for some algorithms. Some tools will produce a better result when realistic goals are specified. When 0 delay is specified for all output signals, the tools will work very hard to produce that result. In the process, outputs which are not needed until later will be optimized for speed. Therefore, the resultant design may be unnecessarily large because some of the slower outputs have been heavily buffered, or parallelized, to create a faster output signal.

Timing constraints

Typical uses for timing constraints are to specify maximum delays for particular paths in a circuit. For instance, a typical timing constraint is the maximum delay for an output port. The timing constraint guides the optimization and mapping to produce a netlist that meets the timing constraint. Meeting timing is usually one of the most difficult tasks when designing an ASIC using synthesis tools. There may be no design that meets the timing constraints specified. A typical delay constraint in Synopsys Design Compiler format is as follows:

```
max_delay 1.7 data_out
```

This constraint specifies that the maximum delay for signal *data_out* should be less than or equal to 1.7 library units.

Some synthesis tools (such as the Synopsys Design Compiler) do a static timing analysis to calculate the delay for each of the nodes in the design. The static timing analyzer uses a timing model for each element connected in the netlist. The timing analyzer calculates the worst- and best-case timing for each node by adding the contribution of each cell that it traverses.

The circuit is then checked to see if all delay constraints have been met. If so, the optimization and mapping process is done; otherwise, alternate optimization strategies may be applied, such as adding more parallelism or more buffered outputs to the slow paths, and the timing analysis is executed again. More detail about the typical timing analysis is discussed in the technology library section.

Attributes

Attributes are used to specify the environment in which the design will live. For instance, attributes specify the loading that the output devices will have to drive, the drive capability of the devices driving the design, and the timing of the input signals. All of this information is taken into account by the static timing analyzer to calculate the timing through the circuit paths. A "cloud" diagram showing attributes is shown in Fig. 9.6.

Load

Each output can specify a drive capability that determines how many loads can be driven within a particular time. Each input can have a

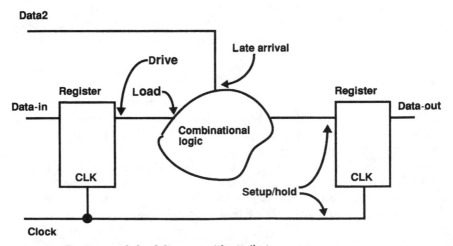

Figure 9.6 Register and cloud diagram with attributes.

load value specified that determines how much it will slow a particular driver. Signals that are arriving later than the clock can have an attribute that specifies this fact.

The Load attribute specifies how much capacitive load exists on a particular output signal. This load value is specified in the units of the technology library in terms of picofarads or standard loads, etc. For instance, the timing analyzer will calculate a long delay for a weak driver and a large capacitive load, and a short delay for a strong driver and a small load. The following is an example of a load specification in Synopsys Design Compiler™ format:

```
set_load 5 xbus
```

This attribute specifies that signal *xbus* will load the driver of this signal with 5 library units of load.

Drive

The Drive attribute specifies the resistance of the driver, which controls how much current it can source. This attribute will also be specified in the units of the technology library. The larger a driver is, the faster a particular path will be, but a larger driver will take more area, so the designer needs to trade off speed and area for the best possible implementation. An example of a drive specification in Synopsys Design Compiler™ format is as follows:

```
set_drive 2.7 ybus
```

This attribute specifies that signal *ybus* has 2.7 library units of drive capability.

Arrival time

Some synthesis tools (Synopsys Design Compiler™) use a static timing analyzer during the synthesis process to check that the logic being created matches the timing constraints the user has specified. Setting the arrival time on a particular node specifies to the static timing analyzer when a particular signal will occur at a node. This is especially important for late-arriving signals. Late-arriving signals drive inputs to the current block at a later time, but the results of the current block still must meet its own timing constraints on its outputs. Therefore, the path to the output of the late-arriving input must be faster than any other inputs, or the timing constraints of the current block cannot be met.

Shown here is the VHDL description of a design:

```
USE WORK.std_logic_1164.ALL;
ENTITY or3 IS
```

```
    PORT (a, b, c, x ,y : IN std_logic;
        d : OUT std_logic);
END or3;

ARCHITECTURE synth OF or3 IS
BEGIN
    d <= a OR b OR ((c and y) and x);
END synth;
```

Figure 9.7 shows the gate-level implementation of the design after synthesis. In this example, all inputs arrive at basically the same time. Figure 9.8 shows the same design with the b input arriving at time 1.5 ns. Notice how in the second example the number of logic levels from input b to the output is much less than in Fig. 9.7. Since input b arrives late, but still has to make the timing constraints for the entire design, the path from input b to the output must be faster than the other inputs.

Technology Libraries

Technology libraries hold all of the information necessary for a synthesis tool to create a netlist for a design based on the desired logical behavior and constraints on the design. Technology libraries contain all of the information that allows the synthesis process to make the correct choices to build a design. Technology libraries contain not only the logical function of an ASIC cell, but the area of the cell, the input-to-output timing of

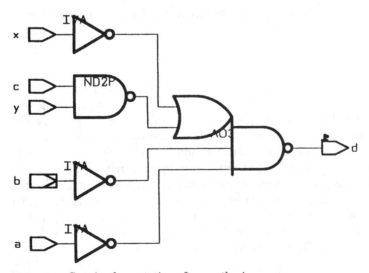

Figure 9.7 Gate implementation after synthesis.

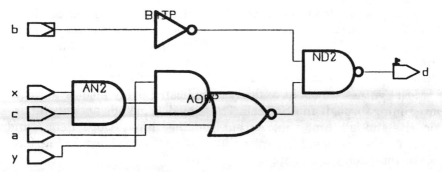

Figure 9.8 Gate implementation with late signal arrival.

the cell, any constraints on fanout of the cell, and the timing checks that are required for the cell. Other information stored in the technology library may be the graphical symbol of the cell for use in schematics.

The following is an example technology library description of a two-input AND gate written in Synopsys format:

```
library (xyz) {
cell (and2) {
  area : 5;
  pin (a1, a2) {
        direction : input;
        capacitance : 1;
  }
  pin (o1) {
        direction : output;
        function : "a1 * a2";
        timing () {
        intrinsic_rise : 0.37;
        intrinsic_fall : 0.56;
        rise_resistance : 0.1234;
        fall_resistance : 0.4567;
        related_pin : "a1 a2";
    }
  }
 }
 }
```

This technology library describes a library named *xyz* with one library cell contained in it. The cell is named *and2*, and has two input pins *a1* and *a2*, and one output pin *o1*. The cell requires 5 units of area and the input pins have 1 unit of loading capacitance to the driver driving them. The intrinsic rise and fall delays listed with pin *o1* specify the delay to the output with no loading. The timing analyzer uses the intrinsic delays plus the rise-and-fall resistance with the output loading to calculate the delay through a particular gate. Notice that the function of pin *o1* is listed as the AND of pins *a1* and *a2*. Also notice that pin *o1* is related to pins *a1* and *a2* such that the timing delay through the device is calculated from pins *a1* and *a2* to pin *o1*.

Most synthesis tools have fairly complicated delay models to calculate timing through an ASIC cell. These models include not only intrinsic rise-and-fall time, but output loading, input slope delay, and estimated wire delay. A diagram illustrating this is shown in Fig. 9.9.

The total delay from gate A1 to gate C1 is:

$$\text{intrinsic\_delay} + \text{loading\_delay} + \text{wire\_delay} + \text{slope\_delay}$$

The intrinsic delay is the delay of the gate without any loading. The loading delay is the delay due to the input capacitance of the gate being driven. The wire delay is an estimated delay used to model the delay through a typical wire used to connect cells together. It can be a statistical model of the wire delays, usually based on the size of the chip die. Given a particular die size, the wire loading effect can be calculated and added to the overall delay. The final component in the delay equation is the extra delay needed to handle the case of slowly rising inputs signals due usually to heavy loading or light drive.

In the preceding technology library, the intrinsic delays are given in the cell description. The loading delay is calculated based on the load applied to the output pin *o1* and the resistance values in the cell description. The value calculated for the wire delay will depend on the die size selected by the user. Selecting a wire model will scale the delay values. Finally, the input slope delay is calculated by the size of the

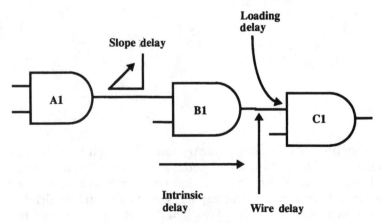

Figure 9.9 Delay effects used in delay model.

driver (in this example, A1) and the capacitance of the gate being driven. The capacitance of the gate being driven will be in the technology library description.

Technology libraries can also contain data about how to scale delay information with respect to process parameters and operating conditions. Operating conditions are the device operating temperature and power supply voltage applied to the device.

Synthesis

To convert the RTL description to gates, three steps typically occur. First the RTL description is translated to an unoptimized boolean description usually consisting of primitive gates such as AND and OR gates, flip-flops, and latches. This is a functionally correct but completely unoptimized description. Then, boolean optimization algorithms are executed on this boolean equivalent description to produce an optimized boolean equivalent description. Finally, this optimized boolean equivalent description is mapped to actual logic gates by making use of a technology library of the target process. This is shown in Fig. 9.10.

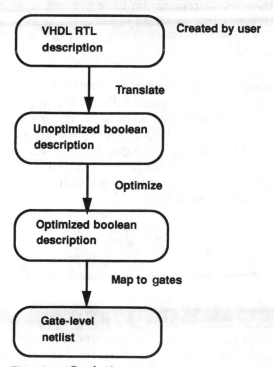

Figure 9.10   Synthesis process.

Translation

The translation from RTL description to boolean equivalent description is usually not user-controllable. The intermediate form that is generated is usually a format that is optimized for a particular tool and may not even be viewable by the user.

All IF, CASE, LOOP statements and conditional signal assignments and selected signal assignment statements are converted to their boolean equivalent in this intermediate form. Flip-flops and latches can either be instantiated or inferred; both cases produce the same flip-flop or latch entry in the intermediate description.

Boolean optimization

The optimization process takes an unoptimized boolean description and converts it to an optimized boolean description. In a lot of designers' eyes, this is where the real work of synthesis gets done. The optimization process uses a number of algorithms and rules to convert the unoptimized boolean description to an optimized one. One technique is to convert the unoptimized boolean description to a very low level description (a *pla* format), optimize that description (using *pla* optimization techniques), and then try to reduce the logic generated by sharing common terms (introducing intermediate variables).

Flattening

The process of converting the unoptimized boolean description to a pla format is known as flattening, because it creates a flat signal representation of only two levels: an AND level and an OR level. The idea is to get the unoptimized boolean description into a format in which optimization algorithms can be used to optimize the logic. A pla structure is a very easy description in which to perform boolean optimization because it has a simple structure and the algorithms are well known. An example of a boolean description is as follows:

```
Original equations

a = b and c;
b = x or (y and z);
c = q or w;
```

This description shows an output "a" that has three equations describing its function. These equations use two intermediate variables b and c to hold temporary values which are then used to calculate the final value for a. These equations describe a particular structure of the design that contains two intermediate nodes or signals, *b* and *c*. The flattening process removes these intermediate nodes to produce a completely flat design, with no intermediate nodes. This is shown as follows:

```
After removing intermediate variables

a = (x and q) or (q and y and z) or (w and x) or (w and y and z);
```

This second description is the boolean equivalent of the first, but it has no intermediate nodes. This design contains only two levels of logic gates, an AND plane and an OR plane. This should result in a very fast design because there are very few logic levels from the input to the output. In fact, the design is usually very fast. There are a number of problems with this type of design, however.

First of all, this type of design can actually be slower than one that has more logic levels. The reason is that this type of design can have a tremendous fanout loading on the input signals because inputs fan out to every term. Second, this type of design can be very large, because there is no sharing between terms. Every term has to calculate its own functionality. Also, there are a number of circuits which are difficult to flatten, because the number of terms created is extremely large. An equation that contains only AND functions will produce one term. A function that contains a large XOR function could produce hundreds or even thousands of terms. A two-input XOR will have the terms A and (not B) or B and (not A). An N input XOR will have $2^{**}(N-1)$ terms. For instance, a 16-input XOR would have 32768 terms, and a 32-bit XOR would have over 2 billion terms. Clearly, designs with these types of functions in them cannot be flattened.

Flattening gets rid of all of the implied structure of design whether it is good or not. Flattening works best with small pieces of random control logic that the designer wants to minimize. Used in conjunction with factoring, a minimal logic description can be generated.

Usually, the designer wants a design that is nearly as fast as the flattened design, but much smaller in area. To reduce the fanout of the input pins, terms are shared. Some synthesis vendors (Synopsys) call this process structuring.

Factoring

Factoring is the process of adding intermediate terms to add structure to a description. It is the opposite of the flattening process. Factoring is usually desirable because, as was mentioned in the last section, flattened designs are usually very big, and may be slower than a factored design because of the amount of fanouts generated. The following is a design before factoring:

```
x = a and b or a and d;
y = z or b or d;
```

After factoring, the common term (*b* or *d*) is factored out to a separate intermediate node. The results are as follows:

```
x = a and q;
y = z or q;
q = b or d;
```

Factoring will usually produce a "better" design but can be very design-dependent. Adding structure adds levels of logic between the inputs and outputs. Adding levels of logic will add more delay. The net result is a smaller design, but a slower design. Typically, the designer wants a design that is nearly as fast as the flattened design if it was driven by large drivers, but as small as the completely factored design. The ideal case would be one in which the critical path was flattened for speed and the rest of the design was factored for small area and low fanout.

After the design has been optimized at the boolean level, it can be mapped to the gate functions in a technology library.

Mapping to gates

The mapping process takes the logically optimized boolean description created by the optimization step and uses the logical and timing information from a technology library to build a netlist. This netlist is targeted to the user's needs for area and speed. There are a number of possible netlists that are functionally the same but vary widely in speed and area. Some netlists are very fast but take a lot of library cells to implement, and others take a small number of library cells to implement but are very slow.

To illustrate this point let's look at a couple of netlists that implement the same functionality. The VHDL description is as follows:

```
ENTITY adder IS
  PORT( a,b : IN BIT_VECTOR(3 DOWNTO 0);
        c : OUT BIT_VECTOR(3 DOWNTO 0)
      );
END adder;

ARCHITECTURE test OF adder IS
BEGIN
  c <= a + b;
END test;
```

Both of the examples implement a 4-bit adder, but the first implementation is a small but slow design, and the second is a big but fast

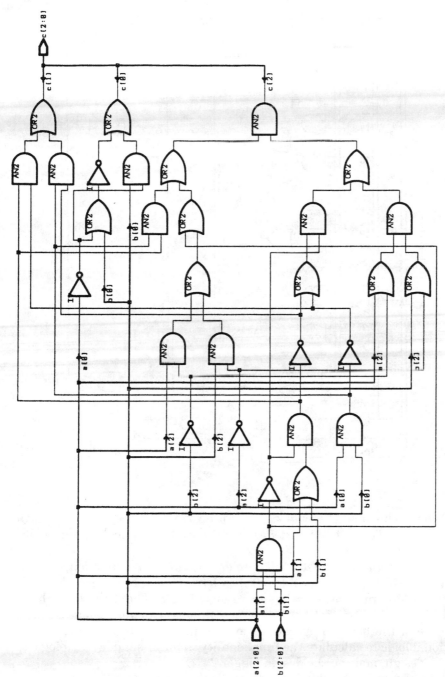

Figure 9.11 Minimum area mapping.

239

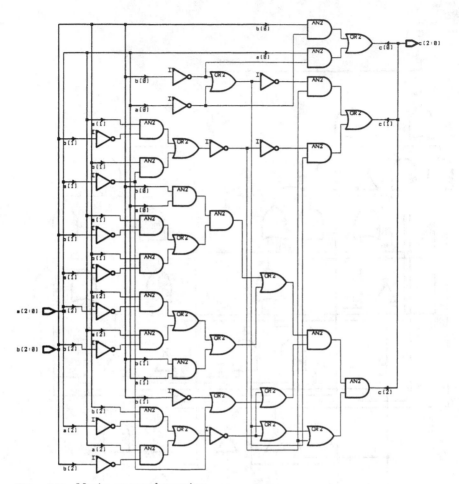

Figure 9.12 Maximum speed mapping.

design. The small, slow design is a 4-bit ripple carry adder shown in Fig. 9.11. The big but fast design is a 4-bit carry look-ahead adder shown in Fig. 9.12.

Both of these netlists will implement the same function, a 4-bit adder. The ripple carry adder takes less cells to implement but is a slower design because it has more logic levels. The carry look-ahead adder takes more cells to implement but is a faster design because more of the boolean operations are calculated in parallel. The additional logic to calculate the functionality in parallel adds extra logic to the design, making the design bigger.

In the Synopsys Design Compiler, the designer has control over which type of adder is selected through the use of constraints. If the designer wants to constrain the design to a very small area, and doesn't need the fastest possible speed, then the ripple carry adder will probably work. If the designer wants the design to be as fast as possible and doesn't care as much about how big the design gets, then the carry look-ahead adder will be selected.

The mapping process takes as input the optimized boolean description, the technology library, and the user constraints; it generates an optimized netlist built entirely from cells in the technology library. During the mapping process, cells are inserted which implement the boolean function from the optimized boolean description. These cells are then locally optimized to meet speed and area requirements. As a final step, the synthesis tool has to make sure that the output does not violate any of the rules of the technology being used to implement the design, such as the maximum number of fanouts a particular cell can have.

In this chapter we have discussed some of the basic principles of the synthesis process. In the next chapter we will take a closer look at how to write models that can be synthesized.

VHDL Synthesis

In this chapter we will focus on how to write VHDL that can be read by synthesis tools. We will start out with some simple combinational logic examples, move on to some sequential models, and end the chapter with a state machine description.

All of the examples were synthesized with the Synopsys VHDL Compiler and Synopsys Design Compiler. The technology library used was a training library used for Synopsys training. All of the output data should be treated simply as sample outputs and not representative of how well the Synopsys Design Compiler™ and VHDL Compiler™ work with real design data.

Simple Gate Using Concurrent Assignment Statement

The first example is a simple description for a three-input OR gate.

```
USE WORK.std_logic_1164.ALL;
ENTITY or3 IS
  PORT (a, b, c : IN std_logic;
        d : OUT std_logic);
END or3;

ARCHITECTURE synth OF or3 IS
BEGIN
  d <= a OR b OR c;
END synth;
```

This model uses a simple concurrent assignment statement to describe the functionality of the OR gate. The model specifies the functionality required for this entity, but not the implementation. The synthesis tool can choose to implement this functionality in a number of ways, depending on the cells available in the technology library and the constraints on the model. For instance, the most obvious implementation is shown in Fig. 10.1.

This implementation uses a three-input OR gate to implement the functionality specified in the concurrent signal assignment statement contained in architecture *synth*.

What if the technology library did not contain a three-input OR device? Two other possible implementations are shown in Figs. 10.2 and 10.3.

The first implementation uses a three-input NOR gate followed by an inverter. The synthesis tool may choose this implementation if there are no three-input OR devices in the technology library. Alternatively, if there are no three-input devices, or if the three-input devices violate a speed constraint, the three-input OR function could be built from four-input devices as shown in Fig. 10.3. Given a technology library of parts, the functionality desired, and design constraints, the synthesis tool is free to choose among any of the implementations that satisfy all the requirements of a design, if such a design exists. There are lots of

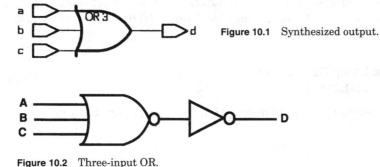

Figure 10.1   Synthesized output.

Figure 10.2   Three-input OR.

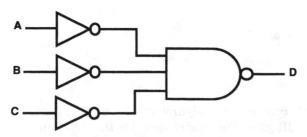

Figure 10.3   Another three-input OR implementation.

cases where the technology or constraints are such that no design can meet all of the design requirements.

IF Control Flow Statements

In this example, control flow statements such as IF THEN ELSE are used to demonstrate how synthesis from a higher-level description is accomplished. This example forms the control logic for a household alarm system. It uses sensor input from a number of sensors to determine whether or not to trigger different types of alarms. The input description is as follows:

```
USE WORK.std_logic_1164.ALL;
ENTITY alarm_cntrl IS
   PORT( smoke, front_door, back_door, side_door,
           alarm_disable, main_disable,
         water_detect : IN std_logic;
           fire_alarm, burg_alarm,
         water_alarm : OUT std_logic);
END alarm_cntrl;

ARCHITECTURE synth OF alarm_cntrl IS
BEGIN
   PROCESS(smoke, front_door, back_door, side_door, alarm_disable,
main_disable,
             water_detect)
  BEGIN
     IF ((smoke = '1') AND (main_disable = '0')) THEN
       fire_alarm <= '1';
    ELSE
       fire_alarm <= '0';
    END IF;

     IF (((front_door = '1') OR (back_door = '1') OR (side_door = '1'))
AND
           ((alarm_disable = '0') AND (main_disable = '0'))) THEN
       burg_alarm <= '1';
    ELSE
       burg_alarm <= '0';
    END IF;

    IF ((water_detect = '1') AND (main_disable = '0')) THEN
      water_alarm <= '1';
    ELSE
      water_alarm <= '0';
    END IF;
  END PROCESS;
END synth;
```

The input description contains a number of sensor input ports such as: a smoke detector input, a number of door switch inputs, a basement water detector, and two disable signals. The *main_disable* port is used to disable all alarms while the *alarm_disable* port is used to disable only the burglar alarm system.

The functionality is described by three separate IF statements. Each IF statement describes the functionality of one or more output ports. Notice that the functionality could also be described very easily with equations, as in the first example. Sometimes, however, the IF statement style is more readable. For instance, the first IF statement can be described by the following two equations:

```
fire_alarm <= smoke and not(main_disable);
```

Since the three IF statements are separate and they generate separate outputs, we can expect that the resulting logic would be three separate pieces of logic. However, the *main_disable* signal is shared between the three pieces of logic. Any operations that make use of this signal may be shared by the other logic pieces. How this sharing takes place is determined by the synthesis tool and is based on the logical functionality of the design and the constraints. Speed constraints may force the logical operations to be performed in parallel.

A sample synthesized output is shown in Fig. 10.4. Notice that signal *main_disable* connects to all three output NOR gates, while signal *alarm_disable* connects only to the alarm control logic. The logic for the water alarm and smoke detector turn out to be quite simple, but we could have guessed that because our equations were so simple. The next example will not be so simple.

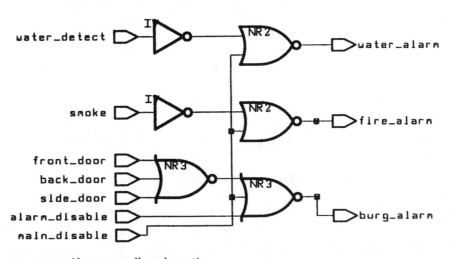

Figure 10.4 Alarm controller schematic.

Case Control Flow Statements

The next example is an implementation of a comparator. There are two 8-bit inputs to be compared, and a CTRL input that determines the type of comparison made. The possible comparison types are: A>B, A<B, A=B, A/= B, A>=B, and A<=B. The design contains one output port for each of the comparison types. If the desired comparison output is true, then the output value on that output port will be a '1'. If false, the output port value will be a '0'. A synthesizable VHDL description of the comparator is as follows:

```
PACKAGE comp_pack IS
  TYPE bit8 is range 0 to 255;
    TYPE t_comp IS (greater_than, less_than, equal, not_equal,
      grt_equal, less_equal);
END comp_pack;

USE WORK.std_logic_1164.ALL;
USE WORK.comp_pack.ALL;
ENTITY compare IS
   PORT( a, b : IN bit8;
          ctrl : IN t_comp;
          gt, lt, eq, neq, gte, lte : OUT std_logic);
  END compare;

ARCHITECTURE synth OF compare IS
BEGIN

  PROCESS(a, b, ctrl)
  BEGIN
    gt <= '0'; lt <= '0'; eq <= '0'; neq <= '0'; gte <= '0'; lte <= '0';
    CASE ctrl IS
      WHEN greater_than =>
        IF (a > b) THEN
          gt <= '1';
        END IF;
      WHEN less_than =>
        IF (a < b) THEN
          lt <= '1';
        END IF;
      WHEN equal =>
        IF (a = b) THEN
          eq <= '1';
        END IF;
      WHEN not_equal =>
        IF (a /= b) THEN
          neq <= '1';
        END IF;
      WHEN grt_equal =>
        IF (a >= b) THEN
          gte <= '1';
        END IF;
```

```
        WHEN less_equal =>
          IF (a > b) THEN
            lte <= '1';
          END IF;
      END CASE;
    END PROCESS;
END synth;
```

Notice that in this example the equations of the inputs and outputs are harder to write because of the comparison operators. It is still possible to do, but will be much less readable than the preceding case statement.

When synthesizing a design, the complexity of the design is related to the complexity of the equations that describe the design function. Typically, the more complex the equations, the more complex the design created. There are exceptions to this rule, especially when the equations reduce to nothing. These, however, are as mentioned, exceptions.

A sample synthesized output from the preceding description is shown in Fig. 10.5. The logic in the upper portion of the plot performs the equality operation, and the logic in the lower left performs the control selection to determine which operator is used. In this example, the Synopsys tool was intelligent enough to create a single comparator element that is shared among all of the less than, greater than, greater than equal, and less than equal operations. For the equality operations, notice that the synthesis tool selected an XOR tree. This design is a very small number of gates for the operation performed.

There are still a number of cases where hand design can create smaller designs, but in most cases today the results of synthesis are very good, and you get the added benefit of using a higher-level design language for easier maintainability and a shorter design cycle.

Simple Sequential Statements

Let's take a closer look at an example that we have already discussed somewhat in the last chapter. This is the inferred D flip-flop. Inferred flip-flops are created by Wait Statements or IF THEN ELSE statements which are surrounded by sensitivities to a clock. By detecting clock edges, the synthesis tool can locate where to insert flip-flops so that the design that is ultimately built behaves the same as the simulation predicts.

An example of a simple sequential design using a Wait Statement is as follows:

```
USE work.std_logic_1164.ALL;
ENTITY dff IS
    PORT( clock, din : IN std_logic;
          dout : OUT std_logic);
```

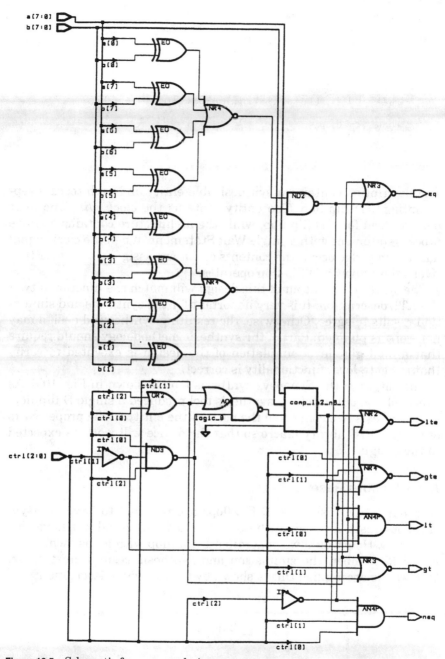

Figure 10.5 Schematic for compare design.

```
END dff;

ARCHITECTURE synth OF dff IS
BEGIN
  PROCESS
  BEGIN
    WAIT UNTIL ((clock'EVENT) AND (clock = '1'));

    dout <= din;

  END PROCESS;
END synth;
```

The description contains a synthesizable entity and architecture representing a D flip-flop. The entity contains the *clock, din,* and *dout* ports needed for a D flip-flop, while the architecture contains a single process statement with a single Wait Statement. When the clock signal has a rising edge occur, the contents of *din* are assigned to *dout.* Effectively, this is how a D flip-flop operates.

The synthesized output of this design will match the functionality of the RTL description. It is very important for the synthesis and simulation results to agree. Otherwise, the resulting synthesized design may not work as planned. Part of the synthesis methodology should require that a final gate-level simulation of the design is executed to verify that the gate-level functionality is correct.

The output of the Synopsys synthesis tool is shown in Fig. 10.6. As expected, the output of the synthesis tool produced a single D flip-flop. The synthesis tool connected the ports of the entity to the proper ports of actual ASIC library macro so that the device will work as expected in the design.

Asynchronous Reset

In a number of instances, D flip-flops are required to have an asynchronous reset capability. The previous D flip-flop did not have this capability. How would we generate a D flip-flop with an asynchronous reset? Remember, the simulation and synthesis results must agree. One way to accomplish this is shown by the following description:

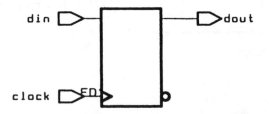

Figure 10.6 Synthesized flip-flop.

```
USE work.std_logic_1164.ALL;
ENTITY dff_asynch IS
    PORT( clock, reset, din : IN std_logic;
          dout : OUT std_logic);
END dff_asynch;

ARCHITECTURE synth OF dff_asynch IS
BEGIN
    PROCESS(rest, clock)
  BEGIN
      IF (reset = '1') THEN
        dout <= '0';
        ELSIF (clock'EVENT) AND (clock = '1') THEN
        dout <= din;
      END IF;
  END PROCESS;
END synth;
```

The entity statement now has an extra input, the *reset* port, which will be used to asynchronously reset the D flip-flop. Notice that *reset* and *clock* are in the process sensitivity list and will cause the process to be evaluated. If an event occurs on either signals *clock* or *reset*, the statements inside the process will be executed.

First, signal *reset* is tested to see if it has an active value ('1'). If active, the output of the flip-flop is reset to '0'. If *reset* is not active ('0'), then the *clock* signal is tested for a rising edge. If signal *clock* has a rising edge, then input *din* is assigned as the new flip-flop output.

The fact that the *reset* signal is tested first in the IF statement gives the *reset* signal a higher priority than the *clock* signal. Also, since the *reset* signal is tested outside of the test for a *clock* edge, the *reset* signal is asynchronous to the *clock*.

The Synopsys Design Compiler™ produces a D flip-flop with an asynchronous reset input, as shown in Fig. 10.7. The resulting design

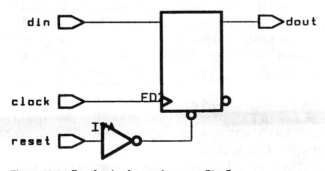

Figure 10.7   Synthesized asynchronous flip-flop.

has an extra inverter in the circuit because the only flip-flop macro that would match the functionality required had a reset input that was active low.

Asynchronous Preset and Clear

Is it possible to describe a flip-flop with an asynchronous preset and clear? As an attempt, we can use the same technique as in the asynchronous reset example. The following example illustrates an attempt to describe a flip-flop with an asynchronous preset and clear inputs.

```
USE work.std_logic_1164.ALL;
ENTITY dff_pc IS
    PORT( preset, clear, clock, din : IN std_logic;
          dout : OUT std_logic);
END dff_pc;

ARCHITECTURE synth OF dff_pc IS
BEGIN
    PROCESS(preset, clear, clock)
  BEGIN
      IF (preset = '1') THEN
         dout <= '1';

      ELSIF (clear = '1') THEN
         dout <= '0';

      ELSIF (clock'EVENT) AND (clock = '1') THEN
         dout <= din;

    END IF;
  END PROCESS;
END synth;
```

The entity contains a *preset* signal which will set the value of the flip-flop to a '1', a *clear* signal which will set the value of the flip-flop to a '0', and the normal *clock* and *din* ports used for the clocked D flip-flop operation. The architecture contains a single process statement with a single IF statement to describe the flip-flop behavior. The IF statement will assign a '1' to the output for a '1' value on the *preset* input, and a '0' to the output for a '1' on the *clear* input. Otherwise, the *clock* input will be checked for a rising edge, and the *din* value clocked to the output *dout*.

What does the output of the synthesis process produce for this VHDL input? The output is shown in Fig. 10.8. We were expecting the output of the synthesis tool in which the design *preset* input was connected to the *preset* input of the flip-flop and the design *clear* input was connected to the *clear* input of the flip-flop. What was output from the syn-

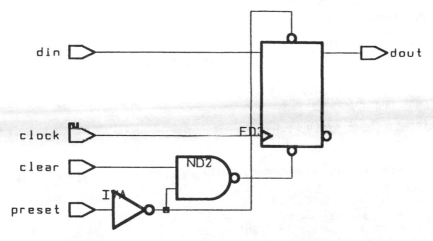

Figure 10.8 Synthesized flip-flop with asynchronous preset and clear.

thesis tool was a design in which the design *preset* and *clear* inputs are separated from the flip-flop *preset* and *clear* inputs by some logic.

This logic circuitry performs a prioritization of the *preset* signal with respect to the *clear* signal. Because the *preset* signal occurs before the *clear* signal in the IF statement, the *preset* signal will be tested before the *clear* signal. If the *preset* signal is active, the flip-flop will preset regardless of the state of the *clear* input. Effectively, the *preset* signal has a higher priority than the *clear* signal. There is currently no way to write a VHDL description to generate a design in which the *preset* and *clear* inputs have the same priority using IF THEN ELSE statements.

More Complex Sequential Statements

The next example is a more complex sequential design of a 4-bit counter. This example makes use of a two-process description style. This style works very well for some synthesis tools, producing very good synthesis results.

Each process has a particular function. One process is clocked and the other is not. The clocked process is used to maintain the present state of the counter, while the unclocked process calculates the next state of the counter.

An example of a counter written in this way is as follows:

```
PACKAGE count_types IS
  TYPE bit4 IS range 0 to 15;
END count_types;
```

```
USE WORK.std_logic_1164.ALL;
USE WORK.count_types.ALL;
ENTITY count IS
  PORT( clock, load, clear : IN std_logic;
        din : IN bit4;
        dout : INOUT bit4);
END count;

ARCHITECTURE synth OF count IS
  SIGNAL count_val : bit4;
BEGIN
   PROCESS(load, clear, din, dout)
   BEGIN
    IF (load = '1') THEN
        count_val <= din;
    ELSIF (clear = '1') THEN
        count_val <= 0;
    ELSIF (dout >= 15) THEN
        count_val <= 0;
    ELSE
        count_val <= dout + 1;
    END IF;
  END PROCESS;

  PROCESS
  BEGIN
     WAIT UNTIL clock'EVENT and clock = '1';

     dout <= count_val;
  END PROCESS;
END synth;
```

The description contains a package that defines a 4-bit range that will cause the synthesis tools to generate a 4-bit counter. Changing the size of the range will cause the synthesis tools to generate different-size counters. By using a constrained universal integer range, the model can take advantage of the built-in arithmetic operators for type universal integer. The other alternative is to define a type that is 4 bits wide and then create a package that overloads the arithmetic operators for the 4-bit type.

The entity contains a *clock* input port to clock the counter, a *load* input port that will allow the counter to be synchronously loaded, a *clear* input port that will synchronously clear the counter, a *din* input port that will allow values to be loaded into the counter, and output port *dout* which presents the current value of the counter to the outside world.

The architecture for the counter contains two processes. The process labeled *synch* is the process that will maintain the current state of the counter. It is the process that is clocked by the clock, and transfers the new calculated output, *count_val,* to the current output, *dout.*

The other process contains a single IF statement that determines whether the counter is being loaded, cleared, or is counting up.

A sample synthesized output is shown in Fig. 10.9. In this example, the generated results were as expected. On the left side of the schematic are shown the inputs to the counter, while the right side of the schematic has the counter output. Notice that the design contains four flip-flops, exactly as specified. Also notice that the logic generated for the counter is very small. This design was optimized for area, thus the number of level of logic would probably be higher than a design optimized for speed.

4-bit shifter. Another sequential example is a 4-bit shifter. This shifter can be loaded with a value, and can be shifted left or right one bit at a time. The model for the shifter is as follows:

```
USE WORK.std_logic_1164.ALL;
PACKAGE shift_types IS
    SUBTYPE bit4 IS std_logic_vector(3 downto 0);
  END shift_types;

USE WORK.shift_types.ALL;
USE WORK.std_logic_1164.ALL;
ENTITY shifter IS
  PORT( din : IN bit4;
        clk, load, left_right : IN std_logic;
        dout : INOUT bit4);
END shifter;

ARCHITECTURE synth OF shifter IS
    SIGNAL shift_val : bit4;
BEGIN
    nxt: PROCESS(load, left_right, din, dout)
  BEGIN
    IF (load = '1') THEN
      shift_val <= din;
    ELSIF (left_right = '0') THEN
      shift_val(2 downto 0) <= dout(3 downto 1);
      shift_val(3) <= '0';
    ELSE
      shift_val(3 downto 1) <= dout(2 downto 0);
      shift_val(0) <= '0';
    END IF;
  END PROCESS;
```

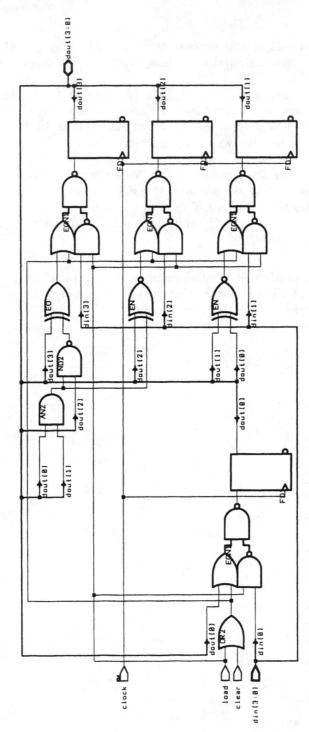

Figure 10.9 Synthesized counter schematic.

```
current: PROCESS
BEGIN
    WAIT UNTIL clk'EVENT AND clk = '1';

    dout <= shift_val;
END PROCESS;
END synth;
```

The 4-bit type used for the input and output of the shifter is declared in package *shift_types*. This package is then used by entity shifter to declare ports *din* and *dout*. Ports *clk, load,* and *left_right* are signals of *std_logic* type used to control the functions of the shifter.

The architecture is organized similarly to the last example, with two processes used to describe the functionality of the architecture. One process keeps track of the current value of the shifter and the other calculates the next value based on the last value and the control inputs.

Process current is used to keep track of the current value of the shifter. It is a process that has a single wait statement and a single signal assignment statement. When the *clk* signal has a rising edge occur, the signal assignment statement is activated and the next calculated value of the *shifter(shift_val)* is written to the signal that holds the current state of the *shifter(dout)*.

Process *nxt* is used to calculate the next value of *shift_val* to be written into *dout*. Load is the highest priority input and, if equal to '1', will cause *shift_val* to receive the value of *din*. Otherwise, signal *left_right* is tested to see if the shifter is shifting left or right. Since this shifter does not contain a carryin or carryout, '0' values are written into the bits whose value has been shifted over. (A good exercise would be to write a shifter that contains a carryin and carryout.)

The synthesis tool produces a schematic for this input description, as shown in Fig. 10.10. By counting the flip-flops on the page, it can be seen that this is indeed a 4-bit shifter.

State Machine Example

The next example is a simple state machine used to control a voicemail system. (This example does not represent any real system in use and is necessarily simple to make it easier to fit in the book.) The voicemail controller will allow the user to send messages, review messages, save messages, and erase messages. A state diagram showing the possible state transitions is shown in Fig. 10.11.

The normal starting state is state *main_st*. From *main_st,* the user can select whether to review messages or send messages. To get to the review menu, the user would press the 1 key on the touch-tone phone.

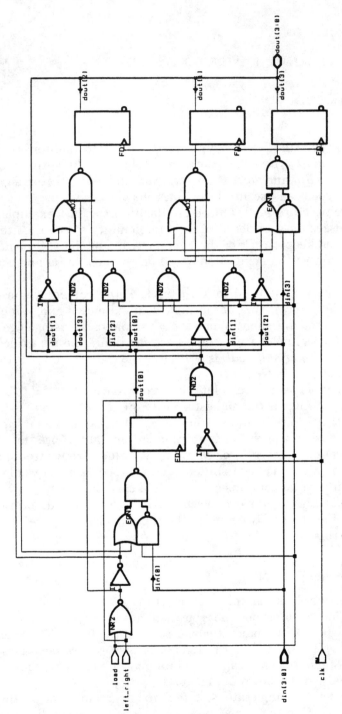

Figure 10.10 Synthesized shifter schematic.

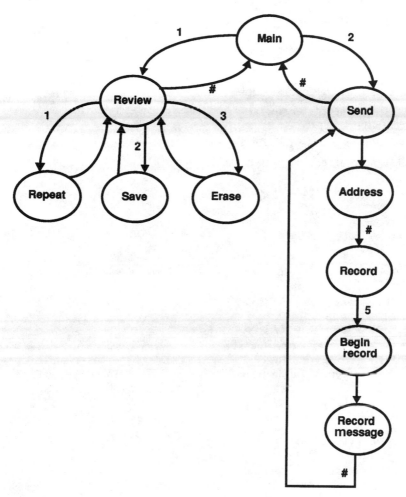

Figure 10.11   State transition diagram for voicemail controller.

To select the send message menu, the user would press the 2 key on the touch-tone phone. Once the user has selected either of these options, further menu options allow the user to perform other functions such as save and erase. For instance, if the user first selected the review menu by pressing key 1, then pressing key 2 will allow the user to save a reviewed message when reviewing is complete.

The VHDL description for the voicemail controller is as follows:

```
PACKAGE vm_pack IS
    TYPE t_vm_state IS (main_st, review_st, repeat_st, save_st,
                        erase_st, send_st, address_st, record_st,
                        begin_rec_st, message_st);
    TYPE t_key IS ('0','1','2','3','4','5','6','7','8','9','*','#');
```

```
END vm_pack;

USE WORK.vm_pack.ALL;
USE WORK.std_logic_1164.ALL;
ENTITY control IS
  PORT( clk : in std_logic;
        key : in t_key;
        play, recrd, erase, save, address : out std_logic);
END control;

ARCHITECTURE synth OF control IS
  SIGNAL next_state, current_state : t_vm_state;
BEGIN
  PROCESS(current_state, key)
  BEGIN
    play <= '0';
    save <= '0';
    erase <= '0';
    recrd <= '0';
    address <= '0';

    CASE current_state IS
    WHEN main_st =>
      IF (key = '1') THEN
          next_state <= review_st;
      ELSIF (key = '2') THEN
          next_state <= send_st;
      ELSE
          next_state <= main_st;
      END IF;

      WHEN review_st =>
       IF (key = '1') THEN
          next_state <= repeat_st;
       ELSIF (key = '2') THEN
          next_state <= save_st;
       ELSIF (key = '3') THEN
          next_state <= erase_st;
       ELSIF (key = '#') THEN
          next_state <= main_st;
      ELSE
          next_state <= review_st;
      END IF;

      WHEN repeat_st =>
       play <= '1';
        next_state <= review_st;

      WHEN save_st =>
       save <= '1';
        next_state <= review_st;
```

```
      WHEN erase_st =>
       erase <= '1';
        next_state <= review_st;

      WHEN send_st =>
        next_state <= address_st;

      WHEN address st =>
       address <= '1';
       IF (key = '#') THEN
           next_state <= record_st;
       ELSE
           next_state <= address_st;
       END IF;

      WHEN record_st =>
       IF (key = '5') THEN
           next_state <= begin_rec_st;
       ELSE
           next_state <= record_st;
       END IF;

      WHEN begin_rec_st =>
       recrd <= '1';
        next_state <= message_st;

      WHEN message_st =>
        recrd <= '1';
        IF (key = '#') THEN
           next_state <= send_st;
        ELSE
           next_state <= message_st;
        END IF;
     END CASE;
   END PROCESS;

   PROCESS
   BEGIN
     WAIT UNTIL clk = '1' AND clk'EVENT;

      current_state <= next_state;
   END PROCESS;
END synth;
```

Package vm_types contains the type declarations for the state values and keys allowed by the voicemail controller. Notice that the states are all named something meaningful, as opposed to S1, S2, S3, etc. This makes the model much more readable.

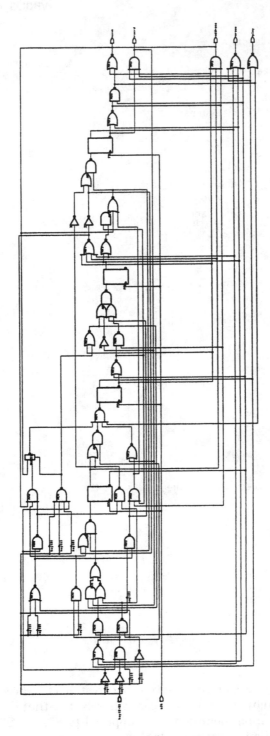

Figure 10.12 Synthesized state machine contoller.

This package is used by the entity to declare local signals and the key input port. The entity has only one input, the *key* input, which represents the possible key values from a touch-tone phone keypad. All of the other ports of the entity are output ports (except *clk*) and are used to control the voicemail system operations.

This model uses the two-process style to describe the operation of the state machine. This style is very useful for describing state machines, as one process represents the current state register and the other process represents the next state logic.

The next-state process starts by initializing all of the output signals to '0'. The reason for this is to provide the synthesis tool with a default value to assign the signal if the signal was not assigned in the case statement.

The rest of the next-state process consists of one case statement. This case statement will describe the action to occur based on the current state of the state machine, and any inputs that affect the state machine. The condition that the case statement keys from is the current state. The state machine can be placed in a different state, depending on the inputs that are being tested by the current state. For instance, if the current state is *main_st;* when the *key* input is '1', the next state will be *review_st;* when the *key* is '2', the next state will be *send_st.*

When this description is synthesized using the Synopsys VHDL Compiler™ and Synopsys Design Compiler,™ the schematic shown in Fig. 10.12 is generated. The *key* and *clk* inputs are shown coming into the right side of the schematic and outputs *save, recrd, address, erase,* and *play* are shown coming out of the right side of the schematic. Intermixed in the design are the state flip-flops that are used to hold the current state of the voicemail controller and the logic used to generate the next state of the controller. This type of output is indicative of state machine descriptions.

In this chapter we looked at a number of different VHDL synthesis examples. They ranged from the simple gate-level descriptions to more complex examples that contained state machines. In the next few chapters we will look at a more complex example that requires a number of state machines, and we will follow the process from start to finish.

Top-Level System Design

In the last few chapters, we have discussed VHDL language features and the VHDL synthesis process. In the next few chapters, we will tie all of these ideas together by developing a top-down design for a vending machine controller. We will start at the system level and continue to break the design down until we reach a level where the design can be synthesized with synthesis tools.

Vending Machine Controller

The vending machine controller we will describe is very similar to the ones that control machines that exist in cafeterias. There are a number of items in the vending machine that can be purchased by inserting the correct amount of money and then selecting the appropriate button to dispense the item. If more money is entered than is needed to purchase the item, the controller will return the correct amount of change.

The controller also has to manage some other functions that may or may not be obvious. For instance, when the money entered is enough to purchase the item with the maximum price, then no more money needs to be entered. The vending machine will activate a signal to the mechanical device that receives coins to reject any further coins.

The vending machine also has to keep track of how many of each item has been dispensed. When all of a particular item has been dispensed, a light on the front of the machine lights up, signifying that the machine has no more of that particular item.

The controller also has to keep track of how much change has been given out to a customer so that, when a customer enters too much money for an item, the machine has enough change internally to return the correct amount. If the machine does not have enough change, then a light on the front of the machine will light up to signal that the machine needs exact change only.

To save writing a lot of redundant VHDL code, we will use a vending machine that supports only four items for this example. The four items and their cost will be

- Pretzels, 50 cents
- Chips, 45 cents
- Cookies, 55 cents
- Doughnuts, 60 cents

The machine is initially stocked with five of each of these items, but can be configured to hold more of each.

The kinds of coins that can be input to the machine are as follows:

- Nickel
- Dime
- Quarter
- Half dollar

The first step in the controller description will be to describe a package that contains descriptions of the preceding items.

Top-Level Package

The first step in describing the system from the top down is to describe all of the object types that will be used in the design. At the very beginning of the design process, it is usually advantageous to use as much of the abstract modeling capability of VHDL as possible. This includes using as many of the abstract types, such as enumerated types, composite types, etc., as possible. This will make writing the VHDL description easier, and will make the model more efficient in runtime (if done correctly). When the design is correct, the abstract types can be replaced with concrete types, and the design can be produced.

Using the description of the objects from the previous section, the top-level package can be described as follows:

```
PACKAGE p_vending IS
   TYPE t_coin IS ( no_coin, nickel, dime, quarter, half_dollar);
   TYPE t_item IS ( no_item, pretzels, chips, cookies, doughnut);
   SUBTYPE t_value IS INTEGER;
```

```
FUNCTION coin_to_int( coin : IN t_coin) RETURN t_value;

FUNCTION int_to_coin( val : IN t_value) RETURN t_coin;

CONSTANT zero : t_value := 0;
END p_vending;
PACKAGE BODY p_vending IS
  FUNCTION int_to_coin( val : IN t_value) RETURN t_coin IS
  BEGIN
    IF (val = 5) THEN
      RETURN nickel;
    ELSIF (val = 10) THEN
      RETURN dime;
    ELSIF (val = 25) THEN
      RETURN quarter;
    ELSIF (val = 50) THEN
      RETURN half_dollar;
    ELSE
      RETURN no_coin;
    END IF;
  END int_to_coin;

  FUNCTION coin_to_int( coin : IN t_coin) RETURN t_value IS
BEGIN
  CASE coin IS
    WHEN no_coin =>
      RETURN 0;
    WHEN nickel =>
      RETURN 5;
    WHEN dime =>
      RETURN 10;
    WHEN quarter =>
      RETURN 25;
    WHEN half_dollar =>
      RETURN 50;
  END CASE;
  END coin_to_int;
END p_vending;
```

Two types, *t_coin* and *t_item,* describe the objects that will be used in the controller. Type *t_coin* is an enumerated type that describes the possible coin values to be input. Type *t_item* describes all of the possible items that can be purchased.

Subtype *t_value* will be used for all of the numeric values used in the design, such as how much money has been entered, how much change needs to be returned, etc. The type specified initially is a constrained range of an integer type, to make use of the built-in mathematical functions provided with the integer type.

Two functions are also included in the top-level package. These functions make it possible to convert from the coins entered into a mathematical value for these coins, and back again. This will facilitate keeping track of how much money has been entered and how much change has been returned.

Top-Level Entity

The next step in any top-down design description is to describe the system interface at the top level. As shown in Fig. 11.1, the system interface consists of input signals, output signals, any inout signals, and any parameters that need to be passed into the top level. Along with the direction of the signals, the type of the signals also needs to be described.

The system interface in VHDL is described by the entity. The first step in the system-level description will be to create the top-level entity. The top-level entity will describe the inputs and outputs of the system and any parameters that need to be passed into the system.

A top-level entity can be created from the symbol shown in Fig. 11.1, using the types described by the top-level package, *p_vending*. This entity is as follows:

```
USE WORK.std_logic_1164.ALL;
USE WORK.p_vending.ALL;
ENTITY vend_control IS
  GENERIC( p_price : t_value := 50;
        ch_price : t_value := 45;
        c_price : t_value := 55;
        d_price : t_value := 60;
        p_total : t_value := 5;
        ch_total : t_value := 5;
        c_total : t_value := 5;
        d_total : t_value := 5;
         num_nickels : t_value := 25;
         num_dimes : t_value := 25;
         max_price : t_value := 60);
    PORT( coin_in : IN t_coin;
       coin_stb : IN std_logic;
       item_stb : IN std_logic;
       item_sel : IN t_item;
       clock : IN std_logic;
       reset : IN std_logic;
       change_out : OUT t_coin;
       change_stb : OUT std_logic;
       item_out : OUT t_item;
       item_out_stb : OUT std_logic;
```

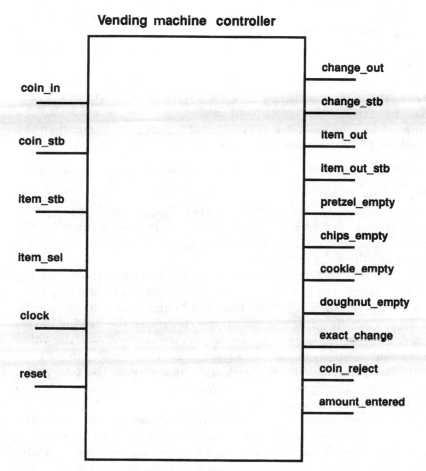

Vending machine controller

coin_in

coin_stb

item_stb

item_sel

clock

reset

change_out

change_stb

item_out

item_out_stb

pretzel_empty

chips_empty

cookie_empty

doughnut_empty

exact_change

coin_reject

amount_entered

Figure 11.1   Vending machine controller symbol.

```
    pretzel_empty : OUT std_logic;
    chips_empty : OUT std_logic;
    cookie_empty : OUT std_logic;
     doughnut_empty : OUT std_logic;
    exact_change : OUT std_logic;
    coin_reject : OUT std_logic;
     amount_entered : OUT t_value);
  END vend_control;
```

Generics

The entity begins with the generics used to control the price of an item, the number of items in the machine, and the number of coins kept for change. Generic *p_price* is the price of pretzels, *ch_price* is the price of chips, etc. In the same fashion, generic *p_total* relates how many pretzel items exist in the machine when it is stocked. The other generics with a total in their names describe the total items stocked for these items as well.

Generics *num_nickels* and *num_dimes* determine how many of each coin are kept in the machine to give out as change. Generic *max_price,* is used to determine when enough money has been entered into the machine to buy the most expensive item. This generic affects when the machine will no longer accept any more coins.

Ports

The ports described by the port clause are only input and output ports. There are no ports which are inout. Port *reset* is used to initialize the controller to a known state. It is active high and, when equal to '1', the system will initialize itself.

Port *clock* is used to synchronize all of the activity of the controller. All of the output signals will be a variation of the *clock* signal.

Ports *coin_in* and *coin_stb* act together to allow coins to be entered into the system. To enter a coin into the controller, the driving device will put the coin value on the *coin_in* port and then strobe the value into the controller by submitting a rising edge on the *coin_stb* port.

Ports *item_sel* and *item_stb* work the same way as the coin ports. Port *item_sel* is the item value input, and *item_stb* is the strobe line to enter the value into the controller.

Ports *change_out, change_stb, item_out,* and *item_out_stb* work the same way as the coin and item input ports, except that these ports are output ports. The change lines are used to drive the change-dispensing device in the vending machine. When a change value is output, the type of change will be output on the *change_out* port, and then a rising edge will be driven from port *change_stb*. The same is true of the item ports, *item_out* and *item_out_stb*.

The *pretzel_empty, chips_empty,* etc. ports are output ports used to drive lights on the front panel of the vending machine. If the machine is out of cookies, then the *cookie_empty* will be a '1' value; otherwise, it will be a '0' value.

The *exact_change* port is used to tell the potential customer of the vending machine that the machine does not have enough change to output, so the customer should enter only correct change. It is a '1' value when the machine is low on change, and a '0' value otherwise.

Port *coin_reject* is not seen externally by the customer. When the customer has entered enough money to buy the most expensive item, no more money needs to be entered to buy any item. Therefore, the machine should reject any new coins. The *coin_reject* port will cause the coin entry mechanism to reject any new coins when the maximum price has been reached. Coins will be rejected when the *coin_reject* value is '1', and not rejected when the value is '0'.

The last port is the *amount_entered* port. This port is used to display the amount of money currently entered by the customer. It will drive a display on the front of the machine.

Now that the interface to the controller has been specified, the input port to output port behavior can be specified by a behavioral architecture for the controller.

Top-Level Architecture

The top-level architecture for the vending machine controller will be written at a very high level so that the concept of the controller can be verified before a lot of time and effort go into the actual construction of the controller. This top-level architecture can be thought of as the system specification for the design. Together with the top-level entity, the complete behavior of the design will be documented.

The architecture of the top level has been expressed as a single process to facilitate the transfer of information from the various pieces of the architecture. With a single process, variables are global to all parts of the architecture. The various pieces of the behavioral description are activated by using the 'EVENT attribute of the input signals in an IF statement.

The behavioral architecture for the top-level design is as follows:

```
ARCHITECTURE a_vend_control OF vend_control IS
BEGIN
  coin_proc : PROCESS
     VARIABLE current_total : t_value;
     VARIABLE p_sold, ch_sold, c_sold, d_sold : t_value;
     VARIABLE dime_out, nickel_out : t_value := 0;

   PROCEDURE strobe_item is
   BEGIN
      item_out_stb <= '1';
      WAIT UNTIL clock = '1';
      WAIT UNTIL clock = '0';
      item_out_stb <= '0';
   END strobe_item;

   PROCEDURE make_change(change : t_value) is
      variable change_val : t_value;
   BEGIN
      change_val := change;
      WHILE change_val > 0 LOOP
```

```
  IF (change_val > 5) THEN
    change_out <= dime;
    change_stb <= '1';
    change_val := change_val - 10;
    dime_out := dime_out + 1;

    ASSERT dime_out <= num_dimes REPORT
    "out of dimes" SEVERITY ERROR;

  ELSE
      change_out <= nickel;
      change_stb <= '1';
      change_val := change_val - 5;
      nickel_out := nickel_out + 1;

      ASSERT nickel_out <= num_nickels REPORT
      "out of nickels" SEVERITY ERROR;

  END IF;

    WAIT UNTIL clock = '1';
    WAIT UNTIL clock = '0';

    change_stb <= '0';
  END LOOP;
  END make_change;

BEGIN

  IF reset = '1' THEN
    current_total := 0;
    p_sold := 0;
    ch_sold := 0;
    c_sold := 0;
    d_sold := 0;
    dime_out := 0;
    nickel_out := 0;

  ELSIF (clock = '1') AND (clock'EVENT) THEN

    IF (coin_stb = '1') THEN
      IF current_total >= max_price THEN
      coin_reject <= '1';
    ELSE
      coin_reject <= '0';

      CASE coin_in IS

        WHEN nickel =>
          current_total := current_total + 5;

        WHEN dime =>
          current_total := current_total + 10;
```

```
        WHEN quarter =>
          current_total := current_total + 25;

        WHEN half_dollar =>
          current_total := current_total + 50;

        WHEN no_coin =>
         null;

     END CASE;
    END IF;

 ELSIF (item_stb = '1') THEN

   CASE item_sel IS

     WHEN pretzels =>
       IF current_total >= p_price THEN
         IF p_sold < p_total THEN

           item_out <= pretzels;
           p_sold := p_sold + 1;
           current_total := current_total - p_price;
           strobe_item;
           make_change(current_total);
         ELSE
           pretzel_empty <= '1';
         END IF;
       END IF;

     WHEN cookies =>
       IF current_total >= c_price THEN
         IF c_sold < c_total THEN

           item_out <= cookies;
           c_sold := c_sold + 1;
           current_total := current_total - c_price;
           strobe_item;
           make_change(current_total);
         ELSE
           cookie_empty <= '1';
         END IF;
       END IF;

     WHEN chips =>
       IF current_total >= ch_price THEN
         IF ch_sold < ch_total THEN

           item_out <= chips;
           ch_sold := ch_sold + 1;
           current_total := current_total - ch_price;
           strobe_item;
```

```
          make_change(current_total);
        ELSE
          chips_empty <= '1';
        END IF;
      END IF;

    WHEN doughnut =>
      IF current_total >= d_price THEN
        IF d_sold < d_total THEN

          item_out <= doughnut;
          d_sold := d_sold + 1;
          current_total := current_total - d_price;
          strobe_item;
          make_change(current_total);
        ELSE
          doughnut_empty <= '1';
        END IF;
      END IF;

    WHEN no_item =>
      null;

    END CASE;
   END IF;
  END IF;
  WAIT ON clock, reset;

END PROCESS;
END a_vend_control;
configuration c_vend_control of vend_control is
    for a_vend_control
    end for;
end c_vend_control;
```

The main process, *coin_proc,* has been implemented using WAIT statements inside the process. Therefore, the process statement cannot have a sensitivity list. However, at the end of the process, a WAIT statement exists that makes the process sensitive to *clock* and *reset.*

When *reset* changes, process *coin_proc* will be invoked. If reset is a '1', then the first IF statement will be satisfied, and all internal variables of the process will be initialized. This allows the vending machine to be reset to a known state.

The other input that can cause the process to be invoked is input *clock.* When an event occurs on input *clock,* process *coin_proc* will be invoked. If *coin_stb* is equal to '1', execution of the process will then proceed to the IF statement that checks to make sure that the amount of money entered cannot buy the most expensive item. If the most expensive item can already be bought, then no more money needs to be entered; otherwise, it will be returned as change. If the most expensive item can be bought, then the *coin_reject* signal is set to a '1' value (forcing strength); otherwise, the *coin_reject* signal is set to a '0' (forcing strength) value.

If the coin is not rejected, then execution continues with the CASE statement. The CASE statement will add the amount of the coin to the *current_total* variable, based on the kind of the coin entered. The *current_total* variable keeps track of the total amount of money entered into the vending machine. This variable is used to determine whether enough money has been entered into the vending machine to buy an item or if coins should be rejected.

If the *item_stb* port is equal to '1', then the following statement will be satisfied:

```
ELSIF (item_stb = '1') THEN
```

The VHDL statements following this statement will handle the processing needed to purchase an item. These statements will update the total money in the vending machine, update the number of items sold, and place the appropriate item on the *item_out* port.

A case statement selects the appropriate statements to execute based on the type of item being purchased.

```
CASE item_sel IS
```

The next check makes sure that enough money has been entered into the vending machine to purchase the item.

```
IF current_total >= p_price THEN
```

Another check is then performed to make sure that at least one item is available for purchase.

```
IF p_sold < p_total THEN
```

If execution proceeds to this point, then the item can be purchased. The *item_out* port receives the value of the item.

```
item_out <= pretzels;
```

Next, the appropriate counter is updated to reflect the fact that an item was sold.

```
p_sold := p_sold + 1;
```

Now that an item has been sold, the purchase price of the item must be subtracted from the total money that has been entered.

```
current_total := current_total - p_price;
```

Finally, a check needs to be made to ensure that the current sale did not exhaust the vending machine of a particular item.

```
IF p_sold < p_total THEN
  pretzel_empty <= '0';
ELSE
  pretzel_empty <= '1';
END IF;
```

If it did, then the empty light for that particular item needs to be lit; otherwise, keep it turned off.

The preceding description showed how the statements for the pretzel item worked. The other items in the vending machine work the same way.

Next, let's examine the statements that provide the output strobe for the item and the change. These statements are contained in the procedure *strobe_item*.

```
item_out_stb <= '1';
```

This first statement will schedule the *item_out_stb* to a '1' value (forcing strength). The next statement will cause this process to suspend until an event whose value is '1' is detected on the *clock* signal.

```
WAIT UNTIL clock = '1';
item_out_stb <= '0';
```

These three statements will create a strobe pulse on the *item_out_stb* port that is at least one clock pulse long. The WAIT statement causes the process to suspend until the next rising edge of the *clock* signal. Then the *item_out_stb* signal is set to a '0' value (forcing strength).

The next operation for the vending machine controller is to output change from the purchase, if required. Since change is returned one coin at a time, a loop will be used to provide the necessary return mechanism. The change return loop is contained in procedure *make_change* and starts with the following statement:

```
WHILE change_val > 0 LOOP
```

If variable *change_val* is equal to 0, then the purchase completely exhausted the money entered into the vending machine, and no change need be returned. However, if *change_val* is nonzero and positive, the amount of change to be returned is the value of *change_val*. If *change_val* is greater than a nickel value, then at least one dime needs to be returned.

```
IF (change_val > 5) THEN
```

Otherwise, just one nickel can be returned. The appropriate coin is placed on the *change_out* port, and the *change_stb* port is set to a '1' value. Then, the change value needs to be subtracted from the *change_val*.

```
change_val := change_val - 10;
```

The counter for the change that was given out has to be updated to reflect the number of each type of coins that were given out.

```
dime_out := dime_out + 1;
```

The model also contains error-checking code to report when a particular type of change coin has been exhausted.

```
ASSERT dime_out <= num_dimes
  REPORT "out of dimes"
SEVERITY ERROR;
```

Finally, the *exact_change* light needs to be illuminated when the amount of change drops below a predefined value. In this example, when there are more than four of each type of coin left, the *exact_change* light is unlit, but when the amount of either of the two types of change drops below 5, the *exact_change* light will be lit. At the end of the IF statement, inside the change loop, is another WAIT statement that will allow the *change_stb* signal to last at least one clock.

When *change_val* drops to zero as change is given, the loop will terminate, and the procedure will return to the calling process and wait for events on the *clock,* or *reset* ports.

Vending Machine Configuration

The configuration *c_vend_control* for entity *vend_control* is shown here, and represents a default configuration for *vend_control*. Architecture *a_vend_control* contains no component instantiations, or blocks, and therefore this configuration need only bind the architecture to the entity.

```
CONFIGURATION c_vend_control OF vend_control IS
  FOR a_vend_control
  END FOR;
END c_vend_control;
```

This configuration is not required if architecture *a_vend_control* has just been compiled into the working library. However, when more than one architecture exists for entity *vend_control,* the architecture will need to be uniquely specified.

Now that we have the top-level description of the vending machine, we can verify that the design works at the behavioral level. This level of description can become the system-level specification that will be used to drive the lower-level specifications. At some point, it will be possible for this description to generate the lower levels of abstraction automatically through a process called synthesis. At the time of this writing, the synthesis tools were not quite able to handle this level of abstraction.

In the next few chapters, this design will be refined to lower and lower levels of abstraction, and synthesized to a gate-level description.

Vending Machine:
First Decomposition

In this chapter we will use the system-level specification from the last chapter as a guide to further break down the description of the vending machine controller. By looking at how the statements are grouped together, we can see that there are three logical pieces that the controller can be broken into:

- Coin handler
- Item processor
- Change maker

The coin handler accepts coins and keeps track of the total amount of money in the vending machine. The item dispenser accepts purchase requests and determines if the money entered is enough to purchase an item. If so, the item dispenser outputs the item. The change maker outputs change, if needed, following a purchase.

Figure 12.1 shows how these components are wired together with signals to form a vending machine controller.

Coin Handler

The *coin_handler* component is used to maintain the total amount of money currently held in the vending machine. The symbol shown in Fig. 12.2 shows the input and output signals to the *coin_handler*. An entity and architecture that implement the function of the *coin_handler* are shown later.

There are only two output ports from the *coin_handler*. The total money in the vending machine at any time is output on port *total*. Port

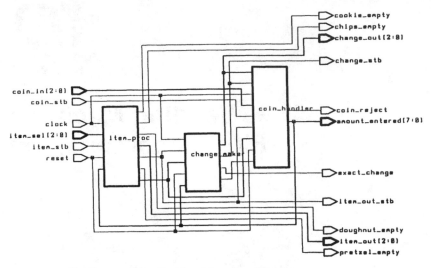

Figure 12.1 Vending machine first-level decomposition.

coin_reject is a '1' when the money entered into the machine can buy the most expensive item, or if input *sell_en* is a '0' value.

Ports *coin_in* and *coin_stb* are used to enter coin values into the *coin_handler.* The coin value is placed on port *coin_in,* and then strobed into the *coin_handler* component, with a rising edge on signal *clock* when signal *coin_stb* is equal to a '1'.

Ports *item_out_stb* and *price* are used to subtract the price of an item from the total when an item has been purchased. The price of the item purchased is placed on signal *price* and strobed into component *coin_handler* with a rising edge on signal *clock* when signal *item_out_stb* is equal to '1'.

Ports *change* and *change_stb* are used to subtract change given out after a purchase from the total. The change value is placed on the change signal and strobed into the *coin_handler* component, with a rising edge on signal *clock* when signal *change_stb* is equal to '1'.

Signal *sell_en* is used to control the input of coins. When *sell_en* is equal to a '1' value, coin values can be entered into the *coin_handler.* When *sell_en* is equal to a '0', coins will be rejected from the vending machine. The only time that *sell_en* is equal to '0' is when the *change_maker* is making change.

Item Processor

The *item_proc* component is used to dispense a purchased item. Ports *item_sel* and *item_stb* are used to select an item to be purchased. The rising edge of signal *clock* when signal *item_stb* is equal to '1' will

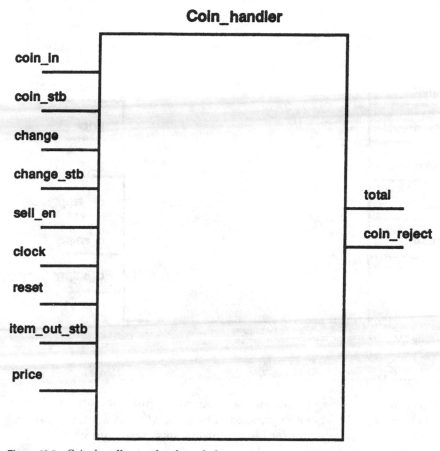

Coin_handler

coin_in
coin_stb
change
change_stb
sell_en
clock
reset
item_out_stb
price

total
coin_reject

Figure 12.2   Coin_handler top-level symbol.

trigger the *item_proc* component to check the *total* signal and make sure that enough money has been entered into the machine to buy the requested item.

If an item can be purchased, the item is sent out on the *item_out* signal and strobed by the *item_out_stb* signal and signal *clock*. Signal *price* is used to communicate to the *coin_handler* and *change_maker* components the value of the purchase price of the item.

The last function of the *item_proc* component is to output the correct status of the *item_empty* signals, where *item* is one of the four items in the vending machine. These signals tell the customer whether the supply of an item has been exhausted or not.

A symbol for the *item_proc* component is shown in Fig. 12.3. This symbol shows the input and output signals of the component. An entity and architecture that match the symbol are shown later.

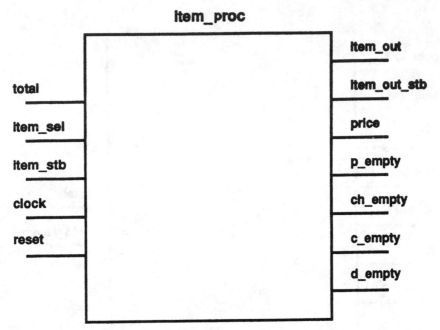

Figure 12.3   Item_proc top-level symbol.

Change Maker

The *change_maker* component is used to output the correct change when an item has been purchased. The *item_stb_out* signal is used to alert the *change_maker* that an item has been purchased. The *change_maker* component will then look at the *price* and *total* inputs to determine how much change needs to be returned. A symbol for the *change_maker* component is shown in Fig. 12.4.

The change is returned a single coin at a time from the *change* and *change_stb* signals. The *change* signal contains the coin to be returned, and the *change_stb* signal and signal *clock* are used to strobe the coin out.

The *clock* signal is used to synchronize the operation of the *change_maker* component with all of the other components. The *reset* signal will initialize the *change_maker* component to a known state.

The *exact_change* signal will be a ' 1 ' value whenever the change available to return to the customer drops below a preset limit for each type of coin returned. In this design, whenever the change drops below five units of either dimes or nickels, the *exact_change* signal will illuminate.

The *sell_en* signal is used to inhibit coins from being entered while change is being returned to the customer. This signal will be ' 0 ' while change is being made, and ' 1 ' otherwise.

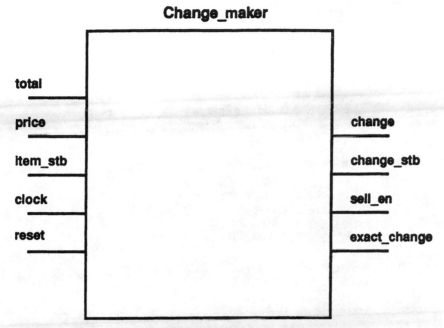

Figure 12.4 Change_maker top-level symbol.

Structural Architecture

A structural architecture that defines the three components and instantiates them is as follows:

```
ARCHITECTURE first_level OF vend_control IS

COMPONENT coin_handler
    GENERIC( max_price : t_value);
    PORT( change_in : IN t_coin;
          change_stb : IN std_logic;
          coin_in : IN t_coin;
          coin_stb : IN std_logic;
          clock : IN std_logic;
          reset : IN std_logic;
          sell_en : IN std_logic;
          price : IN t_value;
          item_out_stb : IN std_logic;
          total : OUT t_value;
          coin_reject : OUT std_logic);
END COMPONENT;

COMPONENT change_maker
    GENERIC( num_dimes, num_nickels : t_value);
```

```
      PORT( total : IN t_value;
            price : IN t_value;
            item_stb : IN std_logic;
            clock : IN std_logic;
            reset : IN std_logic;
            exact_change : OUT std_logic;
            change : OUT t_coin;
            change_stb : OUT std_logic;
            sell_en : OUT std_logic);
  END COMPONENT;

  COMPONENT item_proc
      GENERIC( p_price, ch_price, c_price, d_price, p_total,
               ch_total, c_total, d_total : t_value);
      PORT( total : IN t_value;
            item_sel : IN t_item;
            item_stb : IN std_logic;
            item_out : OUT t_item;
            item_out_stb : OUT std_logic;
            clock : IN std_logic;
            reset : IN std_logic;
            price : OUT t_value;
            p_empty, ch_empty, c_empty, d_empty : OUT std_logic);
    END COMPONENT;

    SIGNAL total, price : t_value;
    SIGNAL sell_en : std_logic;
    SIGNAL change_int : t_coin;
    SIGNAL change_stb_int, item_stb_int : std_logic;

  BEGIN

    u1 : coin_handler GENERIC MAP( max_price)
      PORT MAP( change_in => change_int,
                change_stb => change_stb_int,
                coin_in => coin_in,
                coin_stb => coin_stb,
                clock => clock,
                reset => reset,
                sell_en => sell_en,
                price => price,
                item_out_stb => item_stb_int,
                total => total,
                coin_reject => coin_reject);

    u2 : change_maker GENERIC MAP( num_dimes, num_nickels)
      PORT MAP( total => total,
                price => price,
                item_stb => item_stb_int,
                exact_change => exact_change,
```

```
            change => change_int,
            change_stb => change_stb_int,
            clock => clock,
            reset => reset,
            sell_en => sell_en);

  u3 : item_proc GENERIC MAP( p_price, ch_price, c_price, d_price,
                    p_total, ch_total, c_total, d_total)
     PORT MAP( total => total,
            item_sel => item_sel,
            item_stb => item_stb,
            item_out => item_out,
            item_out_stb => item_stb_int,
            clock => clock,
            reset => reset,
            price =>price,
            p_empty => pretzel_empty,
            ch_empty => chips_empty,
            c_empty => cookie_empty,
            d_empty => doughnut_empty);

    change_out <= change_int;
    change_stb <= change_stb_int;
    item_out_stb <= item_stb_int;
    amount_entered <= total;

END first_level;
```

Notice that the same entity is used for the interface signals as was used for the behavioral architecture. Now, instead of behavioral statements being used to define the behavior of the vending machine, three components will be used.

The architecture declaration contains the component declarations for the three components and the local signals that will be used to tie the components together. In the architecture statement part are the three component instantiations.

Also in the architecture statement part are the following four concurrent signal assignment statements:

```
change_out <= change_int;
change_stb <= change_stb_int;
item_out_stb <= item_stb_int;
amount_entered <= total;
```

These statements are necessary because the signals that drive these ports are also used internally. In VHDL, an output port (e.g., *change_out*) cannot have its value read inside the architecture that drives the port. Since the value of this output port is needed internally as well as externally, an internal signal (e.g., *change_int*) is used to drive the output port, and also the ports internally where the value is needed. The internal signal is also assigned to the external port.

Another method to solve this problem is to buffer the output signals with an actual buffer component. This was not done, because the buffer component is not needed in the final design. Another alternative is to use a port type of BUFFER on the output ports instead of type OUT. Ports of type BUFFER can be assigned to and read from, but can have only one driver.

Next, let's examine the VHDL descriptions for the three components instantiated in the structural architecture. For each component, an entity, architecture, and configuration will be presented that describes the next level of the hierarchy.

Coin handler

The entity for the *coin_handler* component uses the std_logic_1164 package and the *p_vending* packages to access the types and functions provided by each. The entity contains one generic which specifies to the *coin_handler* the price of the most expensive item. When the money collected reaches this price, the *coin_handler* can reject any further coins.

```
USE work.std_logic_1164.ALL;
USE work.p_vending.ALL;
ENTITY coin_handler IS
  GENERIC( max_price : t_value);
  PORT( change_in : IN t_coin;
        change_stb : IN std_logic;
        coin_in : IN t_coin;
        coin_stb : IN std_logic;
        clock : IN std_logic;
        reset : IN std_logic;
        sell_en : IN std_logic;
        price : IN t_value;
        item_out_stb : IN std_logic;
        total : OUT t_value;
        coin_reject : OUT std_logic);
END coin_handler;
```

The *coin_handler* entity matches the architecture component declaration exactly in terms of port names and types. This is not necessary, but it will make the configuration simpler.

The architecture for the *coin_handler* described in this chapter will be a synthesizable one. It can be read by the Synopsys Design Computer™ and Synopsys VHDL Computer™, and produces a gate-level result. The architecture is as follows:

```
ARCHITECTURE behave OF coin_handler IS
BEGIN
  change_proc : PROCESS( reset, clock)
    VARIABLE local_change : t_value := 0;
    VARIABLE int_total : t_value := 0;
  BEGIN

    IF reset = '1' THEN
      int_total := 0;
      total <= 0;
    ELSIF clock'event and clock = '1' THEN
      IF sell_en = '1' THEN
        IF (coin_stb = '1') THEN
          IF int_total >= 75 THEN
            coin_reject <= '1';
          ELSE
            coin_reject <= '0';
            int_total := int_total + coin_to_int(coin_in);
            total <= int_total;
          END IF;
        END IF;
      END IF;

      IF ( change_stb = '1') THEN
        local_change := coin_to_int( change_in);
        IF ( int_total >= local_change )THEN
          int_total := int_total - local_change;
          total <= int_total;
        ELSE
          ASSERT FALSE REPORT "error: change too large"
            SEVERITY ERROR;
        END IF;
      END IF;
      IF ( item_out_stb = '1') THEN
        IF ( int_total >= price )THEN
          int_total := int_total - price;
          total <= int_total;
        ELSE
          ASSERT FALSE REPORT "error: price too large"
            SEVERITY ERROR;
        END IF;
      END IF;
    END IF;
  END PROCESS change_proc;
END behave;
```

```
CONFIGURATION coin_handle_con OF coin_handler IS
  FOR behave
  END FOR;
END coin_handle_con;
```

The *coin_handler* architecture consists of a single process sensitive to signals *clock* and *reset*. When the *reset* signal changes to the value '1', the *coin_handler* is initialized so that the vending machine contains no money. If the *reset* line is not a '1' value, then the *clock* input will be checked for a rising edge. If a rising edge is detected on signal *clock,* execution will start with the IF statement as follows:

```
IF sell_en = '1' THEN
```

This statement will be true if the *change_maker* is not currently making change. If the *change_maker* is making change, then this signal will be '0' and no coins can be entered.

If signal *sell_en* is '1' , then the next IF statement will check for a '1' value on the *coin_stb* port. A '1' value will signify that a coin has been entered. If the total money in the vending machine is already greater than or equal to *max_price,* then *coin_reject* will be activated.

If the maximum price has not been reached, then the coin from the *coin_in* port is converted to type *t_value* and added to the internal total. The internal total value in variable *int_total* is then assigned to output port *total,* where it will be communicated to the other components in the design. If *sell_en* is not equal to '1', then change is being returned from the *change_maker,* so any coins entered will be rejected.

If the *change_stb* port is equal to '1', the *change_maker* is sending change. The change that is sent out needs to be subtracted from the total. The coin being sent out is first converted to type *t_value* so that the integer subtract operation can be performed. The change value is also range-checked to make sure that the value is not too large.

When the *item_out_stb* port is equal to '1', an item has been purchased. The price of the item will be subtracted from the total.

The *coin_handler* has only one behavioral architecture, with no blocks or components instantiated. Therefore, the default configuration which follows is enough to specify the configuration for the entity. Currently, this configuration is not needed, but it may be useful later when more than one architecture exists for component *coin_handler.*

```
CONFIGURATION coin_handle_con OF coin_handler IS
  FOR behave
  END FOR;
END coin_handle_con;
```

The preceding description has been synthesized and produced the schematic shown in Figs. 12.5, 12.6, and 12.7. Although the schematic is hard to read because it is so small, it gives the reader an idea of how much logic was generated by the RTL description. Notice the register in the middle of Fig. 12.5. Its value is the amount of money currently entered into the vending machine.

The VHDL netlist for this block is in App. A. It uses the class library supplied with the Synopsys tools as the ASIC library to which the design is mapped.

The synthesis tool also produced a report on how fast the design was and how much area this part of the design would consume. This block took 557 gates; the slowest path was from clock to *coin_reject,* which took 1.37 ns. Since a vending machine controller can be extremely slow, this design was not optimized for speed, only for area. Therefore, the design could be made faster with an appropriate increase in area.

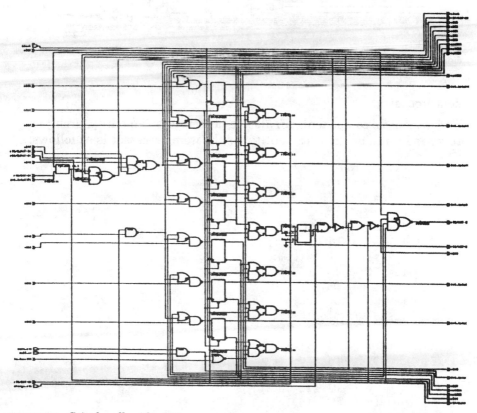

Figure 12.5   Coin_handler (sheet 1).

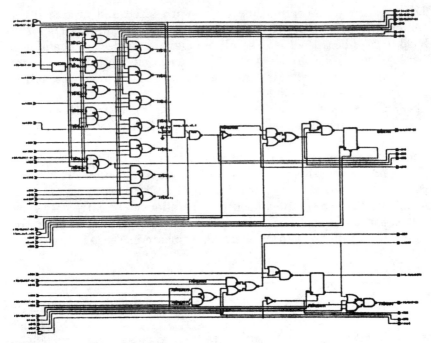

Figure 12.6   Coin_handler (sheet 2).

Item processor

The *item_proc* component can also be described by an entity, architecture, and configuration. The entity for the item processor is as follows:

```
USE work.std_logic_1164.ALL;
USE work.p_vending.ALL;
ENTITY item_proc IS
  GENERIC( p_price, ch_price, c_price, d_price, p_total,
      ch_total, c_total, d_total : t_value);
  PORT( total : IN t_value;
     item_sel : IN t_item;
     item_stb : IN std_logic;
     item_out : OUT t_item;
     item_out_stb : OUT std_logic;
     clock : IN std_logic;
     reset : IN std_logic;
     price : OUT t_value;
     p_empty : OUT std_logic;
     ch_empty : OUT std_logic;
     c_empty : OUT std_logic;
     d_empty : OUT std_logic);
  END item_proc;
```

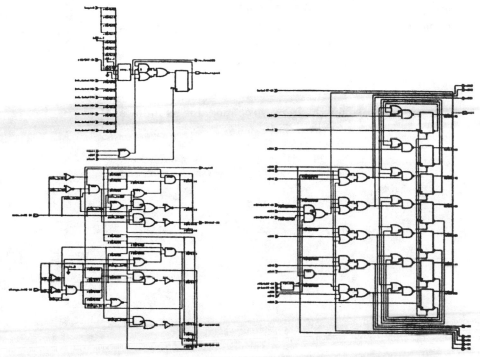

Figure 12.7 Coin_handler (sheet 3).

The entity for the *item_proc* component passes eight of the generic values from the vending machine entity into the *item_proc* entity. Four of these generics, *p_price, ch_price, c_price,* and *d_price,* are used to pass the prices of the items to purchase to the *item_proc* entity. The other four generics, *p_total, ch_total, c_total,* and *d_total,* are used to specify how many of each item were loaded into the vending machine when it was stocked.

Port *total* is used to pass in the current amount of money entered into the vending machine. Entity *item_proc* will compare the value on signal *total* with the price of an item being purchased to determine if the purchase can be made.

Ports *item_stb* and *item_sel* are used to purchase an item. Port *clock* is used to synchronize the components, and port *reset* is used to initialize the *item_proc* model.

The outputs generated are as follows:

item_out	the item purchased
item_out_stb	strobe for the item out

price	the cost of the item purchased
p_empty	empty indicator for pretzels
ch_empty	empty indicator for chips
c_empty	empty indicator for cookies
d_empty	empty indicator for doughnuts

The architecture for the *item_proc* model is as follows:

```
ARCHITECTURE behave OF item_proc IS
  TYPE item_state IS (idle, select_item, strobe_item);
  SIGNAL next_state, present_state : item_state;
  SIGNAL p_sold, ch_sold, c_sold, d_sold : t_value;
  SIGNAL nxt_p_sold, nxt_ch_sold, nxt_c_sold, nxt_d_sold : t_value;
BEGIN
  item_process : PROCESS(present_state, item_stb)
  BEGIN
    item_out_stb <= '0';
    next_state <= idle;
    nxt_p_sold <= p_sold;
    nxt_c_sold <= c_sold;
    nxt_ch_sold <= ch_sold;
    nxt_d_sold <= d_sold;

    CASE present_state IS
    WHEN idle =>
     IF ( item_stb = '1') THEN
      next_state <= select_item;
     END IF;

    WHEN select_item =>
     CASE item_sel IS
      WHEN pretzels =>
        IF p_sold < p_total THEN
          IF total >= p_price THEN
            item_out <= pretzels;
            price <= p_price;
            nxt_p_sold <= p_sold + 1;
            next_state <= strobe_item;
            IF p_sold >= p_total THEN
              p_empty <= '1';
            END IF;
          END IF;
        END IF;
      WHEN chips =>
        IF ch_sold < ch_total THEN
          IF total >= ch_price THEN
            item_out <= chips;
```

```vhdl
            price <= ch_price;
            nxt_ch_sold <= ch_sold + 1;
            next_state <= strobe_item;
            IF ch_sold >= ch_total THEN
              ch_empty <= '1';
            END IF;
          END IF;
        END IF;
    WHEN cookies =>
      IF c_sold < c_total THEN
        IF total >= c_price THEN
          item_out <= cookies;
          price <= c_price;
          nxt_c_sold <= c_sold + 1;
          next_state <= strobe_item;
          IF c_sold >= c_total THEN
            c_empty <= '1';
          END IF;
        END IF;
      END IF;
    WHEN doughnut =>
      IF d_sold < d_total THEN
        IF total >= d_price THEN
            item_out <= doughnut;
            price <= d_price;
            nxt_d_sold <= d_sold + 1;
            next_state <= strobe_item;
            IF d_sold >= d_total THEN
              d_empty <= '1';
            END IF;
          END IF;
        END IF;
      WHEN OTHERS =>
        ASSERT FALSE REPORT "illegal item selected"
          SEVERITY ERROR;
    END CASE;

  WHEN strobe_item =>
    item_out_stb <= '1';
    next_state <= idle;

 END CASE;

END PROCESS item_process;

PROCESS(clock, reset)
BEGIN
  IF reset = '1' THEN
    p_sold <= 0;
    ch_sold <= 0;
```

```
          c_sold <= 0;
          d_sold <= 0;
          present_state <= idle;

       ELSIF clock'EVENT and clock = '1' THEN
          p_sold <= nxt_p_sold;
          ch_sold <= nxt_ch_sold;
          c_sold <= nxt_c_sold;
          d_sold <= nxt_d_sold;

          present_state <= next_state;
       END IF;

    END PROCESS;

  END behave;

  CONFIGURATION item_proc_con OF item_proc IS
    FOR behave
    END FOR;
  END item_proc_con;
```

Architecture *behave* of *item_proc* has four local variables, *p_sold,*
ch_sold, c_sold, and *d_sold,* that track how many of each item have
been purchased. These variables are initialized to zero whenever signal *reset* is a '1'. When a rising edge occurs on the clock, these variables are set to the value determined from the state machine based on
the *present_state* variable.

If the *item_stb* input is equal to '1', then the state machine will
change from the idle state to the *select_item* state. Once this occurs, the
CASE statement will execute the appropriate statements based on the
value of the *item_sel* port. Let's examine what will happen if the input
item is *chips*.

The CASE statement alternative that follows will match, and execution will begin on the statement following this statement.

```
WHEN chips =>
```

The first step is to make sure that all of the chip items have not
already been sold. If there is an item to purchase, then the next check
makes sure that enough money has been entered by checking the value
of signal *total* versus the price of the chips item.

If both of these tests pass, then the item can be purchased. The
item_out port is assigned the value *chips,* and the sold counter for
chips, *ch_sold,* is incremented to reflect the sale. The sold counter is
checked one more time to make sure that the current sale did not
exhaust the vending machine of this item.

After the CASE statement alternative code has been executed, the state machine will be set to the *strobe_item* state. In this state, output *item_out_stb* will be set to a ' 1 ' value to signal the other units that an item has been selected. The *strobe_item* state makes sure that the output signal on *item_out_stb* is at least one clock cycle wide.

Since the architecture of the *item_proc* entity also does not instantiate any components or contain any blocks, the default configuration shown here will configure this entity. Again, this configuration is not currently needed.

```
CONFIGURATION item_proc_con OF item_proc IS
  FOR behave
  END FOR;
END item_proc_con;
```

This description was also synthesized as shown in Figs. 12.8 through 12.12. Again, the output is too small to really understand, but will give the designer an idea of how much logic has been generated. (The synthesis tool will make schematics in which all of the schematics can be read, but it requires too many pages to include in the book.) Again, a few of the registers that were generated can be seen in the schematic.

The resulting VHDL netlist is in App. A. It was also mapped into the class library from Synopsys. The synthesis tool reported that the design took 639 gates to implement, and the slowest path was from *clock* to *price* (0), which took 19.04 ns. Since speed was not an issue in a vending machine controller, the design could be made much faster by optimizing for speed.

Change maker

This section will examine the entity, architecture, and configuration for the *change_maker* component. The entity for the *change_maker* is as follows:

```
USE work.std_logic_1164.ALL;
USE work.p_vending.ALL;
ENTITY change_maker IS
  GENERIC( num_dimes, num_nickels : t_value);
  PORT( total : IN t_value;
      price : IN t_value;
      item_stb : IN std_logic;
      clock : IN std_logic;
      reset : IN std_logic;
      exact_change : OUT std_logic;
```

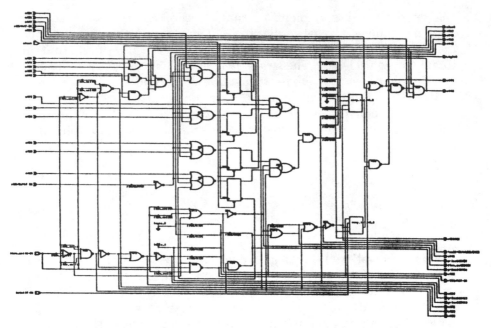

Figure 12.8   Item processor (sheet 1).

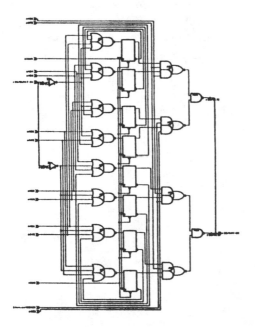

Figure 12.9   Item processor (sheet 2).

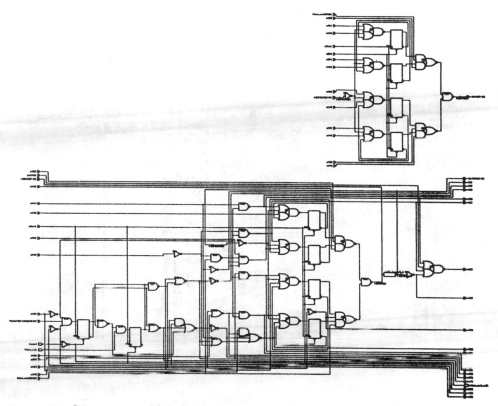

Figure 12.10   Item processor (sheet 3).

```
        change : OUT t_coin;
        change_stb : OUT std_logic;
        sell_en : OUT std_logic);

END change_maker;
```

The generics *num_nickels* and *num_dimes* are used to communicate to the *change_maker* model how many of each type of coin used to make change were entered into the vending machine.

Ports *total* and *price* are used by the model to determine how much change to return. The difference between these two signal values is the change that needs to be returned.

Port *item_stb* alerts the *change_maker* that an item has been sold and that the *change_maker* needs to act on this event. Ports *clock* and *reset* are used in the same way as in components *item_proc* and *coin_handler*. Port *exact_change* communicates to the customer of the vending machine that the amount of change held internally has

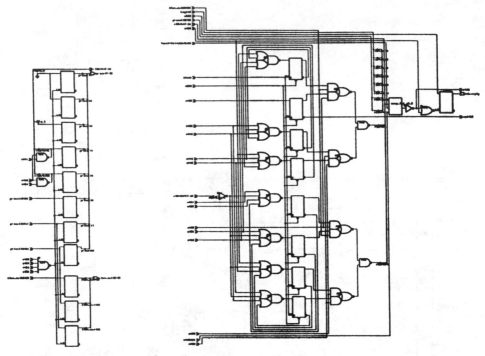

Figure 12.11   Item processor (sheet 4).

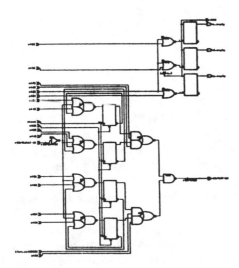

Figure 12.12   Item processor (sheet 5).

dropped below a specified level. The *change* and *change_stb* ports are used to output the coin as change.

The *sell_en* port is used to disable the vending machine from accepting coins while change is being made.

The architecture for the *change_maker* is a behavioral architecture, and is as follows:

```
ARCHITFCTURE behave OF change_maker IS
  TYPE change_state IS (idle, make_change, strobe_wait);
  SIGNAL present_state, next_state : change_state;
BEGIN
  change_mak_proc : PROCESS(clock, item_stb, total, price)
    VARIABLE int_change : t_value;
  BEGIN

    CASE present_state IS
      WHEN idle =>
        change_stb <= '0';
        sell_en <= '1';
        IF (item_stb = '1') THEN
          IF (total > price) THEN
            int_change := total - price;
            sell_en <= '0';
            next_state <= make_change;
          ELSE
            next_state <= idle;
          END IF;
        ELSE
          next_state <= idle;
        END IF;

      WHEN make_change =>
        IF (int_change > 0) THEN
          IF (int_change >= 10) THEN
            change <= dime;
            change_stb <= '1';
            int_change := int_change - 10;
            next_state <= strobe_wait;
          ELSE
            change <= nickel;
            change_stb <= '1';
            int_change := int_change - 5;
            next_state <= strobe_wait;
          END IF;
        ELSE
          next_state <= idle;
          change_stb <= '1';
        END IF;
```

```
        WHEN strobe_wait =>
           change_stb <= '0';
           next_state <= make_change;
     END CASE;
   END PROCESS;

   chng_reg_proc : PROCESS
   BEGIN
     WAIT UNTIL (clock'EVENT AND clock = '1');
     present_state <= next_state;

   END PROCESS;

END behave;

CONFIGURATION change_mak_con OF change_maker IS
   FOR behave
   END FOR;
END change_mak_con;
```

This architecture keeps track of two internal variables, *dime_out* and *nickel_out,* to record how many of each coin has been given out as change. When port *reset* is a '1', these two internal variables are set to the amount of each type of change that is stocked in the vending machine. These values are passed in through the two generic values, *num_dimes* and *num_nickels.*

If an item is sold, the *item_stb* port will be set to a '1' value and will kick off *change_maker* processing. The *change_maker* first makes sure that *total* is greater than *price.* If *total* is equal to *price,* no change needs to be given. If *total* is less than *price,* an internal error has occurred.

Next, an internal variable, *int_change,* is set to the amount of change that needs to be returned, which is the total money in the machine minus the price of the item sold. The *sell_en* port is now set to '0' to prevent any more money from entering the vending machine while change is being made.

The state machine will continue to stay in the *make_change* state as long as the *int_change* value is greater than 0. The state machine allows change to be given sequentially, one coin at a time. Inside the state machine, the change is checked for greater than or equal to 10. If true, a dime will be returned as change. If not, a single nickel will be returned as change.

If a dime is to be returned, the *change_out* port is set to the value of a dime, and the *dime_out* counter is decremented by 1. Then the *int_change* value has a dime, 10, in change subtracted from it. For a nickel change value, the processing is the same, using different values for the change.

The state machine will continue to output dimes and a nickel until the *int_change* value is zero. Once this happens, the state machine will be set to the idle state.

At the end of this processing, the *sell_en* port will be set to a '1' value again, and the process will wait for the next item to be purchased.

The configuration for the *change_maker* is a simple default configuration like all the other components, as follows:

```
CONFIGURATION change_mak_con OF change_maker IS
  FOR behave
  END FOR;
END change_mak_con;
```

The schematic that results from the synthesis of the *change_maker* is shown in Fig. 12.13. This is a considerably smaller design and it fits on one schematic sheet.

The resulting netlist is shown in App. A. The design took only 238 gates. The slowest port was from clock to change (0) and took 4.52 ns.

Next-Level Configuration

Now that the three components that make up the vending machine have been described and instantiated, the configuration that binds these components to the respective entities needs to be described. A typical configuration is as follows:

```
CONFIGURATION first_level_con OF vend_control IS
 FOR first_level
  FOR U1 : coin_handler
   USE CONFIGURATION WORK.coin_handle_con;
  END FOR;

  FOR U2 : change_maker
   USE CONFIGURATION WORK.change_mak_con;
  END FOR;

  FOR U3 : item_proc
   USE CONFIGURATION WORK.item_proc_con;
  END FOR;
 END FOR;
END first_level_con;
```

Each of the component instances is paired with a configuration for the lower-level entity that will be used for each instance. This configuration will allow the vending machine simulation to execute, using behavioral models for the three lower-level components.

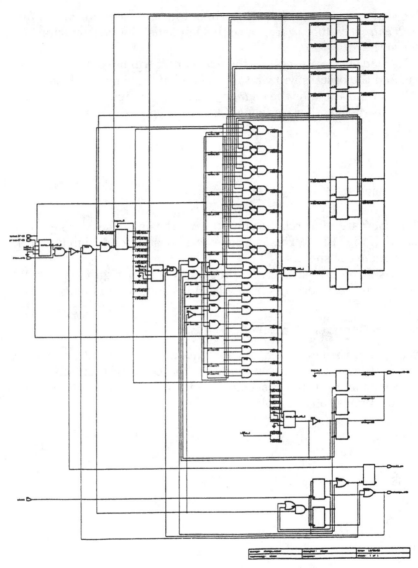

Figure 12.13   Change_maker schematic.

Group Configurations

When a design has been broken down to this level of abstraction, the entity-architecture pair of the lower-level components act as the specification for the next level of the design. Each of the lower-level components can be designed and tested independently of the other components, but tested in the system level by using the proper configurations.

The specification for the current level of the design contains three behavioral components connected together by a higher-level structural architecture. This is shown in Fig. 12.14.

Configuration *c_vend_control* configures the vending machine at the top level with a behavioral architecture. Configuration *first_level_con* configures the vending machine at the next level down, where the design now consists of three subcomponents.

Each of these three subcomponents can now be handed off to different design teams to complete the lower-level design. Each design team can use a behavioral version of the components that they are not working on and the structural version of the component being designed. For instance, let's look at a possible design hierarchy for the design team working on a structural description of the *item_proc* component. This is shown in Fig. 12.15.

The *item_proc* design team is using a structural architecture for component *item_proc,* but a behavioral architecture for components *change_maker* and *coin_handler.*

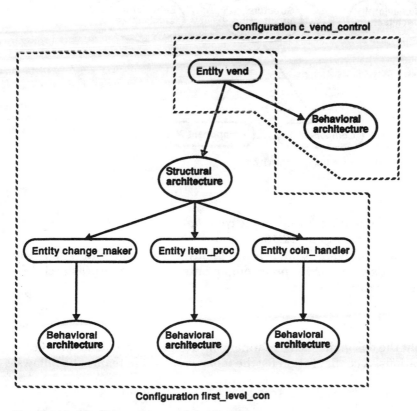

Figure 12.14 Vending machine configurations.

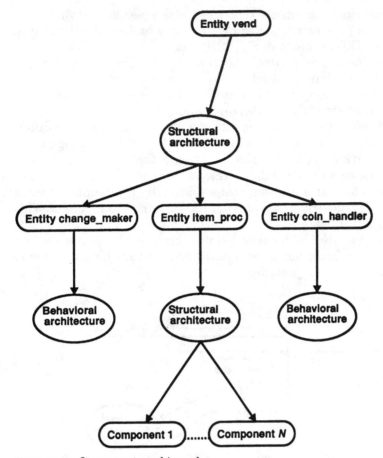

Figure 12.15 Item_proc team hierarchy.

The design team working on the *coin_handler* would have the design hierarchy shown in Fig. 12.16.

This design team would have behavioral architectures for the *change_maker* and *item_proc* components and a structural architecture for the *coin_handler*.

Team Configurations

To split the design in such a manner, the designers can make use of configurations. A configuration for the *item_proc* design team is as follows:

```
CONFIGURATION item_design_team OF vend_control IS
 FOR first_level
```

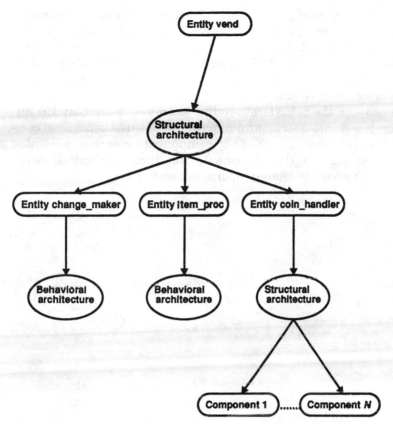

Figure 12.16   Coin_handler team hierarchy.

```
-- behavioral architecture
FOR U1 : coin_handler
  USE CONFIGURATION WORK.coin_handle_con;
END FOR;

-- behavioral architecture
FOR U2 : change_maker
  USE CONFIGURATION WORK.change_mak_con;
END FOR;

-- structural architecture
FOR U3 : item_proc
  USE CONFIGURATION WORK.item_struc_con;
END FOR;

 END FOR;
END item_design_team;
```

Notice that this configuration specifies all the same configuration items for components U1 and U2 as configuration *first_level_con,* but that for component U3, a structural version of the *item_proc* component is selected. Components U1 and U2 of the design will use their behavioral versions, while component U3 can be refined to whatever level the design team chooses.

In this chapter, the behavioral vending machine description was further decomposed into a structural description of three behavioral components. The behavior of each of the components was then presented and described. Each of the components was then synthesized to the gate level, and area and timing reports generated.

Standard Logic Package

This is a copy of the IEEE 1164 standard logic package. It is used in all of the examples in the book and is listed here for reference.

```
-- -------------------------------------------------
--
-- Title : std_logic_1164 multi-value logic system
-- Library  : This package shall be compiled into a library
--       : symbolically named IEEE.
--       :
-- Developers: IEEE model standards group (par 1164)
-- Purpose : This packages defines a standard for designers
--       : to use in describing the interconnection data types
--       : used in vhdl modeling.
--       :
-- Limitation: The logic system defined in this package may
--       : be insufficient for modeling switched transistors,
--       : since such a requirement is out of the scope of this
--       : effort. Furthermore, mathematics, primitives,
--       : timing standards, etc. are considered orthogonal
--       : issues as it relates to this package and are therefore
--       : beyond the scope of this effort.
--       :
-- Note  : No declarations or definitions shall be included in,
--       : or excluded from this package. The "package declaration"
--       : defines the types, subtypes and declarations of
--       : std_logic_1164. The std_logic_1164 package body shall be
--       : considered the formal definition of the semantics of
--       : this package. Tool developers may choose to implement
--       : the package body in the most efficient manner available
--       : to them.
--       :
-- -------------------------------------------------
-- modification history:
-- -------------------------------------------------
```

```
-- version|mod. date:|
-- v4.200|01\02\92 |
-- ----------------------------------------------------

PACKAGE std_logic_1164 IS

  ----------------------------------------------------
  -- logic state system (unresolved)
  ----------------------------------------------------
  TYPE std_ulogic IS ( 'U', -- Uninitialized
            'X', -- Forcing Unknown
            '0', -- Forcing 0
            '1', -- Forcing 1
            'Z', -- High Impedance
            'W', -- Weak    Unknown
            'L', -- Weak    0
            'H', -- Weak    1
            '-' -- Don't care
          );
  ----------------------------------------------------
  -- unconstrained array of std_ulogic for use with the resolution function
  ----------------------------------------------------
  TYPE std_ulogic_vector IS ARRAY ( NATURAL RANGE <> ) OF std_ulogic;

  ----------------------------------------------------
  -- resolution function
  ----------------------------------------------------
  FUNCTION resolved ( s : std_ulogic_vector ) RETURN std_ulogic;

  ----------------------------------------------------
  -- *** industry standard logic type ***
  ----------------------------------------------------
  SUBTYPE std_logic IS resolved std_ulogic;

  ----------------------------------------------------
  -- unconstrained array of std_logic for use in declaring signal arrays
  ----------------------------------------------------
  TYPE std_logic_vector IS ARRAY ( NATURAL RANGE <>) OF std_logic;

  ----------------------------------------------------
  -- common subtypes
  ----------------------------------------------------
  SUBTYPE X01   IS resolved std_ulogic RANGE 'X' TO '1'; -- ('X','0','1')
  SUBTYPE X01Z  IS resolved std_ulogic RANGE 'X' TO 'Z'; -- ('X','0','1','Z')
  SUBTYPE UX01  IS resolved std_ulogic RANGE 'U' TO '1'; -- ('U','X','0','1')
  SUBTYPE UX01Z IS resolved std_ulogic RANGE 'U' TO 'Z'; -- ('U','X','0',
    '1','Z')

  ----------------------------------------------------
  -- overloaded logical operators
  ----------------------------------------------------

  FUNCTION"and" ( l : std_ulogic; r : std_ulogic ) RETURN UX01;
  FUNCTION"nand" ( l : std_ulogic; r : std_ulogic ) RETURN UX01;
  FUNCTION"or" ( l : std_ulogic; r : std_ulogic ) RETURN UX01;
  FUNCTION"nor" ( l : std_ulogic; r : std_ulogic ) RETURN UX01;
```

```
  FUNCTION"xor" ( l : std_ulogic; r : std_ulogic ) RETURN UX01;
--function"xnor" ( l : std_ulogic; r : std_ulogic ) return ux01;
  FUNCTION"not" ( l : std_ulogic                  ) RETURN UX01;

  --------------------------------------------------
  -- vectorized overloaded logical operators
  --------------------------------------------------
  FUNCTION"and" ( l, r : std_logic_vector ) RETURN std_logic_vector;
  FUNCTION"and" ( l, r : std_ulogic_vector ) RETURN std_ulogic_vector;

  FUNCTION"nand" ( l, r : std_logic_vector ) RETURN std_logic_vector;
  FUNCTION"nand" ( l, r : std_ulogic_vector ) RETURN std_ulogic_vector;

  FUNCTION"or" ( l, r : std_logic_vector ) RETURN std_logic_vector;
  FUNCTION"or" ( l, r : std_ulogic_vector ) RETURN std_ulogic_vector;

  FUNCTION"nor" ( l, r : std_logic_vector ) RETURN std_logic_vector;
  FUNCTION"nor" ( l, r : std_ulogic_vector ) RETURN std_ulogic_vector;

  FUNCTION"xor" ( l, r : std_logic_vector ) RETURN std_logic_vector;
  FUNCTION"xor" ( l, r : std_ulogic_vector ) RETURN std_ulogic_vector;

-- --------------------------------------------------- ---
   Note : The declaration and implementation of the "xnor" function is
-- specifically commented until at which time the VHDL language has been
-- officially adopted as containing such a function. At such a point,
-- the following comments may be removed along with this notice without
-- further "official" balloting of this std_logic_1164 package. It is
-- the intent of this effort to provide such a function once it becomes
-- available in the VHDL standard.
-- ---------------------------     ------------------
-- function"xnor" ( l, r : std_logic_vector ) return std_logic_vector;
-- function"xnor" ( l, r : std_ulogic_vector ) return std_ulogic_vector;

  FUNCTION"not" ( l : std_logic_vector ) RETURN std_logic_vector;
  FUNCTION"not" ( l : std_ulogic_vector ) RETURN std_ulogic_vector;

  --------------------------------------------------
  -- conversion functions
  --------------------------------------------------
  FUNCTION To_bit    ( s : std_ulogic;    xmap : BIT := '0') RETURN BIT;
  FUNCTION To_bitvector ( s : std_logic_vector ; xmap : BIT := '0') RETURN
    BIT_VECTOR;
  FUNCTION To_bitvector ( s : std_ulogic_vector; xmap : BIT := '0') RETURN
    BIT_VECTOR;

  FUNCTION To_StdULogic ( b : BIT         ) RETURN std_ulogic;
  FUNCTION To_StdLogicVector ( b : BIT_VECTOR   ) RETURN std_logic_vector;
  FUNCTION To_StdLogicVector ( s : std_ulogic_vector ) RETURN
    std_logic_vector;
  FUNCTION To_StdULogicVector ( b : BIT_VECTOR    ) RETURN std_ulogic_vector;
  FUNCTION To_StdULogicVector ( s : std_logic_vector ) RETURN
    std_ulogic_vector;

  --------------------------------------------------
  -- strength strippers and type convertors
  --------------------------------------------------
```

```
FUNCTION To_X01 ( s : std_logic_vector ) RETURN std_logic_vector;
FUNCTION To_X01 ( s : std_ulogic_vector ) RETURN std_ulogic_vector;
FUNCTION To_X01 ( s : std_ulogic   ) RETURN X01;
FUNCTION To_X01 ( b : BIT_VECTOR   ) RETURN std_logic_vector;
FUNCTION To_X01 ( b : BIT_VECTOR   ) RETURN std_ulogic_vector;
FUNCTION To_X01 ( b : BIT        ) RETURN X01;

FUNCTION To_X01Z ( s : std_logic_vector ) RETURN std_logic_vector;
FUNCTION To_X01Z ( s : std_ulogic_vector ) RETURN std_ulogic_vector;
FUNCTION To_X01Z ( s : std_ulogic   ) RETURN X01Z;
FUNCTION To_X01Z ( b : BIT_VECTOR   ) RETURN std_logic_vector;
FUNCTION To_X01Z ( b : BIT_VECTOR   ) RETURN std_ulogic_vector;
FUNCTION To_X01Z ( b : BIT        ) RETURN X01Z;

FUNCTION To_UX01 ( s : std_logic_vector ) RETURN std_logic_vector;
FUNCTION To_UX01 ( s : std_ulogic_vector ) RETURN std_ulogic_vector;
FUNCTION To_UX01 ( s : std_ulogic   ) RETURN UX01;
FUNCTION To_UX01 ( b : BIT_VECTOR   ) RETURN std_logic_vector;
FUNCTION To_UX01 ( b : BIT_VECTOR   ) RETURN std_ulogic_vector;
FUNCTION To_UX01 ( b : BIT        ) RETURN UX01;

-----------------------------------------------------
-- edge detection
-----------------------------------------------------
FUNCTION rising_edge (SIGNAL s : std_ulogic) RETURN BOOLEAN;
FUNCTION falling_edge (SIGNAL s : std_ulogic) RETURN BOOLEAN;


-----------------------------------------------------
-- object contains an unknown
-----------------------------------------------------
FUNCTION Is_X ( s : std_ulogic_vector ) RETURN BOOLEAN;
FUNCTION Is_X ( s : std_logic_vector ) RETURN BOOLEAN;
FUNCTION Is_X ( s : std_ulogic   ) RETURN BOOLEAN;

END std_logic_1164;

-- -------------------------------------------------
--
-- Title  : std_logic_1164 multi-value logic system
-- Library : This package shall be compiled into a library
--      : symbolically named IEEE.
--      :
-- Developers: IEEE model standards group (par 1164)
-- Purpose : This packages defines a standard for designers
--      : to use in describing the interconnection data types
--      : used in vhdl modeling.
--      :
-- Limitation: The logic system defined in this package may
--      : be insufficient for modeling switched transistors,
--      : since such a requirement is out of the scope of this
--      : effort. Furthermore, mathematics, primitives,
--      : timing standards, etc. are considered orthogonal
--      : issues as it relates to this package and are therefore
--      : beyond the scope of this effort.
--      :
```

```
-- Note  : No declarations or definitions shall be included in,
--       : or excluded from this package. The "package declaration"
--       : defines the types, subtypes and declarations of
--       : std_logic_1164. The std_logic_1164 package body shall be
--       : considered the formal definition of the semantics of
--       : this package. Tool developers may choose to implement
--       : the package body in the most efficient manner available
--       : to them.
--       :
-- ------------------     ------------------------ ---
-- modification history :
-- ------------------------------------------------------
-- version | mod. date:|
-- v4.200  | 01\02\91  |
-- ------------------------------------------------------


PACKAGE BODY std_logic_1164 IS

  ------------------------------------------------------
  -- local types
  ------------------------------------------------------
  TYPE stdlogic_1d IS ARRAY (std_ulogic) OF std_ulogic;
  TYPE stdlogic_table IS ARRAY (std_ulogic, std_ulogic) OF std_ulogic;

  ------------------------------------------------------
  -- resolution function
  ------------------------------------------------------
  CONSTANT resolution_table : stdlogic_table := (
  -- -----------------------------------------------------
  --   | U  X  0  1  Z  W  L  H -   | |
  -- -----------------------------------------------------
       ( 'U', 'U', 'U', 'U', 'U', 'U', 'U', 'U', 'U' ), -- | U |
       ( 'U', 'X', 'X', 'X', 'X', 'X', 'X', 'X', 'X' ), -- | X |
       ( 'U', 'X', '0', 'X', '0', '0', '0', '0', 'X' ), -- | 0 |
       ( 'U', 'X', 'X', '1', '1', '1', '1', '1', 'X' ), -- | 1 |
       ( 'U', 'X', '0', '1', 'Z', 'W', 'L', 'H', 'X' ), -- | Z |
       ( 'U', 'X', '0', '1', 'W', 'W', 'W', 'W', 'X' ), -- | W |
       ( 'U', 'X', '0', '1', 'L', 'W', 'L', 'W', 'X' ), -- | L |
       ( 'U', 'X', '0', '1', 'H', 'W', 'W', 'H', 'X' ), -- | H |
       ( 'U', 'X', 'X', 'X', 'X', 'X', 'X', 'X', 'X' )  -- | - |
  );

  FUNCTION resolved ( s : std_ulogic_vector ) RETURN std_ulogic IS
    VARIABLE result : std_ulogic := 'Z'; -- weakest state default
  BEGIN
    -- the test for a single driver is essential otherwise the
    -- loop would return 'X' for a single driver of '-' and that
    -- would conflict with the value of a single driver unresolved
    -- signal.
    IF  (s'LENGTH = 1) THEN    RETURN s(s'LOW);
    ELSE
      FOR i IN s'RANGE LOOP
        result := resolution_table(result, s(i));
      END LOOP;
```

```vhdl
  END IF;
  RETURN result;
END resolved;

-------------------------------------------------------
-- tables for logical operations
-------------------------------------------------------

-- truth table for "and" function
CONSTANT and_table : stdlogic_table := (
--  -------------------------------------------------
--  |  U  X  0  1  Z  W  L  H  -  | |
--  -------------------------------------------------
      ( 'U', 'U', '0', 'U', 'U', 'U', '0', 'U', 'U' ), -- | U |
      ( 'U', 'X', '0', 'X', 'X', 'X', '0', 'X', 'X' ), -- | X |
      ( '0', '0', '0', '0', '0', '0', '0', '0', '0' ), -- | 0 |
      ( 'U', 'X', '0', '1', 'X', 'X', '0', '1', 'X' ), -- | 1 |
      ( 'U', 'X', '0', 'X', 'X', 'X', '0', 'X', 'X' ), -- | Z |
      ( 'U', 'X', '0', 'X', 'X', 'X', '0', 'X', 'X' ), -- | W |
      ( '0', '0', '0', '0', '0', '0', '0', '0', '0' ), -- | L |
      ( 'U', 'X', '0', '1', 'X', 'X', '0', '1', 'X' ), -- | H |
      ( 'U', 'X', '0', 'X', 'X', 'X', '0', 'X', 'X' )  -- | - |
);

-- truth table for "or" function
CONSTANT or_table : stdlogic_table := (
--  -------------------------------------------------
--  |  U  X  0  1  Z  W  L  H  -  | |
--  -------------------------------------------------
      ( 'U', 'U', 'U', '1', 'U', 'U', 'U', '1', 'U' ), -- | U |
      ( 'U', 'X', 'X', '1', 'X', 'X', 'X', '1', 'X' ), -- | X |
      ( 'U', 'X', '0', '1', 'X', 'X', '0', '1', 'X' ), -- | 0 |
      ( '1', '1', '1', '1', '1', '1', '1', '1', '1' ), -- | 1 |
      ( 'U', 'X', 'X', '1', 'X', 'X', 'X', '1', 'X' ), -- | Z |
      ( 'U', 'X', 'X', '1', 'X', 'X', 'X', '1', 'X' ), -- | W |
      ( 'U', 'X', '0', '1', 'X', 'X', '0', '1', 'X' ), -- | L |
      ( '1', '1', '1', '1', '1', '1', '1', '1', '1' ), -- | H |
      ( 'U', 'X', 'X', '1', 'X', 'X', 'X', '1', 'X' )  -- | - |
);

-- truth table for "xor" function
CONSTANT xor_table : stdlogic_table := (
--  -------------------------------------------------
--  |  U  X  0  1  Z  W  L  H  -  | |
--  -------------------------------------------------
      ( 'U', 'U', 'U', 'U', 'U', 'U', 'U', 'U', 'U' ), -- | U |
      ( 'U', 'X', 'X', 'X', 'X', 'X', 'X', 'X', 'X' ), -- | X |
      ( 'U', 'X', '0', '1', 'X', 'X', '0', '1', 'X' ), -- | 0 |
      ( 'U', 'X', '1', '0', 'X', 'X', '1', '0', 'X' ), -- | 1 |
      ( 'U', 'X', 'X', 'X', 'X', 'X', 'X', 'X', 'X' ), -- | Z |
      ( 'U', 'X', 'X', 'X', 'X', 'X', 'X', 'X', 'X' ), -- | W |
      ( 'U', 'X', '0', '1', 'X', 'X', '0', '1', 'X' ), -- | L |
      ( 'U', 'X', '1', '0', 'X', 'X', '1', '0', 'X' ), -- | H |
      ( 'U', 'X', 'X', 'X', 'X', 'X', 'X', 'X', 'X' )  -- | - |
);
```

```
-- truth table for "not" function
CONSTANT not_table: stdlogic_1d :=
-- -----------------------------------------------------
-- | U X 0 1 Z W L H -  |
-- -----------------------------------------------------
      ( 'U', 'X', '1', '0', 'X', 'X', '1', '0', 'X' );

-- -----------------------------------------------------
-- overloaded logical operators ( with optimizing hints )
-- -----------------------------------------------------
FUNCTION "and" ( 1 : std_ulogic; r : std_ulogic ) RETURN UX01 IS
BEGIN
  RETURN (and_table(1, r));
END "and";

FUNCTION "nand" ( 1 : std_ulogic; r : std_ulogic ) RETURN UX01 IS
BEGIN
  RETURN (not_table ( and_table(1, r)));
END "nand";

FUNCTION "or" ( 1 : std_ulogic; r : std_ulogic ) RETURN UX01 IS
BEGIN
  RETURN (or_table(1, r));
END "or";

FUNCTION "nor" ( 1 : std_ulogic; r : std_ulogic ) RETURN UX01 IS
BEGIN
  RETURN (not_table ( or_table( 1, r)));
END "nor";

FUNCTION "xor" ( 1 : std_ulogic; r : std_ulogic ) RETURN UX01 IS
BEGIN
  RETURN (xor_table(1, r));
END "xor";

-- function "xnor" ( 1 : std_ulogic; r : std_ulogic ) return ux01 is
-- begin
--   return not_table(xor_table(1, r));
-- end "xnor";

FUNCTION "not" ( 1 : std_ulogic ) RETURN UX01 IS
BEGIN
  RETURN (not_table(1));
END "not";

-- -----------------------------------------------------
-- and
-- -----------------------------------------------------
FUNCTION "and" ( 1,r : std_logic_vector ) RETURN std_logic_vector IS
  ALIAS lv : std_logic_vector ( 1 TO 1'LENGTH ) IS 1;
  ALIAS rv : std_logic_vector ( 1 TO r'LENGTH ) IS r;
  VARIABLE result : std_logic_vector ( 1 TO 1'LENGTH );
BEGIN
  IF ( 1'LENGTH \= r'LENGTH ) THEN
    ASSERT FALSE
    REPORT "arguments of overloaded 'and' operator are not of the same length"
```

```
    SEVERITY FAILURE;
  ELSE
    FOR i IN result'RANGE LOOP
      result(i) := and_table (lv(i), rv(i));
    END LOOP;
  END IF;
  RETURN result;
END "and";
-----------------------------------------------------
FUNCTION "and" ( l,r : std_ulogic_vector ) RETURN std_ulogic_vector IS
  ALIAS lv : std_ulogic_vector ( 1 TO l'LENGTH ) IS l;
  ALIAS rv : std_ulogic_vector ( 1 TO r'LENGTH ) IS r;
  VARIABLE result : std_ulogic_vector ( 1 TO l'LENGTH );
BEGIN
  IF ( l'LENGTH \= r'LENGTH ) THEN
    ASSERT FALSE
    REPORT "arguments of overloaded 'and' operator are not of the same length"
    SEVERITY FAILURE;
  ELSE
    FOR i IN result'RANGE LOOP
      result(i) := and_table (lv(i), rv(i));
    END LOOP;
  END IF;
  RETURN result;
END "and";
-----------------------------------------------------
-- nand
-----------------------------------------------------
FUNCTION "nand" ( l,r : std_logic_vector ) RETURN std_logic_vector IS
  ALIAS lv : std_logic_vector ( 1 TO l'LENGTH ) IS l;
  ALIAS rv : std_logic_vector ( 1 TO r'LENGTH ) IS r;
  VARIABLE result : std_logic_vector ( 1 TO l'LENGTH );
BEGIN
  IF ( l'LENGTH \= r'LENGTH ) THEN
    ASSERT FALSE
    REPORT "arguments of overloaded 'nand' operator are not of the same length"
    SEVERITY FAILURE;
  ELSE
    FOR i IN result'RANGE LOOP
      result(i) := not_table(and_table (lv(i), rv(i)));
    END LOOP;
  END IF;
  RETURN result;
END "nand";
-----------------------------------------------------
FUNCTION "nand" ( l,r : std_ulogic_vector ) RETURN std_ulogic_vector IS
  ALIAS lv : std_ulogic_vector ( 1 TO l'LENGTH ) IS l;
  ALIAS rv : std_ulogic_vector ( 1 TO r'LENGTH ) IS r;
  VARIABLE result : std_ulogic_vector ( 1 TO l'LENGTH );
BEGIN
  IF ( l'LENGTH \= r'LENGTH ) THEN
    ASSERT FALSE
```

```
      REPORT "arguments of overloaded 'nand' operator are not of the same length"
      SEVERITY FAILURE;
    ELSE
      FOR i IN result'RANGE LOOP
        result(i) := not_table(and_table (lv(i), rv(i)));
      END LOOP;
    END IF;
    RETURN result;
  END "nand";
  -------------------- ----------------------------- --
  -- or
  ----- ------------------------------------------------
  FUNCTION "or" ( l,r : std_logic_vector ) RETURN std_logic_vector IS
    ALIAS lv : std_logic_vector ( 1 TO l'LENGTH ) IS l;
    ALIAS rv : std_logic_vector ( 1 TO r'LENGTH ) IS r;
    VARIABLE result : std_logic_vector ( 1 TO l'LENGTH );
  BEGIN
    IF ( l'LENGTH \= r'LENGTH ) THEN
      ASSERT FALSE
      REPORT "arguments of overloaded 'or' operator are not of the same length"
      SEVERITY FAILURE;
    ELSE
      FOR i IN result'RANGE LOOP
        result(i) := or_table (lv(i), rv(i));
      END LOOP;
    END IF;
    RETURN result;
  END "or";
  ------------------- -----------------------------------
  FUNCTION "or" ( l,r : std_ulogic_vector ) RETURN std_ulogic_vector IS
    ALIAS lv : std_ulogic_vector ( 1 TO l'LENGTH ) IS l;
    ALIAS rv : std_ulogic_vector ( 1 TO r'LENGTH ) IS r;
    VARIABLE result : std_ulogic_vector ( 1 TO l'LENGTH );
  BEGIN
    IF ( l'LENGTH \= r'LENGTH ) THEN
      ASSERT FALSE
      REPORT "arguments of overloaded 'or' operator are not of the same length"
      SEVERITY FAILURE;
    ELSE
      FOR i IN result'RANGE LOOP
        result(i) := or_table (lv(i), rv(i));
      END LOOP;
    END IF;
    RETURN result;
  END "or";
  ------------------------------------------------------
  -- nor
  ------------------------------------------------------
  FUNCTION "nor" ( l,r : std_logic_vector ) RETURN std_logic_vector IS
    ALIAS lv : std_logic_vector ( 1 TO l'LENGTH ) IS l;
    ALIAS rv : std_logic_vector ( 1 TO r'LENGTH ) IS r;
    VARIABLE result : std_logic_vector ( 1 TO l'LENGTH );
```

```
BEGIN
  IF ( l'LENGTH \= r'LENGTH ) THEN
    ASSERT FALSE
    REPORT "arguments of overloaded 'nor' operator are not of the same length"
    SEVERITY FAILURE;
  ELSE
    FOR i IN result'RANGE LOOP
      result(i) := not_table(or_table (lv(i), rv(i)));
    END LOOP;
  END IF;
  RETURN result;
END "nor";
----------------------------------------------------
FUNCTION "nor" ( l,r : std_ulogic_vector ) RETURN std_ulogic_vector IS
  ALIAS lv : std_ulogic_vector ( 1 TO l'LENGTH ) IS l;
  ALIAS rv : std_ulogic_vector ( 1 TO r'LENGTH ) IS r;
  VARIABLE result : std_ulogic_vector ( 1 TO l'LENGTH );
BEGIN
  IF ( l'LENGTH \= r'LENGTH ) THEN
    ASSERT FALSE
    REPORT "arguments of overloaded 'nor' operator are not of the same length"
    SEVERITY FAILURE;
  ELSE
    FOR i IN result'RANGE LOOP
      result(i) := not_table(or_table (lv(i), rv(i)));
    END LOOP;
  END IF;
  RETURN result;
END "nor";
----------------------------------------------------
-- xor
----------------------------------------------------
FUNCTION "xor" ( l,r : std_logic_vector ) RETURN std_logic_vector IS
  ALIAS lv : std_logic_vector ( 1 TO l'LENGTH ) IS l;
  ALIAS rv : std_logic_vector ( 1 TO r'LENGTH ) IS r;
  VARIABLE result : std_logic_vector ( 1 TO l'LENGTH );
BEGIN
  IF ( l'LENGTH \= r'LENGTH ) THEN
    ASSERT FALSE
    REPORT "arguments of overloaded 'xor' operator are not of the same length"
    SEVERITY FAILURE;
  ELSE
    FOR i IN result'RANGE LOOP
      result(i) := xor_table (lv(i), rv(i));
    END LOOP;
  END IF;
  RETURN result;
END "xor";
----------------------------------------------------
FUNCTION "xor" ( l,r : std_ulogic_vector ) RETURN std_ulogic_vector IS
  ALIAS lv : std_ulogic_vector ( 1 TO l'LENGTH ) IS l;
  ALIAS rv : std_ulogic_vector ( 1 TO r'LENGTH ) IS r;
  VARIABLE result : std_ulogic_vector ( 1 TO l'LENGTH );
```

```
BEGIN
  IF ( l'LENGTH \= r'LENGTH ) THEN
    ASSERT FALSE
    REPORT "arguments of overloaded 'xor' operator are not of the same length"
    SEVERITY FAILURE;
  ELSE
    FOR i IN result'RANGE LOOP
      result(i) := xor_table (lv(i), rv(i));
    END LOOP;
  END IF;
  RETURN result;
END "xor";
-- ----------------------------------------------------
-- -- xnor
-- ----------------------------------------------------
-- ----------------------------------------------------
-- Note : The declaration and implementation of the "xnor" function is
-- specifically commented until at which time the VHDL language has been
-- officially adopted as containing such a function. At such a point,
-- the following comments may be removed along with this notice without
-- further "official" balloting of this std_logic_1164 package. It is
-- the intent of this effort to provide such a function once it becomes
-- available in the VHDL standard.
-- ----------------------------------------------------
-- function "xnor" ( l,r : std_logic_vector ) return std_logic_vector is
--    alias lv : std_logic_vector ( 1 to l'length ) is l;
--    alias rv : std_logic_vector ( 1 to r'length ) is r;
--    variable result : std_logic_vector ( 1 to l'length );
-- begin
--   if ( l'length \= r'length ) then
--      assert false
--      report "arguments of overloaded 'xnor' operator are not of the same
--         length"
--      severity failure;
--   else
--      for i in result'range loop
--        result(i) := not_table(xor_table (lv(i), rv(i)));
--      end loop;
--   end if;
--   return result;
-- end "xnor";
-- ----------------------------------------------------
-- function "xnor" ( l,r : std_ulogic_vector ) return std_ulogic_vector is
--    alias lv : std_ulogic_vector ( 1 to l'length ) is l;
--    alias rv : std_ulogic_vector ( 1 to r'length ) is r;
--    variable result : std_ulogic_vector ( 1 to l'length );
-- begin
--   if ( l'length \= r'length ) then
--      assert false
--      report "arguments of overloaded 'xnor' operator are not of the same
--         length"
--      severity failure;
--   else
```

```
--    for i in result'range loop
--       result(i) := not_table(xor_table (lv(i), rv(i)));
--    end loop;
--  end if;
--   return result;
-- end "xnor";


  ---------------------------------------------------
  -- not
  ---------------------------------------------------
FUNCTION "not" ( l : std_logic_vector ) RETURN std_logic_vector IS
  ALIAS lv : std_logic_vector ( 1 TO l'LENGTH ) IS l;
  VARIABLE result : std_logic_vector ( 1 TO l'LENGTH ) := (OTHERS => 'X');
BEGIN
  FOR i IN result'RANGE LOOP
    result(i) := not_table( lv(i) );
  END LOOP;
  RETURN result;
END;
  ---------------------------------------------------
FUNCTION "not" ( l : std_ulogic_vector ) RETURN std_ulogic_vector IS
  ALIAS lv : std_ulogic_vector ( 1 TO l'LENGTH ) IS l;
  VARIABLE result : std_ulogic_vector ( 1 TO l'LENGTH ) := (OTHERS => 'X');
BEGIN
  FOR i IN result'RANGE LOOP
    result(i) := not_table( lv(i) );
  END LOOP;
  RETURN result;
END;
  ---------------------------------------------------
  -- conversion tables
  ---------------------------------------------------
TYPE logic_x01_table IS ARRAY (std_ulogic'LOW TO std_ulogic'HIGH) OF X01;
TYPE logic_x01z_table IS ARRAY (std_ulogic'LOW TO std_ulogic'HIGH) OF X01Z;
TYPE logic_ux01_table IS ARRAY (std_ulogic'LOW TO std_ulogic'HIGH) OF UX01;
  ---------------------------------------------------
  -- table name : cvt_to_x01
  --
  -- parameters :
  -- in : std_ulogic -- some logic value
  -- returns  : x01    -- state value of logic value
  -- purpose  : to convert state-strength to state only
  --
  -- example  : if (cvt_to_x01 (input_signal) = '1' ) then ...
  --
  ---------------------------------------------------
CONSTANT cvt_to_x01 : logic_x01_table := (
          'X', -- 'U'
          'X', -- 'X'
          '0', -- '0'
          '1', -- '1'
          'X', -- 'Z'
          'X', -- 'W'
```

```
                '0', -- 'L'
                '1', -- 'H'
                'X', -- '_'
            );

----------------------------------------------------
-- table name : cvt_to_x01z
--
-- parameters :
--      in : std_ulogic -- some logic value
-- returns : x01z    -- state value of logic value
-- purpose  : to convert state-strength to state only
--
-- example  : if (cvt_to_x01z (input_signal) = '1' ) then ...
--
----------------------------------------------------
CONSTANT cvt_to_x01z : logic_x01z_table := (
                'X', -- 'U'
                'X', -- 'X'
                '0', -- '0'
                '1', -- '1'
                'Z', -- 'Z'
                'X', -- 'W'
                '0', -- 'L'
                '1', -- 'H'
                'X', -- '_'
            );

----------------------------------------------------
-- table name : cvt_to_ux01
--
-- parameters :
--      in : std_ulogic -- some logic value
-- returns : ux01    -- state value of logic value
-- purpose : to convert state-strength to state only
--
-- example : if (cvt_to_ux01 (input_signal) = '1' ) then ...
--
----------------------------------------------------
CONSTANT cvt_to_ux01 : logic_ux01_table := (
                'U', -- 'U'
                'X', -- 'X'
                '0', -- '0'
                '1', -- '1'
                'X', -- 'Z'
                'X', -- 'W'
                '0', -- 'L'
                '1', -- 'H'
                'X', -- '_'
            );

----------------------------------------------------
-- conversion functions
----------------------------------------------------
```

```
FUNCTION To_bit    ( s : std_ulogic;    xmap : BIT := '0') RETURN BIT IS
BEGIN
    CASE s IS
        WHEN '0' | 'L' => RETURN ('0');
        WHEN '1' | 'H' => RETURN ('1');
      WHEN OTHERS => RETURN xmap;
    END CASE;
END;
----------------------------------------------------
FUNCTION To_bitvector ( s : std_logic_vector ; xmap : BIT := '0') RETURN
  BIT_VECTOR
IS
    ALIAS sv : std_logic_vector ( s'LENGTH-1 DOWNTO 0 ) IS s;
    VARIABLE result : BIT_VECTOR ( s'LENGTH-1 DOWNTO 0 );
BEGIN
  FOR i IN result'RANGE LOOP
    CASE sv(i) IS
        WHEN '0' | 'L' => result(i) := '0';
        WHEN '1' | 'H' => result(i) := '1';
      WHEN OTHERS => result(i) := xmap;
    END CASE;
  END LOOP;
  RETURN result;
END;
----------------------------------------------------
FUNCTION To_bitvector ( s : std_ulogic_vector; xmap : BIT := '0') RETURN
  BIT_VECTOR
IS
    ALIAS sv : std_ulogic_vector ( s'LENGTH-1 DOWNTO 0 ) IS s;
    VARIABLE result : BIT_VECTOR ( s'LENGTH-1 DOWNTO 0 );
BEGIN
  FOR i IN result'RANGE LOOP
    CASE sv(i) IS
        WHEN '0' | 'L' => result(i) := '0';
        WHEN '1' | 'H' => result(i) := '1';
      WHEN OTHERS => result(i) := xmap;
    END CASE;
  END LOOP;
  RETURN result;
END;
----------------------------------------------------
FUNCTION To_StdULogic     ( b : BIT     ) RETURN std_ulogic IS
BEGIN
  CASE b IS
    WHEN '0' => RETURN '0';
    WHEN '1' => RETURN '1';
  END CASE;
END;
----------------------------------------------------
FUNCTION To_StdLogicVector ( b : BIT_VECTOR   ) RETURN std_logic_vector IS
    ALIAS bv : BIT_VECTOR ( b'LENGTH-1 DOWNTO 0 ) IS b;
    VARIABLE result : std_logic_vector ( b'LENGTH-1 DOWNTO 0 );
```

```vhdl
BEGIN
  FOR i IN result'RANGE LOOP
    CASE bv(i) IS
      WHEN '0' => result(i) := '0';
      WHEN '1' => result(i) := '1';
    END CASE;
  END LOOP;
  RETURN result;
END;
-------------------------------------------------------
FUNCTION To_StdLogicVector ( s : std_ulogic_vector ) RETURN std_logic_vector
  ALIAS sv : std_ulogic_vector ( s'LENGTH-1 DOWNTO 0 ) IS s;
  VARIABLE result : std_logic_vector ( s'LENGTH-1 DOWNTO 0 );
BEGIN
  FOR i IN result'RANGE LOOP
    result(i) := sv(i);
  END LOOP;
  RETURN result;
END;
-------------------------------------------------------
FUNCTION To_StdULogicVector ( b : BIT_VECTOR ) RETURN std_ulogic_vector IS
  ALIAS bv : BIT_VECTOR ( b'LENGTH-1 DOWNTO 0 ) IS b;
  VARIABLE result : std_ulogic_vector ( b'LENGTH-1 DOWNTO 0 );
BEGIN
  FOR i IN result'RANGE LOOP
    CASE bv(i) IS
      WHEN '0' => result(i) := '0';
      WHEN '1' => result(i) := '1';
    END CASE;
  END LOOP;
  RETURN result;
END;
-------------------------------------------------------
FUNCTION To_StdULogicVector ( s : std_logic_vector ) RETURN std_ulogic_vector
  ALIAS sv : std_logic_vector ( s'LENGTH-1 DOWNTO 0 ) IS s;
  VARIABLE result : std_ulogic_vector ( s'LENGTH-1 DOWNTO 0 );
BEGIN
  FOR i IN result'RANGE LOOP
    result(i) := sv(i);
  END LOOP;
  RETURN result;
END;

-------------------------------------------------------
-- strength strippers and type convertors
-------------------------------------------------------
-- to_x01
-------------------------------------------------------
FUNCTION To_X01 ( s : std_logic_vector ) RETURN std_logic_vector IS
  ALIAS sv : std_logic_vector ( 1 TO s'LENGTH ) IS s;
  VARIABLE result : std_logic_vector ( 1 TO s'LENGTH );
BEGIN
```

```
  FOR i IN result'RANGE LOOP
    result(i) := cvt_to_x01 (sv(i));
  END LOOP;
  RETURN result;
END;
------------------------------------------------------
FUNCTION To_X01 ( s : std_ulogic_vector ) RETURN std_ulogic_vector IS
  ALIAS sv : std_ulogic_vector ( 1 TO s'LENGTH ) IS s;
  VARIABLE result : std_ulogic_vector ( 1 TO s'LENGTH );
BEGIN
  FOR i IN result'RANGE LOOP
    result(i) := cvt_to_x01 (sv(i));
  END LOOP;
  RETURN result;
END;
------------------------------------------------------
FUNCTION To_X01 ( s : std_ulogic ) RETURN X01 IS
BEGIN
  RETURN (cvt_to_x01(s));
END;
------------------------------------------------------
FUNCTION To_X01 ( b : BIT_VECTOR ) RETURN std_logic_vector IS
  ALIAS bv : BIT_VECTOR ( 1 TO b'LENGTH ) IS b;
  VARIABLE result : std_logic_vector ( 1 TO b'LENGTH );
BEGIN
  FOR i IN result'RANGE LOOP
    CASE bv(i) IS
      WHEN '0' => result(i) := '0';
      WHEN '1' => result(i) := '1';
    END CASE;
  END LOOP;
  RETURN result;
END;
------------------------------------------------------
FUNCTION To_X01 ( b : BIT_VECTOR ) RETURN std_ulogic_vector IS
  ALIAS bv : BIT_VECTOR ( 1 TO b'LENGTH ) IS b;
  VARIABLE result : std_ulogic_vector ( 1 TO b'LENGTH );
BEGIN
  FOR i IN result'RANGE LOOP
    CASE bv(i) IS
      WHEN '0' => result(i) := '0';
      WHEN '1' => result(i) := '1';
    END CASE;
  END LOOP;
  RETURN result;
END;
------------------------------------------------------
FUNCTION To_X01 ( b : BIT ) RETURN X01 IS
BEGIN
    CASE b IS
      WHEN '0' => RETURN('0');
      WHEN '1' => RETURN('1');
    END CASE;
END;
```

```
----------------------------------------------------
-- to_x01z
----------------------------------------------------
FUNCTION To_X01Z ( s : std_logic_vector ) RETURN std_logic_vector IS
  ALIAS sv : std_logic_vector ( 1 TO s'LENGTH ) IS s;
  VARIABLE result : std_logic_vector ( 1 TO s'LENGTH );
BEGIN
  FOR i IN result'RANGE LOOP
    result(i) := cvt_to_x01z (sv(i));
  END LOOP;
  RETURN result;
END;
----------------------------------------------------
FUNCTION To_X01Z ( s : std_ulogic_vector ) RETURN std_ulogic_vector IS
  ALIAS sv : std_ulogic_vector ( 1 TO s'LENGTH ) IS s;
  VARIABLE result : std_ulogic_vector ( 1 TO s'LENGTH );
BEGIN
  FOR i IN result'RANGE LOOP
    result(i) := cvt_to_x01z (sv(i));
  END LOOP;
  RETURN result;
END;
----------------------------------------------------
FUNCTION To_X01Z ( s : std_ulogic ) RETURN X01Z IS
BEGIN
  RETURN (cvt_to_x01z(s));
END;
----------------------------------------------------
FUNCTION To_X01Z ( b : BIT_VECTOR ) RETURN std_logic_vector IS
  ALIAS bv : BIT_VECTOR ( 1 TO b'LENGTH ) IS b;
  VARIABLE result : std_logic_vector ( 1 TO b'LENGTH );
BEGIN
  FOR i IN result'RANGE LOOP
    CASE bv(i) IS
      WHEN '0' => result(i) := '0';
      WHEN '1' => result(i) := '1';
    END CASE;
  END LOOP;
  RETURN result;
END;
----------------------------------------------------
FUNCTION To_X01Z ( b : BIT_VECTOR ) RETURN std_ulogic_vector IS
  ALIAS bv : BIT_VECTOR ( 1 TO b'LENGTH ) IS b;
  VARIABLE result : std_ulogic_vector ( 1 TO b'LENGTH );
BEGIN
  FOR i IN result'RANGE LOOP
    CASE bv(i) IS
      WHEN '0' => result(i) := '0';
      WHEN '1' => result(i) := '1';
    END CASE;
  END LOOP;
  RETURN result;
END;
----------------------------------------------------
```

```vhdl
FUNCTION To_X01Z ( b : BIT ) RETURN X01Z IS
BEGIN
   CASE b IS
     WHEN '0' => RETURN('0');
     WHEN '1' => RETURN('1');
   END CASE;
END;
------------------------------------------------------
-- to_ux01
------------------------------------------------------
FUNCTION To_UX01 ( s : std_logic_vector ) RETURN std_logic_vector IS
  ALIAS sv : std_logic_vector ( 1 TO s'LENGTH ) IS s;
  VARIABLE result : std_logic_vector ( 1 TO s'LENGTH );
BEGIN
  FOR i IN result'RANGE LOOP
    result(i) := cvt_to_ux01 (sv(i));
  END LOOP;
  RETURN result;
END;
------------------------------------------------------
FUNCTION To_UX01 ( s : std_ulogic_vector ) RETURN std_ulogic_vector IS
  ALIAS sv : std_ulogic_vector ( 1 TO s'LENGTH ) IS s;
  VARIABLE result : std_ulogic_vector ( 1 TO s'LENGTH );
BEGIN
  FOR i IN result'RANGE LOOP
    result(i) := cvt_to_ux01 (sv(i));
  END LOOP;
  RETURN result;
END;
------------------------------------------------------
FUNCTION To_UX01 ( s : std_ulogic ) RETURN UX01 IS
BEGIN
  RETURN (cvt_to_ux01(s));
END;
------------------------------------------------------
FUNCTION To_UX01 ( b : BIT_VECTOR ) RETURN std_logic_vector IS
  ALIAS bv : BIT_VECTOR ( 1 TO b'LENGTH ) IS b;
  VARIABLE result : std_logic_vector ( 1 TO b'LENGTH );
BEGIN
  FOR i IN result'RANGE LOOP
    CASE bv(i) IS
      WHEN '0' => result(i) := '0';
      WHEN '1' => result(i) := '1';
    END CASE;
  END LOOP;
  RETURN result;
END;
------------------------------------------------------
FUNCTION To_UX01 ( b : BIT_VECTOR ) RETURN std_ulogic_vector IS
  ALIAS bv : BIT_VECTOR ( 1 TO b'LENGTH ) IS b;
  VARIABLE result : std_ulogic_vector ( 1 TO b'LENGTH );
BEGIN
  FOR i IN result'RANGE LOOP
```

```
      CASE bv(i) IS
        WHEN '0' => result(i) := '0';
        WHEN '1' => result(i) := '1';
      END CASE;
    END LOOP;
    RETURN result;
END;
--------------------------------------------------------
FUNCTION To_UX01 ( b : BIT ) RETURN UX01 IS
BEGIN
    CASE b IS
      WHEN '0' => RETURN('0');
      WHEN '1' => RETURN('1');
    END CASE;
END;

--------------------------------------------------------
-- edge detection
--------------------------------------------------------
FUNCTION rising_edge (SIGNAL s : std_ulogic) RETURN BOOLEAN IS
BEGIN
  RETURN (s'EVENT AND (To_X01(s) = '1') AND
          (To_X01(s'LAST_VALUE) = '0'));
END;

FUNCTION falling_edge (SIGNAL s : std_ulogic) RETURN BOOLEAN IS
BEGIN
  RETURN (s'EVENT AND (To_X01(s) = '0') AND
          (To_X01(s'LAST_VALUE) = '1'));
END;

--------------------------------            -------------
-- object contains an unknown
--------------------------------------------------------
FUNCTION Is_X ( s : std_ulogic_vector ) RETURN BOOLEAN IS
BEGIN
  FOR i IN s'RANGE LOOP
    CASE s(i) IS
        WHEN 'U' | 'X' | 'Z' | 'W' | '-' => RETURN TRUE;
      WHEN OTHERS => NULL;
    END CASE;
  END LOOP;
  RETURN FALSE;
END;
--------------------------------------------------------
FUNCTION Is_X ( s : std_logic_vector ) RETURN BOOLEAN IS
BEGIN
  FOR i IN s'RANGE LOOP
    CASE s(i) IS
        WHEN 'U' | 'X' | 'Z' | 'W' | '-' => RETURN TRUE;
      WHEN OTHERS => NULL;
    END CASE;
  END LOOP;
  RETURN FALSE;
```

```
END;
-------------------------------------------------
FUNCTION Is_X ( s : std_ulogic ) RETURN BOOLEAN IS
BEGIN
  CASE s IS
     WHEN 'U' | 'X' | 'Z' | 'W' | '-' => RETURN TRUE;
    WHEN OTHERS => NULL;
  END CASE;
  RETURN FALSE;
END;

END std_logic_1164;
```

Vending Machine Netlists

Listed here are the gate-level netlists produced by the Synopsys Design Compiler for the VHDL source code in Chap. 12. The synthesis process used a sample library called class.db provided by Synopsys to produce these results. This library is not optimized for any particular gate array and, therefore, the results generated are purely for reference.

The first netlist is for the item processor. This netlist will initially define some components that will be used later, and then connect all these components to produce the netlist for the design.

```vhdl
entity rpl_inc_n8_1 is

  port( A_7_port, A_6_port, A_5_port, A_4_port, A_3_port, A_2_port, A_1_port,
      A_0_port : in BIT; SUM_7_port, SUM_6_port, SUM_5_port, SUM_4_port,
      SUM_3_port, SUM_2_port, SUM_1_port, SUM_0_port : out BIT);

end rpl_inc_n8_1;

architecture STRUCTURAL_VIEW of rpl_inc_n8_1 is

  component AN3
    port( A, B, C : in BIT; Z : out BIT);
  end component;

  component MUX21L
    port( A, B, S : in BIT; Z : out BIT);
  end component;

  component NR2
    port( A, B : in BIT; Z : out BIT);
  end component;

  component IV
    port( A : in BIT; Z : out BIT);
  end component;
```

```
component ND2
  port( A, B : in BIT; Z : out BIT);
end component;

component EN
  port( A, B : in BIT; Z : out BIT);
end component;

component EO
  port( A, B : in BIT; Z : out BIT);
end component;

component EO1
  port( A, B, C, D : in BIT; Z : out BIT);
end component;

signal n40, n34, n35, n36, n37, n38, n39 : BIT;

begin

  U40 : NR2 port map( A => n36, B => n37, Z => n35);
  U41 : AN3 port map( A => A_1_port, B => A_0_port, C => A_2_port, Z =>
            n38);
  U42 : AN3 port map( A => n38, B => A_4_port, C => A_3_port, Z => n39);
  U43 : ND2 port map( A => A_5_port, B => n39, Z => n36);
  U44 : EO1 port map( A => A_0_port, B => A_1_port, C => A_0_port, D =>
            A_1_port, Z => SUM_1_port);
  U45 : EO port map( A => A_7_port, B => n35, Z => SUM_7_port);
  U46 : EO port map( A => n39, B => A_5_port, Z => SUM_5_port);
  U33 : EN port map( A => n40, B => A_4_port, Z => SUM_4_port);
  U34 : EO port map( A => n38, B => A_3_port, Z => SUM_3_port);
  U35 : EN port map( A => n34, B => A_2_port, Z => SUM_2_port);
  U36 : ND2 port map( A => A_3_port, B => n38, Z => n40);
  U37 : ND2 port map( A => A_1_port, B => A_0_port, Z => n34);
  U38 : IV port map( A => A_0_port, Z => SUM_0_port);
  U39 : IV port map( A => A_6_port, Z => n37);
  U2 : MUX21L port map( A => A_6_port, B => n37, S => n36, Z => SUM_6_port
            );

end STRUCTURAL_VIEW;

entity comp_1m2_n8_7 is

  port( A_7_port, A_6_port, A_5_port, A_4_port, A_3_port, A_2_port, A_1_port,
      A_0_port, B_7_port, B_6_port, B_5_port, B_4_port, B_3_port, B_2_port,
      B_1_port, B_0_port, LEQ, TC : in BIT; LT_LE, GE_GT : out BIT);

end comp_1m2_n8_7;

architecture STRUCTURAL_VIEW of comp_1m2_n8_7 is

  component AN2
    port( A, B : in BIT; Z : out BIT);
  end component;

  component AO1P
    port( A, B, C, D : in BIT; Z : out BIT);
  end component;
```

```
component NR2
  port( A, B : in BIT; Z : out BIT);
end component;

component EON1
  port( A, B, C, D : in BIT; Z : out BIT);
end component;

component AN2P
  port( A, B : in BIT; Z : out BIT);
end component;

component AO4
  port( A, B, C, D : in BIT; Z : out BIT);
end component;

component IVA
  port( A : in BIT; Z : out BIT);
end component;

component IV
  port( A : in BIT; Z : out BIT);
end component;

component EO1
  port( A, B, C, D : in BIT; Z : out BIT);
end component;

signal n140, n141, n142, n143, n130, n144, n131, n132, n133, n134, n135,
  n136, n137, n138, n139, n129 : BIT;

begin

  U30 : NR2 port map( A => B_4_port, B => n140, Z => n139);
  U31 : AO1P port map( A => B_5_port, B => n142, C => B_6_port, D =>
          B_7_port, Z => n141);
  U32 : AN2P port map( A => n129, B => A_3_port, Z => n143);
  U20 : IV port map( A => A_2_port, Z => n138);
  U21 : IV port map( A => A_1_port, Z => n136);
  U22 : AN2 port map( A => n133, B => LEQ, Z => n144);
  U23 : IV port map( A => A_0_port, Z => n133);
  U24 : NR2 port map( A => B_1_port, B => n136, Z => n135);
  U25 : IV port map( A => n141, Z => LT_LE);
  U26 : AN2 port map( A => n138, B => B_2_port, Z => n137);
  U13 : IV port map( A => n134, Z => n142);
  U14 : AO4 port map( A => A_3_port, B => n129, C => n143, D => n130, Z =>
          n140);
  U15 : AO4 port map( A => LEQ, B => n133, C => B_0_port, D => n144, Z =>
          n131);
  U16 : EON1 port map( A => n135, B => n131, C => n136, D => B_1_port, Z
          => n132);
  U17 : AO4 port map( A => B_2_port, B => n138, C => n137, D => n132, Z =>
          n130);
  U18 : EO1 port map( A => n140, B => B_4_port, C => A_4_port, D => n139,
          Z => n134);
  U19 : IVA port map( A => B_3_port, Z => n129);
```

```
end STRUCTURAL_VIEW;

entity comp_1m2_n8_8 is

  port( A_7_port, A_6_port, A_5_port, A_4_port, A_3_port, A_2_port, A_1_port,
     A_0_port, B_7_port, B_6_port, B_5_port, B_4_port, B_3_port, B_2_port,
     B_1_port, B_0_port, LEQ, TC : in BIT; LT_LE, GE_GT : out BIT);

end comp_1m2_n8_8;

architecture STRUCTURAL_VIEW of comp_1m2_n8_8 is

  component NR2
    port( A, B : in BIT; Z : out BIT);
  end component;

  component NR3
    port( A, B, C : in BIT; Z : out BIT);
  end component;

  component AO3
    port( A, B, C, D : in BIT; Z : out BIT);
  end component;

  component AO6
    port( A, B, C : in BIT; Z : out BIT);
  end component;

  component IV
    port( A : in BIT; Z : out BIT);
  end component;

  signal n125, n126, n127, n128 : BIT;

begin
    U8 : AO6 port map( A => LEQ, B => B_0_port, C => B_1_port, Z => n125);
    U9 : NR3 port map( A => B_4_port, B => B_6_port, C => B_5_port, Z =>
            n128);
    U10 : NR2 port map( A => B_3_port, B => B_7_port, Z => n127);
    U11 : IV port map( A => B_2_port, Z => n126);
    U12 : AO3 port map( A => n125, B => n126, C => n127, D => n128, Z =>
            LT_LE);

end STRUCTURAL_VIEW;


entity comp_1m2_n8_9 is

  port( A_7_port, A_6_port, A_5_port, A_4_port, A_3_port, A_2_port, A_1_port,
     A_0_port, B_7_port, B_6_port, B_5_port, B_4_port, B_3_port, B_2_port,
     B_1_port, B_0_port, LEQ, TC : in BIT; LT_LE, GE_GT : out BIT);

end comp_1m2_n8_9;

architecture STRUCTURAL_VIEW of comp_1m2_n8_9 is

  component NR2
    port( A, B : in BIT; Z : out BIT);
  end component;
```

```
component NR4
  port( A, B, C, D : in BIT; Z : out BIT);
end component;

component OR3
  port( A, B, C : in BIT; Z : out BIT);
end component;

component AO6
  port( A, B, C : in BIT; Z : out BIT);
end component;

component IV
  port( A : in BIT; Z : out BIT);
end component;

signal n121, n122, n123, n124 : BIT;

begin

  U7 : NR4 port map( A => n121, B => n122, C => B_4_port, D => B_3_port, Z
          => GE_GT);
  U3 : AO6 port map( A => LEQ, B => B_0_port, C => B_1_port, Z => n123);
  U4 : NR2 port map( A => n123, B => n124, Z => n122);
  U5 : OR3 port map( A => B_7_port, B => B_6_port, C => B_5_port, Z =>
          n121);
  U6 : IV port map( A => B_2_port, Z => n124);

end STRUCTURAL_VIEW;
```

Here is the actual entity for the item processor.

```
entity item_proc is

  port( total_7_port, total_6_port, total_5_port, total_4_port, total_3_port,
     total_2_port, total_1_port, total_0_port, item_sel_2_port,
     item_sel_1_port, item_sel_0_port, item_stb : in BIT; item_out_2_port,
     item_out_1_port, item_out_0_port, item_out_stb : out BIT; clock,
     reset : in BIT; price_7_port, price_6_port, price_5_port,
     price_4_port, price_3_port, price_2_port, price_1_port, price_0_port,
     p_empty, ch_empty, c_empty, d_empty : out BIT);

end item_proc;

architecture STRUCTURAL_VIEW of item_proc is

  component rpl_inc_n8_1
    port( A_7_port, A_6_port, A_5_port, A_4_port, A_3_port, A_2_port,
       A_1_port, A_0_port : in BIT; SUM_7_port, SUM_6_port, SUM_5_port,
       SUM_4_port, SUM_3_port, SUM_2_port, SUM_1_port, SUM_0_port : out
       BIT);
  end component;

  component OR2
    port( A, B : in BIT; Z : out BIT);
  end component;
```

```
component OR3
  port( A, B, C : in BIT; Z : out BIT);
end component;

component AN2P
  port( A, B : in BIT; Z : out BIT);
end component;

component LD1
  port( D, G : in BIT; Q, QN : out BIT);
end component;

component comp_1m2_n8_7
  port( A_7_port, A_6_port, A_5_port, A_4_port, A_3_port, A_2_port,
     A_1_port, A_0_port, B_7_port, B_6_port, B_5_port, B_4_port,
     B_3_port, B_2_port, B_1_port, B_0_port, LEQ, TC : in BIT; LT_LE,
     GE_GT : out BIT);
end component;

component comp_1m2_n8_8
  port( A_7_port, A_6_port, A_5_port, A_4_port, A_3_port, A_2_port,
     A_1_port, A_0_port, B_7_port, B_6_port, B_5_port, B_4_port,
     B_3_port, B_2_port, B_1_port, B_0_port, LEQ, TC : in BIT; LT_LE,
     GE_GT : out BIT);
end component:

component comp_1m2_n8_9
  port( A_7_port, A_6_port, A_5_port, A_4_port, A_3_port, A_2_port,
     A_1_port, A_0_port, B_7_port, B_6_port, B_5_port, B_4_port,
     B_3_port, B_2_port, B_1_port, B_0_port, LEQ, TC : in BIT; LT_LE,
     GE_GT : out BIT);
end component;

component IV
  port( A : in BIT; Z : out BIT);
end component;

component ND2
  port( A, B : in BIT; Z : out BIT);
end component;

component ND3
  port( A, B, C : in BIT; Z : out BIT);
end component;

component ND4
  port( A, B, C, D : in BIT; Z : out BIT);
end component;

component AN3
  port( A, B, C : in BIT; Z : out BIT);
end component;

component AN4
  port( A, B, C, D : in BIT; Z : out BIT);
end component;
```

```
component AO1P
  port( A, B, C, D : in BIT; Z : out BIT);
end component;

component NR2
  port( A, B : in BIT; Z : out BIT);
end component;

component NR3
  port( A, B, C : in BIT; Z : out BIT);
end component;

component AO1
  port( A, B, C, D : in BIT; Z : out BIT);
end component;

component AO2
  port( A, B, C, D : in BIT; Z : out BIT);
end component;

component AO4
  port( A, B, C, D : in BIT; Z : out BIT);
end component;

component IVA
  port( A : in BIT; Z : out BIT);
end component;

component FD2
  port( D, CP, CD : in BIT; Q, QN : out BIT);
end component;

component IVP
  port( A : in BIT; Z : out BIT);
end component;

signal n437, n438, n439, n510, n511, n512, n513, n514, n515, n516, n517,
n518, n519, ch_sold_1_port, ch_sold_5_port, p_sold_0_port,
price118_5_port, p_sold_4_port, price118_1_port, X_cell_814_U60_Z_3_port,
c_sold_0_port, present_state_0_port, net420, net421, net423,
c_sold_4_port, net425, net429, Logic0, n419_0_port, d_sold_7_port,
d_sold_3_port, n164, n480, n481, n482, n483, n484, n485, n486, n487, n488
, n489, sum326_4_port, n440, n441, n442, n443, is_less333, n444, n445,
n446, n447, n448, n449, sum326_0_port, n520, n521, n522, n523,
ch_sold_0_port, ch_sold_4_port, n94_2_port, p_sold_3_port,
price118_2_port, p_sold_7_port, item_out_stb_port,
X_cell_814_U60_Z_4_port, item_out93_2_port, net430, net431,
X_cell_814_U60_Z_0_port, net433, c_sold_3_port, net434, net435, net436,
net437, c_sold_7_port, d_sold_4_port, d_sold_0_port, n490, n491, n492,
n493, n494, n495, n496, n497, n498, n499, sum326_5_port, n450, n451, n452
, n453, n454, n455, n456, n457, n458, n459, sum326_1_port,
X_cell_814_U52_Z_0_port, ch_sold_3_port, ch_sold_7_port, p_sold_2_port,
price118_3_port, p_sold_6_port, X_cell_814_U60_Z_5_port, net440, net441,
X_cell_814_U60_Z_1_port, net442, net443, c_sold_2_port, net444, net445,
net447, net449, net400, net403, c_sold_6_port, net404, net405, net406,
net407, net408, net409, d_sold_5_port, n181, d_sold_1_port, n147,
```

```
sum326_6_port, n460, n461, n462, n463, n464, n465, n466, n467, n468, n469
, sum326_2_port, is_less236, n424, n425, n426, n427, n428, n429, n500,
n501, n502, n503, n504, n505, n506, n507, n508, n509, ch_sold_2_port,
ch_sold_6_port, p_sold_1_port, price118_4_port, p_sold_5_port,
price118_0_port, X_cell_814_U60_Z_6_port, X_cell_814_U60_Z_2_port,
c_sold_1_port, present_state_1_port, net410, c_sold_5_port, net416,
net417, net418, net419, X_cell_814_U53_Z_7_port, d_sold_6_port, n198,
d_sold_2_port, sum326_7_port, n470, n471, n472, n473, n474, n475, n476,
n477, n478, n479, sum326_3_port, n430, n431, is_less228, n432, n433, n434
, n435, n436 : BIT;

begin

  item_out_stb <= item_out_stb_port;

  c_sold_reg_7_label : FD2 port map( D => n520, CP => clock, CD => n508, Q
          => c_sold_7_port, QN => net449);
  price_reg_1_label : LD1 port map( D => price118_1_port, G => n94_2_port,
          Q => price_1_port, QN => open);
  c_sold_reg_3_label : FD2 port map( D => n518, CP => clock, CD => n508, Q
          => c_sold_3_port, QN => net445);
  p_sold_reg_6_label : FD2 port map( D => n516, CP => clock, CD => n508, Q
          => p_sold_6_port, QN => net443);
  p_sold_reg_2_label : FD2 port map( D => n514, CP => clock, CD => n508, Q
          => p_sold_2_port, QN => net441);
  item_out_reg_2_label : LD1 port map( D => item_out93_2_port, G =>
          n94_2_port, Q => item_out_2_port, QN => open);
  leq_170 : AO4 port map( A => n460, B => n480, C => n448, D => net423, Z
          => n501);
  leq_171 : AO2 port map( A => ch_sold_6_port, B => n472, C =>
          d_sold_6_port, D => item_out93_2_port, Z => n482);
  leq_172 : NR2 port map( A => present_state_1_port, B =>
          present_state_0_port, Z => n424);
  leq_173 : NR2 port map( A => n470, B => n438, Z => n468);
  leq_174 : AO1 port map( A => n449, B => n426, C => item_out_stb_port, D
          => n424, Z => n467);
  leq_175 : ND2 port map( A => n438, B => n425, Z => n451);
  leq_176 : ND2 port map( A => n466, B => n425, Z => n464);
  leq_177 : ND2 port map( A => n466, B => n437, Z => n478);
  leq_178 : ND2 port map( A => n444, B => n425, Z => n460);
  leq_179 : AN4 port map( A => n468, B => n475, C => n443, D => n477, Z =>
          n448);
  leq_130 : OR3 port map( A => item_sel_1_port, B => item_sel_0_port, C =>
          n434, Z => n469);
  leq_131 : AO2 port map( A => c_sold_2_port, B => n432, C =>
          ch_sold_2_port, D => n472, Z => n428);
  d_sold_reg_0_label : FD2 port map( D => n512, CP => clock, CD => n508, Q
          => d_sold_0_port, QN => net437);
  leq_132 : AO4 port map( A => n464, B => n452, C => n465, D => net440, Z
          => n513);
  leq_133 : AO2 port map( A => ch_sold_3_port, B => n472, C =>
          c_sold_3_port, D => n432, Z => n430);
  leq_134 : AO4 port map( A => n465, B => net416, C => n464, D => n442, Z
          => n495);
```

```
leq_135 : AO2 port map( A => d_sold_3_port, B => item_out93_2_port, C =>
          p_sold_3_port, D => n433, Z => n431);
leq_136 : AO2 port map( A => p_sold_4_port, B => n433, C =>
          d_sold_4_port, D => item_out93_2_port, Z => n454);
leq_137 : AO2 port map( A => ch_sold_4_port, B => n472, C =>
          c_sold_4_port, D => n432, Z => n455);
leq_138 : AO2 port map( A => p_sold_5_port, B => n433, C =>
          d_sold_5_port, D => item_out93_2_port, Z => n456);
leq_139 : AO2 port map( A => ch_sold_5_port, B => n472, C =>
          c_sold_5_port, D => n432, Z => n457);
d_sold_reg_4_label : FD2 port map( D => n509, CP => clock, CD => n508, Q
          => d_sold_4_port, QN => net434);
leq_210 : AO4 port map( A => n451, B => n447, C => n453, D => net408, Z
          => n492);
ch_sold_reg_3_label : FD2 port map( D => n507, CP => clock, CD => n508,
          Q => ch_sold_3_port, QN => net433);
leq_211 : IVA port map( A => n443, Z => n466);
leq_212 : NR2 port map( A => n429, B => n461, Z => n164);
leq_213 : AO4 port map( A => n451, B => n446, C => n453, D => net436, Z
          => n511);
leq_214 : IV port map( A => n440, Z => n477);
leq_215 : ND2 port map( A => n456, B => n457, Z =>
          X_cell_814_U60_Z_5_port);
Logic0 <= '0';
leq_216 : AO4 port map( A => n453, B => net410, C => n451, D => n442, Z
          => n494);
price118_5_port <= '1';
leq_217 : IVP port map( A => n484, Z => n472);
leq_218 : NR2 port map( A => n429, B => n460, Z => n181);
leq_219 : AO4 port map( A => n451, B => n452, C => n453, D => net437, Z
          => n512);
ch_sold_reg_7_label : FD2 port map( D => n504, CP => clock, CD => n508,
          Q => ch_sold_7_port, QN => net429);
price_reg_6_label : LD1 port map( D => n521, G => n94_2_port, Q =>
          price_6_port, QN => open);
price_reg_2_label : LD1 port map( D => price118_2_port, G => n94_2_port,
          Q => price_2_port, QN => open);
c_sold_reg_4_label : FD2 port map( D => n501, CP => clock, CD => n508, Q
          => c_sold_4_port, QN => net423);
p_sold_reg_7_label : FD2 port map( D => n498, CP => clock, CD => n508, Q
          => p_sold_7_port, QN => net419);
c_sold_reg_0_label : FD2 port map( D => n499, CP => clock, CD => n508, Q
          => c_sold_0_port, QN => net420);
p_sold_reg_3_label : FD2 port map( D => n496, CP => clock, CD => n508, Q
          => p_sold_3_port, QN => net417);
p_empty_reg : LD1 port map( D => n522, G => n147, Q => p_empty, QN =>
          open);
leq_180 : ND2 port map( A => n440, B => n425, Z => n461);
leq_181 : ND2 port map( A => n444, B => n437, Z => n475);
leq_182 : NR2 port map( A => n483, B => n435, Z => n444);
leq_183 : NR2 port map( A => net400, B => present_state_0_port, Z =>
          item_out_stb_port);
leq_184 : ND3 port map( A => item_sel_0_port, B => n434, C =>
          item_sel_1_port, Z => n483);
```

```
leq_185 : OR3 port map( A => n444, B => n440, C => n466, Z => n473);
leq_186 : AO2 port map( A => ch_sold_7_port, B => n472, C =>
            p_sold_7_port, D => n433, Z => n474);
leq_187 : IVA port map( A => sum326_6_port, Z => n436);
leq_188 : AO2 port map( A => d_sold_7_port, B => item_out93_2_port, C =>
            c_sold_7_port, D => n432, Z => n476);
leq_189 : AO2 port map( A => ch_sold_0_port, B => n472, C =>
            p_sold_0_port, D => n433, Z => n458);
leq_140 : AO2 port map( A => c_sold_6_port, B => n432, C =>
            p_sold_6_port, D => n433, Z => n479);
leq_141 : IV port map( A => item_sel_2_port, Z => n434);
leq_142 : AN4 port map( A => n468, B => n450, C => n481, D => n443, Z =>
            n445);
leq_143 : ND2 port map( A => n440, B => n437, Z => n450);
leq_144 : AO1P port map( A => n437, B => n438, C => n470, D => n473, Z
            => n453);
leq_145 : AN4 port map( A => n468, B => n478, C => n481, D => n477, Z =>
            n465);
leq_146 : AN3 port map( A => n425, B => X_cell_814_U52_Z_0_port, C =>
            n426, Z => n486);
leq_147 : AN2P port map( A => n424, B => item_stb, Z => n503);
leq_148 : IVA port map( A => sum326_3_port, Z => n447);
leq_149 : IVA port map( A => sum326_7_port, Z => n441);
d_sold_reg_3_label : FD2 port map( D => n492, CP => clock, CD => n508, Q
            => d_sold_3_port, QN => net408);
leq_220 : IV port map( A => n437, Z => n425);
ch_sold_reg_2_label : FD2 port map( D => n491, CP => clock, CD => n508,
            Q => ch_sold_2_port, QN => net407);
leq_221 : ND2 port map( A => n454, B => n455, Z =>
            X_cell_814_U60_Z_4_port);
leq_222 : IVP port map( A => n435, Z => n426);
leq_223 : NR2 port map( A => n429, B => n451, Z => n198);
leq_224 : IVA port map( A => n469, Z => item_out93_2_port);
leq_225 : AO4 port map( A => n464, B => n446, C => n465, D => net441, Z
            => n514);
leq_226 : ND2 port map( A => n430, B => n431, Z =>
            X_cell_814_U60_Z_3_port);
leq_227 : AO4 port map( A => n464, B => n447, C => n465, D => net417, Z
            => n496);
leq_228 : NR2 port map( A => n429, B => n464, Z => n147);
leq_229 : AO4 port map( A => n445, B => net429, C => n461, D => n441, Z
            => n504);
d_sold_reg_7_label : FD2 port map( D => n488, CP => clock, CD => n508, Q
            => d_sold_7_port, QN => net404);
r18 : comp_1m2_n8_9 port map( A_7_port => Logic0, A_6_port => Logic0,
            A_5_port => Logic0, A_4_port => Logic0, A_3_port =>
            Logic0, A_2_port => price118_5_port, A_1_port =>
            Logic0, A_0_port => price118_5_port, B_7_port =>
            X_cell_814_U53_Z_7_port, B_6_port =>
            X_cell_814_U60_Z_6_port, B_5_port =>
            X_cell_814_U60_Z_5_port, B_4_port =>
            X_cell_814_U60_Z_4_port, B_3_port =>
            X_cell_814_U60_Z_3_port, B_2_port =>
```

```
            X_cell_814_U60_Z_2_port, B_1_port =>
            X_cell_814_U60_Z_1_port, B_0_port =>
            X_cell_814_U60_Z_0_port, LEQ =>
            X_cell_814_U52_Z_0_port, TC => n419_0_port, LT_LE =>
            open, GE_GT => is_less228);
ch_sold_reg_6_label : FD2 port map( D => n487, CP => clock, CD => n508,
            Q => ch_sold_6_port, QN => net403);
r104 : comp_lm2_n8_8 port map( A_7_port => Logic0, A_6_port => Logic0,
            A_5_port => Logic0, A_4_port => Logic0, A_3_port =>
            Logic0, A_2_port => price118_5_port, A_1_port =>
            Logic0, A_0_port => price118_5_port, B_7_port =>
            X_cell_814_U53_Z_7_port, B_6_port =>
            X_cell_814_U60_Z_6_port, B_5_port =>
            X_cell_814_U60_Z_5_port, B_4_port =>
            X_cell_814_U60_Z_4_port, B_3_port =>
            X_cell_814_U60_Z_3_port, B_2_port =>
            X_cell_814_U60_Z_2_port, B_1_port =>
            X_cell_814_U60_Z_1_port, B_0_port =>
            X_cell_814_U60_Z_0_port, LEQ =>
            X_cell_814_U52_Z_0_port, TC => n419_0_port, LT_LE =>
            is_less333, GE_GT => open);
r106 : comp_lm2_n8_7 port map( A_7_port => Logic0, A_6_port => Logic0,
            A_5_port => price118_5_port, A_4_port =>
            price118_4_port, A_3_port => price118_3_port,
            A_2_port => price118_2_port, A_1_port =>
            price118_1_port, A_0_port => price118_0_port,
            B_7_port => total_7_port, B_6_port => total_6_port,
            B_5_port => total_5_port, B_4_port => total_4_port,
            B_3_port => total_3_port, B_2_port => total_2_port,
            B_1_port => total_1_port, B_0_port => total_0_port,
            LEQ => X_cell_814_U52_Z_0_port, TC => n419_0_port,
            LT_LE => is_less236, GE_GT => open);
price_reg_7_label : LD1 port map( D => n521, G => n94_2_port, Q =>
            price_7_port, QN => open);
price_reg_3_label : LD1 port map( D => price_118_3_port, G => n94_2_port,
            Q => price_3_port, QN => open);
c_sold_reg_5_label : FD2 port map( D => n519, CP => clock, CD => n508, Q
            => c_sold_5_port, QN => net447);
c_sold_reg_1_label : FD2 port map( D => n517, CP => clock, CD => n508, Q
            => c_sold_1_port, QN => net444);
p_sold_reg_4_label : FD2 port map( D => n515, CP => clock, CD => n508, Q
            => p_sold_4_port, QN => net442);
p_sold_reg_0_label : FD2 port map( D => n513, CP => clock, CD => n508, Q
            => p_sold_0_port, QN => net440);
leq_190 : AO2 port map( A => d_sold_0_port, B => item_out93_2_port, C =>
            c_sold_0_port, D => n432, Z => n459);
item_out_reg_0_label : LD1 port map( D => price118_1_port, G =>
            n94_2_port, Q => item_out_0_port, QN => open);
leq_191 : AO2 port map( A => d_sold_1_port, B => item_out93_2_port, C =>
            p_sold_1_port, D => n433, Z => n462);
leq_192 : IVA port map( A => sum326_0_port, Z => n452);
leq_193 : IV port map( A => is_less333, Z => n429);
leq_194 : IVP port map( A => item_sel_0_port, Z => n439);
```

```
leq_195 : IVA port map( A => sum326_5_port, Z => n485);
leq_196 : IVA port map( A => n471, Z => price118_1_port);
leq_197 : IVA port map( A => sum326_4_port, Z => n480);
leq_198 : OR2 port map( A => item_out93_2_port, B => price118_0_port, Z
          => price118_2_port);
leq_199 : IVA port map( A => sum326_1_port, Z => n442);
leq_150 : ND4 port map( A => n460, B => n464, C => n461, D => n451, Z =>
          n94_2_port);
leq_151 : IVA port map( A => n449, Z => X_cell_814_U52_Z_0_port);
leq_152 : ND2 port map( A => n458, B => n459, Z =>
          X_cell_814_U60_Z_0_port);
leq_153 : NR2 port map( A => n432, B => n433, Z => n471);
leq_154 : AO4 port map( A => n465, B => net419, C => n464, D => n441, Z
          => n498);
leq_155 : AO4 port map( A => n464, B => n436, C => n465, D => net443, Z
          => n516);
leq_156 : AO4 port map( A => n464, B => n485, C => n465, D => net418, Z
          => n497);
leq_157 : AO4 port map( A => n460, B => n485, C => n448, D => net447, Z
          => n519);
leq_158 : AO4 port map( A => n464, B => n480, C => n465, D => net442, Z
          => n515);
leq_159 : AO4 port map( A => n461, B => n442, C => n445, D => net435, Z
          => n510);
d_sold_reg_2_label : FD2 port map( D => n511, CP => clock, CD => n508, Q
          => d_sold_2_port, QN => net436);
leq_230 : ND2 port map( A => n427, B => n428, Z =>
          X_cell_814_U60_Z_2_port);
ch_sold_reg_1_label : FD2 port map( D => n510, CP => clock, CD => n508,
          Q => ch_sold_1_port, QN => net435);
leq_231 : AO4 port map( A => n461, B => n436, C => n445, D => net403, Z
          => n487);
leq_232 : ND2 port map( A => n462, B => n463, Z =>
          X_cell_814_U60_Z_1_port);
leq_233 : AO4 port map( A => n461, B => n485, C => n445, D => net430, Z
          => n505);
leq_234 : AO4 port map( A => n461, B => n480, C => n445, D => net405, Z
          => n489);
leq_235 : AO4 port map( A => n460, B => n441, C => n448, D => net449, Z
          => n520);
leq_236 : AO4 port map( A => n461, B => n447, C => n445, D => net433, Z
          => n507);
leq_237 : AO4 port map( A => n460, B => n436, C => n448, D => net425, Z
          => n502);
d_empty_reg : LD1 port map( D => n522, G => n198, Q => d_empty, QN =>
          open);
leq_238 : AO4 port map( A => n461, B => n446, C => n445, D => net407, Z
          => n491);
n419_0_port <= '0';
d_sold_reg_6_label : FD2 port map( D => n506, CP => clock, CD => n508, Q
          => d_sold_6_port, QN => net431);
ch_sold_reg_5_label : FD2 port map( D => n505, CP => clock, CD => n508,
          Q => ch_sold_5_port, QN => net430);
```

```
present_state_reg_0_label : FD2 port map( D => n503, CP => clock, CD =>
          n508, Q => present_state_0_port, QN => open);
price_reg_4_label : LD1 port map( D => price118_4_port, G => n94_2_port,
          Q => price_4_port, QN => open);
c_sold_reg_6_label : FD2 port map( D => n502, CP => clock, CD => n508, Q
          => c_sold_6_port, QN => net425);
price_reg_0_label : LD1 port map( D => price118_0_port, G => n94_2_port,
          Q => price_0_port, QN => open);
c_sold_reg_2_label : FD2 port map( D => n500, CP => clock, CD => n508, Q
          => c_sold_2_port, QN => net421);
p_sold_reg_5_label : FD2 port map( D => n497, CP => clock, CD => n508, Q
          => p_sold_5_port, QN => net418);
p_sold_reg_1_label : FD2 port map( D => n495, CP => clock, CD => n508, Q
          => p_sold_1_port, QN => net416);
n523 <= '1';
n522 <= '1';
n521 <= '0';
item_out_reg_1_label : LD1 port map( D => price118_0_port, G =>
          n94_2_port, Q => item_out_1_port, QN => open);
leq_160 : ND2 port map( A => n479, B => n482, Z =>
          X_cell_814_U60_Z_6_port);
leq_161 : AO4 port map( A => n461, B => n452, C => n445, D => net409, Z
          => n493);
leq_162 : ND2 port map( A => n474, B => n476, Z =>
          X_cell_814_U53_Z_7_port);
leq_163 : IVA port map( A => reset, Z => n508);
leq_164 : ND2 port map( A => n469, B => n471, Z => price118_4_port);
leq_165 : AO4 port map( A => n460, B => n452, C => n448, D => net420, Z
          => n499);
leq_166 : AO4 port map( A => n460, B => n442, C => n448, D => net444, Z
          => n517);
leq_167 : AO4 port map( A => n460, B => n446, C => n448, D => net421, Z
          => n500);
leq_168 : AO4 port map( A => n460, B => n447, C => n448, D => net445, Z
          => n518);
leq_169 : NR2 port map( A => price118_2_port, B => n433, Z => n449);
leq_121 : ND2 port map( A => n433, B => n426, Z => n443);
d_sold_reg_1_label : FD2 port map( D => n494, CP => clock, CD => n508, Q
          => d_sold_1_port, QN => net410);
leq_122 : NR3 port map( A => item_sel_1_port, B => item_sel_2_port, C =>
          n439, Z => n433);
leq_123 : NR2 port map( A => n484, B => n435, Z => n440);
ch_sold_reg_0_label : FD2 port map( D => n493, CP => clock, CD => n508,
          Q => ch_sold_0_port, QN => net409);
leq_124 : ND3 port map( A => n434, B => n439, C => item_sel_1_port, Z =>
          n484);
leq_125 : NR2 port map( A => n435, B => n469, Z => n438);
leq_126 : ND2 port map( A => is_less228, B => is_less236, Z => n437);
leq_127 : AO2 port map( A => c_sold_1_port, B => n432, C =>
          ch_sold_1_port, D => n472, Z => n463);
leq_128 : ND2 port map( A => present_state_0_port, B => net400, Z =>
          n435);
r33 : rpl_inc_n8_1 port map( A_7_port => X_cell_814_U53_Z_7_port,
```

```
            A_6_port => X_cell_814_U60_Z_6_port, A_5_port =>
            X_cell_814_U60_Z_5_port, A_4_port =>
            X_cell_814_U60_Z_4_port, A_3_port =>
            X_cell_814_U60_Z_3_port, A_2_port =>
            X_cell_814_U60_Z_2_port, A_1_port =>
            X_cell_814_U60_Z_1_port, A_0_port =>
            X_cell_814_U60_Z_0_port, SUM_7_port => sum326_7_port
            , SUM_6_port => sum326_6_port, SUM_5_port =>
            sum326_5_port, SUM_4_port => sum326_4_port,
            SUM_3_port => sum326_3_port, SUM_2_port =>
            sum326_2_port, SUM_1_port => sum326_1_port,
            SUM_0_port => sum326_0_port);
    leq_129 : AO2 port map( A => d_sold_2_port, B => item_out93_2_port, C =>
            p_sold_2_port, D => n433, Z => n427);
    d_sold_reg_5_label : FD2 port map( D => n490, CP => clock, CD => n508, Q
            => d_sold_5_port, QN => net406);
    leq_200 : AO4 port map( A => n451, B => n441, C => n453, D => net404, Z
            => n488);
    ch_sold_reg_4_label : FD2 port map( D => n489, CP => clock, CD => n508,
            Q => ch_sold_4_port, QN => net405);
    leq_201 : AO4 port map( A => n451, B => n436, C => n453, D => net431, Z
            => n506);
    leq_202 : AO4 port map( A => n451, B => n485, C => n453, D => net406, Z
            => n490);
    leq_203 : IV port map( A => n467, Z => n470);
    leq_204 : ND2 port map( A => n483, B => n484, Z => price118_0_port);
    leq_205 : IV port map( A => n444, Z => n481);
    leq_206 : IVA port map( A => sum326_2_port, Z => n446);
    leq_207 : AO4 port map( A => n451, B => n480, C => n453, D => net434, Z
            => n509);
    leq_208 : IVA port map( A => n483, Z => n432);
    leq_209 : ND2 port map( A => n469, B => n484, Z => price118_3_port);
    ch_empty_reg : LD1 port map( D => n522, G => n164, Q => ch_empty, QN =>
            open);
    c_empty_reg : LD1 port map( D => n522, G => n181, Q => c_empty, QN =>
            open);
    present_state_reg_1_label : FD2 port map( D => n486, CP => clock, CD =>
            n508, Q => present_state_1_port, QN => net400);
    price_reg_5_label : LD1 port map( D => n523, G => n94_2_port, Q =>
            price_5_port, QN => open);

end STRUCTURAL_VIEW;
```

The next netlist is for the *coin_handler*. This netlist will also define some higher-level components first and then instantiate these components to form the netlist.

```
entity rpl_add_n8_1 is

  port( A_7_port, A_6_port, A_5_port, A_4_port, A_3_port, A_2_port, A_1_port,
      A_0_port, B_7_port, B_6_port, B_5_port, B_4_port, B_3_port, B_2_port,
      B_1_port, B_0_port : in BIT; SUM_7_port, SUM_6_port, SUM_5_port,
      SUM_4_port, SUM_3_port, SUM_2_port, SUM_1_port, SUM_0_port : out BIT);
```

```
end rpl_add_n8_1;

architecture STRUCTURAL_VIEW of rpl_add_n8_1 is

  component AN2
    port( A, B : in BIT; Z : out BIT);
  end component;

  component NR2
    port( A, B : in BIT; Z : out BIT);
  end component;

  component AO2
    port( A, B, C, D : in BIT; Z : out BIT);
  end component;

  component AO4
    port( A, B, C, D : in BIT; Z : out BIT);
  end component;

  component MUX21L
    port( A, B, S : in BIT; Z : out BIT);
  end component;

  component IVA
    port( A : in BIT; Z : out BIT);
  end component;

  component IV
    port( A : in BIT; Z : out BIT);
  end component;

  component ND2
    port( A, B : in BIT; Z : out BIT);
  end component;

  component EN
    port( A, B : in BIT; Z : out BIT);
  end component;

  component EO
    port( A, B : in BIT; Z : out BIT);
  end component;

  component IVP
    port( A : in BIT; Z : out BIT);
  end component;

  signal n60, n61, n62, n63, n50, n64, n51, n65, n52, n66, n53, n67, n54,
    n55, n56, n57, n58, n59 : BIT;

begin
  U7 : AO4 port map( A => n57, B => n56, C => n52, D => n55, Z => n51);
  U8 : AO2 port map( A => A_3_port, B => B_3_port, C => n51, D => n58, Z
          => n50);
  U9 : AO4 port map( A => n60, B => n61, C => n50, D => n59, Z => n63);
  U20 : IV port map( A => B_4_port, Z => n61);
  U21 : EN port map( A => n64, B => n54, Z => SUM_1_port);
  U22 : EO port map( A => A_0_port, B => B_0_port, Z => SUM_0_port);
```

```
U23 : EO port map( A => B_7_port, B => n65, Z => SUM_7_port);
U10 : EO port map( A => B_5_port, B => A_5_port, Z => n62);
U24 : AN2 port map( A => B_0_port, B => n54, Z => n53);
U11 : AO2 port map( A => A_5_port, B => B_5_port, C => n63, D => n62, Z
        => n66);
U25 : ND2 port map( A => B_0_port, B => A_0_port, Z => n64);
U12 : IVP port map( A => B_6_port, Z => n67);
U26 : NR2 port map( A => n66, B => n67, Z => n65);
U13 : EO port map( A => n63, B => n62, Z => SUM_5_port);
U27 : EO port map( A => A_1_port, B => B_1_port, Z => n54);
U14 : IV port map( A => A_2_port, Z => n57);
U15 : EO port map( A => n50, B => n59, Z => SUM_4_port);
U16 : IV port map( A => B_2_port, Z => n56);
U17 : EO port map( A => n51, B => n58, Z => SUM_3_port);
U18 : IVA port map( A => A_4_port, Z => n60);
U19 : EO port map( A => n52, B => n55, Z => SUM_2_port);
U2 : MUX21L port map( A => B_6_port, B => n67, S => n66, Z => SUM_6_port
        );
U3 : AO2 port map( A => n56, B => A_2_port, C => B_2_port, D => n57, Z
        => n55);
U4 : EO port map( A => A_3_port, B => B_3_port, Z => n58);
U5 : AO2 port map( A => n60, B => B_4_port, C => A_4_port, D => n61, Z
        => n59);
U6 : AO2 port map( A => A_1_port, B => B_1_port, C => A_0_port, D => n53
        , Z => n52);

end STRUCTURAL_VIEW;

entity comp_1m2_n8_4 is

  port( A_7_port, A_6_port, A_5_port, A_4_port, A_3_port, A_2_port, A_1_port,
      A_0_port, B_7_port, B_6_port, B_5_port, B_4_port, B_3_port, B_2_port,
      B_1_port, B_0_port, LEQ, TC : in BIT; LT_LE, GE_GT : out BIT);

end comp_1m2_n8_4;

architecture STRUCTURAL_VIEW of comp_1m2_n8_4 is

  component AN2
    port( A, B : in BIT; Z : out BIT);
  end component;

  component AO4
    port( A, B, C, D : in BIT; Z : out BIT);
  end component;

  component AO6
    port( A, B, C : in BIT; Z : out BIT);
  end component;

  component IVA
    port( A : in BIT; Z : out BIT);
  end component;

  component IV
    port( A : in BIT; Z : out BIT);
  end component;
```

```
component ND2
  port( A, B : in BIT; Z : out BIT);
end component;

component EO1
  port( A, B, C, D : in BIT; Z : out BIT);
end component;

signal n160, n161, n162, n163, n150, n151, n152, n153, n154, n155, n156,
  n143, n157, n144, n158, n145, n159, n146, n147, n149 : BIT;

begin

U90 : IV port map( A => B_6_port, Z => n153);
U91 : IVA port map( A => A_5_port, Z => n154);
U92 : IV port map( A => B_4_port, Z => n150);
U93 : AO4 port map( A => A_7_port, B => n160, C => n162, D => n163, Z =>
          LT_LE);
U80 : IV port map( A => B_7_port, Z => n160);
U94 : AN2 port map( A => n160, B => A_7_port, Z => n162);
U81 : IV port map( A => B_2_port, Z => n161);
U95 : EO1 port map( A => n149, B => n151, C => n153, D => A_6_port, Z =>
          n163);
U82 : IVA port map( A => A_1_port, Z => n156);
U96 : AO6 port map( A => B_1_port, B => n156, C => B_0_port, Z => n155);
U83 : EO1 port map( A => n143, B => n147, C => n150, D => A_4_port, Z =>
          n146);
U84 : EO1 port map( A => n146, B => n152, C => n154, D => B_5_port, Z =>
          n149);
U85 : ND2 port map( A => A_2_port, B => n161, Z => n159);
U86 : ND2 port map( A => B_3_port, B => n145, Z => n144);
U87 : ND2 port map( A => A_4_port, B => n150, Z => n147);
U88 : ND2 port map( A => B_5_port, B => n154, Z => n152);
U89 : ND2 port map( A => A_6_port, B => n153, Z => n151);
U76 : EO1 port map( A => n155, B => A_0_port, C => n156, D => B_1_port,
          Z => n157);
U77 : EO1 port map( A => n157, B => n159, C => n161, D => A_2_port, Z =>
          n158);
U78 : EO1 port map( A => n158, B => n144, C => n145, D => B_3_port, Z =>
          n143);
U79 : IVA port map( A => A_3_port, Z => n145);

end STRUCTURAL_VIEW;


entity comp_1m2_n8_5 is

  port( A_7_port, A_6_port, A_5_port, A_4_port, A_3_port, A_2_port, A_1_port,
    A_0_port, B_7_port, B_6_port, B_5_port, B_4_port, B_3_port, B_2_port,
    B_1_port, B_0_port, LEQ, TC : in BIT; LT_LE, GE_GT : out BIT);

end comp_1m2_n8_5;

architecture STRUCTURAL_VIEW of comp_1m2_n8_5 is

  component AO1P
    port( A, B, C, D : in BIT; Z : out BIT);
  end component;
```

```
  component A06
    port( A, B, C : in BIT; Z : out BIT);
  end component;

  component IV
    port( A : in BIT; Z : out BIT);
  end component;

  signal n140, n141, n137, n138, n139 : BIT;

begin

  U44 : A06 port map( A => n138, B => B_6_port, C => B_7_port, Z => n137);
  U45 : A06 port map( A => B_0_port, B => B_1_port, C => B_2_port, Z =>
            n139);
  U46 : A01P port map( A => B_3_port, B => n141, C => B_5_port, D =>
            B_4_port, Z => n140);
  U47 : IV port map( A => n137, Z => LT_LE);
  U48 : IV port map( A => n140, Z => n138);
  U49 : IV port map( A => n139, Z => n141);

end STRUCTURAL_VIEW;


entity comp_1m2_n8_6 is

  port( A_7_port, A_6_port, A_5_port, A_4_port, A_3_port, A_2_port, A_1_port,
     A_0_port, B_7_port, B_6_port, B_5_port, B_4_port, B_3_port, B_2_port,
     B_1_port, B_0_port, LEQ, TC : in BIT; LT_LE, GE_GT : out BIT);

end comp_1m2_n8_6;

architecture STRUCTURAL_VIEW of comp_1m2_n8_6 is

  component OR3
    port( A, B, C : in BIT; Z : out BIT);
  end component;

  component AN2P
    port( A, B : in BIT; Z : out BIT);
  end component;

  component A04
    port( A, B, C, D : in BIT; Z : out BIT);
  end component;

  component A06
    port( A, B, C : in BIT; Z : out BIT);
  end component;

  component IVA
    port( A : in BIT; Z : out BIT);
  end component;

  component IV
    port( A : in BIT; Z : out BIT);
  end component;
```

```
component ND2
  port( A, B : in BIT; Z : out BIT);
end component;

component EO1
  port( A, B, C, D : in BIT; Z : out BIT);
end component;

signal n130, n131, n132, n133, n134, n121, n135, n122, n136, n123, n124,
  n125, n126, n127, n128 : BIT;

begin

  U40 : IVA port map( A => A_3_port, Z => n121);
  U41 : IVA port map( A => B_2_port, Z => n131);
  U42 : OR3 port map( A => B_6_port, B => B_7_port, C => n132, Z => LT_LE
          );
  U43 : AN2P port map( A => n135, B => A_5_port, Z => n134);
  U30 : EO1 port map( A => n125, B => A_0_port, C => n126, D => B_1_port,
          Z => n127);
  U31 : IV port map( A => A_1_port, Z => n126);
  U32 : EO1 port map( A => n127, B => n130, C => n131, D => A_2_port, Z =>
          n128);
  U33 : EO1 port map( A => n128, B => n133, C => n121, D => B_3_port, Z =>
          n122);
  U34 : AO4 port map( A => A_5 port, B => n135, C => n134, D => n136, Z =>
          n132);
  U35 : ND2 port map( A => A_2_port, B => n131, Z => n130);
  U36 : ND2 port map( A => B_3_port, B => n121, Z => n133);
  U37 : ND2 port map( A => A_4 port, B => n124, Z => n123);
  U38 : IVA port map( A => B_5_port, Z => n135);
  U39 : IVA port map( A => B_4_port, Z => n124);
  U28 : EO1 port map( A => n122, B => n123, C => n124, D => A_4_port, Z =>
          n136);
  U29 : AO6 port map( A => B_1_port, B => n126, C => B_0_port, Z => n125);
end STRUCTURAL_VIEW;


entity rpl_sub_n8_2 is

  port( A_7_port, A_6_port, A_5_port, A_4_port, A_3_port, A_2_port, A_1_port,
    A_0_port, B_7_port, B_6_port, B_5_port, B_4_port, B_3_port, B_2_port,
    B_1_port, B_0_port : in BIT; SUM_7_port, SUM_6_port, SUM_5_port,
    SUM_4_port, SUM_3_port, SUM_2_port, SUM_1_port, SUM_0_port : out BIT);

end rpl_sub_n8_2;

architecture STRUCTURAL_VIEW of rpl_sub_n8_2 is

  component AO2
    port( A, B, C, D : in BIT; Z : out BIT);
  end component;

  component AO4
    port( A, B, C, D : in BIT; Z : out BIT);
  end component;
```

```
component AO7
  port( A, B, C : in BIT; Z : out BIT);
end component;

component MUX21L
  port( A, B, S : in BIT; Z : out BIT);
end component;

component IVA
  port( A : in BIT; Z : out BIT);
end component;

component IV
  port( A : in BIT; Z : out BIT);
end component;

component ND2
  port( A, B : in BIT; Z : out BIT);
end component;

component EN
  port( A, B : in BIT; Z : out BIT);
end component;

component EO
  port( A, B : in BIT; Z : out BIT);
end component;

component EO1
  port( A, B, C, D : in BIT; Z : out BIT);
end component;

signal n90, n91, n92, n93, n94, n95, n96, n97, n100, n98, n101, n99, n86,
  n102, n87, n103, n88, n104, n89, n105, n106 : BIT;

begin

  U97 : MUX21L port map( A => B_5_port, B => n97, S => A_5_port, Z => n101
          );
  U98 : MUX21L port map( A => B_1_port, B => n89, S => A_1_port, Z => n90
          );
  U99 : MUX21L port map( A => B_3_port, B => n93, S => A_3_port, Z => n86
          );
  U109 : AO2 port map( A => n89, B => A_1_port, C => n105, D => n90, Z =>
          n87);
  U108 : IV port map( A => A_6_port, Z => n99);
  U107 : ND2 port map( A => B_0_port, B => n103, Z => n105);
  U119 : AO4 port map( A => B_6_port, B => n99, C => n96, D => n98, Z =>
          n94);
  U106 : EN port map( A => A_7_port, B => B_7_port, Z => n92);
  U118 : IVA port map( A => B_1_port, Z => n89);
  U105 : EO1 port map( A => A_6_port, B => B_6_port, C => A_6_port, D =>
          B_6_port, Z => n98);
  U117 : AO2 port map( A => n97, B => A_5_port, C => n100, D => n101, Z =>
          n96);
  U104 : EO1 port map( A => A_4_port, B => B_4_port, C => A_4_port, D =>
          B_4_port, Z => n104);
```

```
U116 : IV port map( A => A_2_port, Z => n91);
U103 : IV port map( A => A_0_port, Z => n103);
U115 : AO4 port map( A => B_4_port, B => n95, C => n102, D => n104, Z =>
          n100);
U102 : EO port map( A => n87, B => n88, Z => SUM_2_port);
U114 : IVA port map( A => B_3_port, Z => n93);
U101 : EO port map( A => n106, B => n86, Z => SUM_3_port);
U113 : AO2 port map( A => n93, B => A_3_port, C => n106, D => n86, Z =>
          n102);
U100 : EO port map( A => n102, B => n104, Z => SUM_4_port);
U125 : EO port map( A => n100, B => n101, Z => SUM_5_port);
U112 : IV port map( A => A_4_port, Z => n95);
U124 : EO port map( A => n96, B => n98, Z => SUM_6_port);
U111 : AO4 port map( A => B_2_port, B => n91, C => n87, D => n88, Z =>
          n106);
U123 : EO port map( A => n92, B => n94, Z => SUM_7_port);
U110 : IVA port map( A => B_5_port, Z => n97);
U122 : EO port map( A => n105, B => n90, Z => SUM_1_port);
U121 : AO7 port map( A => B_0_port, B => n103, C => n105, Z =>
          SUM_0_port);
U120 : EO1 port map( A => A_2_port, B => B_2_port, C => A_2_port, D =>
          B_2_port, Z => n88);

end STRUCTURAL_VIEW;


entity rpl_sub_n8_3 is

  port( A_7_port, A_6_port, A_5_port, A_4_port, A_3_port, A_2_port, A_1_port,
     A_0_port, B_7_port, B_6_port, B_5_port, B_4_port, B_3_port, B_2_port,
     B_1_port, B_0_port : in BIT; SUM_7_port, SUM_6_port, SUM_5_port,
     SUM_4_port, SUM_3_port, SUM_2_port, SUM_1_port, SUM_0_port : out BIT);

end rpl_sub_n8_3;

architecture STRUCTURAL_VIEW of rpl_sub_n8_3 is

  component NR2
    port( A, B : in BIT; Z : out BIT);
  end component

  component AO2
    port( A, B, C, D : in BIT; Z : out BIT);
  end component;

  component AO4
    port( A, B, C, D : in BIT; Z : out BIT);
  end component

  component AO7
    port( A, B, C : in BIT; Z : out BIT);
  end component

  component MUX21L
    port( A, B, S : in BIT; Z : out BIT);
  end component;
```

```
component IVA
  port( A : in BIT; Z : out BIT);
end component;

component IV
  port( A : in BIT; Z : out BIT);
end component;

component ND2
  port( A, B : in BIT; Z : out BIT);
end component;

component EN
  port( A, B : in BIT; Z : out BIT);
end component;

component EO
  port( A, B : in BIT; Z : out BIT);
end component;

component EO1
  port( A, B, C, D : in BIT; Z : out BIT);
end component;

signal n80, n81, n82, n83, n70, n84, n71, n85, n72, n73, n74, n75, n76,
  n77, n78, n79, n68, n69 : BIT;

begin
  U70 : AO4 port map( A => B_2_port, B => n69, C => n81, D => n83, Z =>
            n78);
  U71 : AO2 port map( A => n70, B => A_3_port, C => n78, D => n79, Z =>
            n76);
  U72 : EO1 port map( A => n71, B => A_4_port, C => n76, D => n77, Z =>
            n73);
  U73 : AO7 port map( A => B_0_port, B => n80, C => n82, Z => SUM_0_port);
  U60 : EO port map( A => n76, B => n77, Z => SUM_4_port);
  U74 : NR2 port map( A => A_6_port, B => n85, Z => n84);
  U61 : IVA port map( A => B_4_port, Z => n71);
  U75 : AO4 port map( A => B_5_port, B => n72, C => n73, D => n74, Z =>
            n85);
  U62 : EO port map( A => n78, B => n79, Z => SUM_3_port);
  U63 : IVA port map( A => B_3_port, Z => n70);
  U50 : MUX21L port map( A => B_3_port, B => n70, S => A_3_port, Z => n79
            );
  U64 : EO port map( A => n81, B => n83, Z => SUM_2_port);
  U51 : MUX21L port map( A => n71, B => B_4_port, S => A_4_port, Z => n77
            );
  U65 : IVA port map( A => A_2_port, Z => n69);
  U52 : MUX21L port map( A => B_1_port, B => n68, S => A_1_port, Z => n75
            );
  U66 : ND2 port map( A => B_0_port, B => n80, Z => n82);
  U53 : EO port map( A => n75, B => n82, Z => SUM_1_port);
  U67 : IV port map( A => B_1_port, Z => n68);
  U54 : EO port map( A => A_7_port, B => n84, Z => SUM_7_port);
  U68 : AO2 port map( A => n68, B => A_1_port, C => n82, D => n75, Z =>
            n81);
```

```
U55 : EN port map( A => A_6_port, B => n85, Z => SUM_6_port);
U69 : IVA port map( A => A_0_port, Z => n80);
U56 : EO1 port map( A => A_2_port, B => B_2_port, C => A_2_port, D =>
          B_2_port, Z => n83);
U57 : EO1 port map( A => A_5_port, B => B_5_port, C => A_5_port, D =>
          B_5_port, Z => n74);
U58 : EO port map( A => n73, B => n74, Z => SUM_5_port);
U59 : IVA port map( A => A_5_port, Z => n72);

end STRUCTURAL_VIEW;
```

Here is the entity for the *coin_handler.*

```
entity coin_handler is

  port( change_in_2_port, change_in_1_port, change_in_0_port, change_stb,
     coin_in_2_port, coin_in_1_port, coin_in_0_port, coin_stb, clock, reset
     , sell_en, price_7_port, price_6_port, price_5_port, price_4_port,
     price_3_port, price_2_port, price_1_port, price_0_port, item_out_stb :
     in BIT; total_7_port, total_6_port, total_5_port, total_4_port,
     total_3_port, total_2_port, total_1_port, total_0_port, coin_reject :
     out BIT);

end coin_handler;

architecture STRUCTURAL_VIEW of coin_handler is

  component rpl_add_n8_1
    port( A_7_port, A_6_port, A_5_port, A_4_port, A_3_port, A_2_port,
      A_1_port, A_0_port, B_7_port, B_6_port, B_5_port, B_4_port,
      B_3_port, B_2_port, B_1_port, B_0_port : in BIT; SUM_7_port,
      SUM_6_port, SUM_5_port, SUM_4_port, SUM_3_port, SUM_2_port,
      SUM_1_port, SUM_0_port : out BIT);
  end component;

  component EON1
    port( A, B, C, D : in BIT; Z : out BIT);
  end component;

  component AN2P
    port( A, B : in BIT; Z : out BIT);
  end component;

  component comp_1m2_n8_4
    port( A_7_port, A_6_port, A_5_port, A_4_port, A_3_port, A_2_port,
      A_1_port, A_0_port, B_7_port, B_6_port, B_5_port, B_4_port,
      B_3_port, B_2_port, B_1_port, B_0_port, LEQ, TC : in BIT; LT_LE,
      GE_GT : out BIT);
  end component;

  component comp_1m2_n8_5
    port( A_7_port, A_6_port, A_5_port, A_4_port, A_3_port, A_2_port,
      A_1_port, A_0_port, B_7_port, B_6_port, B_5_port, B_4_port,
      B_3_port, B_2_port, B_1_port, B_0_port, LEQ, TC : in BIT; LT_LE,
      GE_GT : out BIT);
  end component;
```

```
component comp_1m2_n8_6
  port( A_7_port, A_6_port, A_5_port, A_4_port, A_3_port, A_2_port,
      A_1_port, A_0_port, B_7_port, B_6_port, B_5_port, B_4_port,
      B_3_port, B_2_port, B_1_port, B_0_port, LEQ, TC : in BIT; LT_LE,
      GE_GT : out BIT);
end component;

component IV
  port( A : in BIT; Z : out BIT);
end component;

component ND2
  port( A, B : in BIT; Z : out BIT);
end component;

component AN3
  port( A, B, C : in BIT; Z : out BIT);
end component;

component NR2
  port( A, B : in BIT; Z : out BIT);
end component;

component AO2
  port( A, B, C, D : in BIT; Z : out BIT);
end component;

component AO6
  port( A, B, C : in BIT; Z : out BIT);
end component;

component AO7
  port( A, B, C : in BIT; Z : out BIT);
end component;

component OR2P
  port( A, B : in BIT; Z : out BIT);
end component;

component IVA
  port( A : in BIT; Z : out BIT);
end component;

component EO1
  port( A, B, C, D : in BIT; Z : out BIT);
end component;

component FD1
  port( D, CP : in BIT; Q, QN : out BIT);
end component;

component FD2
  port( D, CP, CD : in BIT; Q, QN : out BIT);
end component;

component rpl_sub_n8_2
  port( A_7_port, A_6_port, A_5_port, A_4_port, A_3_port, A_2_port,
      A_1_port, A_0_port, B_7_port, B_6_port, B_5_port, B_4_port,
```

```
        B_3_port, B_2_port, B_1_port, B_0_port : in BIT; SUM_7_port,
        SUM_6_port, SUM_5_port, SUM_4_port, SUM_3_port, SUM_2_port,
        SUM_1_port, SUM_0_port : out BIT);
end component;

component rpl_sub_n8_3
  port( A_7_port, A_6_port, A_5_port, A_4_port, A_3_port, A_2_port,
        A_1_port, A_0_port, B_7_port, B_6_port, B_5_port, B_4_port,
        B_3_port, B_2_port, B_1_port, B_0_port : in BIT; SUM_7_port,
        SUM_6_port, SUM_5_port, SUM_4_port, SUM_3_port, SUM_2_port,
        SUM_1_port, SUM_0_port : out BIT);
end component;

component IVP
  port( A : in BIT; Z : out BIT);
end component;

signal coin_to_int_return160_2_port, sum175_7_port, sum175_3_port,
  sum208_1_port, sum208_5_port, a194_1_port, n193_6_port, int_total_5_port
  net340, net341, net342, net343, sum225_6_port, int_total_1_port,
  a211_6_port, sum225_2_port, Logic0, Logic1, a211_2_port, n280, n281, n28
  , n283, n284, coin_to_int_return181_4_port, n240, n241, n242, n243, n244
  coin_t_int_return181_0_port, n245, n246, n247, n248, n249, is_less217,
  coin_to_int_return160_1_port, coin_to_int_return160_5_port, sum175_4_por
  , sum208_0_port, sum175_0_port, sum208_4_port, a194_2_port, n193_5_port,
  int_total_6_port, sum225_7_port, int_total_2_port, a211_7_port,
  sum225_3_port, a211_3_port, coin_to_int_return181_5_port, n250, n251,
  n252, n253, n254, coin_to_int_return181_1_port, n255, n256, n257, n258,
  n259, is_less200, coin_to_int_return160_0_port,
  coin_to_int_return160_4_port, sum175_5_port, sum175_1_port, sum208_3_por
  , sum208_7_port, a194_3_port, n193_4_port, int_total_7_port,
  int_total_3_port, net326, sum225_4_port, net328, net329, a211_4_port,
  sum225_0_port, a211_0_port, n260, n261, n262, n263, n264,
  coin_to_int_return181_2_port, n265, n266, n267, n268, n269, n226, n227,
  n228, n229, coin_to_int_return160_3_port, is_less155, sum175_6_port,
  sum175_2_port, sum208_2_port, sum208_6_port, a194_0_port, n193_7_port,
  int_total_4_port, net330, net331, net332, net333, net334, net335, net336
  sum225_5_port, net337, net338, net339, int_total_0_port, a211_5_port,
  sum225_1_port, a211_1_port, n270, n271, n272, n273, n274,
  coin_to_int_return181_3_port, n275, n276, n277, n278, n279, n230, n231,
  n232, n233, n234, n235, n236, n237, n238, n239 : BIT;

begin

  total_reg_4_label : FD2 port map( D => n278, CP => clock, CD => n265, Q
              => total_4_port, QN => net343);
  total_reg_2_label : FD2 port map( D => n276, CP => clock, CD => n265, Q
              => total_2_port, QN => net341);
  total_reg_0_label : FD2 port map( D => n274, CP => clock, CD => n265, Q
              => total_0_port, QN => net339);
  coin_reject_reg : FD1 port map( D => n273, CP => clock, Q => coin_reject
              , QN => net338);
  int_total_reg_7_label : FD2 port map( D => n272, CP => clock, CD => n265
              , Q => int_total_7_port, QN => net337);
```

```
r40 : comp_1m2_n8_5 port map( A_7_port => Logic0, A_6_port => Logic1,
        A_5_port => Logic0, A_4_port => Logic0, A_3_port =>
        Logic1, A_2_port => Logic0, A_1_port => Logic1,
        A_0_port => Logic1, B_7_port => int_total_7_port,
        B_6_port => int_total_6_port, B_5_port =>
        int_total_5_port, B_4_port => int_total_4_port,
        B_3_port => int_total_3_port, B_2_port =>
        int_total_2_port, B_1_port => int_total_1_port,
        B_0_port => int_total_0_port, LEQ => n281, TC =>
        n282, LT_LE => is_less155, GE_GT => open);
r69 : rpl_sub_n8_3 port map( A_7_port => n193_7_port, A_6_port =>
        n193_6_port, A_5_port => n193_5_port, A_4_port =>
        n193_4_port, A_3_port => a194_3_port, A_2_port =>
        a194_2_port, A_1_port => a194_1_port, A_0_port =>
        a194_0_port, B_7_port => Logic0, B_6_port => Logic0,
        B_5_port => coin_to_int_return181_5_port, B_4_port
        => coin_to_int_return181_4_port, B_3_port =>
        coin_to_int_return181_3_port, B_2_port =>
        coin_to_int_return181_2_port, B_1_port =>
        coin_to_int_return181_1_port, B_0_port =>
        coin_to_int_return181_0_port, SUM_7_port =>
        sum208_7_port, SUM_6_port => sum208_6_port,
        SUM_5_port => sum208_5_port, SUM_4_port =>
        sum208_4_port, SUM_3_port => sum208_3_port,
        SUM_2_port => sum208_2_port, SUM_1_port =>
        sum208_1_port, SUM_0_port => sum208_0_port);
int_total_reg_5_label : FD2 port map( D => n270, CP => clock, CD => n265
        , Q => int_total_5_port, QN => net335);
sub_119 : EON1 port map( A => net335, B => n245, C => sum175_5_port, D
        => n245, Z => n193_5_port);
sub_118 : AO2 port map( A => sum175_0_port, B => n229, C =>
        sum208_0_port, D => n230, Z => n241);
sub_117 : AO2 port map( A => n232, B => n249, C => net337, D => n244, Z
        => a211_7_port);
int_total_reg_3_label : FD2 port map( D => n268, CP => clock, CD => n265
        , Q => int_total_3_port, QN => net333);
sub_116 : AO2 port map( A => sum175_5_port, B => n229, C =>
        sum208_5_port, D => n230, Z => n242);
sub_115 : AO2 port map( A => n233, B => n249, C => net333, D => n244, Z
        => a211_3_port);
sub_114 : AO2 port map( A => sum175_1_port, B => n229, C =>
        sum208_1_port, D => n230, Z => n243);
Logic0 <= '0';
sub_113 : EON1 port map( A => net333, B => n245, C => sum175_3_port, D
        => n245, Z => a194_3_port);
sub_139 : AO2 port map( A => sum175_7_port, B => n229, C =>
        sum208_7_port, D => n230, Z => n232);
Logic1 <= '1';
sub_112 : NR2 port map( A => n254, B => coin_in_2_port, Z =>
        coin_to_int_return160_0_port);
sub_138 : AO6 port map( A => change_in_0_port, B =>
        coin_to_int_return181_3_port, C =>
        coin_to_int_return181_5_port, Z => n256);
```

```
sub_111 : EON1 port map( A => net334, B => n245, C => sum175_4_port, D
          => n245, Z => n193_4_port);
sub_137 : AO2 port map( A => sum175_3_port, B => n229, C =>
          sum208_3_port, D => n230, Z => n233);
int_total_reg_1_label : FD2 port map( D => n266, CP => clock, CD => n265
          , Q => int_total_1_port, QN => net331);
sub_110 : ND2 port map( A => coin_stb, B => sell_en, Z => n227);
sub_136 : AO7 port map( A => n236, B => net328, C => n238, Z => n262);
sub_135 : AO2 port map( A => sum175_4_port, B => n229, C =>
          sum208_4_port, D => n230, Z => n240);
sub_134 : AO7 port map( A => net336, B => n236, C => n238, Z => n271);
sub_133 : A06 port map( A => coin_in_0_port, B =>
          coin_to_int_return160_3_port, C =>
          coin_to_int_return160_5_port, Z => n239);
sub_159 : ND2 port map( A => n244, B => n246, Z => n236);
sub_132 : A06 port map( A => n254, B => coin_to_int_return160_3_port, C
          => coin_to_int_return160_5_port, Z => n253);
sub_158 : AN3 port map( A => n260, B => n257, C => change_in_2_port, Z
          => coin_to_int_return181_5_port);
sub_131 : AO7 port map( A => net330, B => n236, C => n235, Z => n264);
sub_157 : EO1 port map( A => n248, B => sum225_4_port, C => n240, D =>
          n247, Z => n252);
sub_130 : AO7 port map( A => net331, B => n236, C => n237, Z => n266);
sub_156 : ND2 port map( A => change_stb, B => is_less200, Z => n229);
sub_155 : EO1 port map( A => sum225_3_port, B => n248, C => n233, D =>
          n247, Z => n251);
sub_154 : AN3 port map( A => n258, B => n254, C => coin_in_2_port, Z =>
          coin_to_int_return160_5_port);
sub_153 : EO1 port map( A => sum225_2_port, B => n248, C => n231, D =>
          n247, Z => n250);
n282 <= '0';
sub_152 : FO1 port map( A => sum225_1_port, B => n248, C => n243, D =>
          n247, Z => n237);
n281 <= '1';
sub_151 : AO7 port map( A => net337, B => n236, C => n234, Z => n272);
n280 <= '0';
sub_150 : EO1 port map( A => sum225_0_port, B => n248, C => n241, D =>
          n247, Z => n235);
n279 <= '1';
sub_175 : IV port map( A => change_in_0_port, Z => n260);
sub_95 : AO7 port map( A => n236, B => net339, C => n235, Z => n274);
sub_174 : IVP port map( A => n244, Z => n249);
sub_96 : AO7 port map( A => n236, B => net340, C => n237, Z => n275);
sub_173 : IVA port map( A => n239, Z => coin_to_int_return160_4_port);
sub_97 : AO7 port map( A => n236, B => net341, C => n250, Z => n276);
sub_172 : IVA port map( A => n253, Z => coin_to_int_return160_1_port);
sub_98 : AO7 port map( A => n236, B => net342, C => n251, Z => n277);
sub_171 : AO2 port map( A => n240, B => n249, C => net334, D => n244, Z
          => a211_4_port);
sub_99 : AO7 port map( A => net343, B => n236, C => n252, Z => n278);
sub_170 : IVP port map( A => n246, Z => n248);
total_reg_7_label : FD2 port map( D => n263, CP => clock, CD => n265, Q
          => total_7_port, QN => net329);
```

```
total_reg_5_label : FD2 port map( D => n261, CP => clock, CD => n265, Q
          => total_5_port, QN => net326);
total_reg_3_label : FD2 port map( D => n277, CP => clock, CD => n265, Q
          => total_3_port, QN => net342);
total_reg_1_label : FD2 port map( D => n275, CP => clock, CD => n265, Q
          => total_1_port, QN => net340);
r70 : comp_1m2_n8_6 port map( A_7_port => Logic0, A_6_port => Logic0,
          A_5_port => coin_to_int_return181_5_port, A_4_port
          => coin_to_int_return181_4_port, A_3_port =>
          coin_to_int_return181_3_port, A_2_port =>
          coin_to_int_return181_2_port, A_1_port =>
          coin_to_int_return181_1_port, A_0_port =>
          coin_to_int_return181_0_port, B_7_port =>
          n193_7_port, B_6_port => n193_6_port, B_5_port =>
          n193_5_port, B_4_port => n193_4_port, B_3_port =>
          a194_3_port, B_2_port => a194_2_port, B_1_port =>
          a194_1_port, B_0_port => a194_0_port, LEQ => n283,
          TC => n284, LT_LE => is_less200, GE_GT => open);
r72 : comp_1m2_n8_4 port map( A_7_port => price_7_port, A_6_port =>
          price_6_port, A_5_port => price_5_port, A_4_port =>
          price_4_port, A_3_port => price_3_port, A_2_port =>
          price_2_port, A_1_port => price_1_port, A_0_port =>
          price_0_port, B_7_port => a211_7_port, B_6_port =>
          a211_6_port, B_5_port => a211_5_port, B_4_port =>
          a211_4_port, B_3_port => a211_3_port, B_2_port =>
          a211_2_port, B_1_port => a211_1_port, B_0_port =>
          a211_0_port, LEQ => n279, TC => n280, LT_LE =>
          is_less217, GE_GT => open);
r73 : rpl_sub_n8_2 port map( A_7_port => a211_7_port, A_6_port =>
          a211_6_port, A_5_port => a211_5_port, A_4_port =>
          a211_4_port, A_3_port => a211_3_port, A_2_port =>
          a211_2_port, A_1_port => a211_1_port, A_0_port =>
          a211_0_port, B_7_port => price_7_port, B_6_port =>
          price_6_port, B_5_port => price_5_port, B_4_port =>
          price_4_port, B_3_port => price_3_port, B_2_port =>
          price_2_port, B_1_port => price_1_port, B_0_port =>
          price_0_port, SUM_7_port => sum225_7_port,
          SUM_6_port => sum225_6_port, SUM_5_port =>
          sum225_5_port, SUM_4_port => sum225_4_port,
          SUM_3_port => sum225_3_port, SUM_2_port =>
          sum225_2_port, SUM_1_port => sum225_1_port,
          SUM_0_port => sum225_0_port);
int_total_reg_6_label : FD2 port map( D => n271, CP => clock, CD => n265
          , Q => int_total_6_port, QN => net336);
sub_109 : NR2 port map( A => n245, B => n230, Z => n244);
sub_108 : AO7 port map( A => net333, B => n236, C => n251, Z => n268);
sub_107 : NR2 port map( A => n257, B => change_in_2_port, Z =>
          coin_to_int_return181_3_port);
int_total_reg_4_label : FD2 port map( D => n269, CP => clock, CD => n265
          , Q => int_total_4_port, QN => net334);
sub_106 : AO7 port map( A => net334, B => n236, C => n252, Z => n269);
r37 : rpl_add_n8_1 port map( A_7_port => Logic0, A_6_port => Logic0,
          A_5_port => coin_to_int_return160_5_port, A_4_port
```

```
                     => coin_to_int_return160_4_port, A_3_port =>
                     coin_to_int_return160_3_port, A_2_port =>
                     coin_to_int_return160_2_port, A_1_port =>
                     coin_to_int_return160_1_port, A_0_port =>
                     coin_to_int_return160_0_port, B_7_port =>
                     int_total_7_port, B_6_port => int_total_6_port,
                     B_5_port => int_total_5_port, B_4_port =>
                     int_total_4_port, B_3_port => int_total_3_port,
                     B_2_port => int_total_2_port, B_1_port =>
                     int_total_1_port, B_0_port => int_total_0_port,
                     SUM_7_port => sum175_7_port, SUM_6_port =>
                     sum175_6_port, SUM_5_port => sum175_5_port,
                     SUM_4_port => sum175_4_port, SUM_3_port =>
                     sum175_3_port, SUM_2_port => sum175_2_port,
                     SUM_1_port => sum175_1_port, SUM_0_port =>
                     sum175_0_port);
sub_105 : NR2 port map( A => n258, B => coin_in_2_port, Z =>
                     coin_to_int_return160_3_port);
sub_104 : AO7 port map( A => net335, B => n236, C => n255, Z => n270);
sub_103 : NR2 port map( A => n260, B => change_in_2_port, Z =>
                     coin_to_int_return181_0_port);
sub_129 : AO7 port map( A => net332, B => n236, C => n250, Z => n267);
sub_102 : AO7 port map( A => n236, B => net329, C => n234, Z => n263);
sub_128 : NR2 port map( A => n227, B => is_less155, Z => n245);
sub_101 : ND2 port map( A => is_less217, B => item_out_stb, Z => n246);
sub_127 : EON1 port map( A => net331, B => n245, C => sum175_1_port, D
                     => n245, Z => a194_1_port);
int_total_reg_2_label : FD2 port map( D => n267, CP => clock, CD => n265
                     , Q => int_total_2_port, QN => net332);
sub_100 : AO7 port map( A => n236, B => net326, C => n255, Z => n261);
sub_126 : EON1 port map( A => net336, B => n245, C => sum175_6_port, D
                     => n245, Z => n193_6_port);
sub_125 : IV port map( A => change_in_1_port, Z => n257);
sub_124 : AO2 port map( A => n228, B => n249, C => net336, D => n244, Z
                     => a211_6_port);
sub_123 : IV port map( A => coin_in_0_port, Z => n254);
sub_149 : AN2P port map( A => n257, B => coin_to_int_return181_0_port, Z
                     => coin_to_int_return181_2_port);
sub_122 : AO2 port map( A => n231, B => n249, C => net332, D => n244, Z
                     => a211_2_port);
sub_148 : EO1 port map( A => sum225_7_port, B => n248, C => n232, D =>
                     n247, Z => n234);
sub_121 : IV port map( A => coin_in_1_port, Z => n258);
sub_147 : AN2P port map( A => n258, B => coin_to_int_return160_0_port, Z
                     => coin_to_int_return160_2_port);
int_total_reg_0_label : FD2 port map( D => n264, CP => clock, CD => n265
                     , Q => int_total_0_port, QN => net330);
sub_120 : EON1 port map( A => net332, B => n245, C => sum175_2_port, D
                     => n245, Z => a194_2_port);
sub_146 : EO1 port map( A => sum225_6_port, B => n248, C => n228, D =>
                     n247, Z => n238);
sub_145 : AO6 port map( A => n260, B => coin_to_int_return181_3_port, C
                     => coin_to_int_return181_5_port, Z => n259);
```

```
sub_144 : EO1 port map( A => sum225_5_port, B => n248, C => n242, D =>
            n247, Z => n255);
sub_143 : OR2P port map( A => reset, B => n227, Z => n226);
sub_169 : AO2 port map( A => n241, B => n249, C => net330, D => n244, Z
            => a211_0_port);
sub_142 : AO2 port map( A => sum175_6_port, B => n229, C =>
            sum208_6_port, D => n230, Z => n228);
sub_168 : IVA port map( A => n256, Z => coin_to_int_return181_4_port);
sub_141 : AO2 port map( A => sum175_2_port, B => n229, C =>
            sum208_2_port, D => n230, Z => n231);
sub_167 : EON1 port map( A => net330, B => n245, C => sum175_0_port, D
            => n245, Z => a194_0_port);
sub_140 : IVA port map( A => reset, Z => n265);
sub_166 : IVA port map( A => n259, Z => coin_to_int_return181_1_port);
sub_165 : EON1 port map( A => net337, B => n245, C => sum175_7_port, D
            => n245, Z => n193_7_port);
sub_164 : IV port map( A => n229, Z => n230);
sub_163 : AO2 port map( A => n242, B => n249, C => net335, D => n244, Z
            => a211_5_port);
sub_162 : AO2 port map( A => n243, B => n249, C => net331, D => n244, Z
            => a211_1_port);
sub_161 : ND2 port map( A => n246, B => n236, Z => n247);
sub_160 : EO1 port map( A => net338, B => n226, C => is_less155, D =>
            n226, Z => n273);
n284 <= '0';
n283 <= '1';
total_reg_6_label : FD2 port map( D => n262, CP => clock, CD => n265, Q
            => total_6_port, QN => net328);

end STRUCTURAL_VIEW;
```

Finally, we have the netlist for the *change_maker* part of the design. It also declares some components and instantiates them along with library primitives to form the *change_maker* netlist.

```
entity comp_1m2_n8_1 is

  port( A_7_port, A_6_port, A_5_port, A_4_port, A_3_port, A_2_port, A_1_port,
      A_0_port, B_7_port, B_6_port, B_5_port, B_4_port, B_3_port, B_2_port,
      B_1_port, B_0_port, LEQ, TC : in BIT; LT_LE, GE_GT : out BIT);

end comp_1m2_n8_1;

architecture STRUCTURAL_VIEW of comp_1m2_n8_1 is

  component NR2
    port( A, B : in BIT; Z : out BIT);
  end component;

  component AO7
    port( A, B, C : in BIT; Z : out BIT);
  end component;
```

```
  component ND3
    port( A, B, C : in BIT; Z : out BIT);
  end component;

  signal n144, n145, n146 : BIT;

begin

  U60 : NR2 port map( A => B_6_port, B => B_7_port, Z => n146);
  U61 : AO7 port map( A => B_2_port, B => B_1_port, C => B_3_port, Z =>
            n145);
  U58 : ND3 port map( A => n144, B => n145, C => n146, Z => LT_LE);
  U59 : NR2 port map( A => B_5_port, B => B_4_port, Z => n144);

end STRUCTURAL_VIEW;


entity comp_1m2_n8_2 is

  port( A_7_port, A_6_port, A_5_port, A_4_port, A_3_port, A_2_port, A_1_port,
     A_0_port, B_7_port, B_6_port, B_5_port, B_4_port, B_3_port, B_2_port,
     B_1_port, B_0_port, LEQ, TC : in BIT; LT_LE, GE_GT : out BIT);

end comp_1m2_n8_2;

architecture STRUCTURAL_VIEW of comp_1m2_n8_2 is

  component AO3
    port( A, B, C, D : in BIT; Z : out BIT);
  end component;

  component AO6
    port( A, B, C : in BIT; Z : out BIT);
  end component

  component AO7
    port( A, B, C : in BIT; Z : out BIT);
  end component;

  component IVA
    port( A : in BIT; Z : out BIT);
  end component;

  component IV
    port( A : in BIT; Z : out BIT);
  end component;

  component ND2
    port( A, B : in BIT; Z : out BIT);
  end component;

  component EO1
    port( A, B, C, D : in BIT; Z : out BIT);
  end component;

  signal n140, n141, n142, n143, n130, n131, n132, n133, n134, n135, n136,
    n123, n137, n124, n138, n125, n139, n126, n127, n128, n129 : BIT;
```

```
begin

  U7 : IVA port map( A => A_6_port, Z => n126);
  U8 : IVA port map( A => B_5_port, Z => n130);
  U9 : IVA port map( A => A_4_port, Z => n139);
  U20 : IVA port map( A => A_7_port, Z => n142);
  U21 : AO3 port map( A => B_4_port, B => n139, C => n123, D => n140, Z =>
            n124);
  U22 : ND2 port map( A => B_6_port, B => n126, Z => n125);
  U23 : AO3 port map( A => A_5_port, B => n130, C => n124, D => n138, Z =>
            n128);
  U10 : ND2 port map( A => B_2_port, B => n135, Z => n133);
  U24 : ND2 port map( A => A_5_port, B => n130, Z => n132);
  U11 : IVA port map( A => B_3_port, Z => n141);
  U25 : AO3 port map( A => B_6_port, B => n126, C => n132, D => n128, Z =>
            n134);
  U12 : AO7 port map( A => B_2_port, B => n135, C => n131, Z => n137);
  U26 : AO7 port map( A => B_7_port, B => n142, C => n143, Z => GE_GT);
  U13 : IVA port map( A => A_2_port, Z => n135);
  U27 : AO6 port map( A => B_1_port, B => n129, C => B_0_port, Z => n127);
  U28 : EO1 port map( A => n127, B => A_0_port, C => n129, D => B_1_port,
            Z => n131);
  U15 : ND2 port map( A => B_4_port, B => n139, Z => n138);
  U16 : IV port map( A => A_1_port, Z => n129);
  U17 : AO3 port map( A => A_3_port, B => n141, C => n137, D => n133, Z =>
            n140);
  U18 : IVA port map( A => B_7_port, Z => n136);
  U19 : ND2 port map( A => A_3_port, B => n141, Z => n123);
  U6 : AO3 port map( A => A_7_port, B => n136, C => n134, D => n125, Z =>
            n143);
end STRUCTURAL_VIEW;

entity comp_1m2_n8_3 is

  port( A_7_port, A_6_port, A_5_port, A_4_port, A_3_port, A_2_port, A_1_port,
      A_0_port, B_7_port, B_6_port, B_5_port, B_4_port, B_3_port, B_2_port,
      B_1_port, B_0_port, LEQ, TC : in BIT; LT_LE, GE_GT : out BIT);

end comp_1m2_n8_3;

architecture STRUCTURAL_VIEW of comp_1m2_n8_3 is

  component NR4
    port( A, B, C, D : in BIT; Z : out BIT);
  end component;

  component ND2
    port( A, B : in BIT; Z : out BIT);
  end component;

  signal n121, n122 : BIT;

begin

  U3 : ND2 port map( A => n121, B => n122, Z => GE_GT);
  U4 : NR4 port map( A => A_7_port, B => A_6_port, C => A_5_port, D =>
            A_4_port, Z => n122);
```

```
  U5 : NR4 port map( A => A_3_port, B => A_2_port, C => A_0_port, D =>
          A_1_port, Z => n121);

end STRUCTURAL_VIEW;

entity rpl_sub_n8_1 is
  port( A_7_port, A_6_port, A_5_port, A_4_port, A_3_port, A_2_port, A_1_port,
      A_0_port, B_7_port, B_6_port, B_5_port, B_4_port, B_3_port, B_2_port,
      B_1_port, B_0_port : in BIT; SUM_7_port, SUM_6_port, SUM_5_port,
      SUM_4_port, SUM_3_port, SUM_2_port, SUM_1_port, SUM_0_port : out BIT);

end rpl_sub_n8_1;

architecture STRUCTURAL_VIEW of rpl_sub_n8_1 is

  component NR2
    port( A, B : in BIT; Z : out BIT);
  end component;

  component AO2
    port( A, B, C, D : in BIT; Z : out BIT);
  end component;

  component AO4
    port( A, B, C, D : in BIT; Z : out BIT);
  end component;

  component AO6
    port( A, B, C : in BIT; Z : out BIT);
  end component;

  component MUX21L
    port( A, B, S : in BIT; Z : out BIT);
  end component;

  component IVA
    port( A : in BIT; Z : out BIT);
  end component;

  component IV
    port( A : in BIT; Z : out BIT);
  end component;

  component EO
    port( A, B : in BIT; Z : out BIT);
  end component;

  component EO1
    port( A, B, C, D : in BIT; Z : out BIT);
  end component;

  signal n70, n71, n72, n73, n60, n74, n61, n75, n62, n76, n63, n77, n64,
    n78, n65, n79, n66, n67, n68, n69, n58, n59 : BIT;

begin

  U50 : NR2 port map( A => n76, B => A_0_port, Z => n78);
  U51 : AO4 port map( A => B_1_port, B => n66, C => n78, D => n73, Z =>
          n64);
```

```
U52 : AO2 port map( A => n68, B => A_2_port, C => n64, D => n63, Z =>
          n62);
U53 : AO4 port map( A => B_3_port, B => n70, C => n62, D => n61, Z =>
          n60);
U40 : EO port map( A => n67, B => n69, Z => SUM_6_port);
U54 : AO6 port map( A => n76, B => A_0_port, C => n78, Z => n74);
U41 : EO1 port map( A => A_3_port, B => B_3_port, C => A_3_port, D =>
          B_3_port, Z => n61);
U55 : AO2 port map( A => n67, B => n69, C => A_6_port, D => n71, Z =>
          n65);
U42 : EO port map( A => n77, B => n79, Z => SUM_5_port);
U56 : EO1 port map( A => n73, B => n78, C => n73, D => n78, Z =>
          SUM_1_port);
U43 : EO port map( A => n59, B => n60, Z => SUM_4_port);
U30 : MUX21L port map( A => B_6_port, B => n71, S => A_6_port, Z => n67
          );
U57 : EO port map( A => n65, B => n75, Z => SUM_7_port);
U44 : EO1 port map( A => A_5_port, B => B_5_port, C => A_5_port, D =>
          B_5_port, Z => n77);
U31 : IVA port map( A => n74, Z => SUM_0_port);
U45 : EO port map( A => n61, B => n62, Z => SUM_3_port);
U32 : IVA port map( A => A_1_port, Z => n66);
U46 : EO port map( A => n63, B => n64, Z => SUM_2_port);
U33 : IVA port map( A => A_3_port, Z => n70);
U47 : IV port map( A => B_6_port, Z => n71);
U34 : IVA port map( A => B_2_port, Z => n68);
U48 : EO port map( A => B_7_port, B => A_7_port, Z => n75);
U35 : AO2 port map( A => n72, B => A_4_port, C => n60, D => n59, Z =>
          n79);
U49 : IVA port map( A => B_0_port, Z => n76);
U36 : IVA port map( A => A_5_port, Z => n58);
U37 : AO4 port map( A => B_5_port, B => n58, C => n79, D => n77, Z =>
          n69);
U38 : IV port map( A => B_4_port, Z => n72);
U39 : EO1 port map( A => A_1_port, B => B_1_port, C => A_1_port, D =>
          B_1_port, Z => n73);
U29 : MUX21L port map( A => B_4_port, B => n72, S => A_4_port, Z => n59
          );
U2 : MUX21L port map( A => B_2_port, B => n68, S => A_2_port, Z => n63);

end STRUCTURAL_VIEW;
```

Here is the entity for the change maker.

```
entity change_maker is

  port( total_7_port, total_6_port, total_5_port, total_4_port, total_3_port,
      total_2_port, total_1_port, total_0_port, price_7_port, price_6_port,
      price_5_port, price_4_port, price_3_port, price_2_port, price_1_port,
      price_0_port, item_stb, clock, reset : in BIT; exact_change,
      change_2_port, change_1_port, change_0_port, change_stb, sell_en : out
      BIT);

  end change_maker;
```

```vhdl
architecture STRUCTURAL_VIEW of change_maker is

component AN2
  port( A, B : in BIT; Z : out BIT);
end component;

component NR2
  port( A, B : in BIT; Z : out BIT);
end component;

component EON1
  port( A, B, C, D : in BIT; Z : out BIT);
end component;

component AN2P
  port( A, B : in BIT; Z : out BIT);
end component;

component AO7
  port( A, B, C : in BIT; Z : out BIT);
end component;

component comp_1m2_n8_1
  port( A_7_port, A_6_port, A_5_port, A_4_port, A_3_port, A_2_port,
      A_1_port, A_0_port, B_7_port, B_6_port, B_5_port, B_4_port,
      B_3_port, B_2_port, B_1_port, B_0_port, LEQ, TC : in BIT; LT_LE,
      GE_GT : out BIT);
end component;

component comp_1m2_n8_2
  port( A_7_port, A_6_port, A_5_port, A_4_port, A_3_port, A_2_port,
      A_1_port, A_0_port, B_7_port, B_6_port, B_5_port, B_4_port,
      B_3_port, B_2_port, B_1_port, B_0_port, LEQ, TC : in BIT; LT_LE,
      GE_GT : out BIT);
end component;

component comp_1m2_n8_3
  port( A_7_port, A_6_port, A_5_port, A_4_port, A_3_port, A_2_port,
      A_1_port, A_0_port, B_7_port, B_6_port, B_5_port, B_4_port,
      B_3_port, B_2_port, B_1_port, B_0_port, LEQ, TC : in BIT); LT_LE,
      GE_GT : out BIT);
end component;

component LD1
  port( D, G : in BIT; Q, QN : out BIT);
end component;

component IVA
  port( A : in BIT; Z : out BIT);
end component;

component IV
  port( A : in BIT; Z : out BIT);
end component;

component ND2
  port( A, B : in BIT; Z : out BIT);
end component;
```

```
component FD1
  port ( D, CP : in BIT; Q, QN : out BIT);
end component;

component rpl_sub_n8_1
  port( A_7_port, A_6_port, A_5_port, A_4_port, A_3_port, A_2_port,
      A_1_port, A_0_port, B_7_port, B_6_port, B_5_port, B_4_port,
      B_3_port, B_2_port, B_1_port, B_0_port : in BIT; SUM_7_port,
      SUM_6_port, SUM_5_port, SUM_4_port, SUM_3_port, SUM_2_port,
      SUM_1_port, SUM_0_port : out BIT);
end component;

component IVP
  port( A : in BIT; Z : out BIT);
end component;

signal is_less117, X_cell_277_U18_Z_4_port, X_cell_277_U18_Z_3_port,
  X_cell_277_U18_Z_2_port, X_cell_277_U18_Z_1_port, X_cell_277_U18_Z_0_port
  , sell_en32, int_change_0_port, int_change_1_port, int_change_2_port,
  int_change_3_port, int_change_4_port, n70_0_port, is_less89,
  int_change_5_port, int_change_6_port, int_change_7_port,
  X_cell_277_U17_Z_0_port, X_cell_277_U17_Z_1_port, X_cell_277_U17_Z_2_port
  , X_cell_277_U17_Z_3_port, n33, change69_1_port, X_cell_277_U17_Z_4_port,
  net141, change69_0_port, X_cell_277_U17_Z_5_port, net142, net143, net144,
  X_cell_277_U17_Z_6_port, net145, net146, net134, X_cell_277_U17_Z_7_port,
  net135, net136, net138, present_state_0_port, present_state_1_port,
  Logic0, Logic1, n160, n161, n162, n163, n150, n164, n151, n152, n153,
  n154, n155, sum109_0_port, n156, n157, n158, sum109_1_port, n159, n147
  n148, sum109_2_port, n149, sum109_3_port, change_stb_port, sum109_4_port,
  sum109_5_port, sum109_6_port, sum109_7_port, n45_7_port,
  X_cell_277_U18_Z_7_port, X_cell_277_U18_Z_6_port, X_cell_277_U18_Z_5_port
  : BIT;

begin

  change_stb <= change_stb_port;

  int_change_reg_0_label : LD1 port map( D => sum109_0_port, G =>
          n45_7_port, Q => int_change_0_port, QN => net146);
  int_change_reg_1_label : LD1 port map( D => sum109_1_port, G =>
          n45_7_port, Q => int_change_1_port, QN => net145);
  int_change_reg_2_label : LD1 port map( D => sum109_2_port, G =>
          n45_7_port, Q => int_change_2_port, QN => net144);
  int_change_reg_3_label : LD1 port map( D => sum109_3_port, G =>
          n45_7_port, Q => int_change_3_port, QN => net143);
  int_change_reg_4_label : LD1 port map( D => sum109_4_port, G =>
          n45_7_port, Q => int_change_4_port, QN => net142);
  int_change_reg_5_label : LD1 port map( D => sum109_5_port, G =>
          n45_7_port, Q => int_change_5_port, QN => net141);
  int_change_reg_6_label : LD1 port map( D => sum109_6_port, G =>
          n45_7_port, Q => int_change_6_port, QN => net138);
  int_change_reg_7_label : LD1 port map( D => sum109_7_port, G =>
          n45_7_port, Q => int_change_7_port, QN => net136);
  n158 <= '0';
```

```
change_reg_2_label : LD1 port map( D => n158, G => n70_0_port, Q =>
        change_2_port, QN => open);
change_reg_1_label : LD1 port map( D => change69_1_port, G => n70_0_port
        , Q => change_1_port, QN => open);
change_reg_0_label : LD1 port map( D => change69_0_port, G => n70_0_port
        , Q => change_0_port, QN => open);
r50 : comp_1m2_n8_1 port map( A_7_port => Logic0, A_6_port => Logic0,
        A_5_port => Logic0, A_4_port => Logic0, A_3_port =>
        Logic1, A_2_port => Logic0, A_1_port => Logic1,
        A_0_port => Logic0, B_7_port => int_change_7_port,
        B_6_port => int_change_6_port, B_5_port =>
        int_change_5_port, B_4_port => int_change_4_port,
        B_3_port => int_change_3_port, B_2_port =>
        int_change_2_port, B_1_port => int_change_1_port,
        B_0_port => int_change_0_port, LEQ => n159, TC =>
        n160, LT_LE => change69_1_port, GE_GT => open);
r51 : comp_1m2_n8_2 port map( A_7_port => total_7_port, A_6_port =>
        total_6_port, A_5_port => total_5_port, A_4_port =>
        total_4_port, A_3_port => total_3_port, A_2_port =>
        total_2_port, A_1_port => total_1_port, A_0_port =>
        total_0_port, B_7_port => price_7_port, B_6_port =>
        price_6_port, B_5_port => price_5_port, B_4_port =>
        price_4_port, B_3_port => price_3_port, B_2_port =>
        price_2_port, B_1_port => price_1_port, B_0_port =>
        price_0_port, LEQ => n161, TC => n162, LT_LE => open
        , GE_GT => is_less117);
r23 : rpl_sub_n8_1 port map( A_7_port => X_cell_277_U18_Z_7_port,
        A_6_port => X_cell_277_U18_Z_6_port, A_5_port =>
        X_cell_277_U18_Z_5_port, A_4_port =>
        X_cell_277_U18_Z_4_port, A_3_port =>
        X_cell_277_U18_Z_3_port, A_2_port =>
        X_cell_277_U18_Z_2_port, A_1_port =>
        X_cell_277_U18_Z_1_port, A_0_port =>
        X_cell_277_U18_Z_0_port, B_7_port =>
        X_cell_277_U17_Z_7_port, B_6_port =>
        X_cell_277_U17_Z_6_port, B_5_port =>
        X_cell_277_U17_Z_5_port, B_4_port =>
        X_cell_277_U17_Z_4_port, B_3_port =>
        X_cell_277_U17_Z_3_port, B_2_port =>
        X_cell_277_U17_Z_2_port, B_1_port =>
        X_cell_277_U17_Z_1_port, B_0_port =>
        X_cell_277_U17_Z_0_port, SUM_7_port => sum109_7_port
        , SUM_6_port => sum109_6_port, SUM_5_port =>
        sum109_5_port, SUM_4_port => sum109_4_port,
        SUM_3_port => sum109_3_port, SUM_2_port =>
        sum109_2_port, SUM_1_port => sum109_1_port,
        SUM_0_port => sum109_0_port);
r24 : comp_1m2_n8_3 port map( A_7_port => int_change_7_port, A_6_port =>
        int_change_6_port, A_5_port => int_change_5_port,
        A_4_port => int_change_4_port, A_3_port =>
        int_change_3_port, A_2_port => int_change_2_port,
        A_1_port => int_change_1_port, A_0_port =>
```

```
                int_change_0_port, B_7_port => Logic0, B_6_port =>
                Logic0, B_5_port => Logic0, B_4_port => Logic0,
                B_3_port => Logic0, B_2_port => Logic0, B_1_port =>
                Logic0, B_0_port => Logic0, LEQ => n163, TC => n164,
                LT_LE => open, GE_GT => is_less89);
Logic0 <= '0';
Logic1 <= '1';
sub_70 : AN2P port map( A => price_5_port, B => n147, Z =>
                X_cell_277_U17_Z_5_port);
sub_71 : AN2 port map( A => price_6_port, B => n147, Z =>
                X_cell_277_U17_Z_6_port);
n159 <= '1';
sub_60 : AN2P port map( A => n151, B => n154, Z => n155);
n160 <= '0';
sub_61 : ND2 port map( A => is_less117, B => item_stb, Z => sell_en32);
n161 <= '1';
sub_62 : ND2 port map( A => n33, B => n149, Z => n148);
n162 <= '0';
sub_50 : EON1 port map( A => n155, B => net144, C => total_2_port, D =>
                n147, Z => X_cell_277_U18_Z_2_port);
sub_63 : IVP port map( A => change69_1_port, Z => change69_0_port);
n163 <= '1';
sub_51 : IV port map( A => sell_en32, Z => n149);
sub_64 : ND2 port map( A => n153, B => n154, Z =>
                X_cell_277_U17_Z_1_port);
n164 <= '0';
sub_52 : EON1 port map( A => n155, B => net143, C => total_3_port, D =>
                n147, Z => X_cell_277_U18_Z_3_port);
sub_65 : ND2 port map( A => n150, B => n151, Z =>
                X_cell_277_U17_Z_0_port);
sub_40 : ND2 port map( A => n70_0_port, B => change69_1_port, Z => n154
                );
sub_53 : ND2 port map( A => n156, B => n151, Z =>
                X_cell_277_U17_Z_2_port);
sub_66 : AO7 port map( A => present_state_0_port, B => net135, C => n148
                , Z => n157);
sub_41 : ND2 port map( A => n70_0_port, B => change69_0_port, Z => n151
                );
sub_54 : IVA port map( A => n148, Z => n147);
sub_67 : ND2 port map( A => n155, B => n148, Z => n45_7_port);
sub_42 : ND2 port map( A => price_3_port, B => n147, Z => n152);
sub_55 : NR2 port map( A => present_state_1_port, B =>
                present_state_0_port, Z => n33);
sub_68 : AN2 port map( A => price_4_port, B => n147, Z =>
                X_cell_277_U17_Z_4_port);
sub_43 : ND2 port map( A => price_2_port, B => n147, Z => n156);
sub_56 : EON1 port map( A => n155, B => net145, C => total_1_port, D =>
                n147, Z => X_cell_277_U18_Z_1_port);
sub_69 : AN2 port map( A => n147, B => price_7_port, Z =>
                X_cell_277_U17_Z_7_port);
sub_44 : EON1 port map( A => n155, B => net136, C => total_7_port, D =>
                n147, Z => X_cell_277_U18_Z_7_port);
```

```
sub_57 : ND2 port map( A => n152, B => n154, Z =>
            X_cell_277_U17_Z_3_port);
sub_45 : ND2 port map( A => price_1_port, B => n147, Z => n153);
sub_58 : AN2 port map( A => is_less89, B => change_stb_port, Z =>
            n70_0_port);
sub_46 : EON1 port map( A => n155, B => net138, C => total_6_port, D =>
            n147, Z => X_cell_277_U18_Z_6_port);
sub_59 : EON1 port map( A => n155, B => net146, C => total_0_port, D =>
            n147, Z => X_cell_277_U18_Z_0_port);
sub_47 : ND2 port map( A => price_0_port, B => n147, Z => n150);
sub_48 : EON1 port map( A => n155, B => net141, C => total_5_port, D =>
            n147, Z => X_cell_277_U18_Z_5_port);
sub_49 : EON1 port map( A => n155, B => net142, C => total_4_port, D =>
            n147, Z => X_cell_277_U18_Z_4_port);
sub_39 : NR2 port map( A => net134, B => present_state_1_port, Z =>
            change_stb_port);
present_state_reg_1_label : FD1 port map( D => n70_0_port, CP => clock,
            Q => present_state_1_port, QN => net135);
present_state_reg_0_label : FD1 port map( D => n157, CP => clock, Q =>
            present_state_0_port, QN => net134);
sell_en_reg : LD1 port map( D => sell_en32, G => n33, Q => sell_en, QN
            => open);

end STRUCTURAL_VIEW;
```

VHDL Reference Tables

This appendix will focus on tables of information that are useful while writing VHDL descriptions. Most of the information in the tables is available in the text of the book; however, these tables consolidate the information into one area for easy reference.

Table C.1 lists all of the different kinds of statements alphabetically and includes an example usage.

TABLE C.1

Statement or clause	Example(s)
Access type	`TYPE access_type IS ACCESS type_to_be_accessed;`
Aggregate	`record_type := (first, second, third);`
Alias	`ALIAS opcode : BIT_VECTOR(0 TO 3) IS INSTRUCTION(10 TO 13);`

Architecture	`ARCHITECTURE architecture_name OF entity name IS`
	`   -- declare some signals here`
	`BEGIN`
	`   -- put some concurrent statements here`
	`END architecture_name;`

Array type	`TYPE array_type IS ARRAY (0 TO 7) OF BIT;`
Assert	`ASSERT x >10 REPORT "x is too small" SEVERITY ERROR;`
Attribute declaration	`ATTRIBUTE attribute_name : attribute_type;`
Attribute specification	`ATTRIBUTE attribute_name OF` `   entity_name : entity_class IS value;`

Block statement	`block_name : BLOCK`
	`   -- declare some stuff here`
	`BEGIN`
	`   -- put some concurrent statements here`
	`END BLOCK block_name;`

TABLE C.1 (*Continued*)

Statement or clause	Example(s)
| Case statement | ```
CASE some_expression IS
  WHEN some_value =>
    -- do_some_stuff
  WHEN some_other_value =>
    -- do_some_other_stuff
  WHEN OTHERS =>
    -- do_some_default_stuff
END CASE;
``` |
| Component declaration | ```
COMPONENT component_name
  PORT(port1_name : port1_type;
       port2_name : port2_type;
       port3_name : port3_type);
END COMPONENT;
``` |
| Component instantiation | ```
instance_name : component_name PORT MAP (first_port,
  second_port, third_port);

instance_name : component_name PORT MAP
(formal1 => actual1, formal2 => actual2);
``` |
| Conditional signal assignment | ```
target <= first_value WHEN (x = y) ELSE
          second_value WHEN a >= b ELSE
             third_value;
``` |
| Configuration declaration | ```
CONFIGURATION configuration_name OF entity_name IS
  FOR architecture_name
    FOR instance_name : entity_name USE ENTITY
         library_name.entity_name(architecture_name);
    END FOR;
      FOR instance_name : entity_name USE CONFIGURATION
        library_name.configuration_name;
    END FOR;
  END FOR;
END configuration_name;
``` |
| Constant declaration | ```
CONSTANT constant_name : constant_type := value;
``` |
| Entity declaration | ```
ENTITY entity_name IS
  PORT(port1 : port1_type;
       port2 : port2_type);
END entity_name;
``` |
| Exit statement | ```
EXIT;

EXIT WHEN a <= b;

EXIT loop_label WHEN x = z;
``` |
| File type declaration | ```
TYPE file_type_name IS FILE OF data_type;
``` |
| File object declaration | ```
FILE file_object_name : file_type_name IS IN
     "/absolute/path/name";
``` |
| For loop | ```
FOR loop_variable IN start TO end LOOP
  -- do_some_stuff
END LOOP;
``` |
```

TABLE C.1 (*Continued*)

Statement or clause	Example(s)
| Function declaration | ```
FUNCTION function_name (parameter1 : parameter1_type;
                        parameter2 : parameter2_type)
           RETURN return_type;
``` |
| Function body | ```
FUNCTION function_name(parameter1 : parameter1_type;
                       parameter2 : parameter2_type)
           RETURN return_type IS

BEGIN
   -- do some stuff
END function_name;
``` |
| Generate statement | ```
generate_label : FOR gen_var IN start TO end Generate
   label : component_name PORT MAP(.........);
END GENERATE;
``` |
| Generic declaration | ```
GENERIC (generic1_name : generic1_type;
             generic2_name : generic2_type);
``` |
| Generic map | ```
GENERIC MAP(generic1_name => value1, value2);
``` |
| Guarded signal assignment | ```
g1 : BLOCK(clk = '1' AND clk'EVENT)
BEGIN
   q <= GUARDED d AFTER 5 NS;
END BLOCK;
``` |
| IF statement | ```
IF x <= y THEN
   -- some statements
END IF;

IF z > w THEN
   -- some statements
ELSIF q < r THEN
   -- some more statements
END IF;

IF a = b THEN
   -- some statements
ELSIF c = d THEN
   -- some more statements
ELSE
   -- even more statements
END IF;
``` |
| Incomplete type | ```
TYPE type_name;
``` |
| Library declaration | ```
LIBRARY library_name;
``` |
| Loop statement | ```
FOR loop_variable IN start TO end LOOP
   -- do lots of stuff
END LOOP;

WHILE x < y LOOP
   -- modify x and y and do other stuff
END LOOP;
``` |
| Next statement | ```
IF i < 0 THEN
   NEXT;
END IF;
``` |
```

TABLE C.1 (*Continued*)

Statement or clause	Example(s)
Others clause	```WHEN OTHERS =>``` ``` -- do some stuff```

Package declaration	```PACKAGE package_name IS```
	``` -- declare some stuff```
	```END PACKAGE;```

Package body	```PACKAGE BODY package_name IS```
	``` --put subprogram bodies here```
	```END package_name;```

Physical type	```TYPE physical_type_name IS RANGE start TO end```
	``` UNITS```
	``` unit1 ;```
	``` unit2 = 10 unit1;```
	``` unit3 = 10 unit2;```
	``` END UNITS;```

Port clause	```PORT(port1_name : port1_type; port2_name :``` ```port2_type);```
Port map clause	```PORT MAP (port1_name => signal1, signal2);```

Procedure declaration	```PROCEDURE procedure_name(parm1 : in parm1_type;```
	``` parm2 : out parm2_type;```
	``` parm3 : inout parm3_type);```

Procedure body	```PROCEDURE procedure_name(parm1 : in parm1_type;```
	``` parm2 : out parm1_type;```
	``` parm3 : inout parm3_type) IS```
	```BEGIN```
	``` -- do some stuff```
	```END procedure_name;```

Process statement	```PROCESS(signal1, signal2, signal3)```
	``` -- declare some stuff```
	```BEGIN```
	``` -- do some stuff```
	```END PROCESS;```

Record type	```TYPE record_type IS```
	``` RECORD```
	``` field1 : field1_type;```
	``` field2 : field2_type;```
	``` END RECORD;```

Report clause	```ASSERT x = 10 REPORT "some string";```
Return statement	```RETURN;``` ```RETURN (x + 10);```

Selected signal assignment	```WITH z SELECT```
	``` x <= 1 AFTER 5 NS WHEN 0,```
	``` 2 AFTER 5 NS WHEN 1,```
	``` 3 AFTER 5 NS WHEN OTHERS;```

Severity clause	```ASSERT x > 5 REPORT "some string" SEVERITY ERROR;```
Signal assignment	```a <= b AFTER 20 NS;```

TABLE C.1 *(Continued)*

Statement or clause	Example(s)
Signal declaration	`SIGNAL x : xtype;`
Subtype declaration	`SUBTYPE bit8 IS INTEGER RANGE 0 TO 255;`
Transport signal assignment	`x <= TRANSPORT y AFTER 50 NS;`
Type declaration	`TYPE color is (red, yellow, blue, green, orange);` `TYPE small_int is 0 to 65535;`
Use clause	`USE WORK.my_package.all;`
Variable declaration	`VARIABLE variable_name : variable_type;`

Wait statement	`WAIT ON a, b, c;`
	`WAIT UNTIL clock'EVENT AND clock = '1';`
	`WAIT FOR 100 NS;`
	`WAIT ON a, b UNTIL b > 10 FOR 50 NS;`

While loop	`WHILE x > 15 LOOP`
	`   -- do some stuff`
	`END LOOP;`

Table C.2 lists all of the predefined attributes that retrieve information about VHDL type data. The descriptions are necessarily terse to fit into the table cells. (See Chap. 6 for more detailed information.)

TABLE C.2

Attribute	Explanation	Examples
T'BASE	Returns the base type of data type it is attached to	`NATURAL'BASE returns` `INTEGER`

T'LEFT	Returns left value specified in type declaration	`INTEGER'LEFT is`
		`-2147483647`
		
		`BIT'LEFT is '0'`

T'RIGHT	Returns right value specified in type declaration	`INTEGER'RIGHT is`
		`2147483647`
		
		`BIT'RIGHT is '1'`

T'HIGH	Returns largest value specified in declaration	`TYPE bit8 is 255 downto 0` `bit8'HIGH is 255`
T'LOW	Returns smallest value specified in declaration	`TYPE bit8 is 255 downto 0` `bit8'LOW is 0`

TABLE C.2 (*Continued*)

Attribute	Explanation	Examples

T'POS(X)	Returns position number of argument in type (first position is 0)	`TYPE color IS (red,`
		`green, blue, orange);`
		
		`color'POS(green) is 1`

T'VAL(X)	Returns value in type at specified position number	`TYPE color IS (red, green.`
		`blue, orange);`
		
		`color'VAL(2) is blue`

T'SUCC(X)	Returns the successor to the value passed in	`TYPE color IS (red, green`
		`blue, orange);`
		
		`color'SUCC(green) is blue`

T'PRED(X)	Returns the predecessor to the value passed in	`TYPE color IS (red, green,`
		`blue, orange);`
		
		`color'PRED(blue) is green`

T'LEFTOF(X)	Returns the value to the left of the value passed in	`TYPE color IS (red, green,`
		`blue, orange);`
		
		`color'LEFTOF(green) is red`

T'RIGHTOF(X)	Returns the value to the right of the value passed in	`TYPE color IS (red, green,`
		`blue, orange);`
		
		`color'RIGHTOF(blue) is`
		`orange`

Table C.3 lists all predefined attributes that return information about array data types. The N parameter for all attributes specifies to which particular range the attribute is being applied. This makes sense only for multidimensional arrays. For single dimensional arrays, the parameter can be ignored. (For more detailed information, see Chap. 6.)

All of the examples shown apply to the following declaration:

```
TYPE a_type IS ARRAY(0 TO 3, 7 DOWNTO 0) OF BIT;
```

TABLE C.3

Attribute	Explanation	Example
A'LEFT(N)	Returns left array bound of selected index range	`a_type'LEFT(1) is 0` `a_type'LEFT(2) is 7`
A'RIGHT(N)	Returns right array bound of selected index range	`a_type'RIGHT(1) is 3` `a_type'RIGHT(2) is 0`

TABLE C.3 *(Continued)*

Attribute	Explanation	Example
A'HIGH(N)	Returns largest array bound value of selected index range	a_type'HIGH(1) is 3 a_type'HIGH(2) is 7
A'LOW(N)	Returns smallest array bound value of selected index range	a_type'LOW(1) is 0 a_type'LOW(2) is 0
A'RANGE(N)	Returns selected index range	a_type'RANGE(1) is 0 TO 3 a_type'RANGE(2) is 7 DOWNTO 0
A'REVERSE_RANGE(N)	Returns selected index range reversed	a_type' REVERSE_RANGE(1) is 3 DOWNTO 0 a_type' REVERSE_RANGE(2) is 0 TO 7
A'LENGTH(N)	Returns size of selected index range	a_type'LENGTH(1) is 4 a_type'LENGTH(2) is 8

Table C.4 lists all predefined attributes that return information about signals or create new signals. (For more detailed information, see Chap. 6.)

TABLE C.4

Attribute	Explanation	Example
S'DELAYED(T)	Creates a new signal delayed by T	clock'DELAYED(10 ns)
S'QUIET(I)	Creates a new signal that is true when signal S has had no transactions for time T and false otherwise	reset'QUIET(5 ns)
S'STABLE(T)	Creates a new signal that is true when signal S has had no events for time T and false otherwise	clock'STABLE(1 ns)
S'TRANSACTION	Creates a signal of type BIT that toggles for every transaction on signal S	load'TRANSACTION
S'EVENT	Returns true when an event has occurred for signal S this delta	clock'EVENT
S'ACTIVE	Returns true when a transaction has occurred for signal S this delta	load'ACTIVE
S'LAST_EVENT	Returns the elapsed time since the last event on signal S	data'LAST_EVENT
S'LAST_ACTIVE	Returns the elapsed time since the last transaction on signal S	clock'LAST_ACTIVE
S'LAST_VALUE	Returns the previously assigned value of signal S	data'LAST_VALUE

Table C.5 lists all of the operators and their relative precedence.

TABLE C.5

Precedence	Operator class	Operator
Highest	Miscellaneous	`**, ABS, NOT`
	Multiplying	`*, /, MOD, REM`
	Sign	`+, −`
	Adding	`+, −, &`
	Relational	`=, /=, <, <=, >, >=`
Lowest	Logical	`AND, OR, NAND, NOR, XOR`

Table C.6 lists all of the different types of literals and a sample usage.

TABLE C.6

Literal type	Example

Decimal integer	`5 2`
	`0`
	`3E3   -- equals 3000`
	`1_000_000 -- equals 1 million`

Decimal real	`52.0`
	`0.0`
	`.178`
	`1.222_333`

Decimal real with exponent	`1.2E+10` `4.6E-9`

Based integer	`16#FF# -- equals 255`
	`8#777# -- equals 511`
	`2#1101_0101# -- equals 213`
	`16#FF#E1 -- equals 4080`

Based real	`2#11.11#`
	`16#AB.CD#E+2`
	`8#77.66#E-10`

Character	`'a'`
	`'*'`
	`' '   -- the space character`

String	`"this is a string"`
	`" " -- empty string`
	`"ABC" & "CDE" -- concatenation`

Bit string	`X"FFEF"`
	`O"770770"`
	`B"1111_0000_1111"`

In all cases, the _ character is ignored when interpreting the value of a literal. The base to which the exponent in the based integer and based real examples are applied is the base specified for interpreting the number. Bit string literals are used to specify values for types which resemble the BIT_VECTOR type.

Reading VHDL BNF

Once the basic concepts of VHDL are understood, the designer will want to try to write VHDL in a more elegant manner. To fully understand how to apply all of the syntactic constructs available in VHDL, it is helpful to know how to read the VHDL Bachus-Naur format (BNF) of the language. This format is in appendix A of the IEEE Std. 1076-1987 *VHDL Language Reference Manual* (LRM), pages A-1 to A-17. This format will specify which constructs are necessary versus optional or repeatable versus singular, and how constructs can be associated.

BNF is basically a hierarchical description method, where complex constructs are made of successive specifications of lower-level constructs. Our purpose for examining BNF is not to understand every nuance of the BNF but to put the basics to use to help build complex VHDL constructs. To this end, let us examine some BNF and discuss what it means.

The BNF for the IF statement is shown as follows:

```
if_statement ::=
  IF condition THEN
    sequence_of_statements
  {ELSIF condition THEN
    sequence_of_statements}
  [ELSE
    sequence_of_statements]
  END IF;
```

The first line of the BNF description specifies the name of the construct being described. This line is read as follows "the IF statement consists of" or "the IF statement is constructed from." The rest of the description represents the rules for constructing an IF statement.

The second line of the description specifies that the IF statement starts with the keyword IF, is followed by a condition construct, and ends the clause with the keyword THEN. The next line contains the construct SEQUENCE_OF_STATEMENTS (discussed later). All of the constructs discussed so far are required for the IF statement because the constructs are not enclosed in any kind of punctuation.

Statements enclosed in brackets [ ], as in lines 6 and 7, are optional constructs. An optional construct can be specified or left out depending on the functionality required. The ELSE clause of the IF statement is an example of an optional construct. A legal IF statement may or may not have an ELSE clause.

Statements enclosed in curly braces { }, as in lines 4 and 5, are optional and repeatable constructs. An optional and repeatable construct can either be left out, or have one or more of the construct exist. The ELSIF clause is an example of an optional and repeatable construct. The IF statement can be constructed without an ELSIF clause, or have one or more ELSIF clauses, depending on the desired behavior.

The last line of the IF_STATEMENT description contains the END IF clause. This is a required clause because it is not optional [ ], and not optional and repeatable { }.

The IF statement contains two other constructs that need more description. These are the SEQUENCE_OF_STATEMENTS and the CONDITION. The SEQUENCE_OF_STATEMENTS construct is described by the following BNF:

```
sequence_of_statements  ::=
  {sequential_statement}
```

The SEQUENCE_OF_STATEMENTS construct is described by one or more sequential statements, where a sequential statement is described as shown here:

```
sequential_statement  ::=
  wait_statement
  | assertion_statement
  | signal_assignment_statement
  | variable_assignment_statement
  | procedure_call_statement
  | if_statement
  | case_statement
  | loop_statement
  | next_statement
  | exit_statement
  | return_statement
  | null_statement
```

The | character means OR, such that a sequential statement can be a WAIT statement, or an ASSERT statement, or a SIGNAL ASSIGN-MENT statement, etc. From this description, we can see that the statement part of the IF statement can contain one or more sequential statements, such as WAIT statements, ASSERT statements, etc.

The CONDITION construct is specified with the following BNF description:

```
condition   ::= boolean_expression
```

Notice that the keyword *boolean* is italicized. The italics indicate the type of the expression required for the CONDITION. If a designer looks for a boolean expression construct to describe the syntax required, none will be found. The reason is that all expressions share the same syntax description. For our purposes, the boolean type of the expression is ignored, and the construct description can be found under the following description:

```
expression  ::=
    relation {and relation}
    |relation {or relation}
    |relation {xor relation}
    | relation [nand relation]
    |relation [nor relation]
```

To summarize, curly braces { } are optional and repeatable con-structs, square brackets [ ] are optional constructs, and italicized pieces of a construct can be ignored for purposes of finding descrip-tions.

Index

ABOUT THE AUTHOR

Douglas L. Perry is a senior applications engineer with
Redwood Design Automation and has been active in
the CAE field for more than 12 years. He is the author of
the first edition of *VHDL*.